The Witch and the Beast 4 is a v   fiction. Names, characters
places, and incidents are the pr   or are used fictitiously. Any resem
persons, living or dead

A Kodansha Comics T
The Witch and the Beast 4 copyright © 2019 Kousuke Satake
English translation copyright © 2021 Kousuke Satake

Published in the United States by Kodansha Comics, an imprint of
Kodansha USA Publishing, LLC, New York.

Publication rights for this English edition arranged through
Kodansha Ltd., Tokyo.

First published in Japan in 2019 by Kodansha Ltd., Tokyo
as *Majo to yaju*, volume 4.

ISBN 978-1-64651-024-5

Original cover design by Yusuke Kurachi (Astrorb)

Printed in the United States of America.

www.kodanshacomics.com

9 8 7 6 5 4 3 2 1
Translation: Kevin Gifford
Lettering: Phil Christie
Editing: Vanessa Tenazas
Kodansha Comics edition cover design by My Truong

Publisher: Kiichiro Sugawara

Director of publishing services: Ben Applegate
Associate director of operations: Stephen Pakula
Publishing services managing editor: Noelle Webster
Assistant production manager: Emi Lotto, Angela Zurlo
Logo and character art ©Kodansha USA Publishing, LLC

Young characters and steampunk setting, like *Howl's Moving Castle* and *Battle Angel Alita*

Beyond the Clouds © 2018 Nicke / Ki-oon

A boy with a talent for machines and a mysterious girl whose wings he's fixed will take you beyond the clouds! In the tradition of the high-flying, resonant adventure stories of Studio Ghibli comes a gorgeous tale about the longing of young hearts for adventure and friendship!

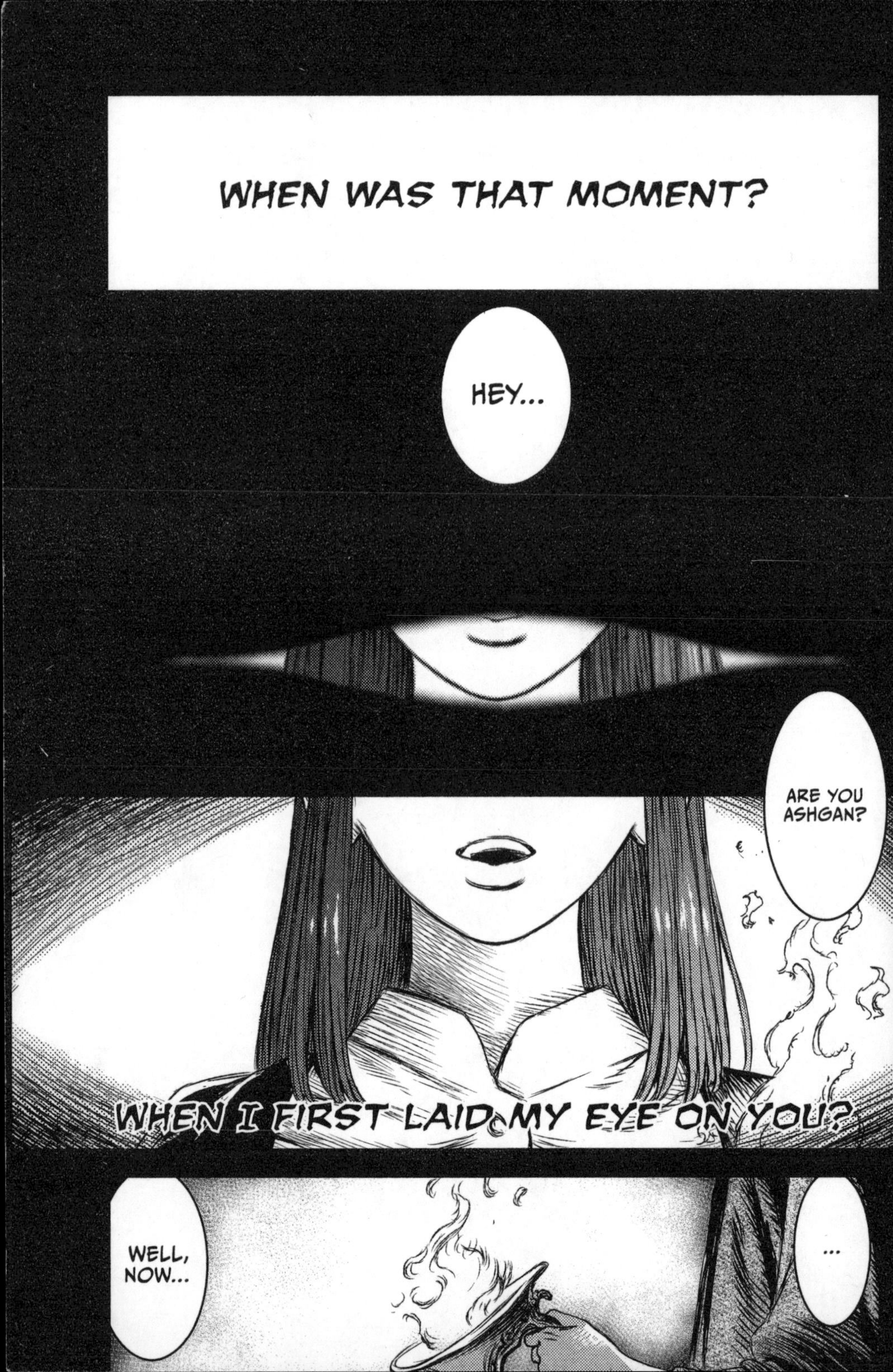
WHEN WAS THAT MOMENT?
HEY...
ARE YOU ASHGAN?
WHEN I FIRST LAID MY EYE ON YOU?
...
WELL, NOW...

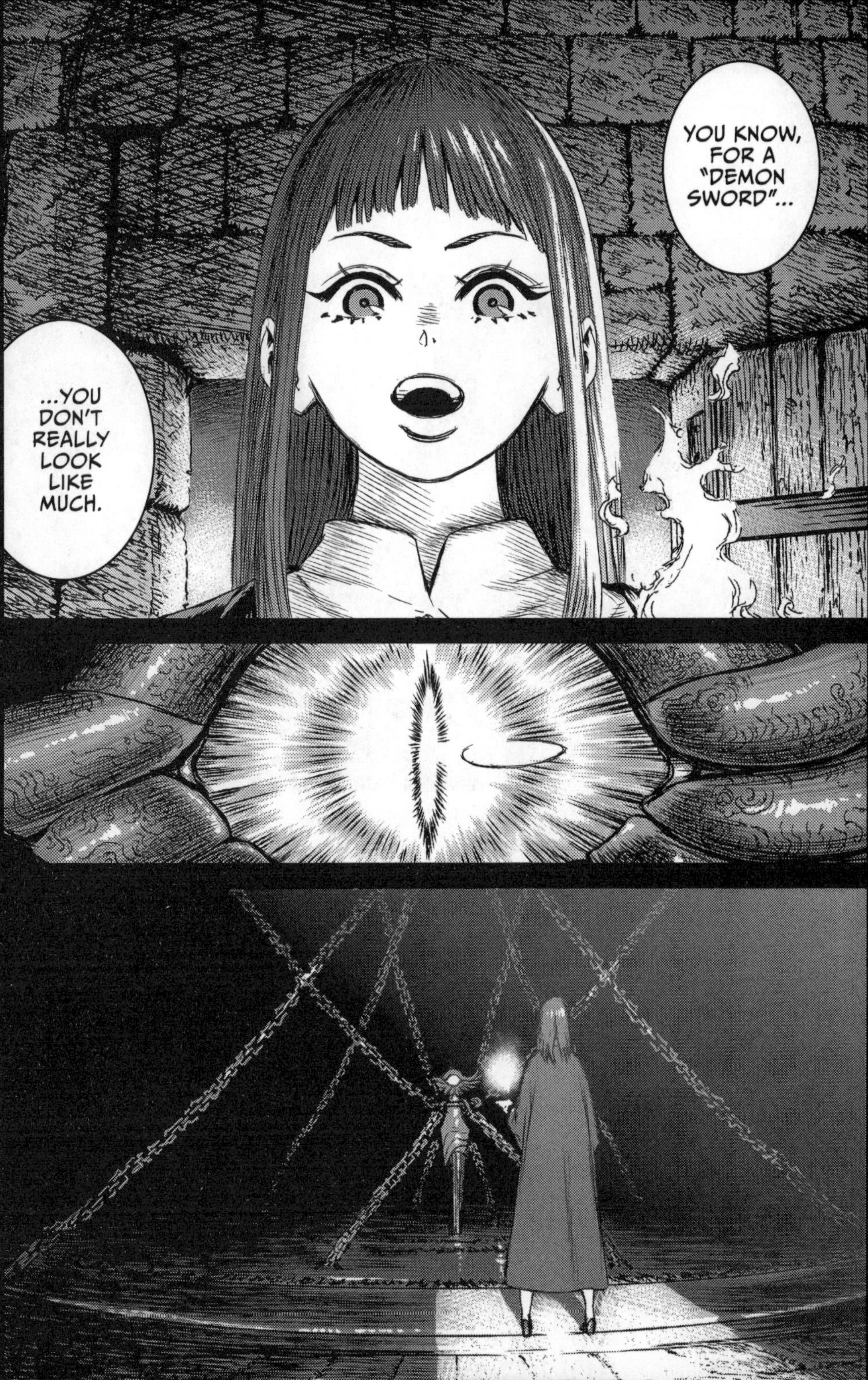
YOU KNOW, FOR A "DEMON SWORD"...
...YOU DON'T REALLY LOOK LIKE MUCH.

THE WITCH AND THE BEAST

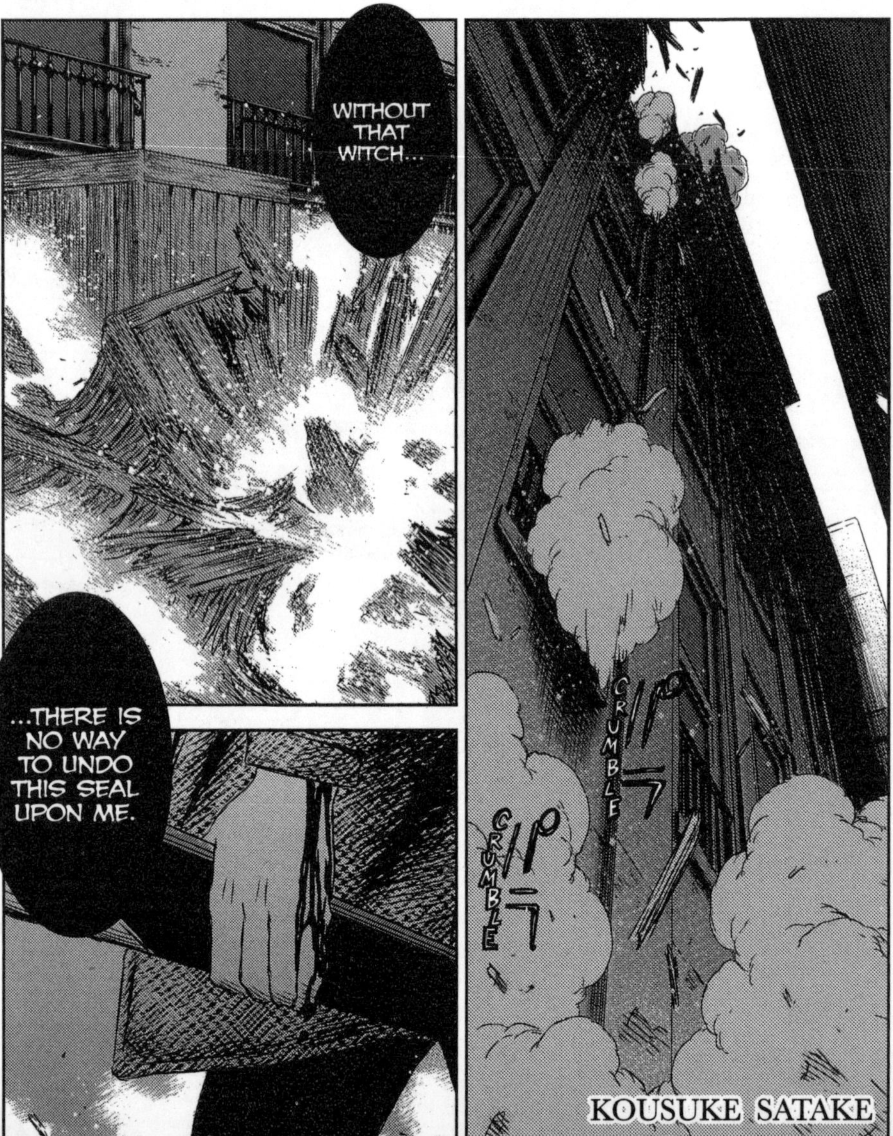
CRUMBLE
CRUMBLE
WITHOUT THAT WITCH...
...THERE IS NO WAY TO UNDO THIS SEAL UPON ME.

KOUSUKE SATAKE

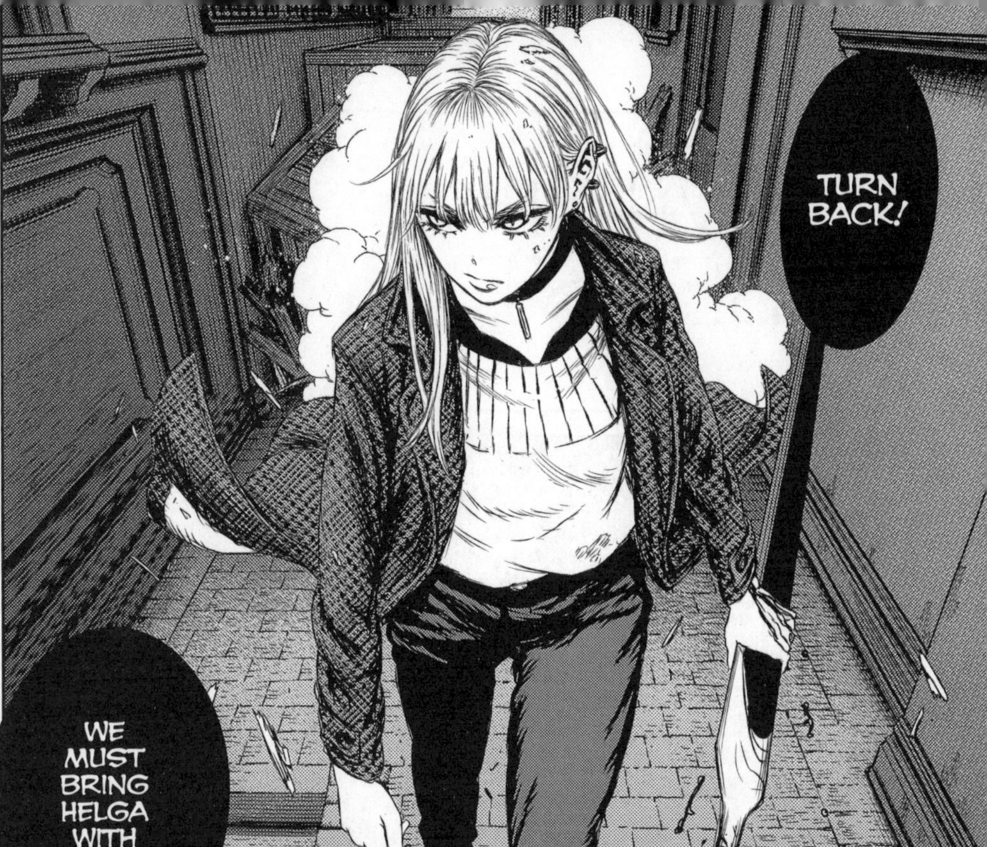
TURN BACK!
WE MUST BRING HELGA WITH US!!

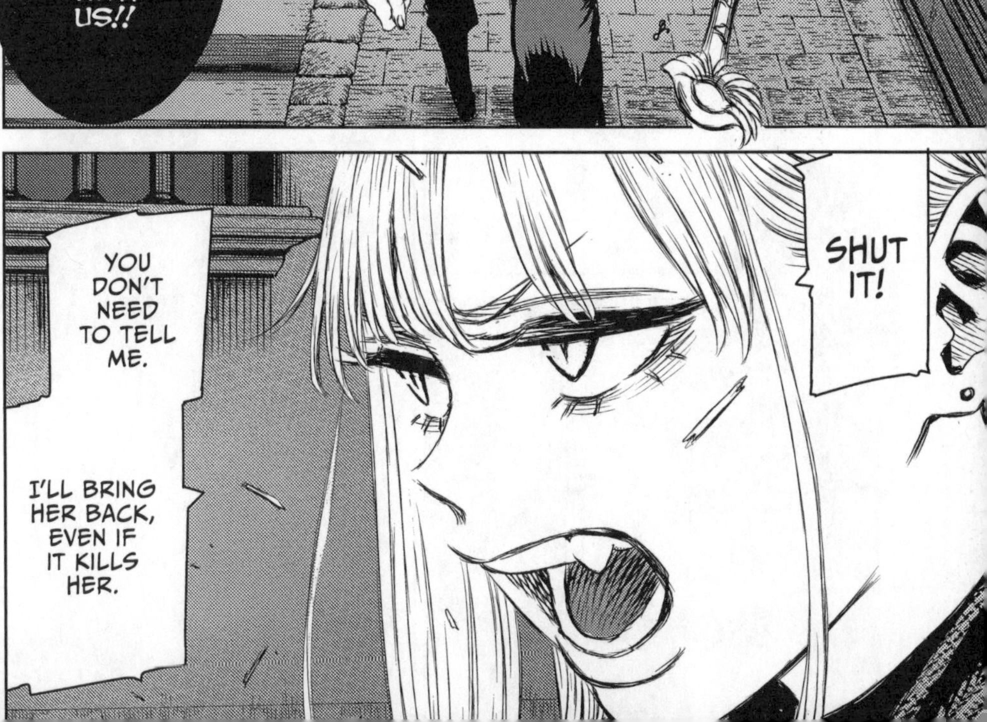
SHUT IT!
YOU DON'T NEED TO TELL ME.
I'LL BRING HER BACK, EVEN IF IT KILLS HER.

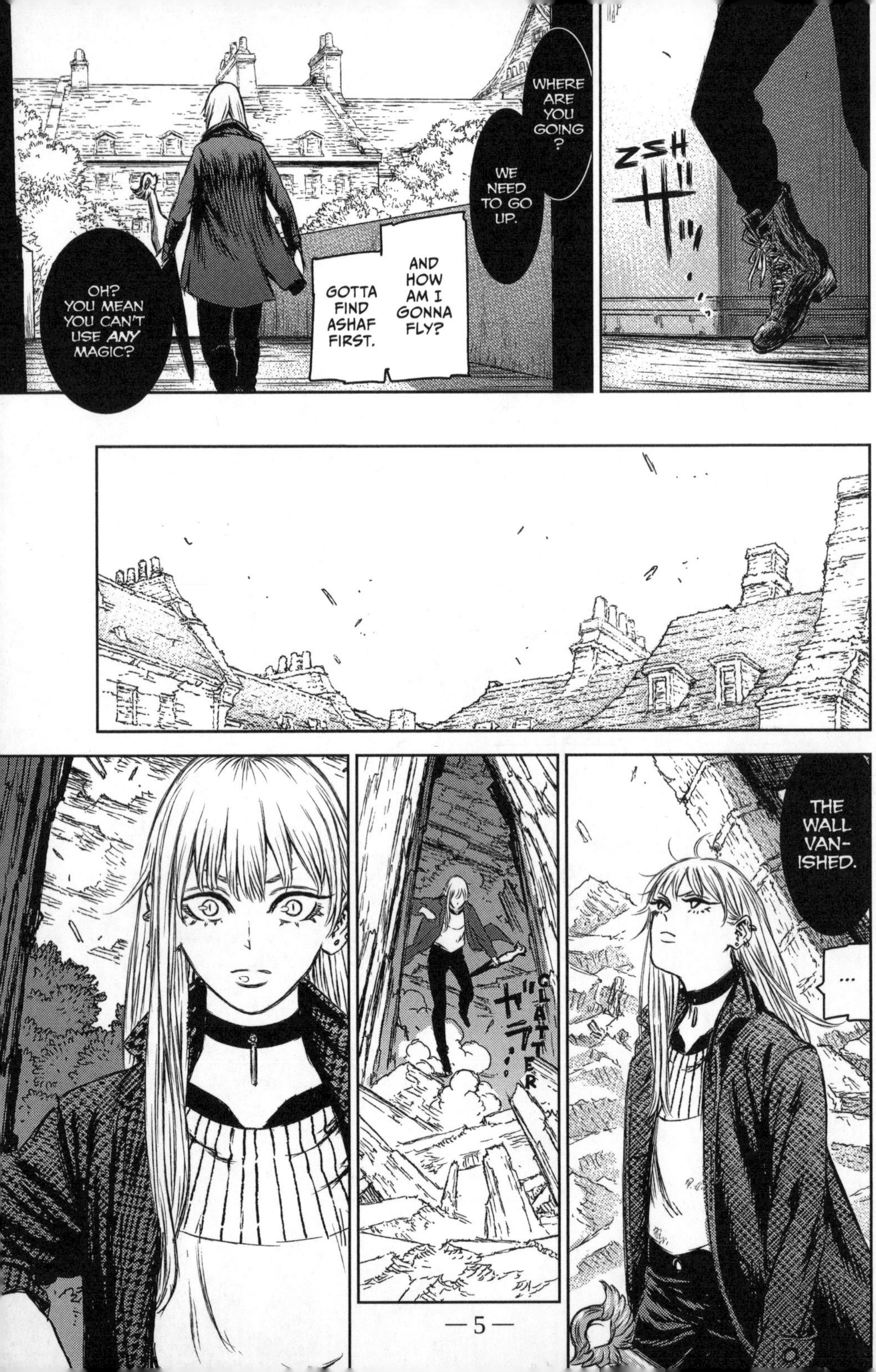
ZSH
WHERE ARE YOU GOING?
WE NEED TO GO UP.
AND HOW AM I GONNA FLY?
GOTTA FIND ASHAF FIRST.
OH? YOU MEAN YOU CAN'T USE *ANY* MAGIC?
THE WALL VAN-ISHED.
...
CLATTER

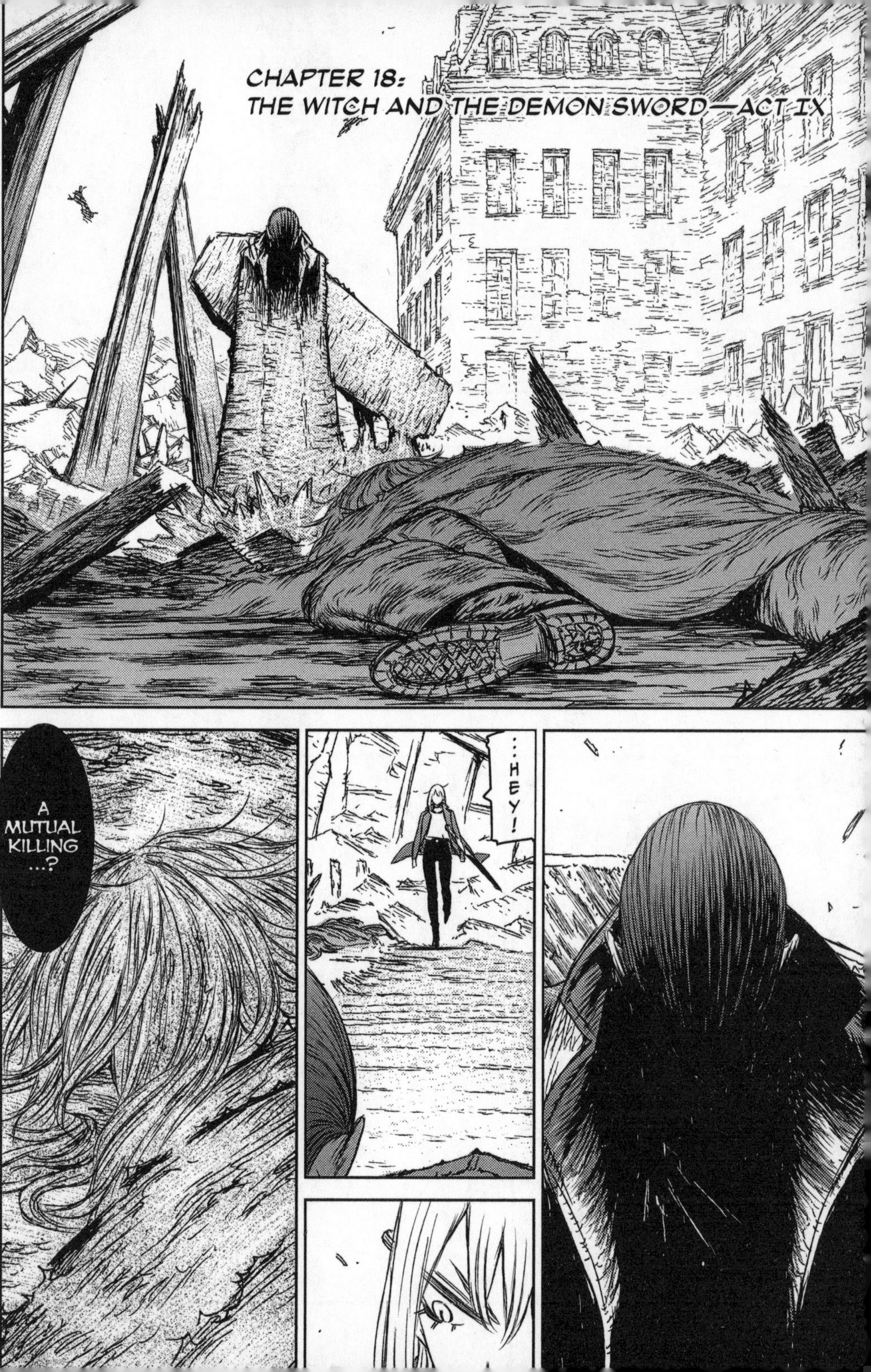
CHAPTER 18:
THE WITCH AND THE DEMON SWORD—ACT IX
...HEY!
A MUTUAL KILLING ...?

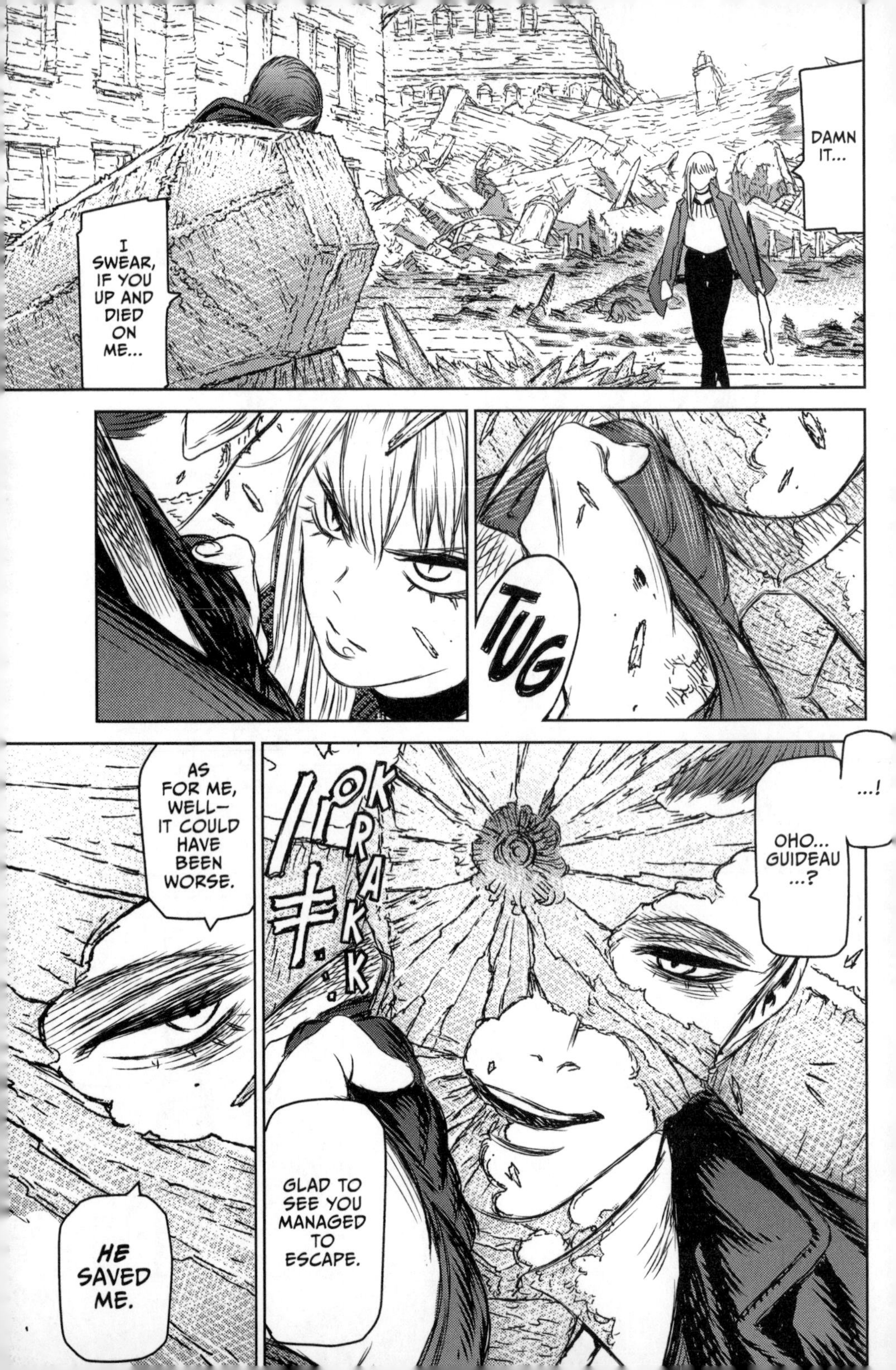
DAMN IT...
I SWEAR, IF YOU UP AND DIED ON ME...
TUG
...!
OHO... GUIDEAU ...?
KRAKK
GLAD TO SEE YOU MANAGED TO ESCAPE.
AS FOR ME, WELL— IT COULD HAVE BEEN WORSE.
HE SAVED ME.

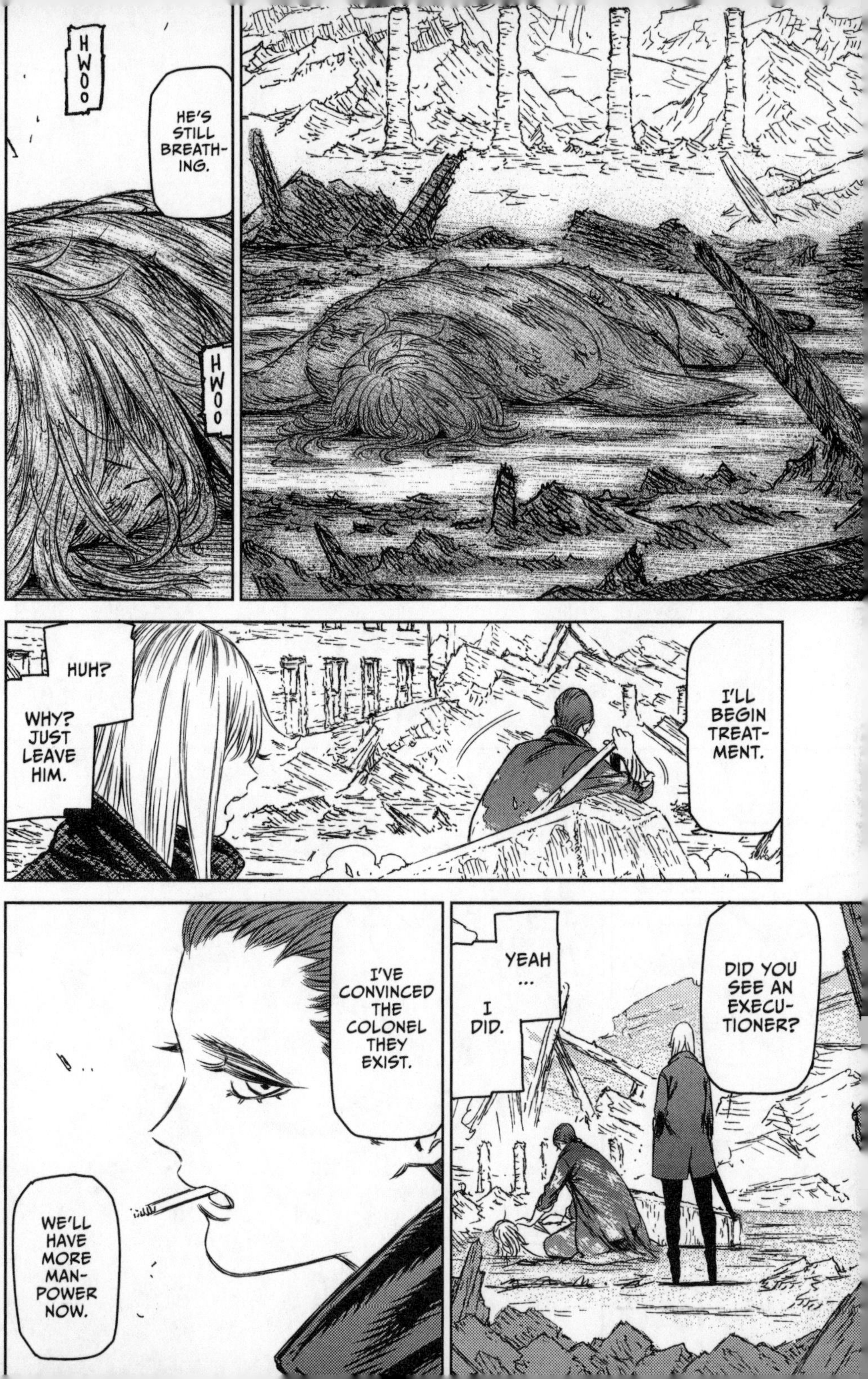
HWOO
HE'S STILL BREATHING.
HWOO
I'LL BEGIN TREATMENT.
HUH?
WHY? JUST LEAVE HIM.
DID YOU SEE AN EXECUTIONER?
YEAH...
I DID.
I'VE CONVINCED THE COLONEL THEY EXIST.
WE'LL HAVE MORE MANPOWER NOW.

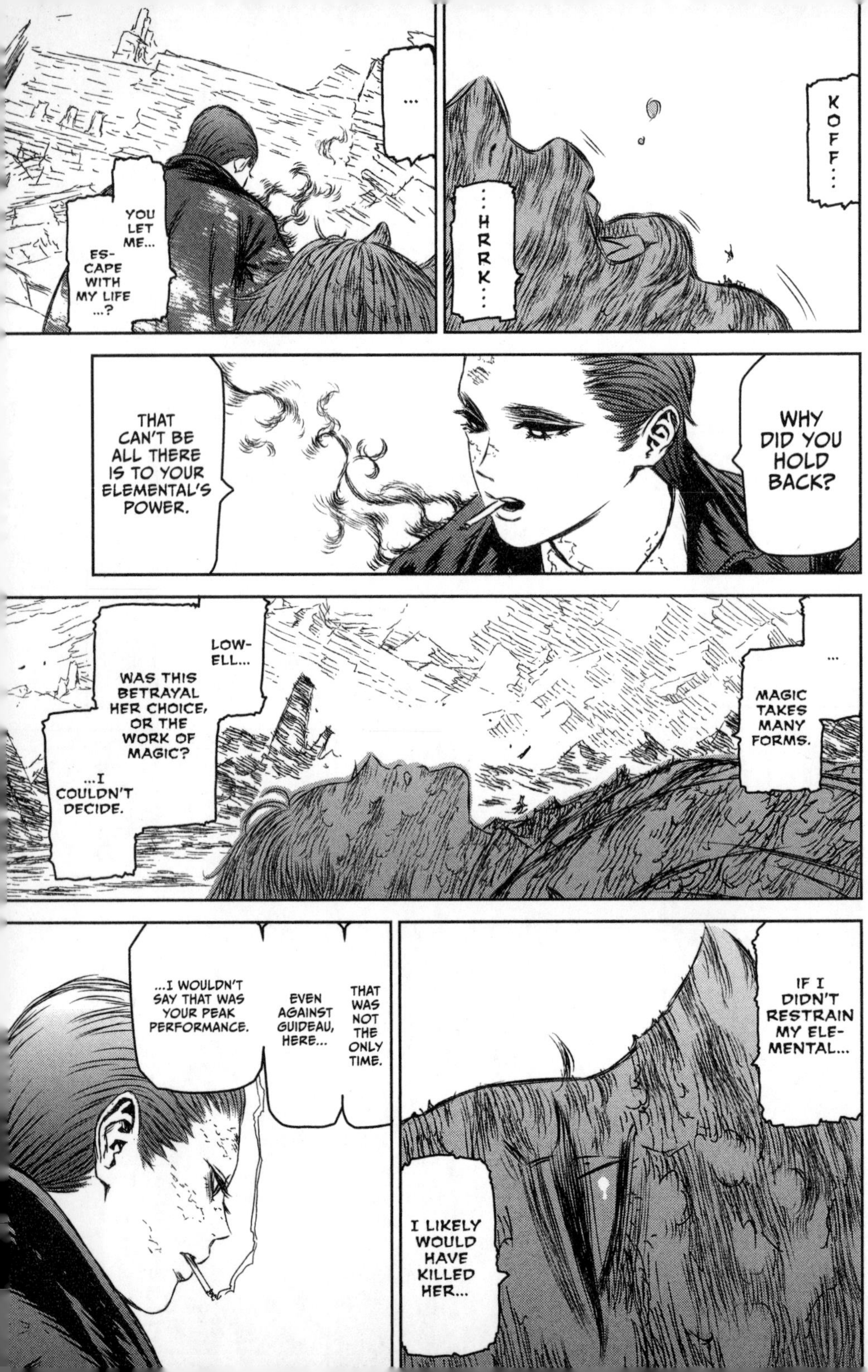
KOFF...
...HRRK...
...
YOU LET ME... ES-CAPE WITH MY LIFE ...?
WHY DID YOU HOLD BACK?
THAT CAN'T BE ALL THERE IS TO YOUR ELEMENTAL'S POWER.
...
MAGIC TAKES MANY FORMS.
LOW-ELL...
WAS THIS BETRAYAL HER CHOICE, OR THE WORK OF MAGIC?
...I COULDN'T DECIDE.
IF I DIDN'T RESTRAIN MY ELE-MENTAL...
I LIKELY WOULD HAVE KILLED HER...
THAT WAS NOT THE ONLY TIME.
EVEN AGAINST GUIDEAU, HERE...
...I WOULDN'T SAY THAT WAS YOUR PEAK PERFORMANCE.

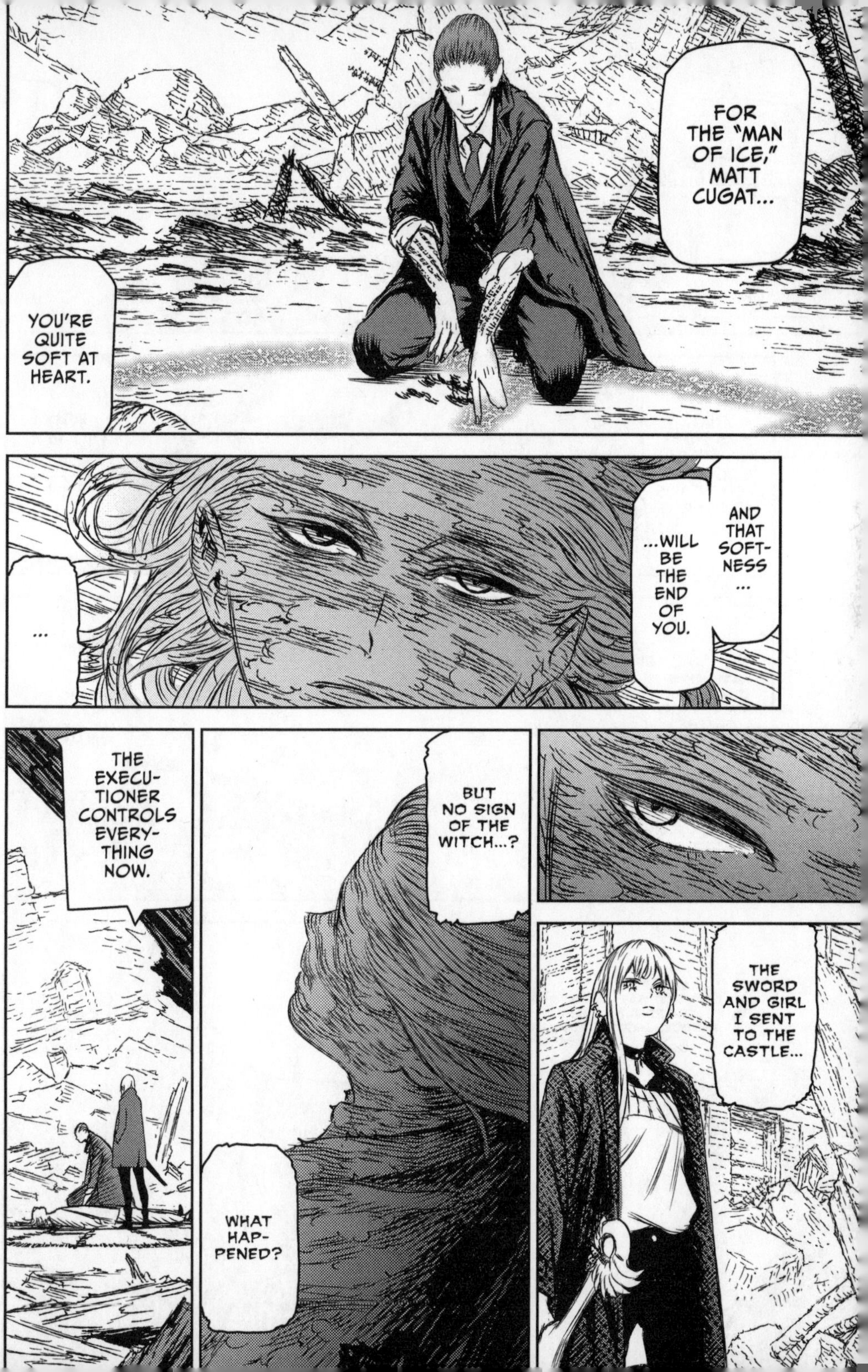
FOR THE "MAN OF ICE," MATT CUGAT...
YOU'RE QUITE SOFT AT HEART.
AND THAT SOFTNESS...
...WILL BE THE END OF YOU.
...
THE SWORD AND GIRL I SENT TO THE CASTLE...
BUT NO SIGN OF THE WITCH...?
WHAT HAPPENED?
THE EXECUTIONER CONTROLS EVERYTHING NOW.

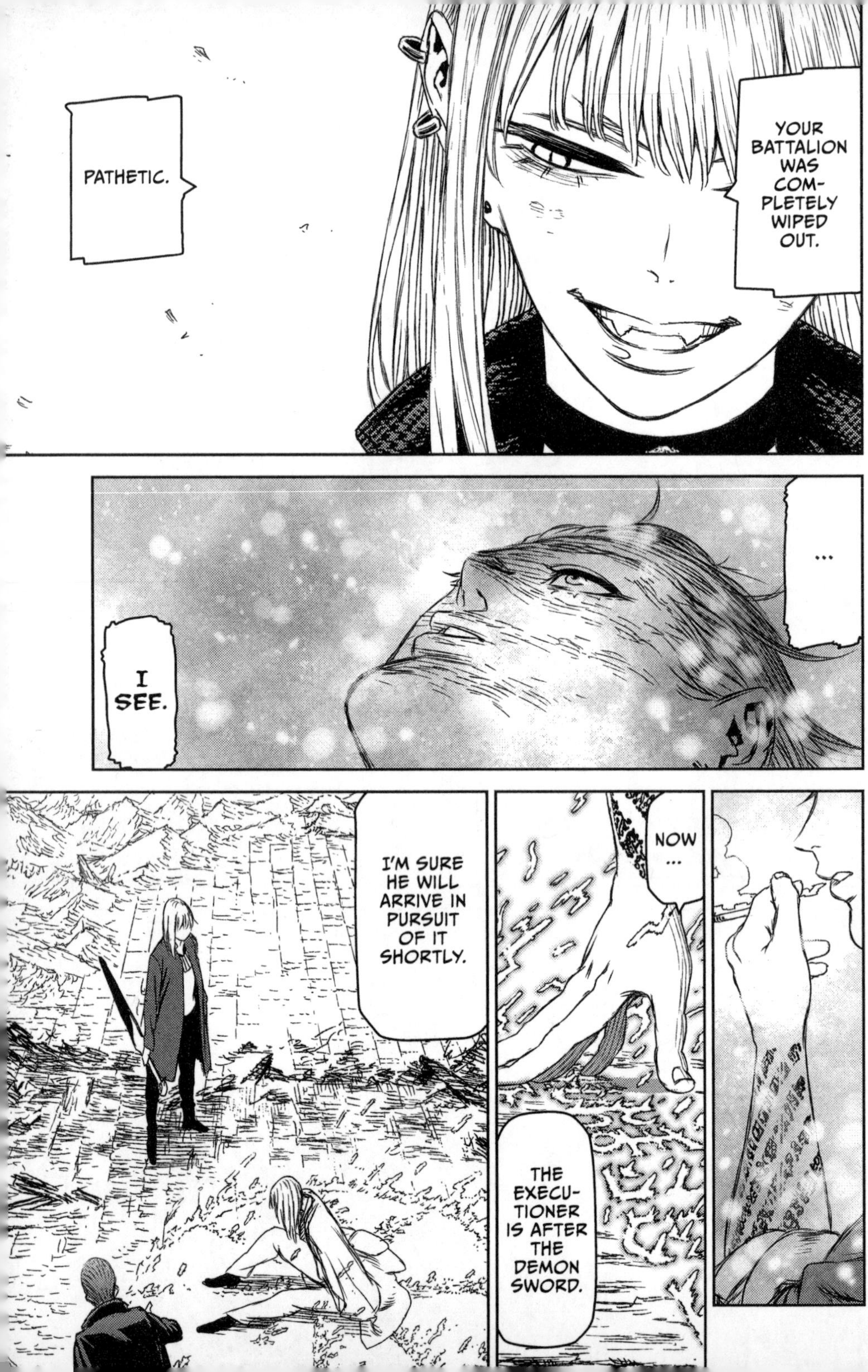
YOUR BATTALION WAS COM-PLETELY WIPED OUT.
PATHETIC.
...
I SEE.
NOW ...
THE EXECU-TIONER IS AFTER THE DEMON SWORD.
I'M SURE HE WILL ARRIVE IN PURSUIT OF IT SHORTLY.

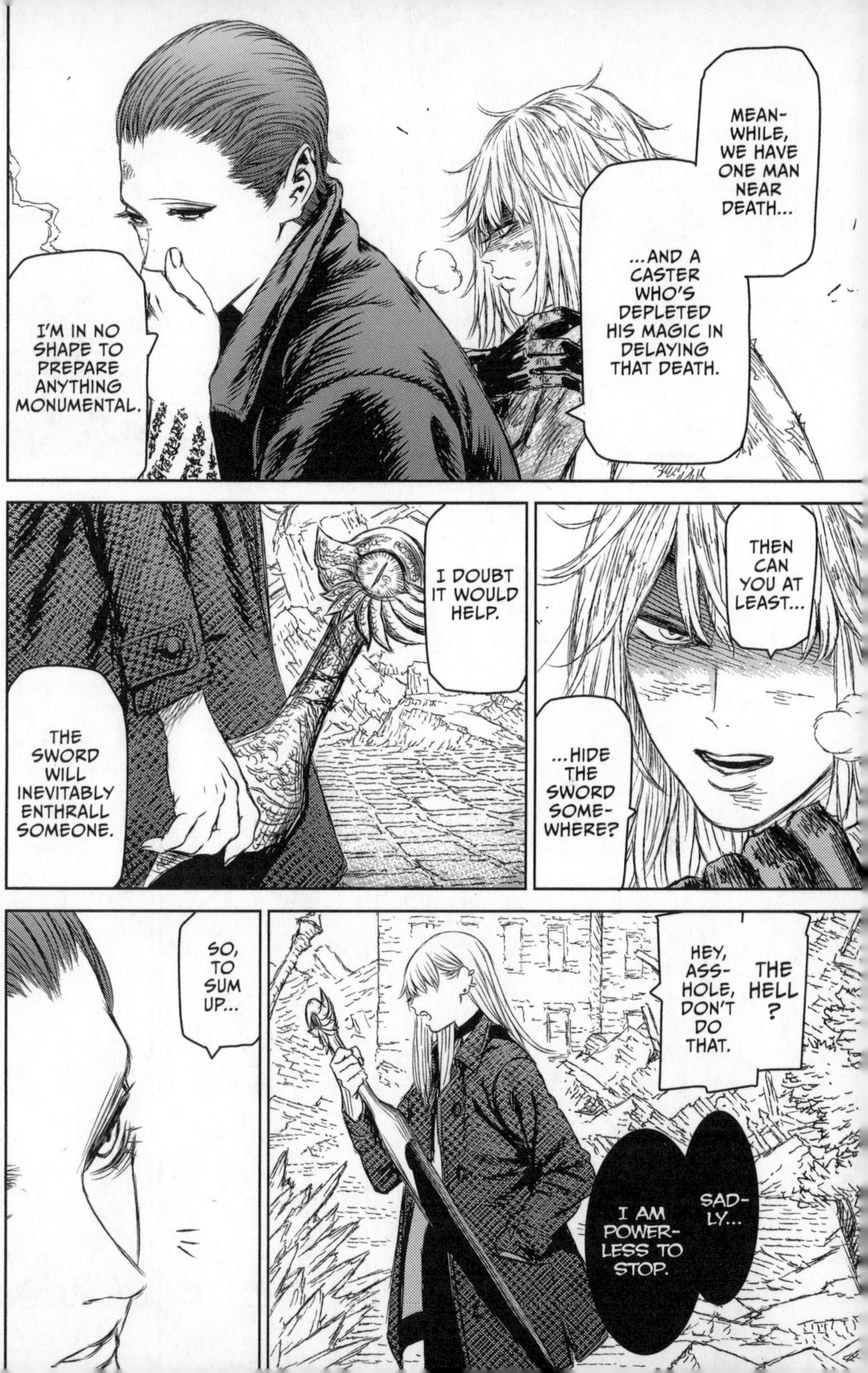

MEANWHILE, WE HAVE ONE MAN NEAR DEATH...
...AND A CASTER WHO'S DEPLETED HIS MAGIC IN DELAYING THAT DEATH.
I'M IN NO SHAPE TO PREPARE ANYTHING MONUMENTAL.
THEN CAN YOU AT LEAST...
...HIDE THE SWORD SOMEWHERE?
I DOUBT IT WOULD HELP.
THE SWORD WILL INEVITABLY ENTHRALL SOMEONE.
THE HELL?
HEY, ASSHOLE, DON'T DO THAT.
SADLY...
I AM POWERLESS TO STOP.
SO, TO SUM UP...

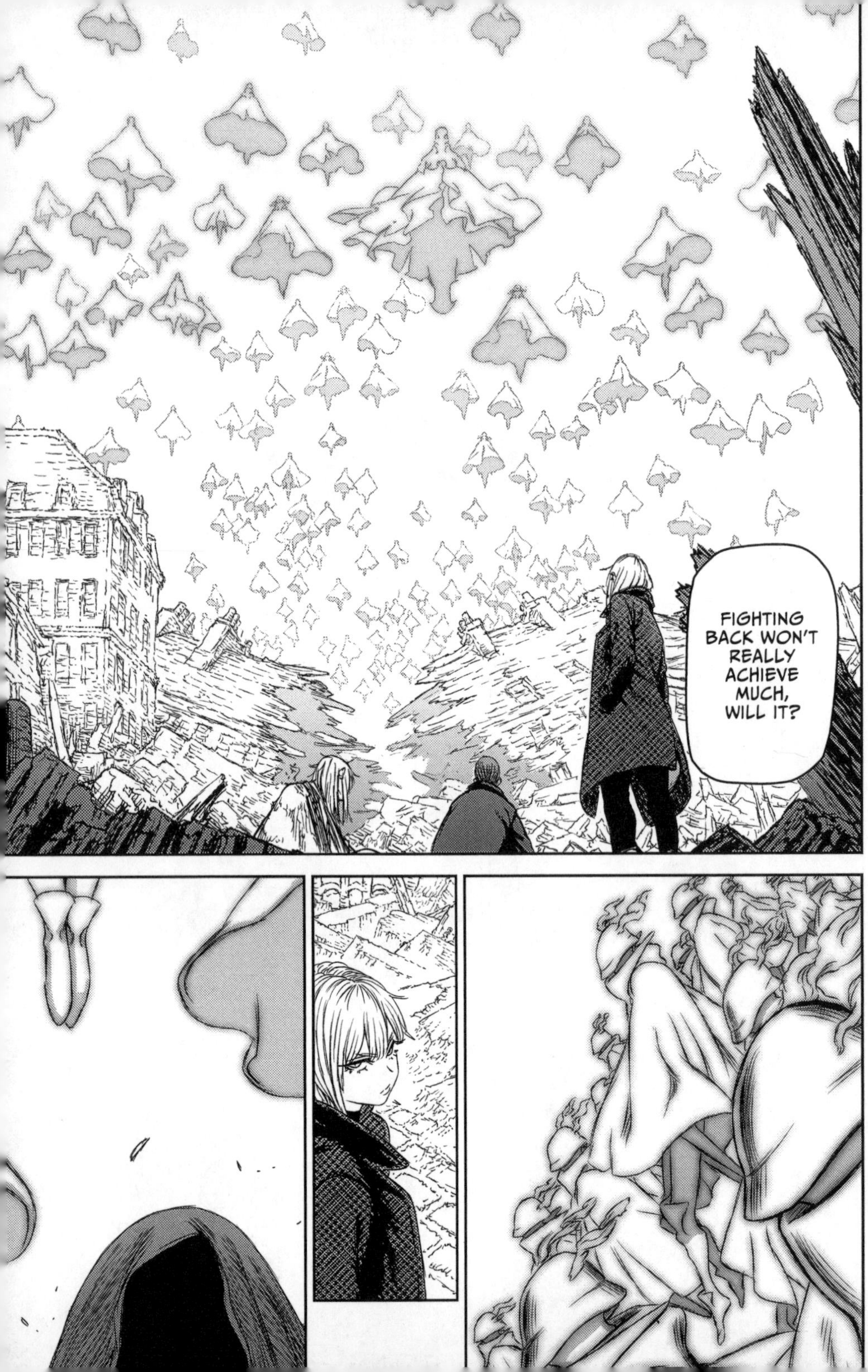
FIGHTING BACK WON'T REALLY ACHIEVE MUCH, WILL IT?

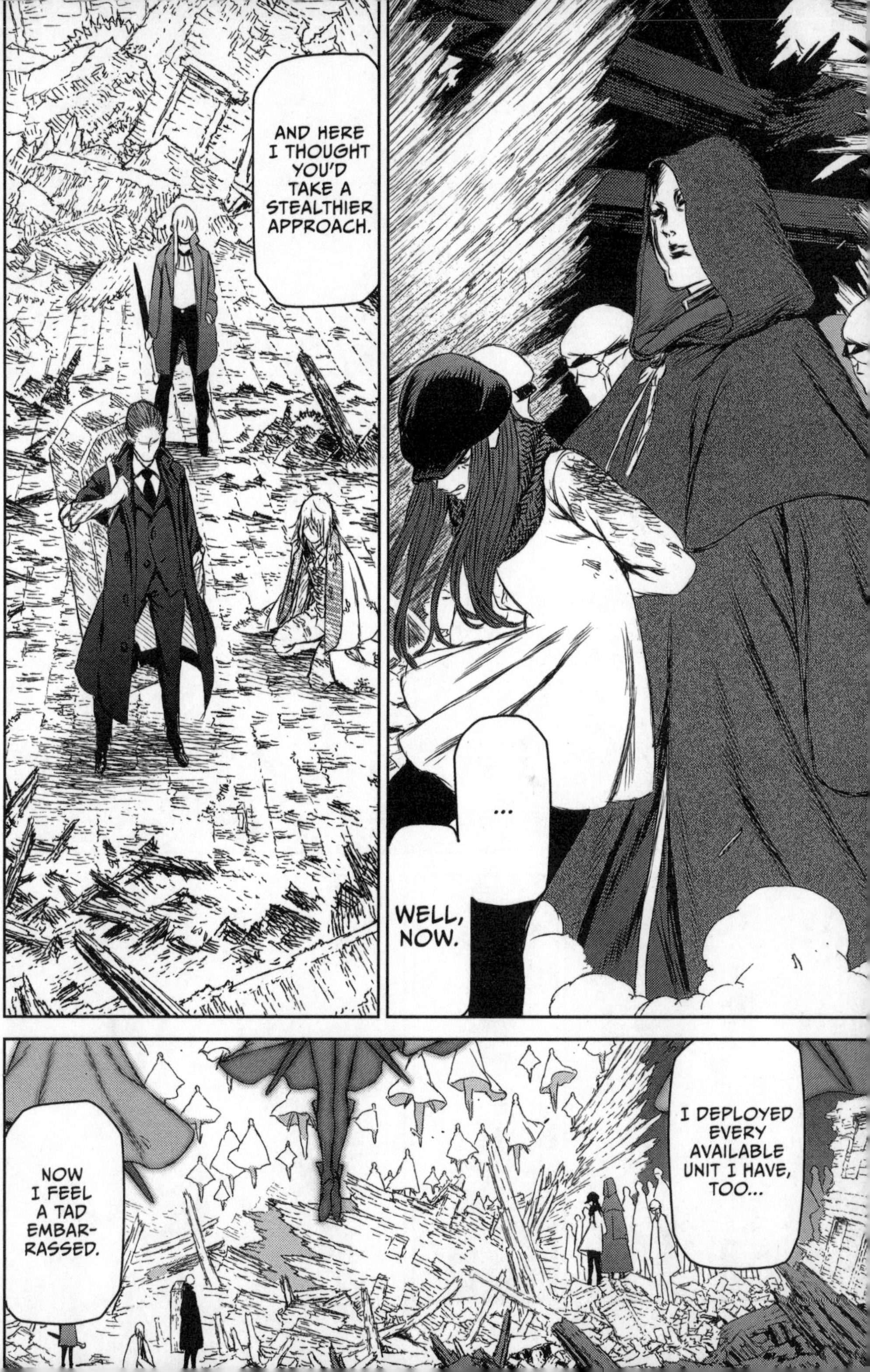
...
WELL, NOW.
AND HERE I THOUGHT YOU'D TAKE A STEALTHIER APPROACH.
I DEPLOYED EVERY AVAILABLE UNIT I HAVE, TOO...
NOW I FEEL A TAD EMBARRASSED.

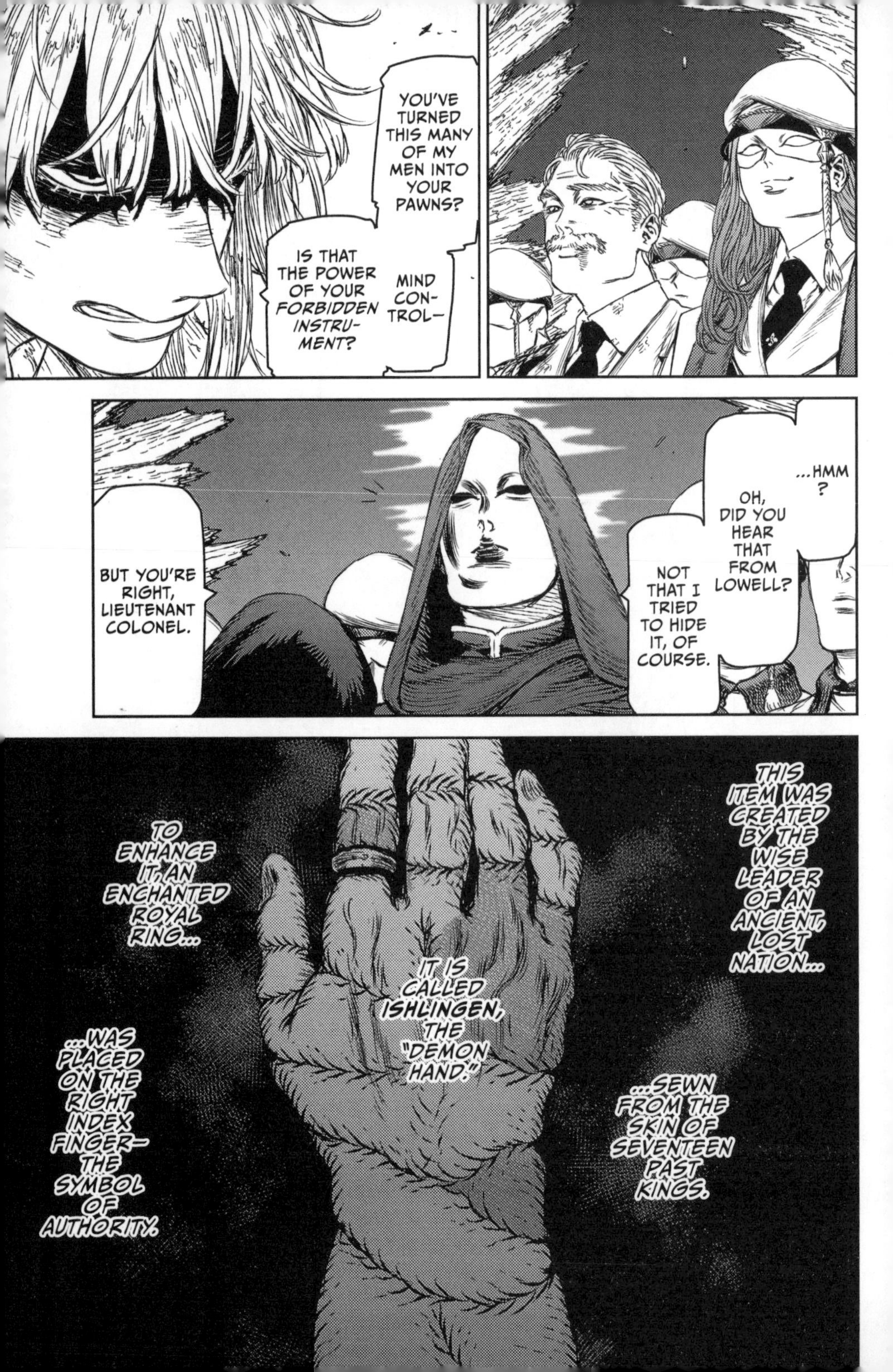
YOU'VE TURNED THIS MANY OF MY MEN INTO YOUR PAWNS?
MIND CON-TROL—
IS THAT THE POWER OF YOUR FORBIDDEN INSTRU-MENT?
...HMM?
OH, DID YOU HEAR THAT FROM LOWELL?
NOT THAT I TRIED TO HIDE IT, OF COURSE.
BUT YOU'RE RIGHT, LIEUTENANT COLONEL.
THIS ITEM WAS CREATED BY THE WISE LEADER OF AN ANCIENT, LOST NATION...
...SEWN FROM THE SKIN OF SEVENTEEN PAST KINGS.
IT IS CALLED ISHLINGEN, THE "DEMON HAND."
TO ENHANCE IT, AN ENCHANTED ROYAL RING...
...WAS PLACED ON THE RIGHT INDEX FINGER— THE SYMBOL OF AUTHORITY.

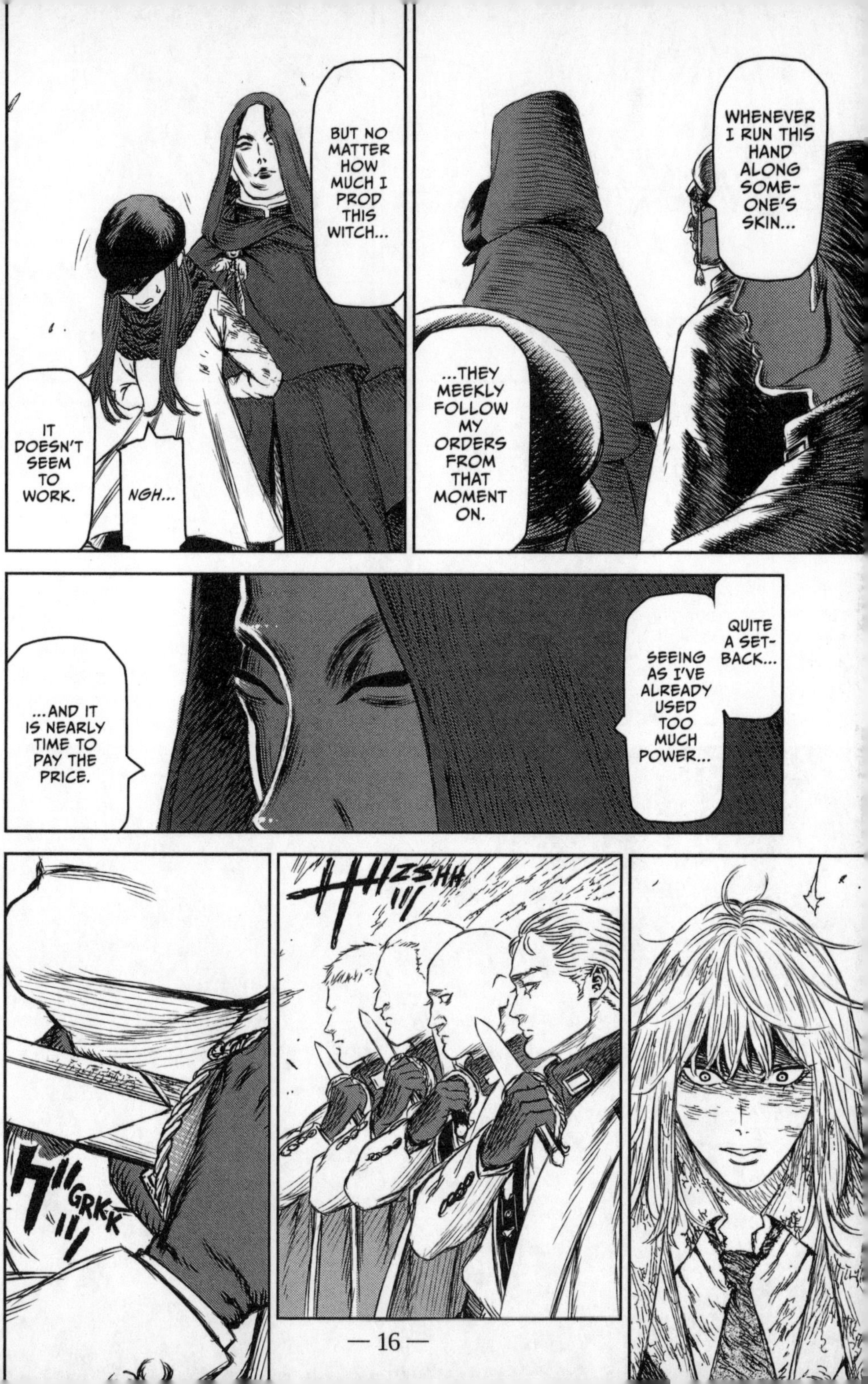
WHENEVER I RUN THIS HAND ALONG SOME-ONE'S SKIN...
...THEY MEEKLY FOLLOW MY ORDERS FROM THAT MOMENT ON.
BUT NO MATTER HOW MUCH I PROD THIS WITCH...
NGH...
IT DOESN'T SEEM TO WORK.
QUITE A SET-BACK...
SEEING AS I'VE ALREADY USED TOO MUCH POWER...
...AND IT IS NEARLY TIME TO PAY THE PRICE.
ZSHH
GRKK

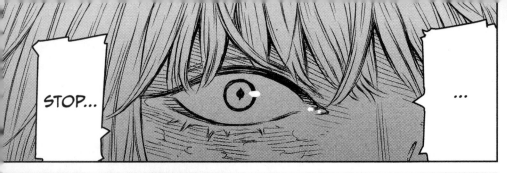

STOP...

...

THRP

THR

THR

THR

SIGH
...

THIS IS ONE SLIGHT DISADVANTAGE TO USING A FORBIDDEN INSTRUMENT.

WHUMP

WHUMP

WHUMP WHUMP

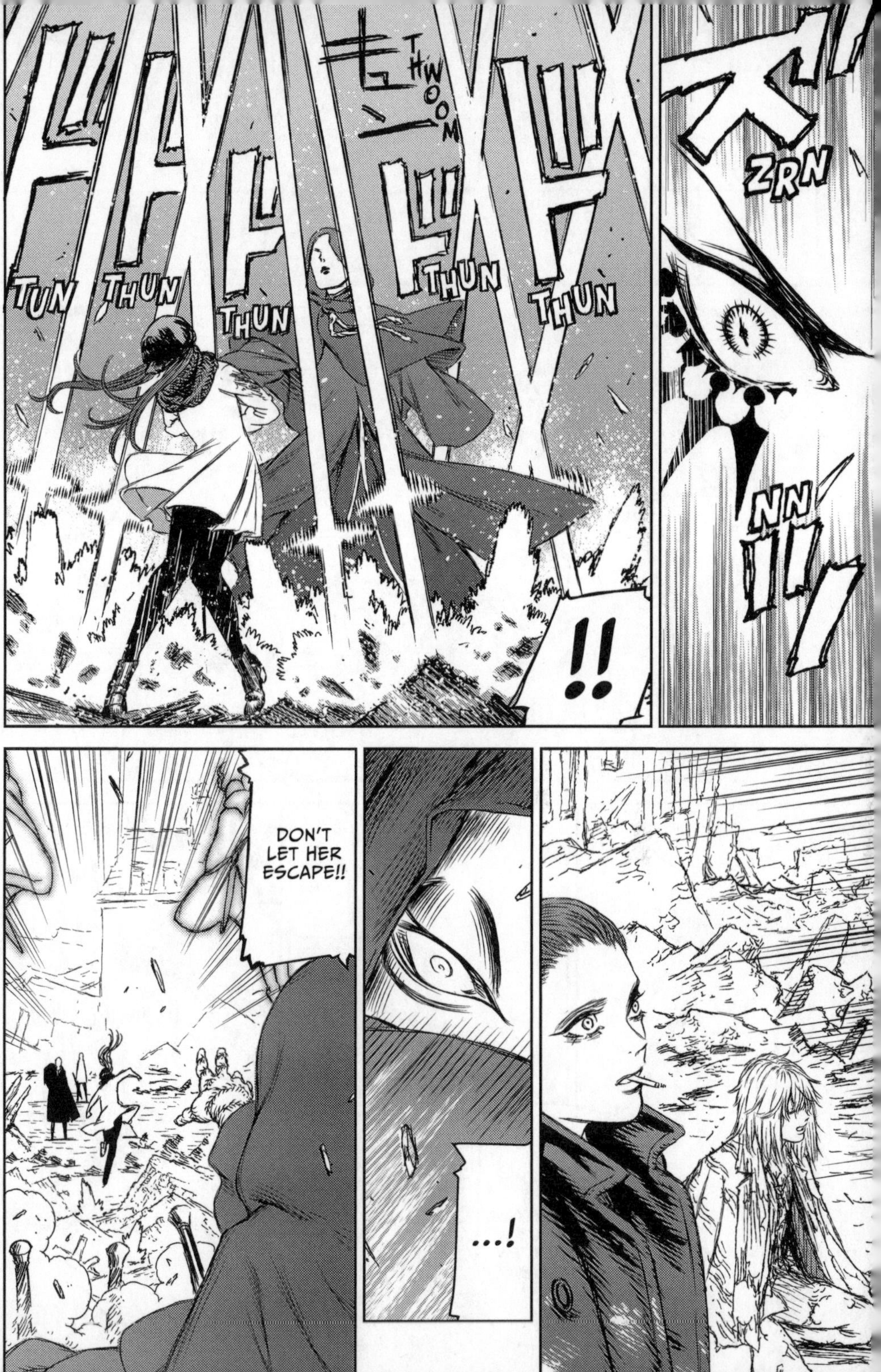
ZRN
NN!!
THWOOM
THUN
THUN
THUN
THUN
TUN
!!
...!
DON'T LET HER ESCAPE!!

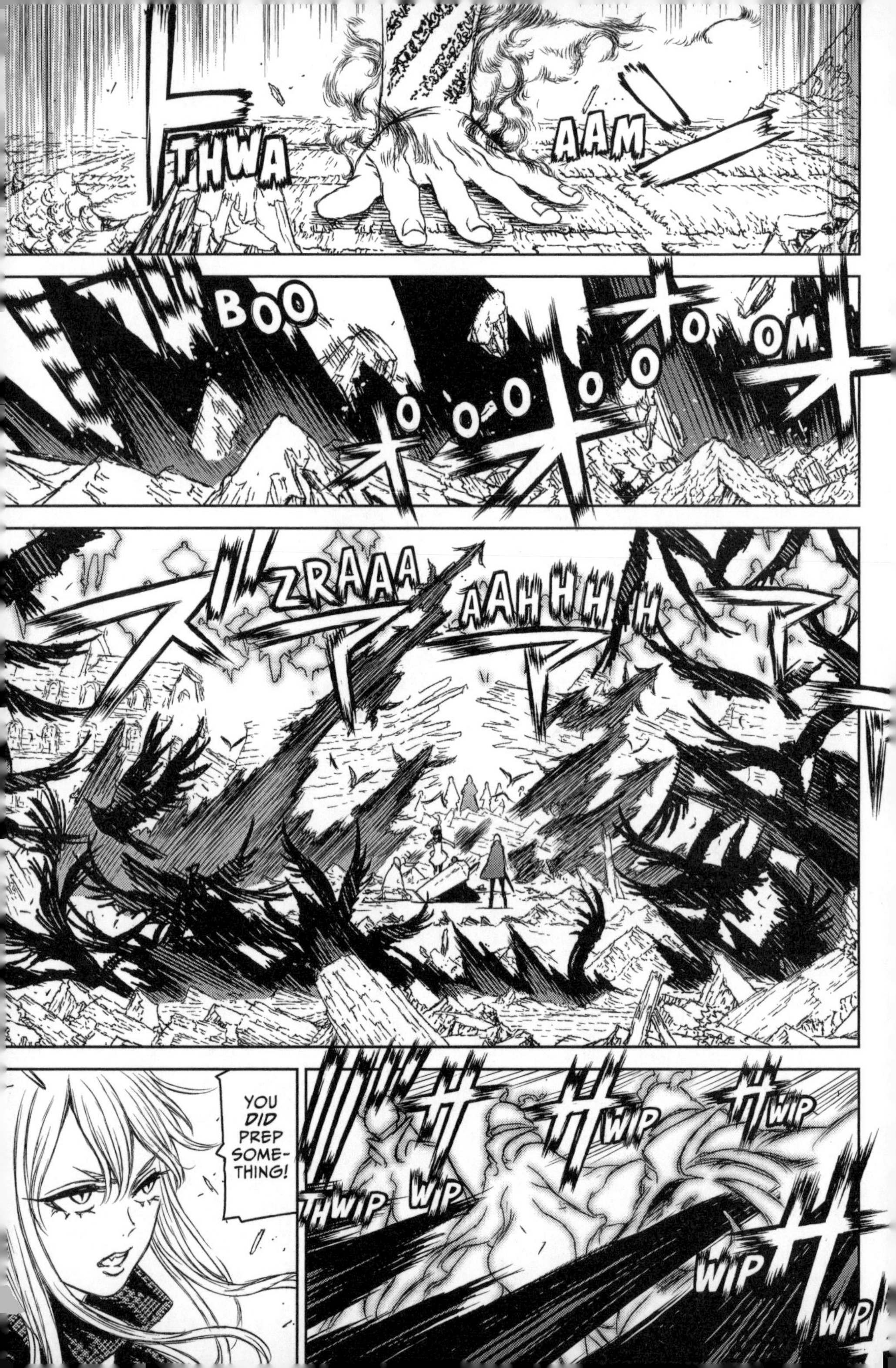
THWA
AAM
BOO
OOOOOO
OM
ZRAAA
AAHHHHH
WIP
WIP
WIP
WIP
THWIP WIP
YOU DID PREP SOME-THING!

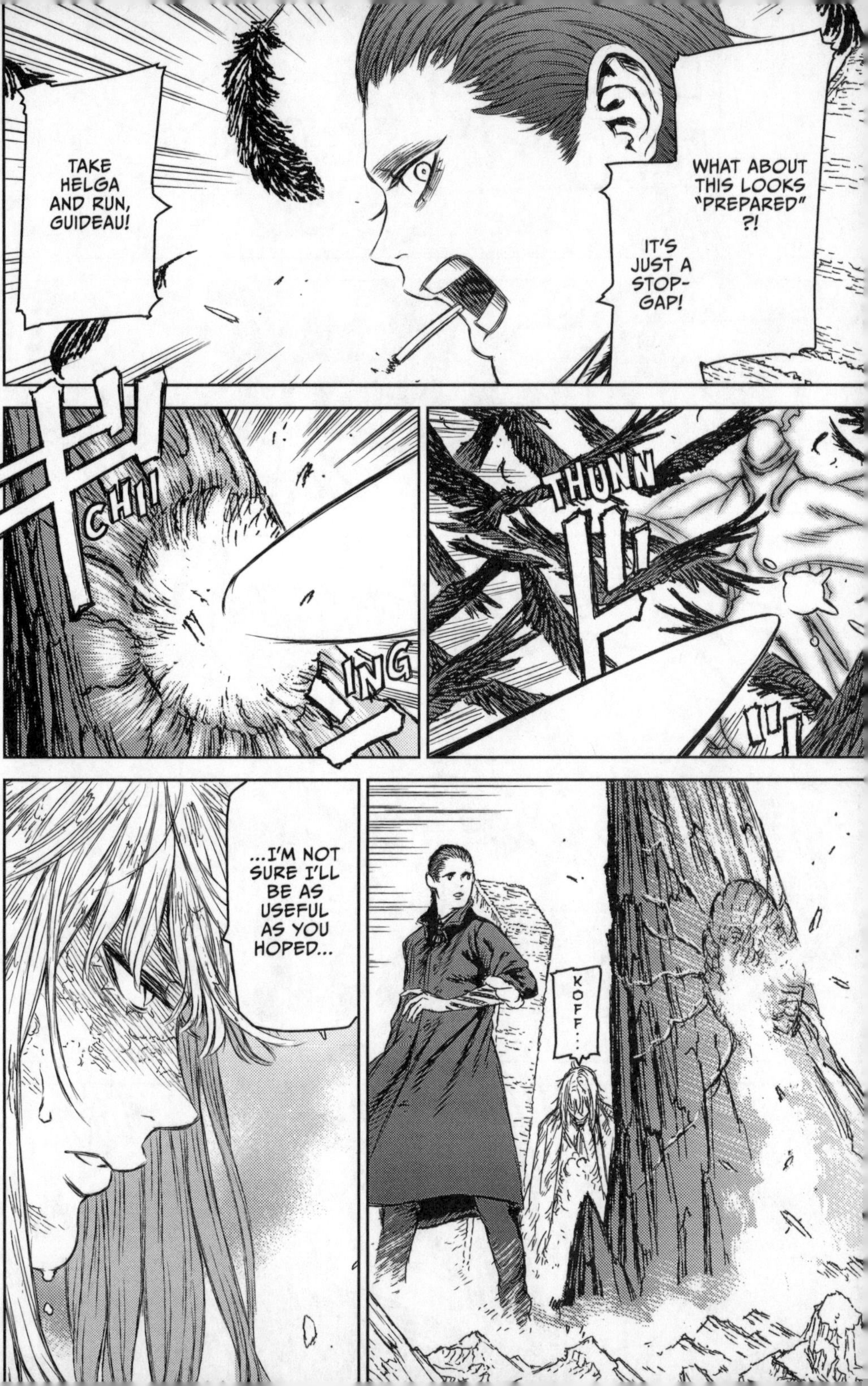
WHAT ABOUT THIS LOOKS "PREPARED" ?!
IT'S JUST A STOP-GAP!
TAKE HELGA AND RUN, GUIDEAU!
THUNN
CHIIING
KOFF...
...I'M NOT SURE I'LL BE AS USEFUL AS YOU HOPED...

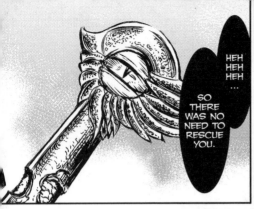

HEH HEH HEH...

SO THERE WAS NO NEED TO RESCUE YOU.

OH?

WERE YOU *REALLY* PLANNING TO COME SAVE ME?

WILL YOU QUIT YAPPING?!

WE GOTTA RUN!

...!!

!

BEHIND YOU!

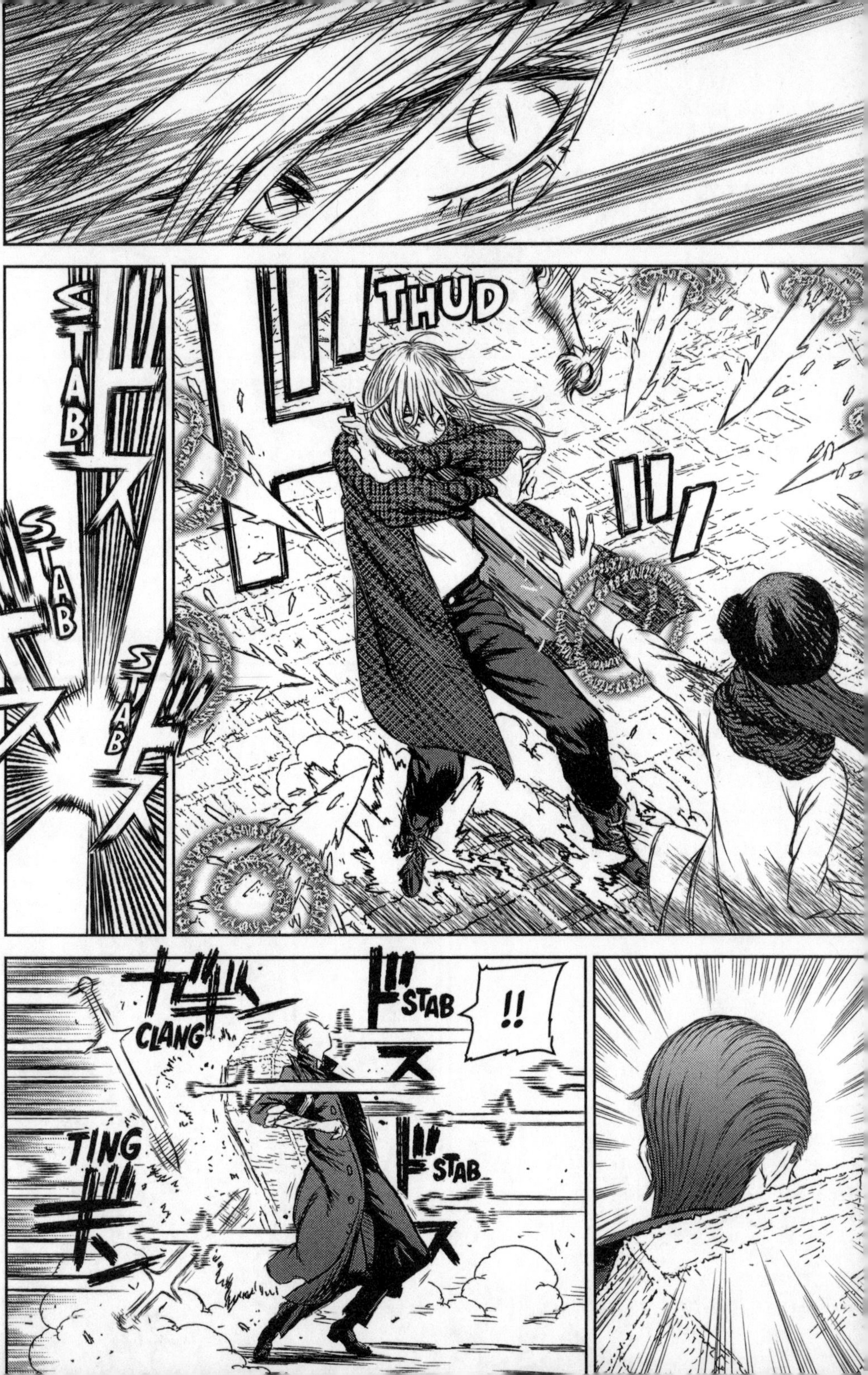
THUD
STAB
STAB
STAB
!!
STAB
CLANG
STAB
TING

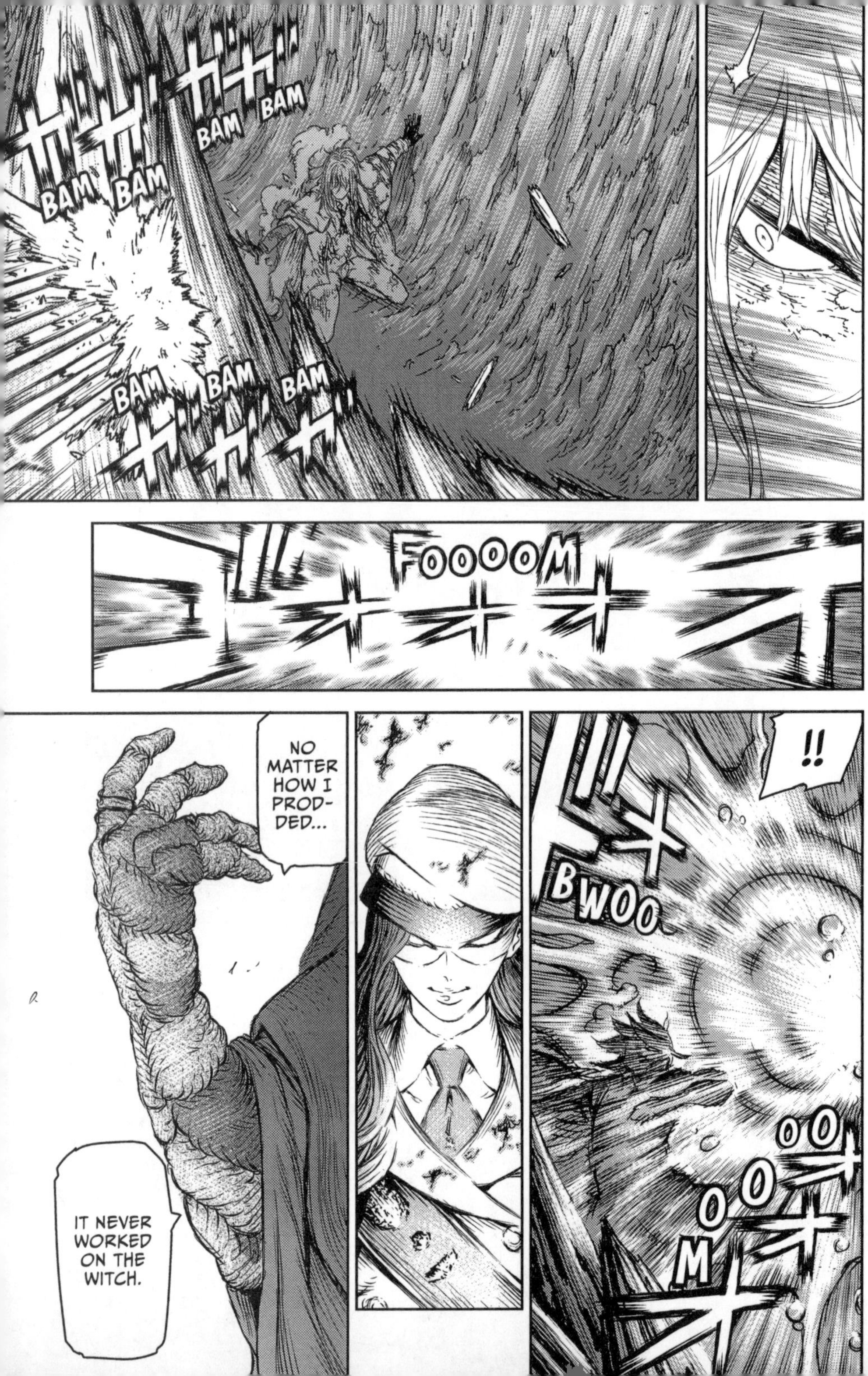
BAM BAM BAM BAM
BAM BAM BAM
FOOOOM
!!
BWOOOOOM
NO MATTER HOW I PRODDED...
IT NEVER WORKED ON THE WITCH.

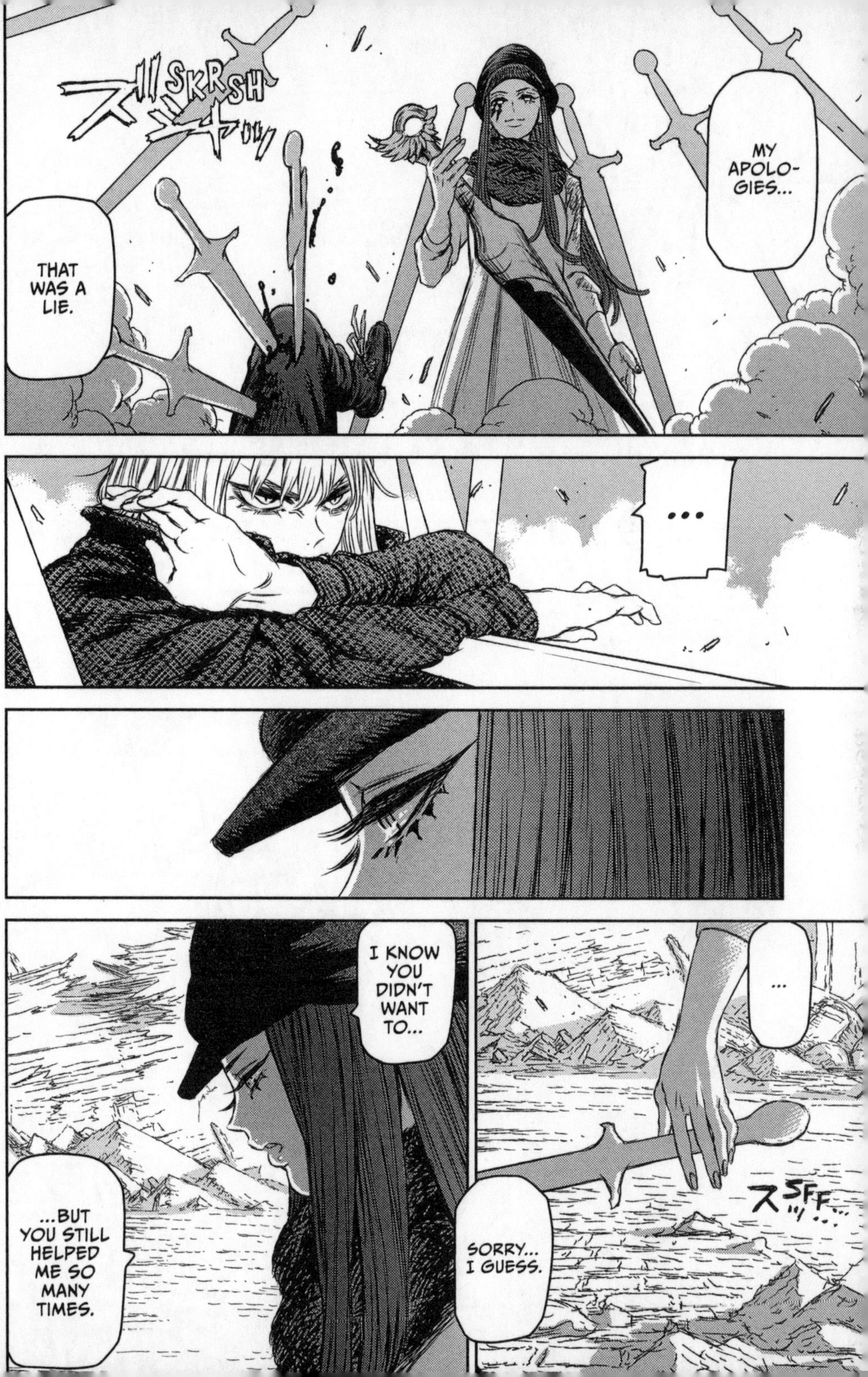
MY APOLO-GIES...
SKRSH
THAT WAS A LIE.
...
...
SFF...
SORRY... I GUESS.
I KNOW YOU DIDN'T WANT TO...
...BUT YOU STILL HELPED ME SO MANY TIMES.

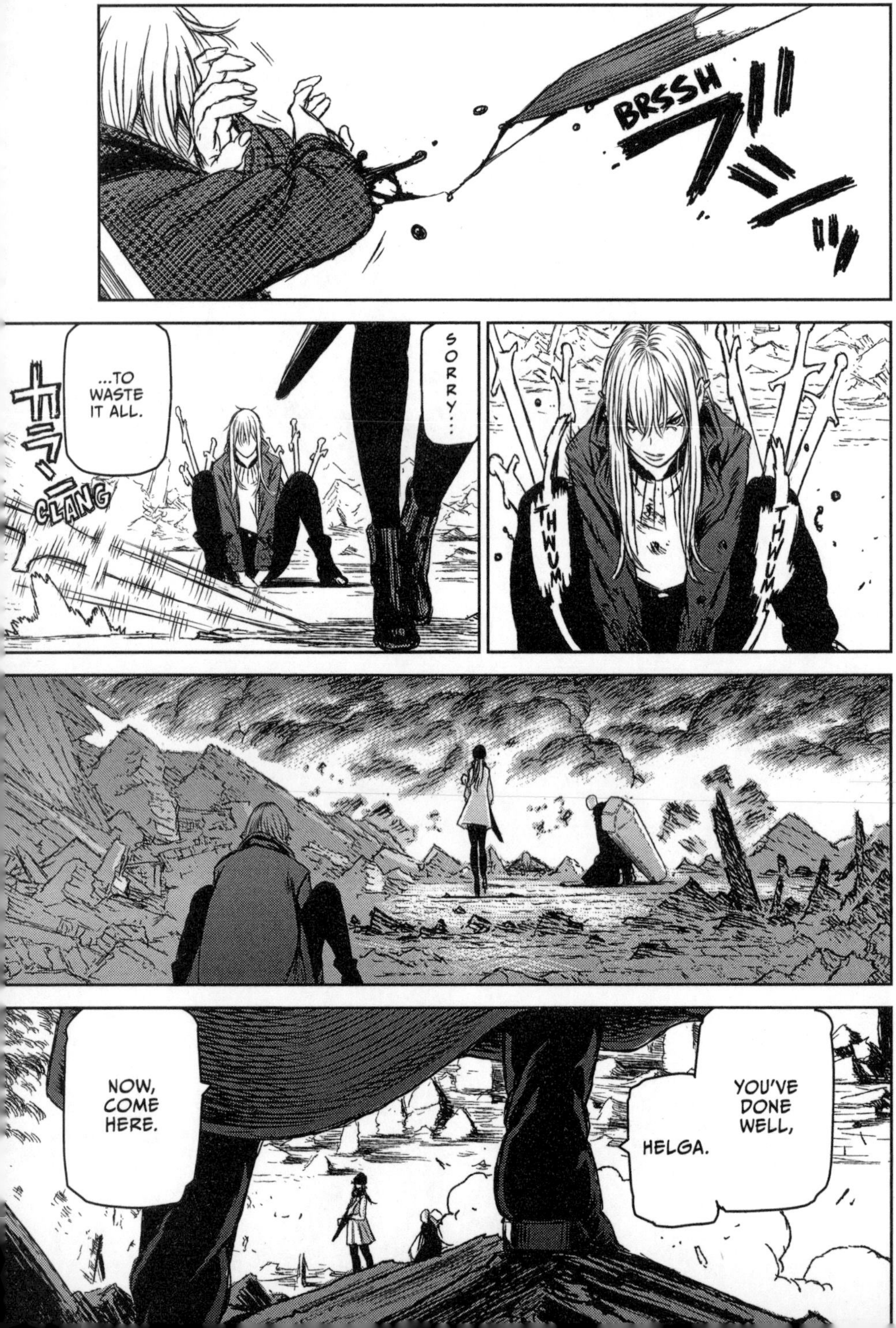
BRSSH
THWUM
THWUM
SORRY...
...TO WASTE IT ALL.
CLANG
YOU'VE DONE WELL,
HELGA.
NOW, COME HERE.

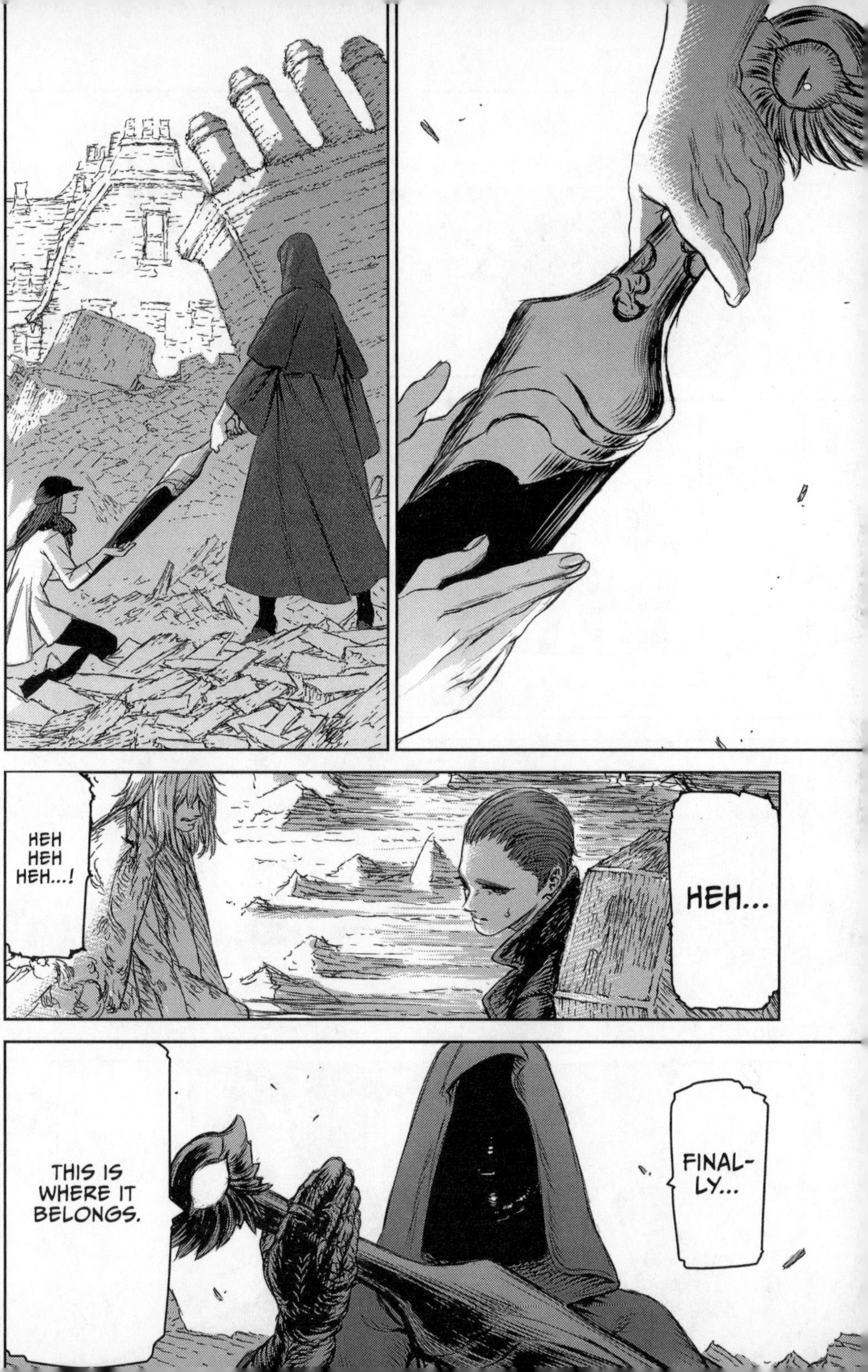
HEH...
HEH HEH HEH...!
FINAL-LY...
THIS IS WHERE IT BELONGS.

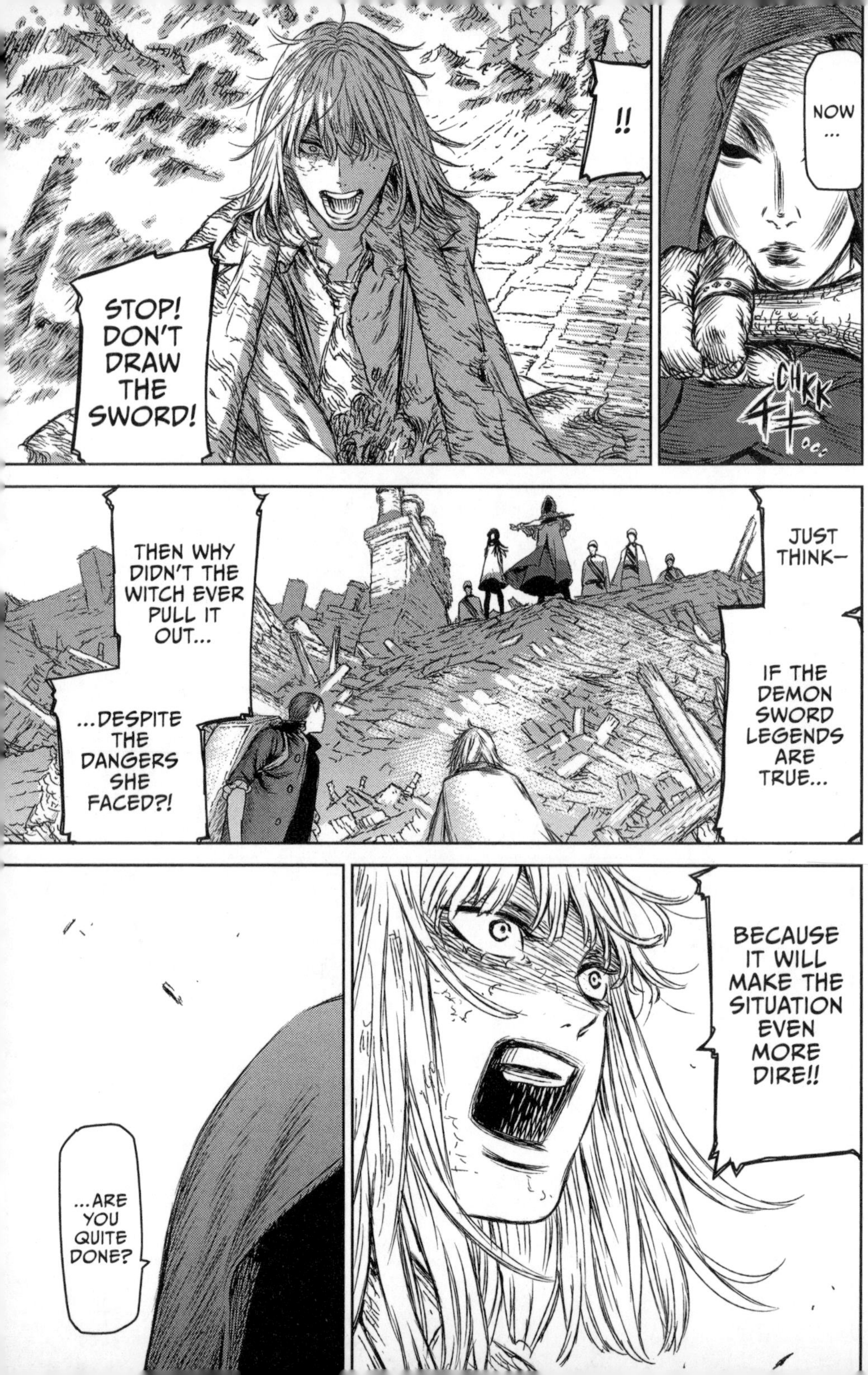

NOW ...
CHKK
!!
STOP! DON'T DRAW THE SWORD!
JUST THINK—
IF THE DEMON SWORD LEGENDS ARE TRUE...
THEN WHY DIDN'T THE WITCH EVER PULL IT OUT...
...DESPITE THE DANGERS SHE FACED?!
BECAUSE IT WILL MAKE THE SITUATION EVEN MORE DIRE!!
...ARE YOU QUITE DONE?

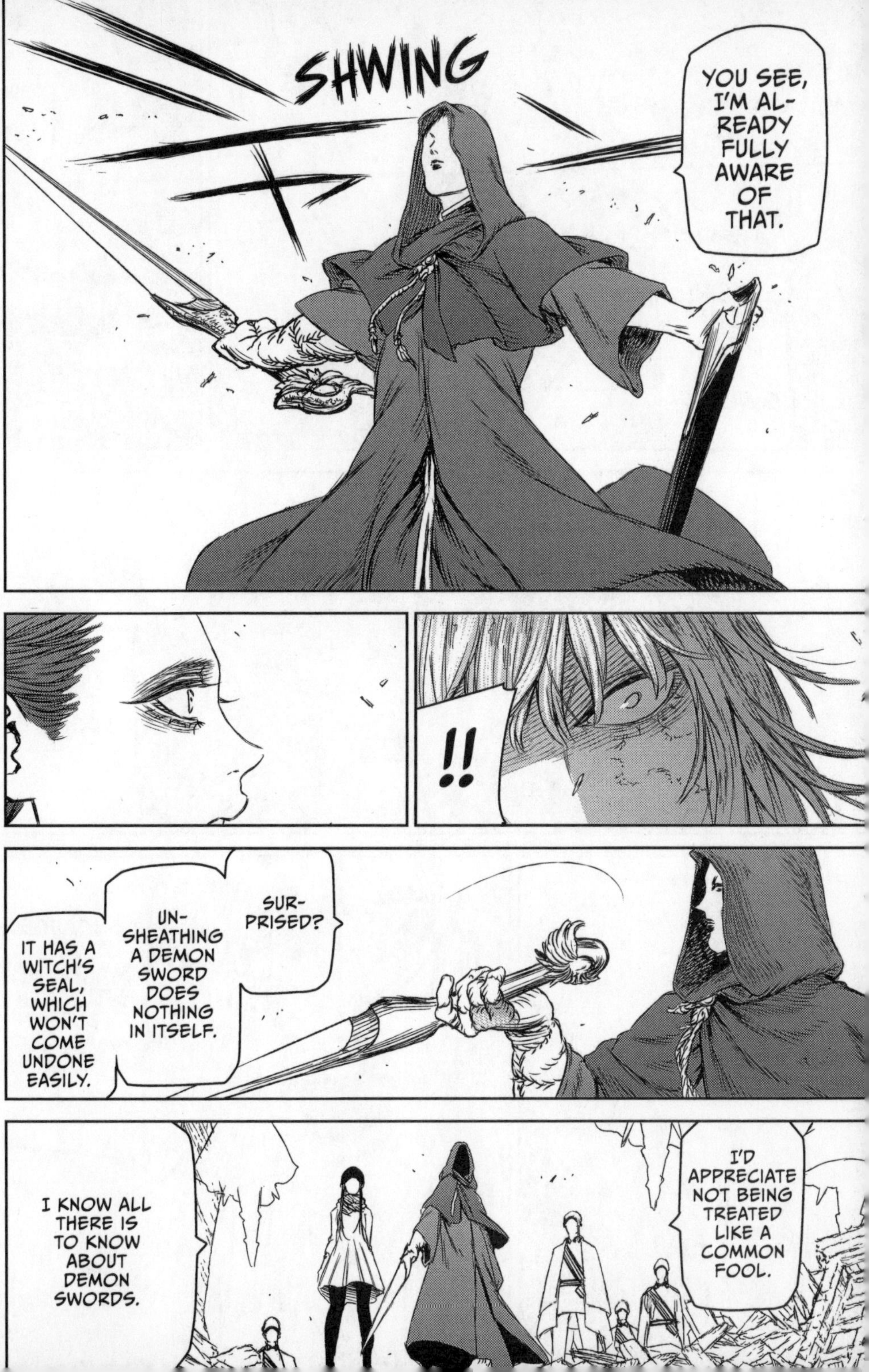
YOU SEE, I'M ALREADY FULLY AWARE OF THAT.
SHWING
!!
SURPRISED?
UNSHEATHING A DEMON SWORD DOES NOTHING IN ITSELF.
IT HAS A WITCH'S SEAL, WHICH WON'T COME UNDONE EASILY.
I'D APPRECIATE NOT BEING TREATED LIKE A COMMON FOOL.
I KNOW ALL THERE IS TO KNOW ABOUT DEMON SWORDS.

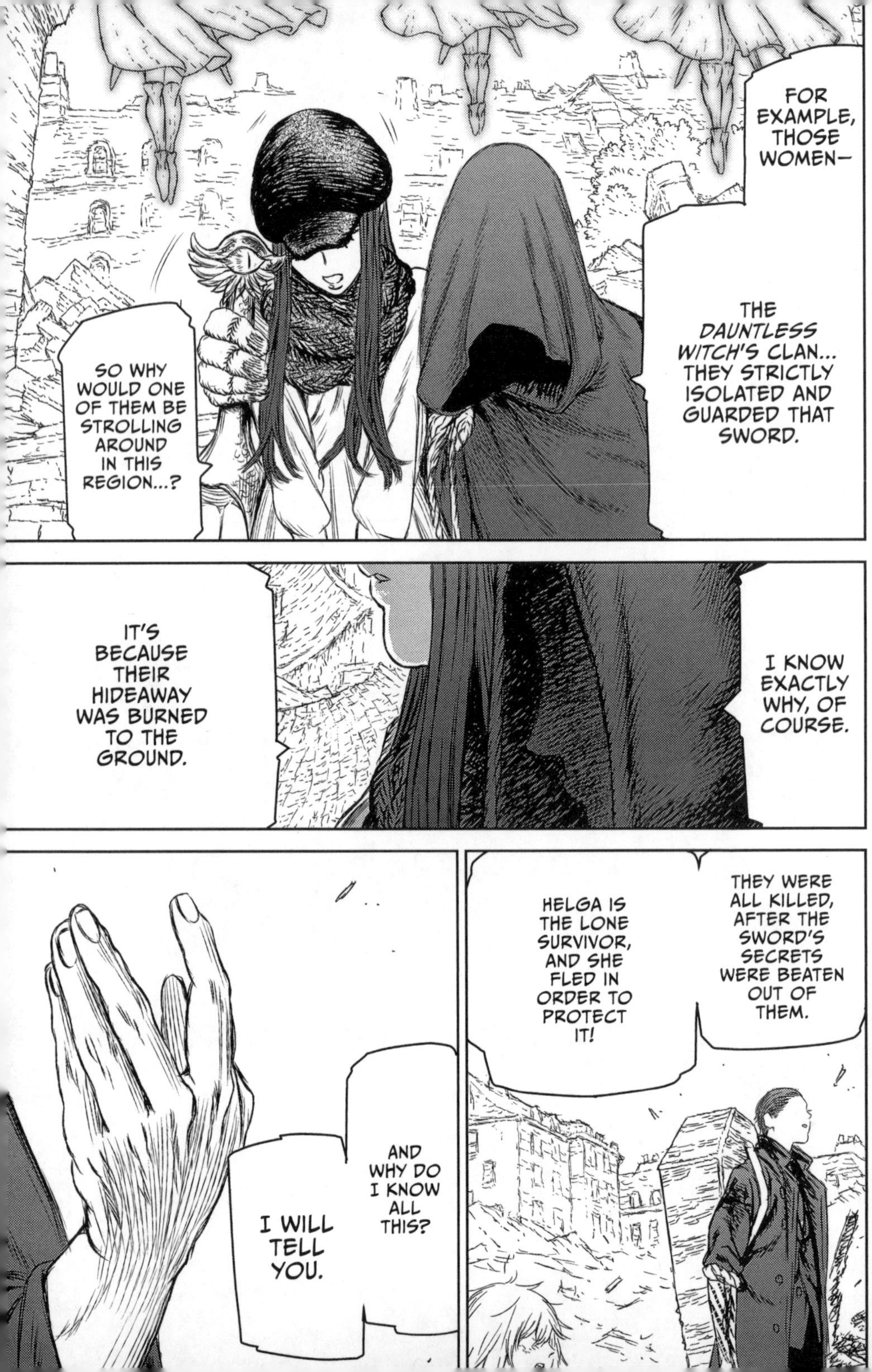

FOR EXAMPLE, THOSE WOMEN—
THE *DAUNTLESS WITCH'S* CLAN... THEY STRICTLY ISOLATED AND GUARDED THAT SWORD.
SO WHY WOULD ONE OF THEM BE STROLLING AROUND IN THIS REGION...?
I KNOW EXACTLY WHY, OF COURSE.
IT'S BECAUSE THEIR HIDEAWAY WAS BURNED TO THE GROUND.
THEY WERE ALL KILLED, AFTER THE SWORD'S SECRETS WERE BEATEN OUT OF THEM.
HELGA IS THE LONE SURVIVOR, AND SHE FLED IN ORDER TO PROTECT IT!
AND WHY DO I KNOW ALL THIS?
I WILL TELL YOU.

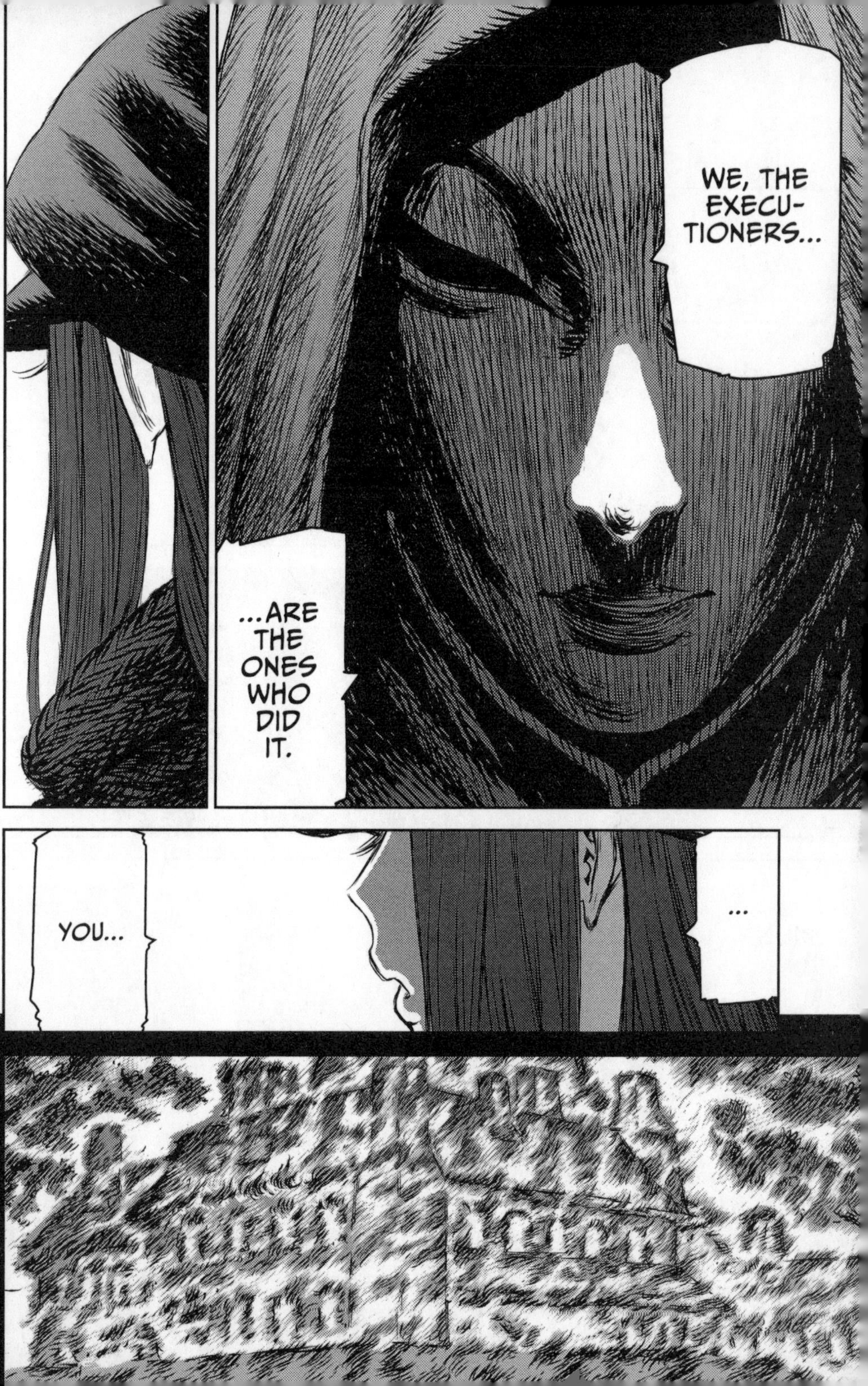
WE, THE EXECUTIONERS...
...ARE THE ONES WHO DID IT.
...
YOU...

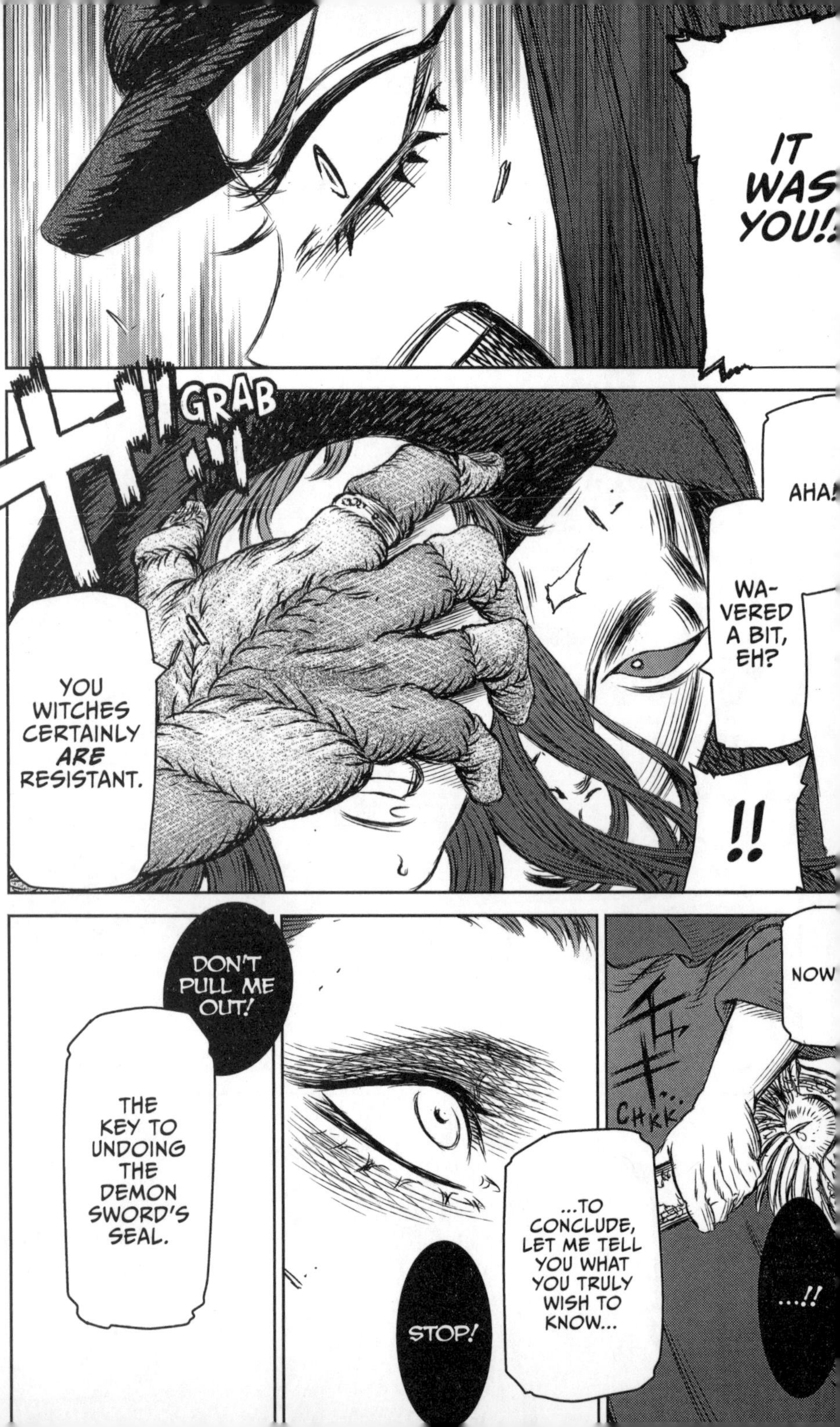
IT WAS YOU!
AHA
WA-VERED A BIT, EH?
!!
GRAB
YOU WITCHES CERTAINLY *ARE* RESISTANT.
NOW
CHKK
...!!
...TO CONCLUDE, LET ME TELL YOU WHAT YOU TRULY WISH TO KNOW...
STOP!
DON'T PULL ME OUT!
THE KEY TO UNDOING THE DEMON SWORD'S SEAL.

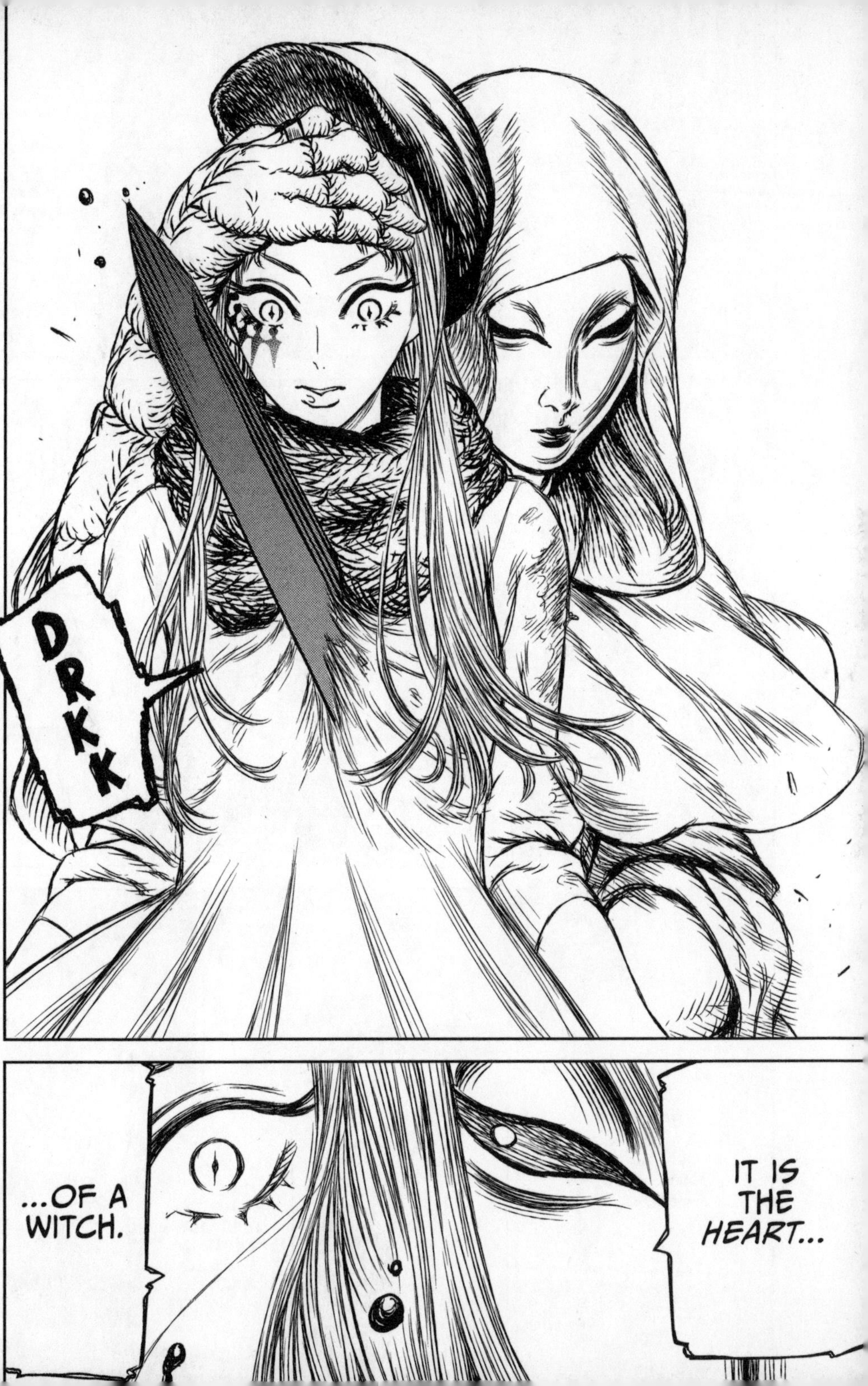
DRKK
IT IS THE HEART...
...OF A WITCH.

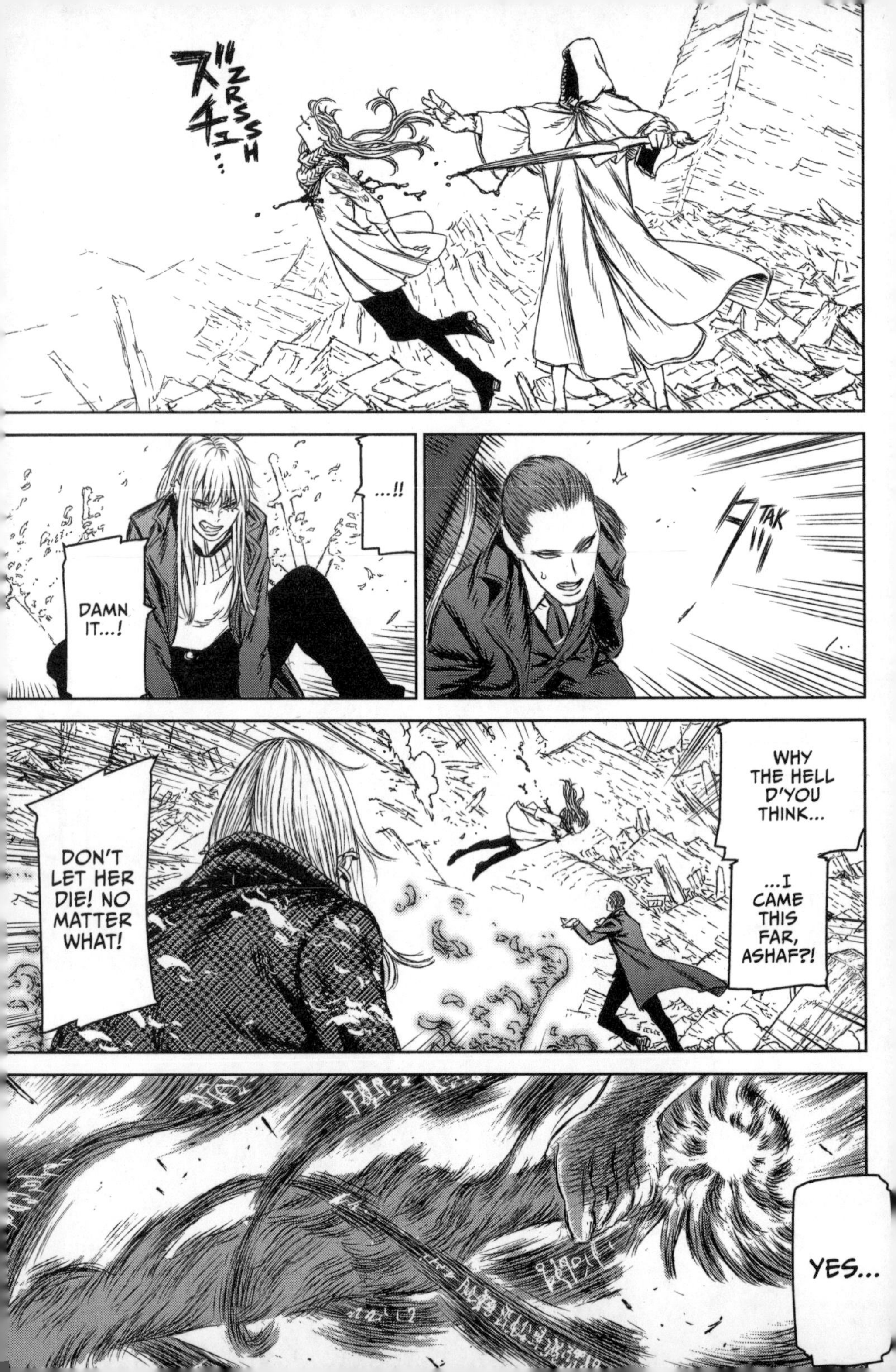
ZRSSH
TAK
...!!
DAMN IT...!
WHY THE HELL D'YOU THINK...
...I CAME THIS FAR, ASHAF?!
DON'T LET HER DIE! NO MATTER WHAT!
YES...

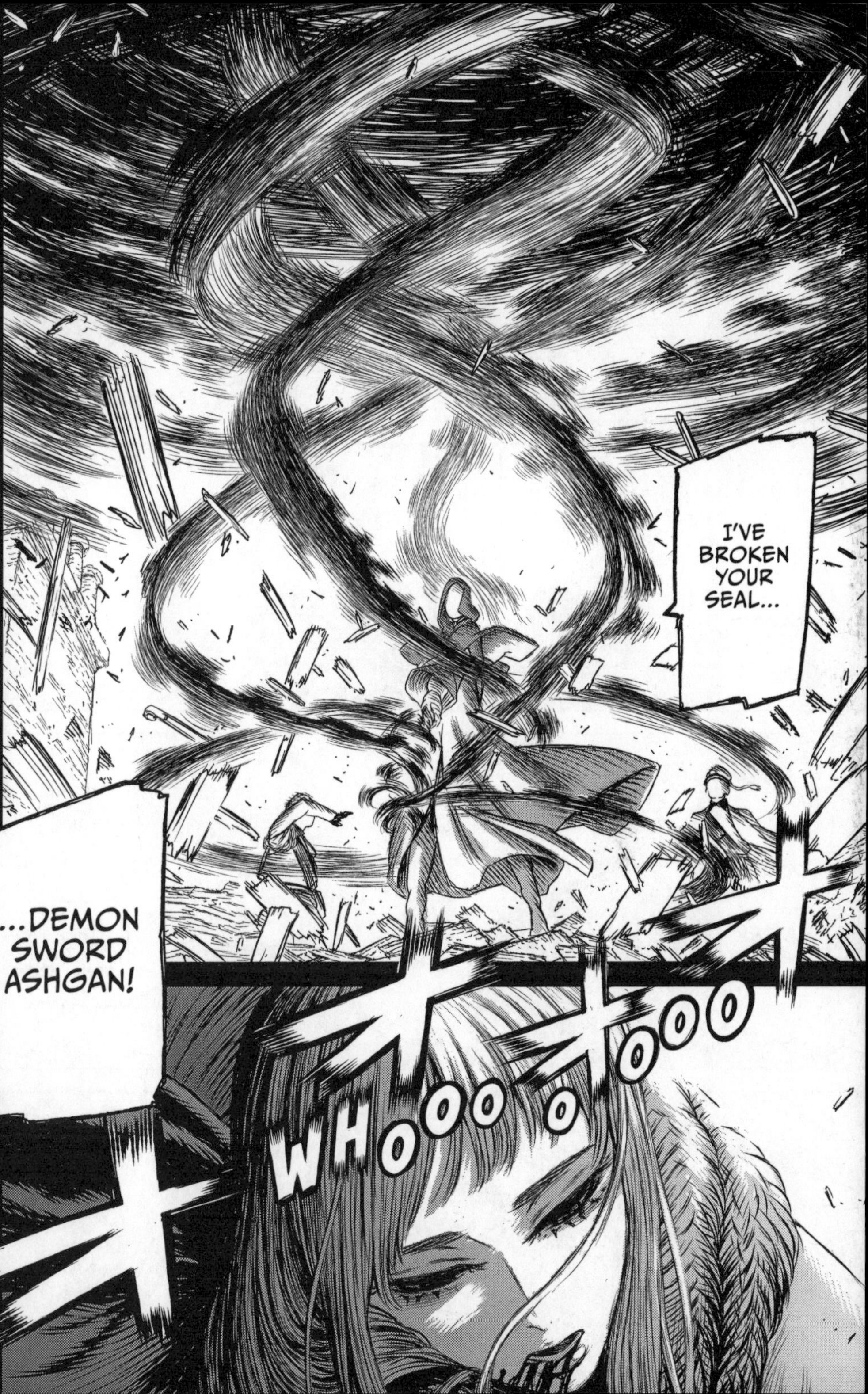
I'VE BROKEN YOUR SEAL...
...DEMON SWORD ASHGAN!
WHOOOOOOOO

THE WITCH AND THE BEAST

THE WITCH AND THE BEAST

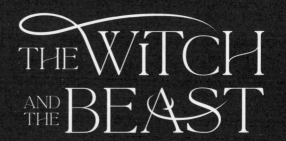

CHAPTER 19: THE WITCH AND THE DEMON SWORD—ACT X

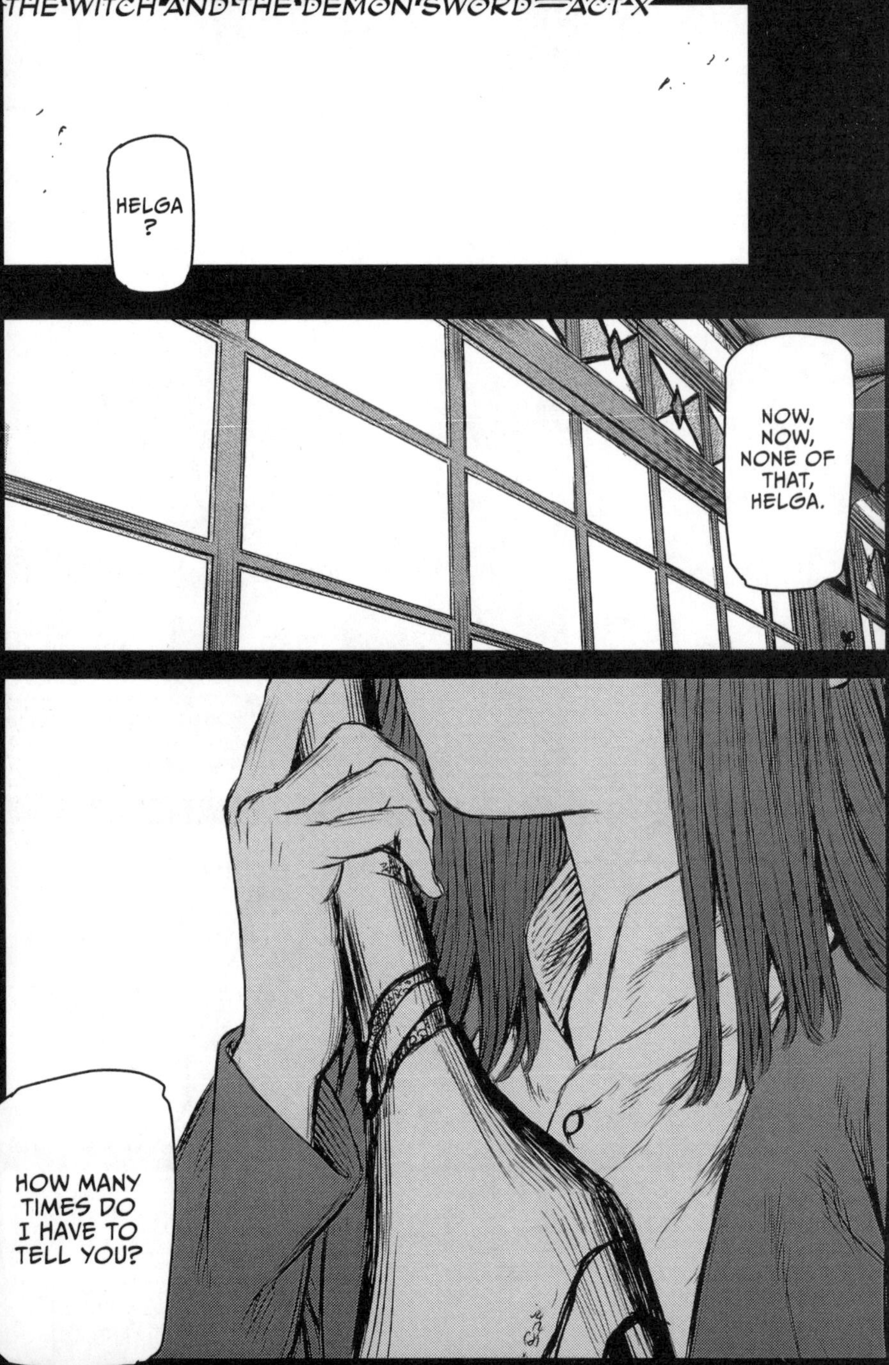
HELGA ?
NOW, NOW, NONE OF THAT, HELGA.
HOW MANY TIMES DO I HAVE TO TELL YOU?

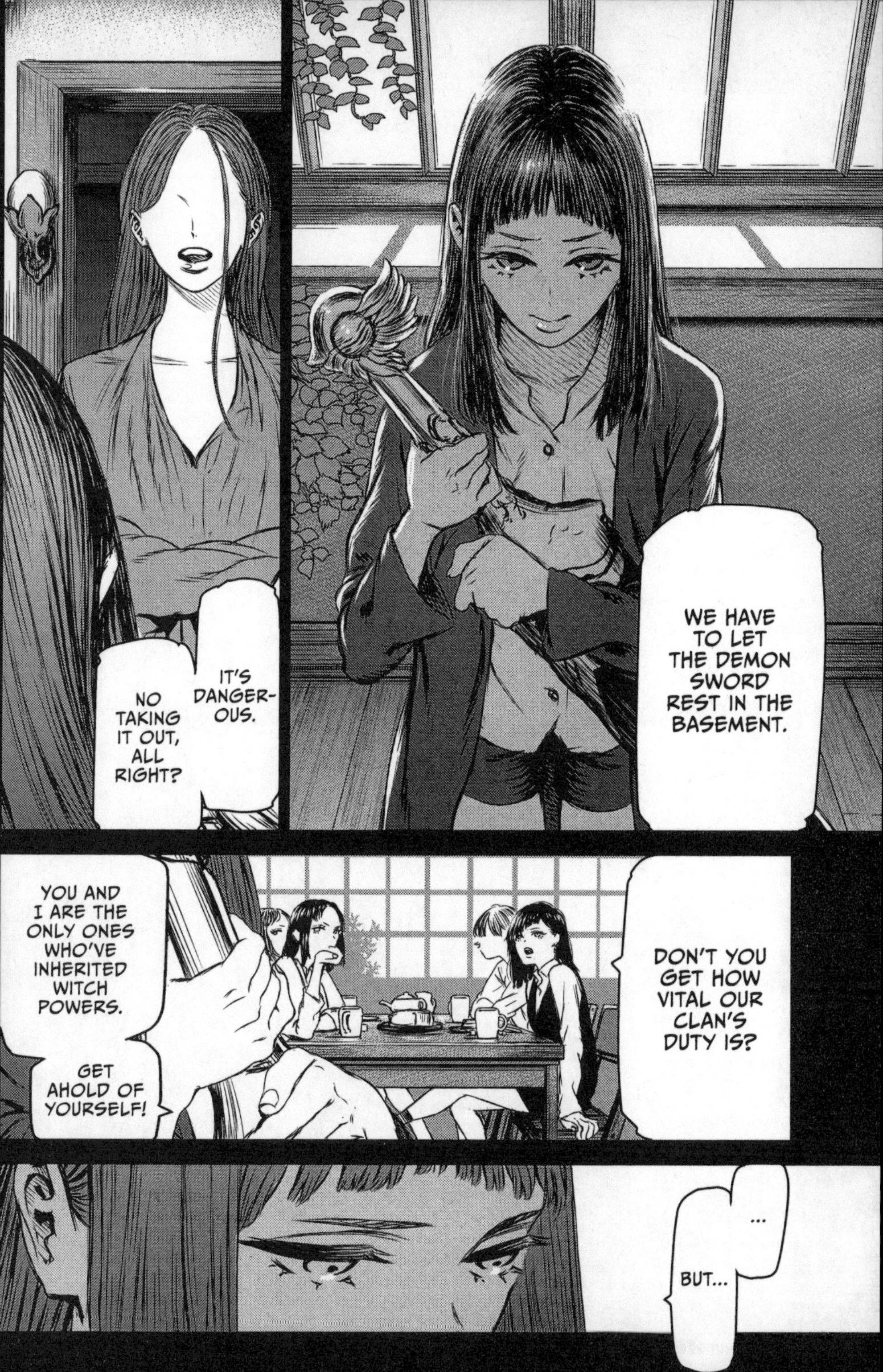
WE HAVE TO LET THE DEMON SWORD REST IN THE BASEMENT.
IT'S DANGER-OUS.
NO TAKING IT OUT, ALL RIGHT?
DON'T YOU GET HOW VITAL OUR CLAN'S DUTY IS?
YOU AND I ARE THE ONLY ONES WHO'VE INHERITED WITCH POWERS.
GET AHOLD OF YOURSELF!
...
BUT...

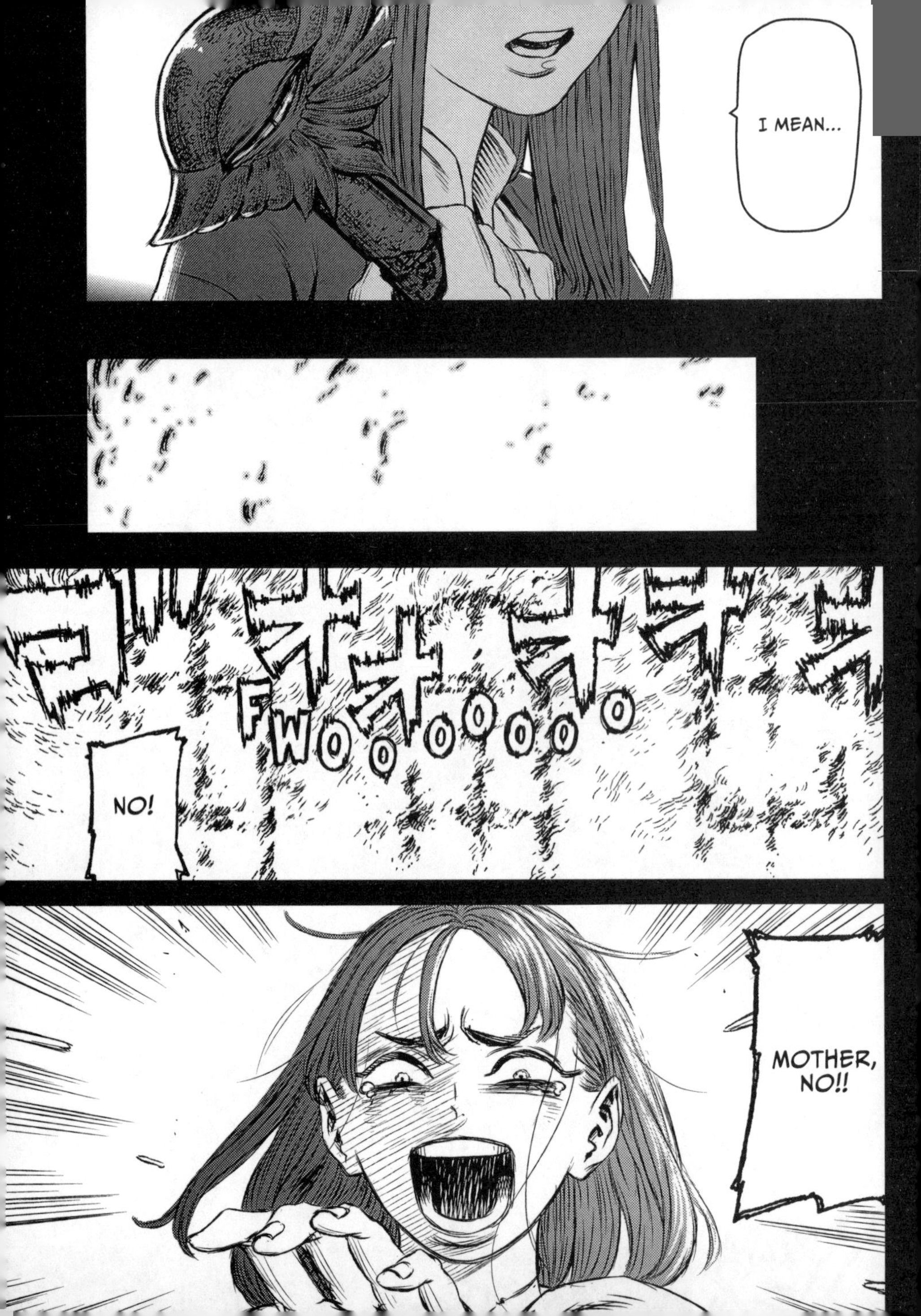
I MEAN...
FWOOOOOOO
NO!
MOTHER, NO!!

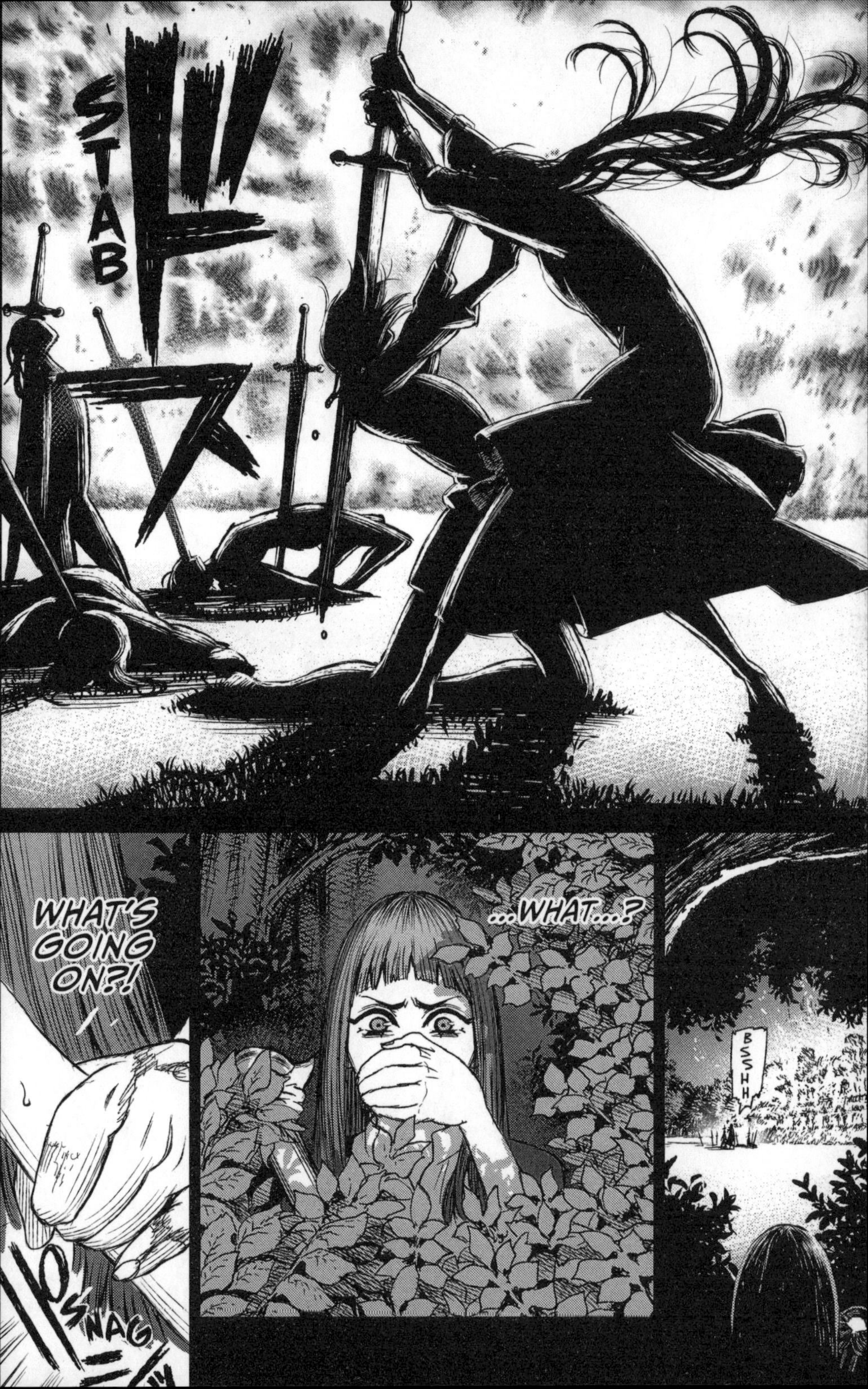
STAB
BSSHH
...WHAT...?
WHAT'S GOING ON?!
SNAG

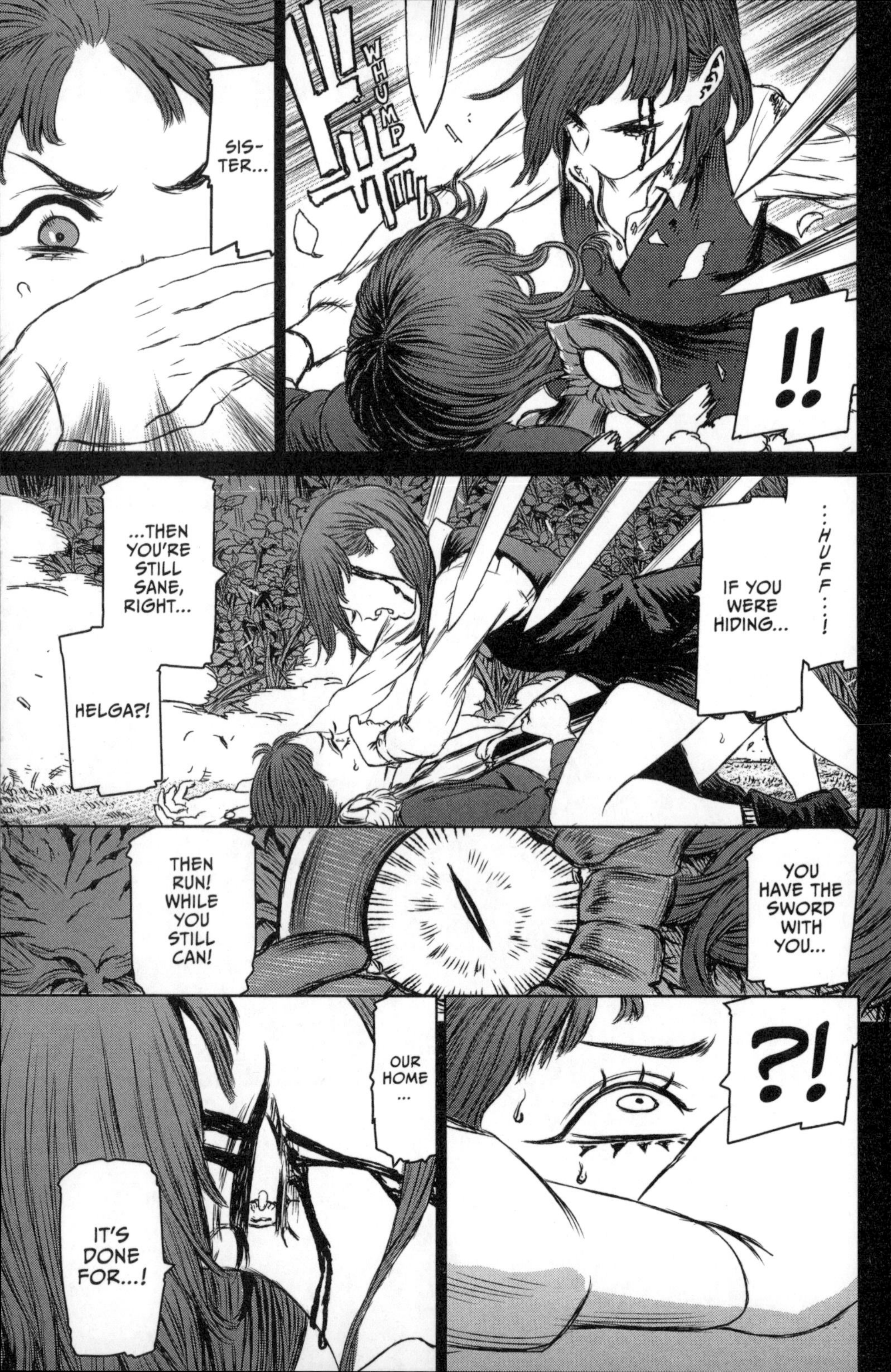
WHUMP
!!
SIS-TER...
...HUFF...!
IF YOU WERE HIDING...
...THEN YOU'RE STILL SANE, RIGHT...
HELGA?!
YOU HAVE THE SWORD WITH YOU...
THEN RUN! WHILE YOU STILL CAN!
?!
OUR HOME ...
IT'S DONE FOR...!

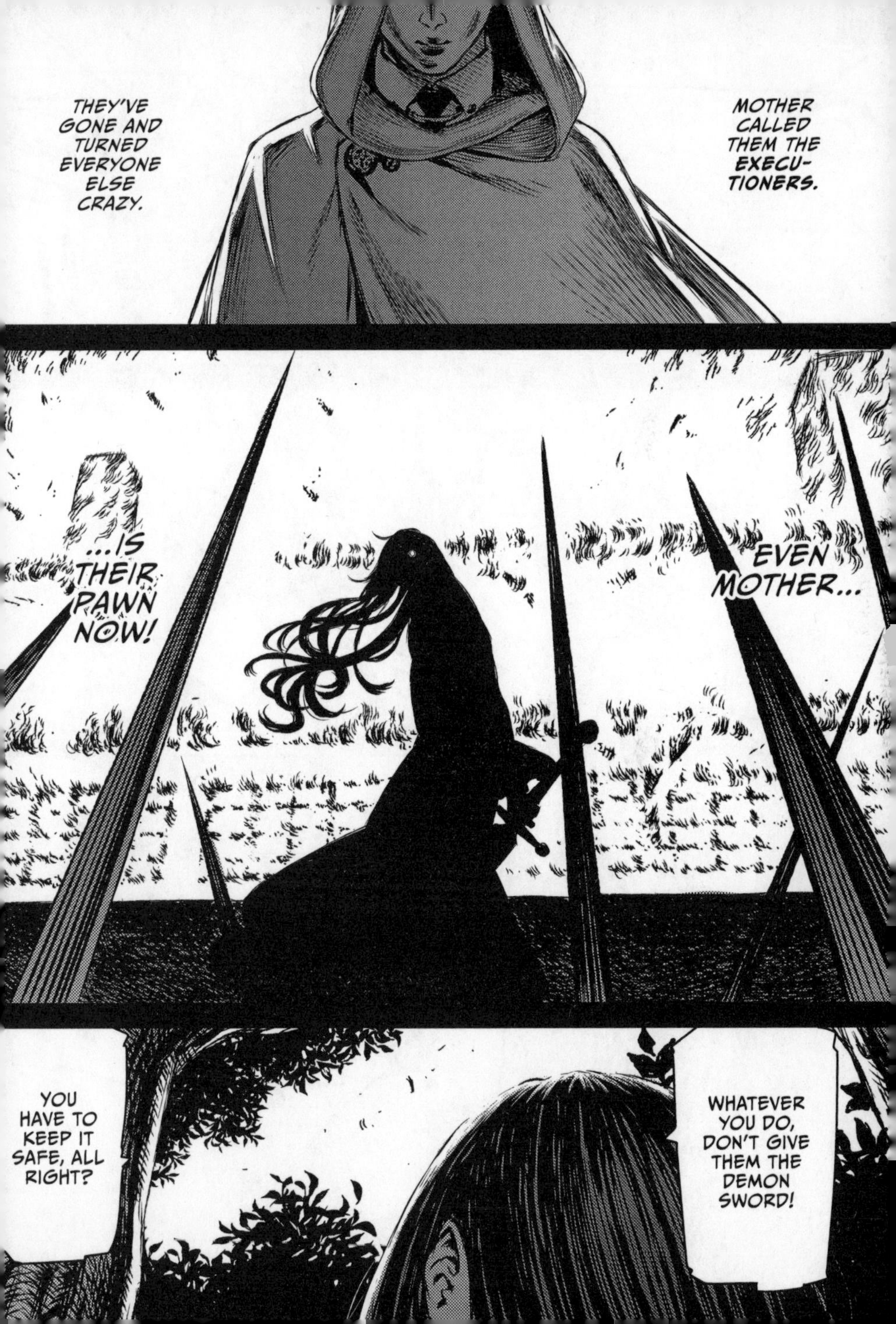
MOTHER CALLED THEM THE EXECUTIONERS.
THEY'VE GONE AND TURNED EVERYONE ELSE CRAZY.
EVEN MOTHER...
...IS THEIR PAWN NOW!
WHATEVER YOU DO, DON'T GIVE THEM THE DEMON SWORD!
YOU HAVE TO KEEP IT SAFE, ALL RIGHT?

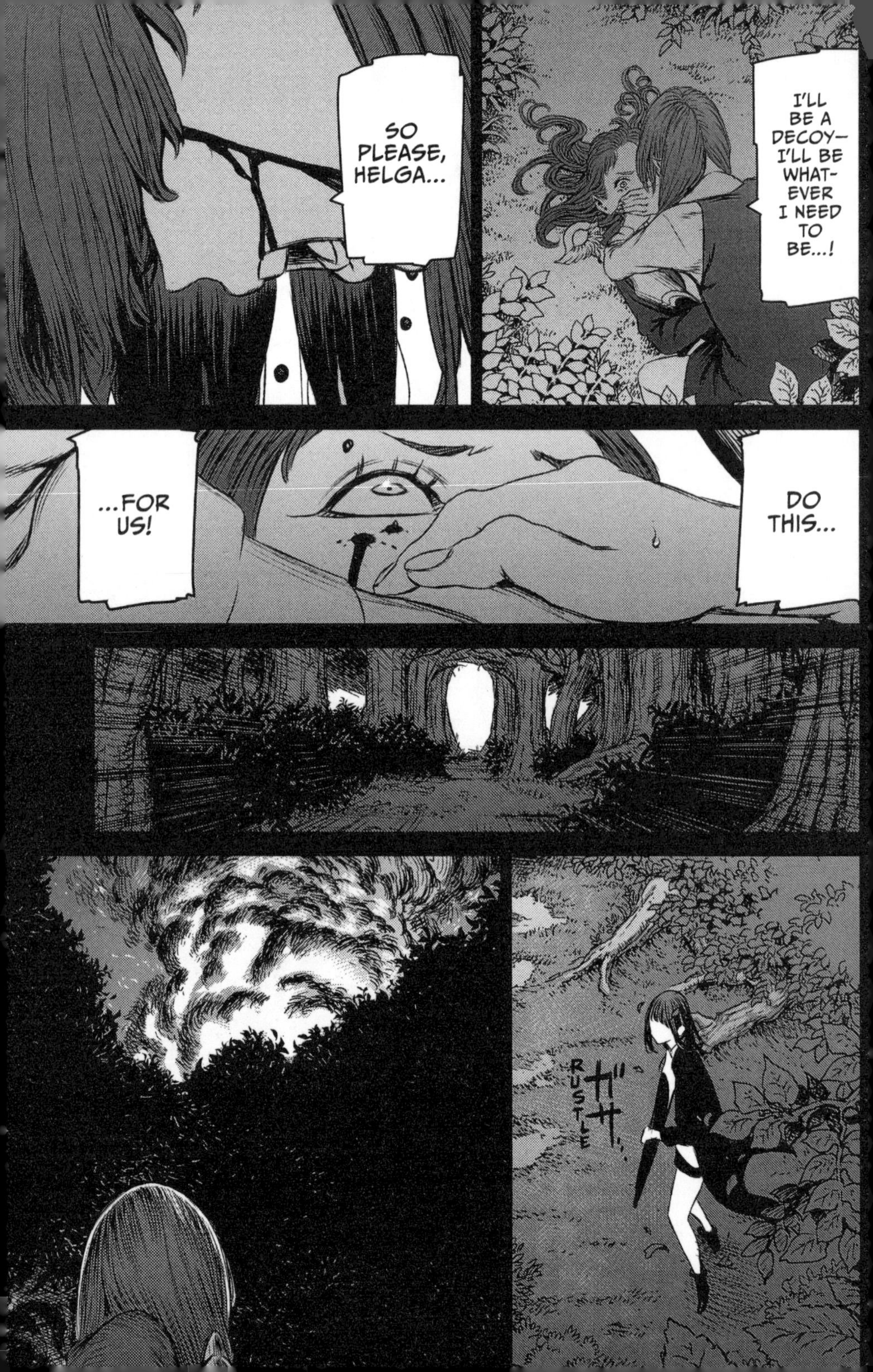
I'LL BE A DECOY—I'LL BE WHATEVER I NEED TO BE...!
SO PLEASE, HELGA...
DO THIS...
...FOR US!
RUSTLE

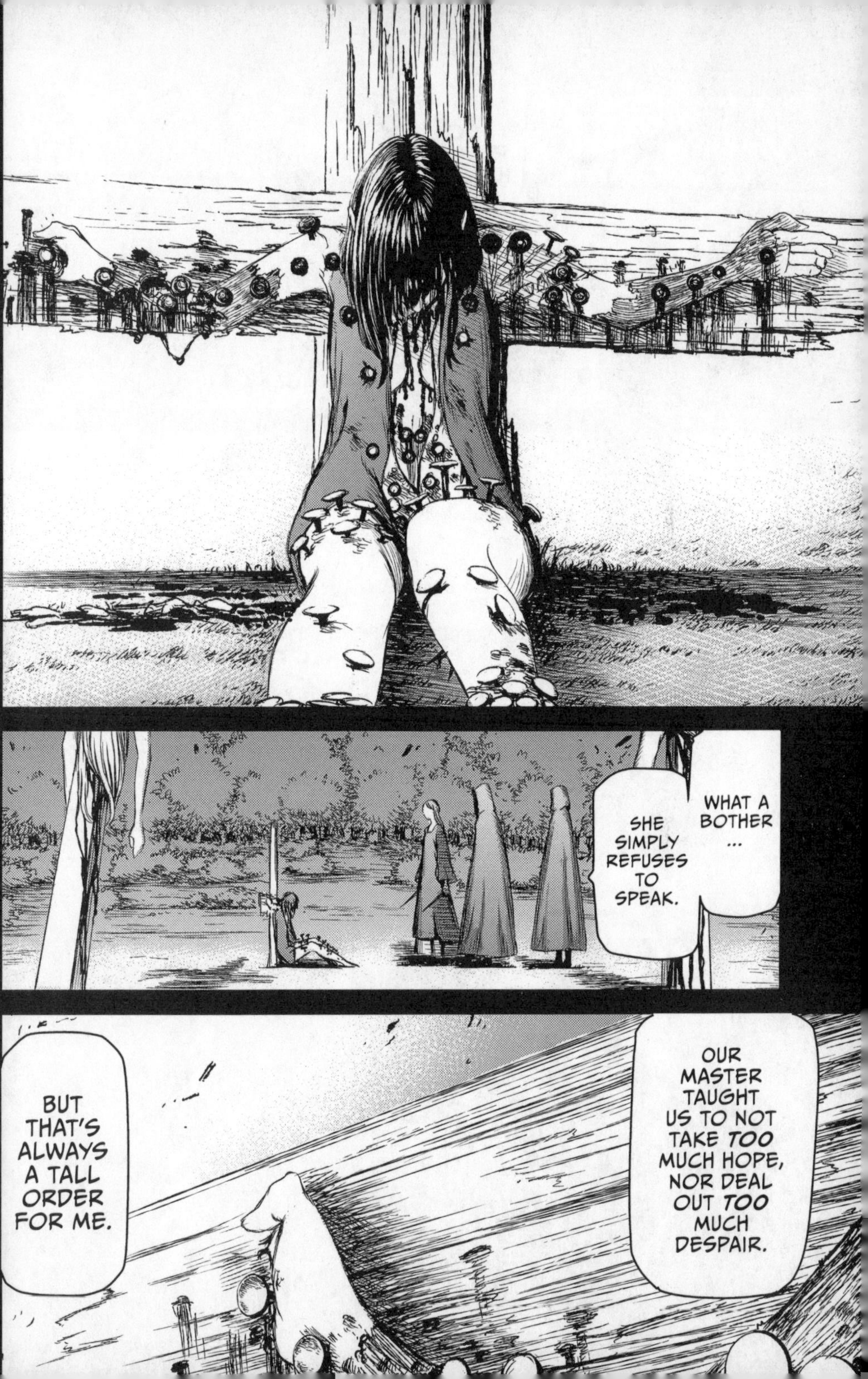
WHAT A BOTHER ...
SHE SIMPLY REFUSES TO SPEAK.
OUR MASTER TAUGHT US TO NOT TAKE *TOO* MUCH HOPE, NOR DEAL OUT *TOO* MUCH DESPAIR.
BUT THAT'S ALWAYS A TALL ORDER FOR ME.

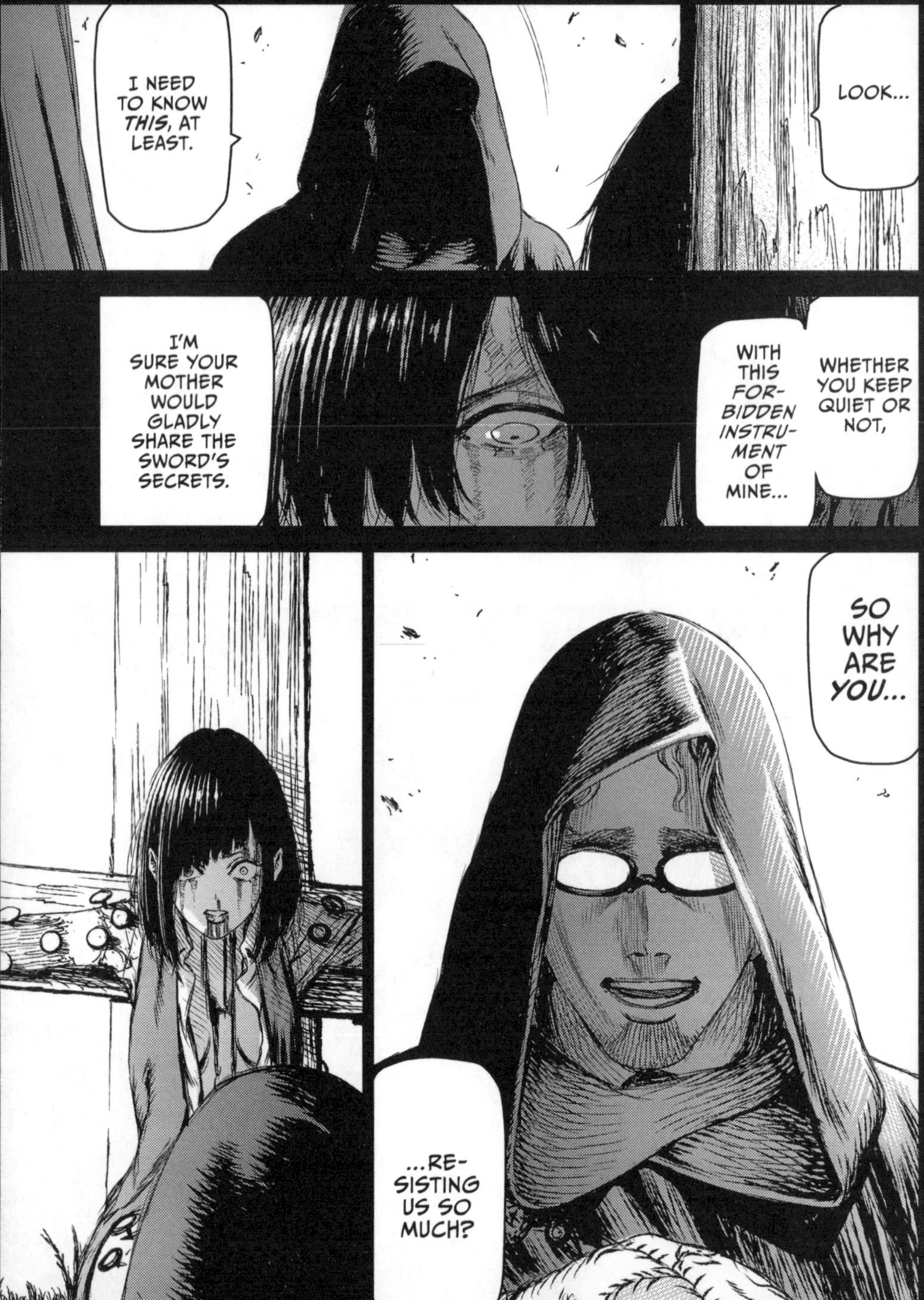
LOOK...
I NEED TO KNOW *THIS*, AT LEAST.
WHETHER YOU KEEP QUIET OR NOT,
WITH THIS FORBIDDEN INSTRUMENT OF MINE...
I'M SURE YOUR MOTHER WOULD GLADLY SHARE THE SWORD'S SECRETS.
SO WHY ARE *YOU*...
...RESISTING US SO MUCH?

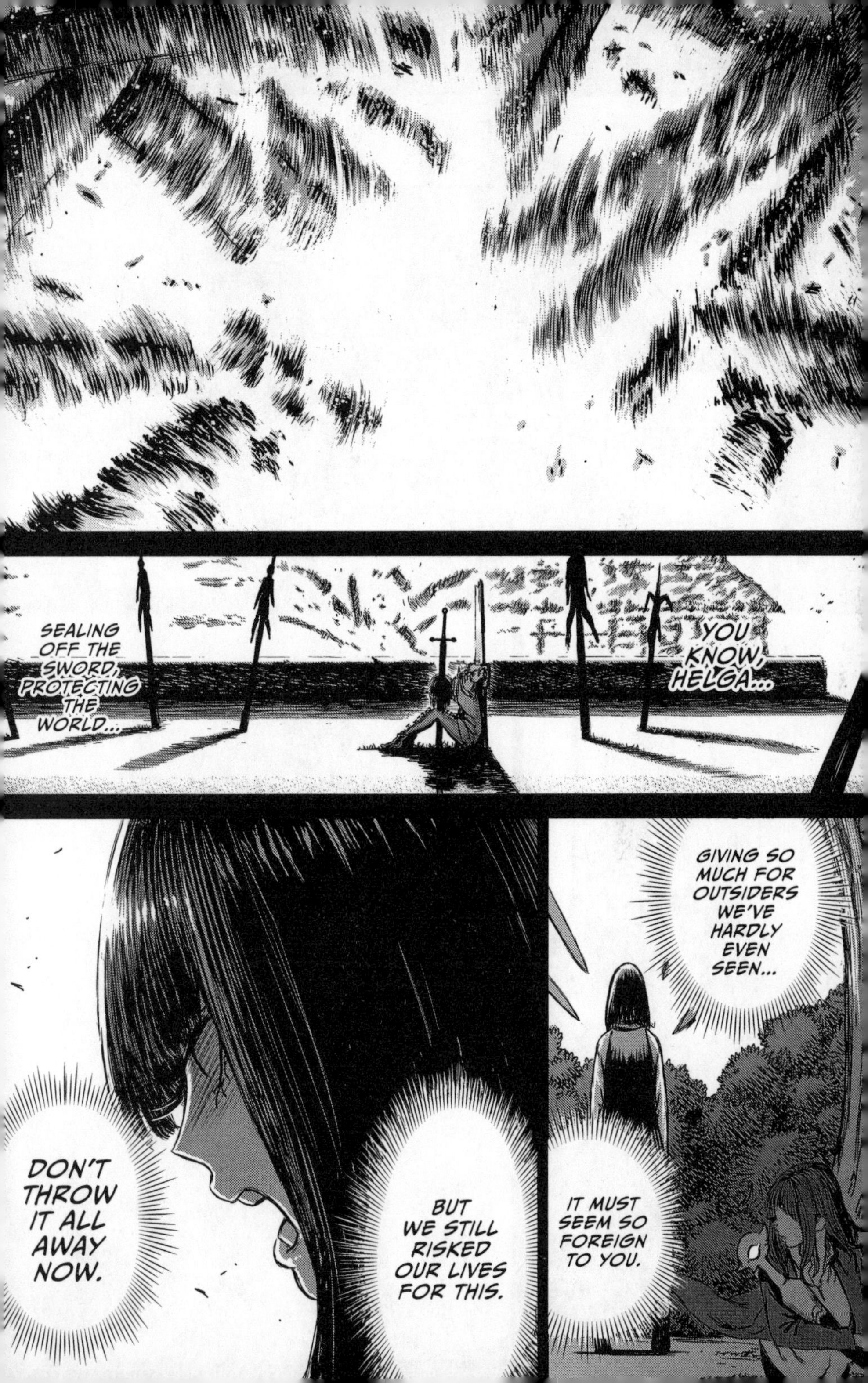
YOU KNOW, HELGA...
SEALING OFF THE SWORD, PROTECTING THE WORLD...
GIVING SO MUCH FOR OUTSIDERS WE'VE HARDLY EVEN SEEN...
IT MUST SEEM SO FOREIGN TO YOU.
BUT WE STILL RISKED OUR LIVES FOR THIS.
DON'T THROW IT ALL AWAY NOW.

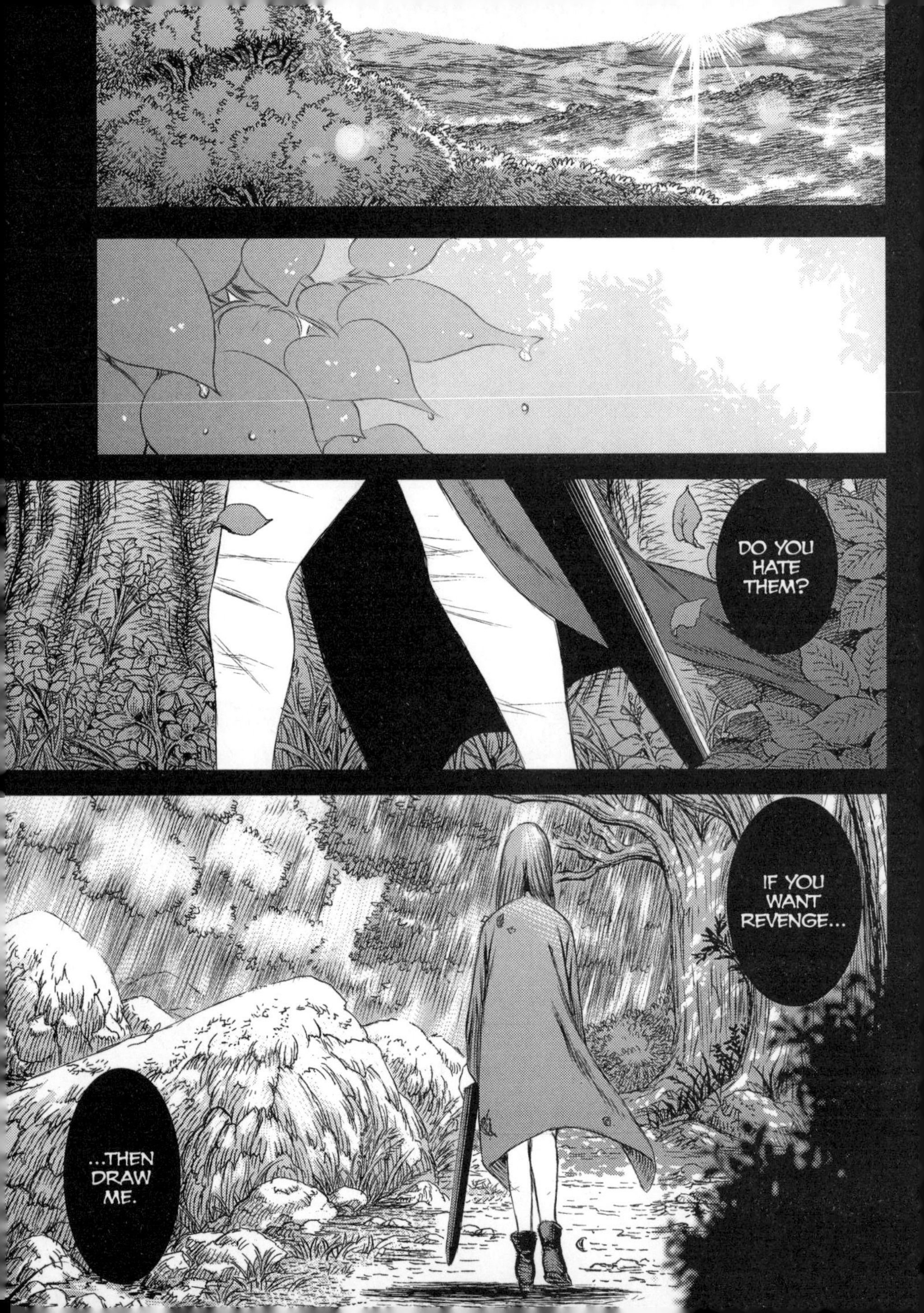
DO YOU HATE THEM?
IF YOU WANT REVENGE...
...THEN DRAW ME.

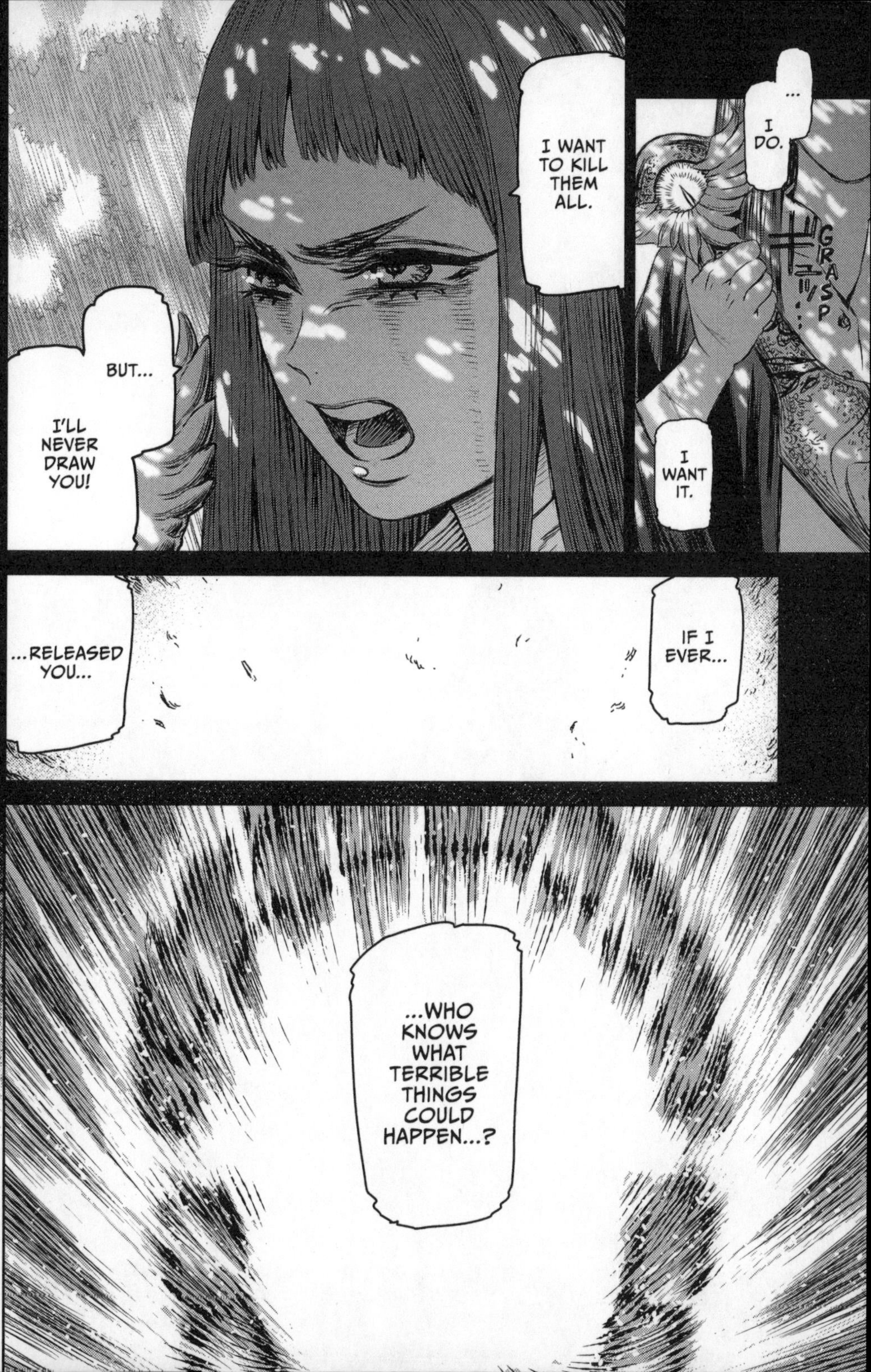
... I DO.
GRASP
I WANT IT.
I WANT TO KILL THEM ALL.
BUT...
I'LL NEVER DRAW YOU!
IF I EVER...
...RELEASED YOU...
...WHO KNOWS WHAT TERRIBLE THINGS COULD HAPPEN...?

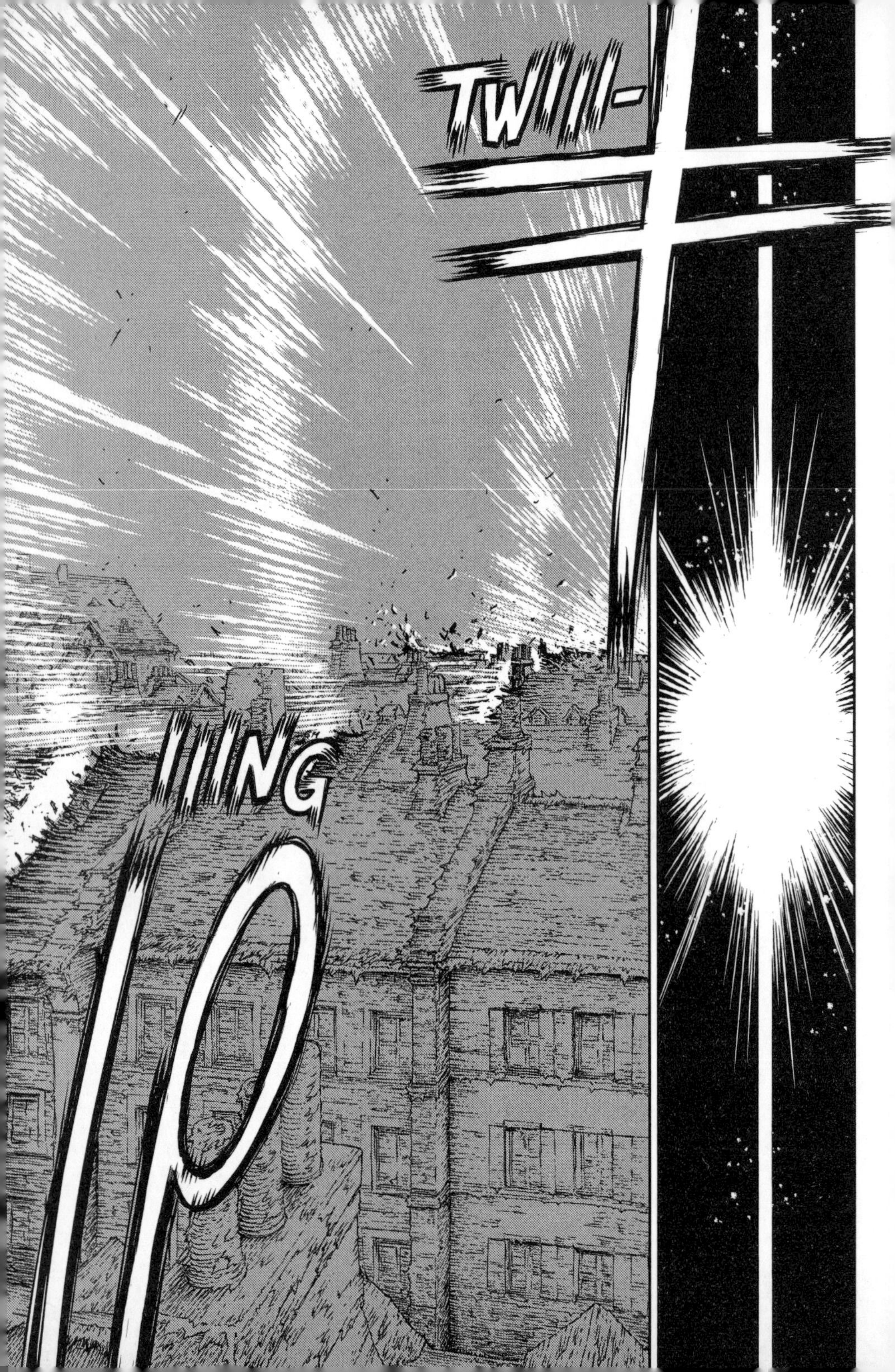
TWIII-IIING

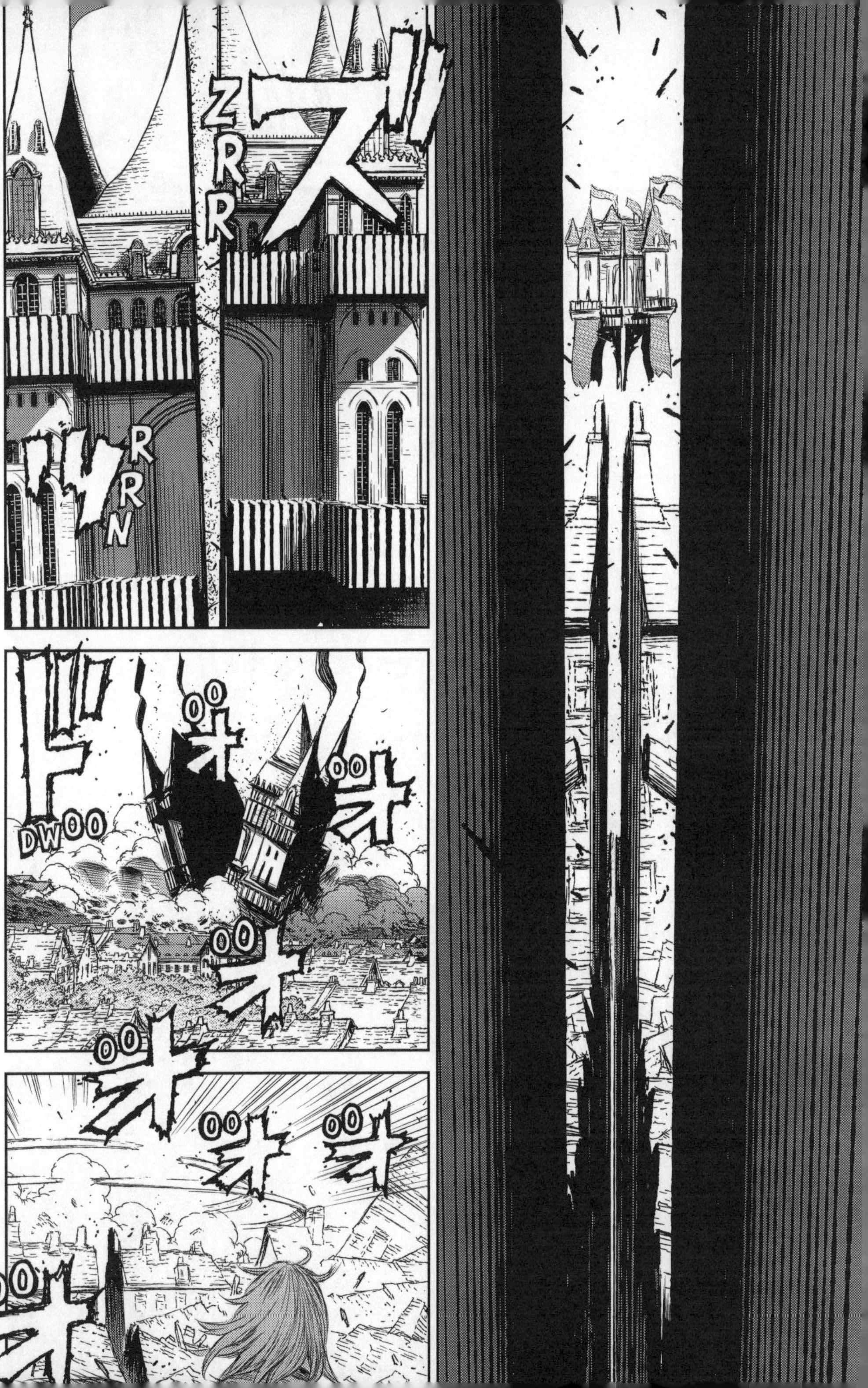

ズ
ZRR
RRN
ド
DWOO
オ
OO
オ
OO
オ
OO
オ
OO
オ
OO
オ
OO
オ
OO

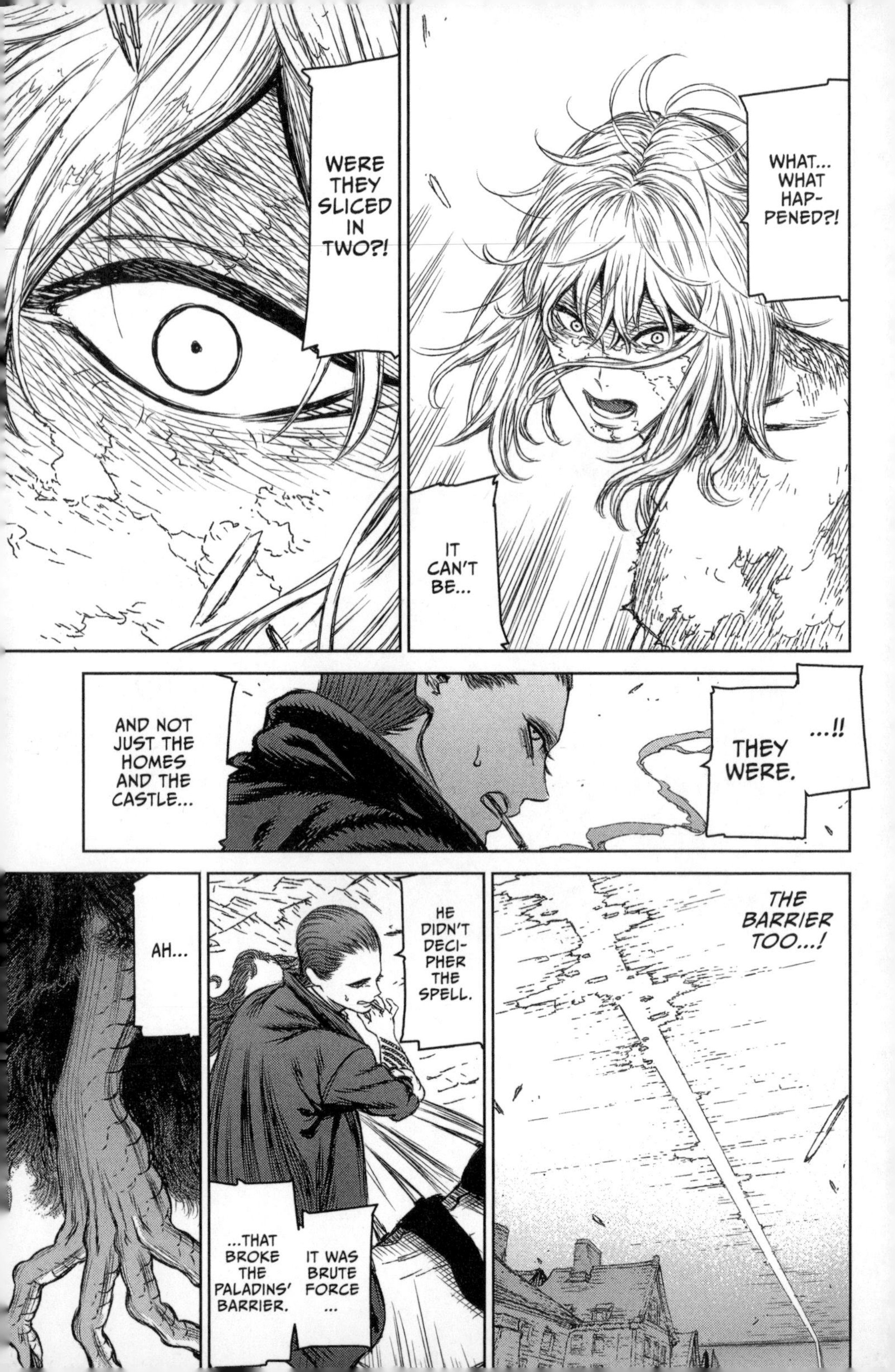
WHAT... WHAT HAP-PENED?!
IT CAN'T BE...
WERE THEY SLICED IN TWO?!
...!!
THEY WERE.
AND NOT JUST THE HOMES AND THE CASTLE...
THE BARRIER TOO...!
HE DIDN'T DECI-PHER THE SPELL.
IT WAS BRUTE FORCE ...
...THAT BROKE THE PALADINS' BARRIER.
AH...

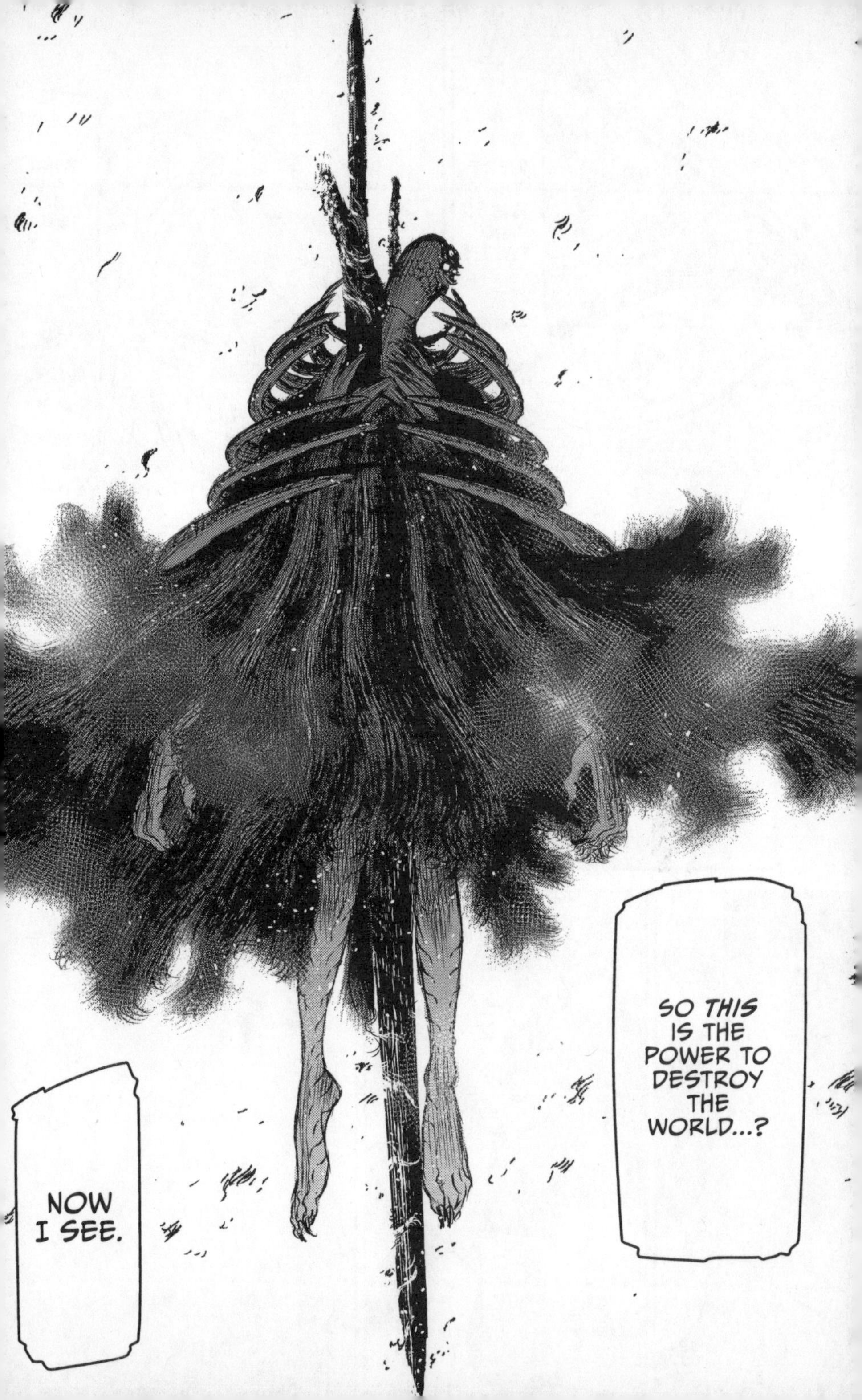
SO THIS IS THE POWER TO DESTROY THE WORLD...?
NOW I SEE.

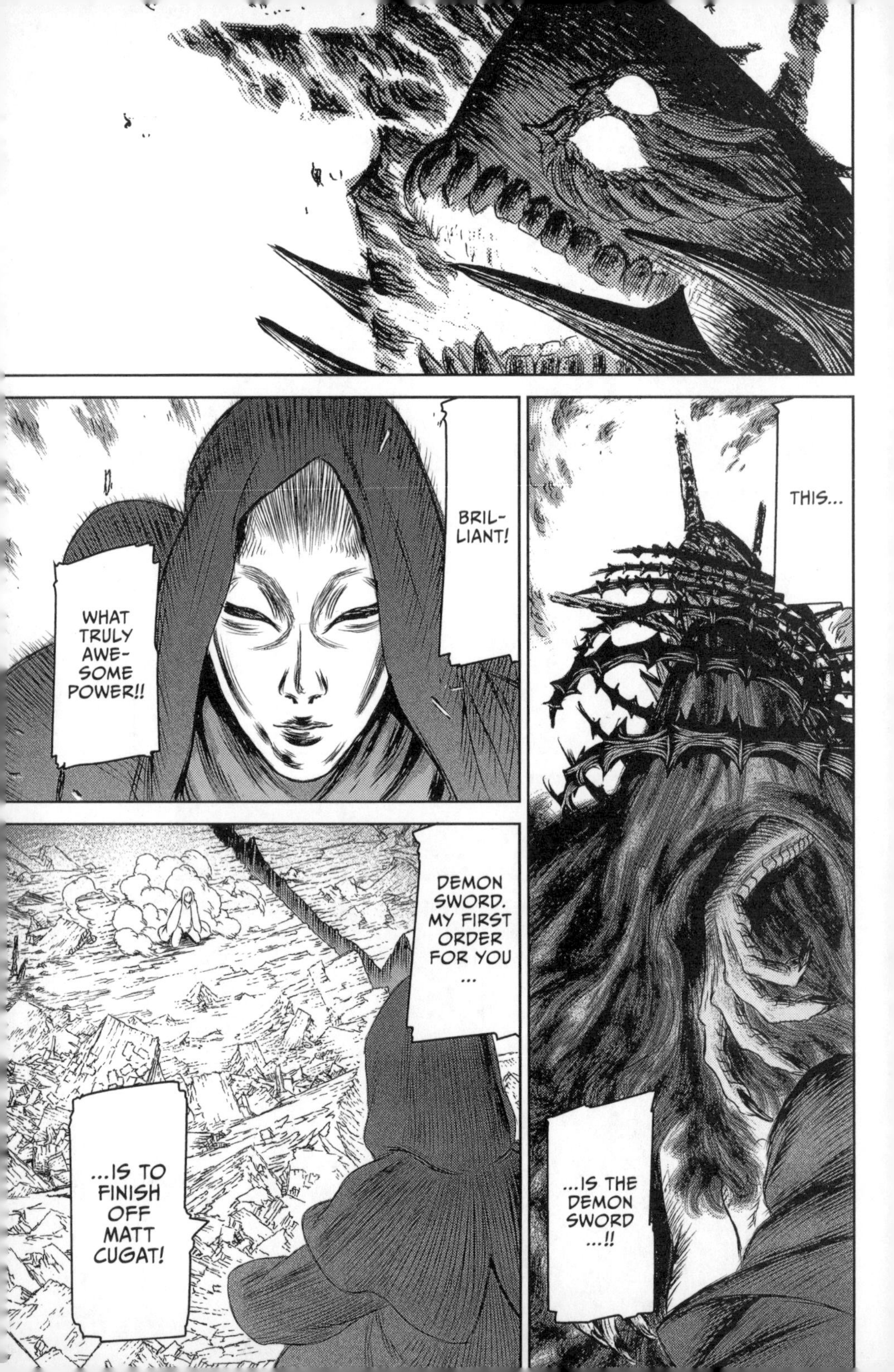
THIS...
...IS THE DEMON SWORD ...!!
BRIL-LIANT!
WHAT TRULY AWE-SOME POWER!!
DEMON SWORD. MY FIRST ORDER FOR YOU ...
...IS TO FINISH OFF MATT CUGAT!

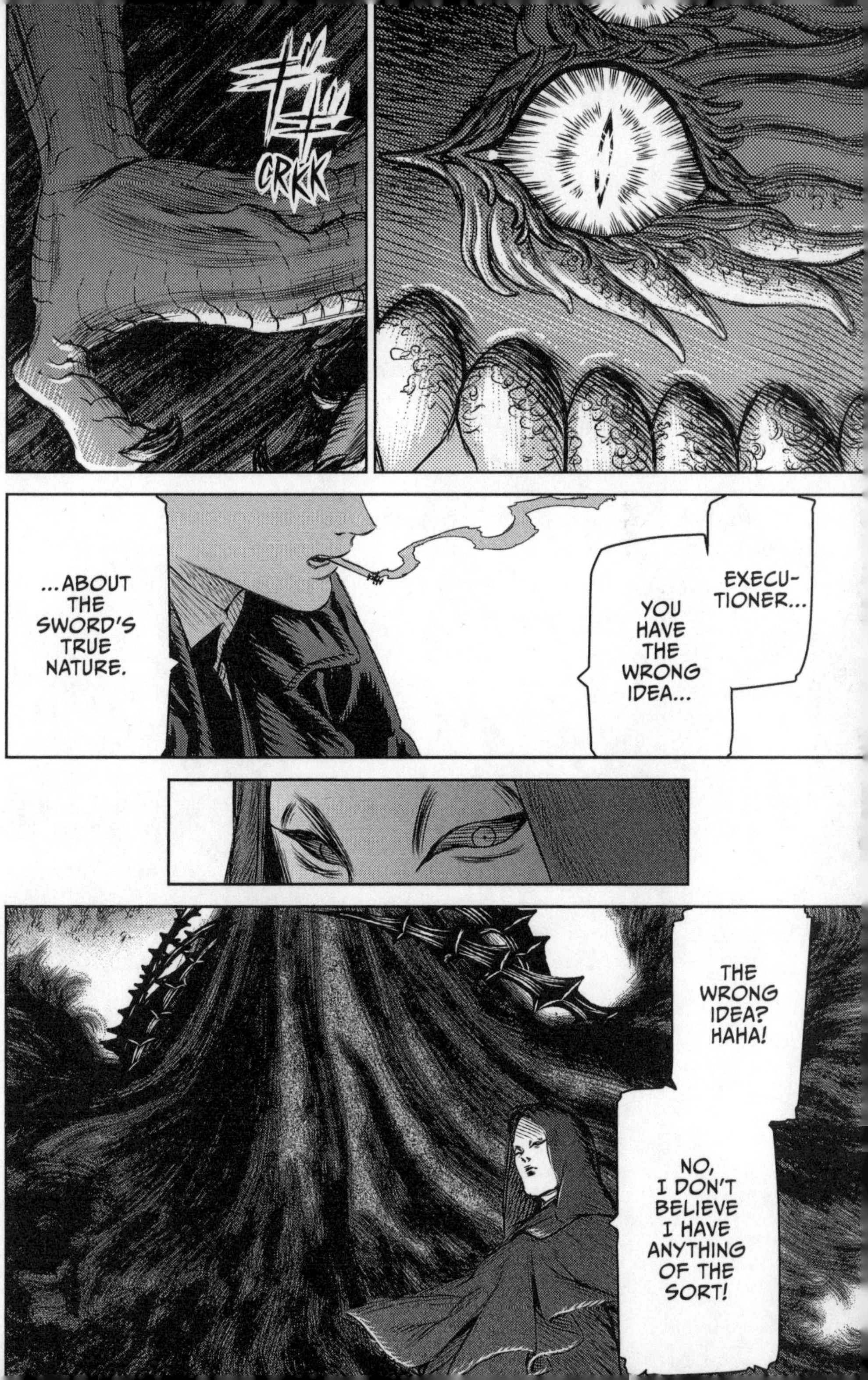
CRKK
EXECUTIONER...
YOU HAVE THE WRONG IDEA...
...ABOUT THE SWORD'S TRUE NATURE.
THE WRONG IDEA? HAHA!
NO, I DON'T BELIEVE I HAVE ANYTHING OF THE SORT!

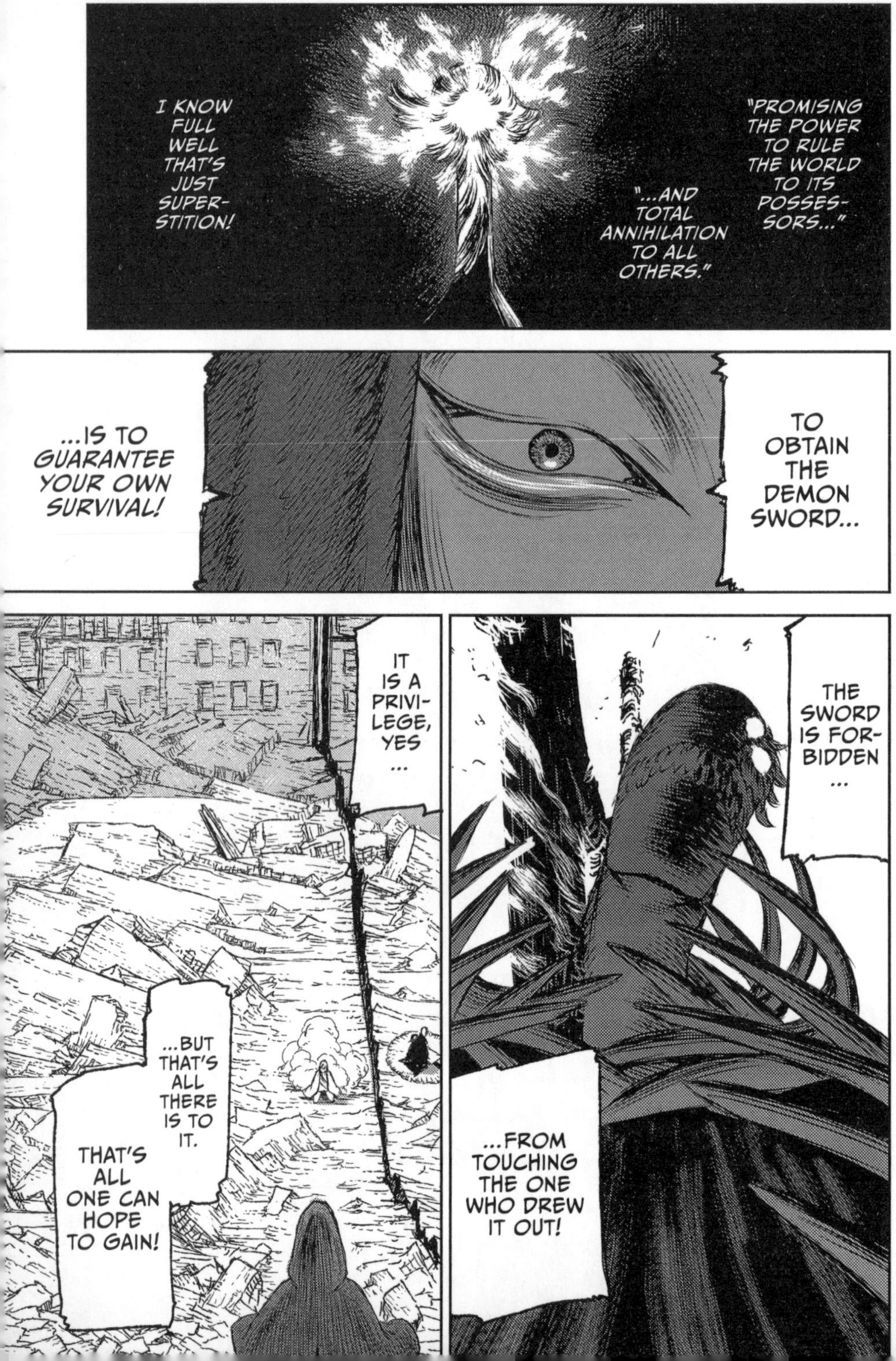
"PROMISING THE POWER TO RULE THE WORLD TO ITS POSSESSORS..."
"...AND TOTAL ANNIHILATION TO ALL OTHERS."
I KNOW FULL WELL THAT'S JUST SUPERSTITION!
TO OBTAIN THE DEMON SWORD...
...IS TO GUARANTEE YOUR OWN SURVIVAL!
THE SWORD IS FORBIDDEN...
...FROM TOUCHING THE ONE WHO DREW IT OUT!
IT IS A PRIVILEGE, YES...
...BUT THAT'S ALL THERE IS TO IT.
THAT'S ALL ONE CAN HOPE TO GAIN!

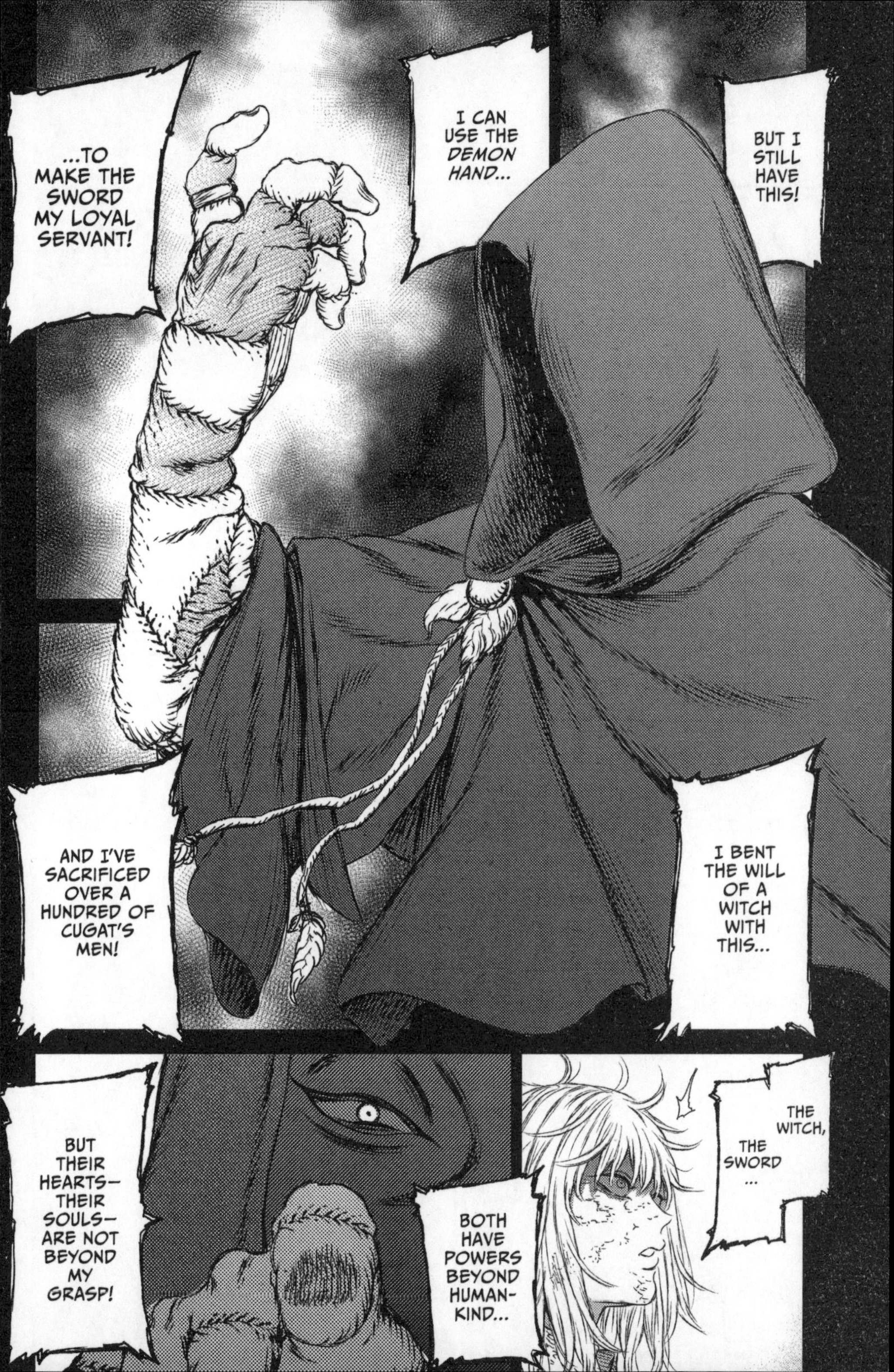
BUT I STILL HAVE THIS!
I CAN USE THE DEMON HAND...
...TO MAKE THE SWORD MY LOYAL SERVANT!
I BENT THE WILL OF A WITCH WITH THIS...
AND I'VE SACRIFICED OVER A HUNDRED OF CUGAT'S MEN!
THE WITCH, THE SWORD ...
BOTH HAVE POWERS BEYOND HUMAN-KIND...
BUT THEIR HEARTS— THEIR SOULS— ARE NOT BEYOND MY GRASP!

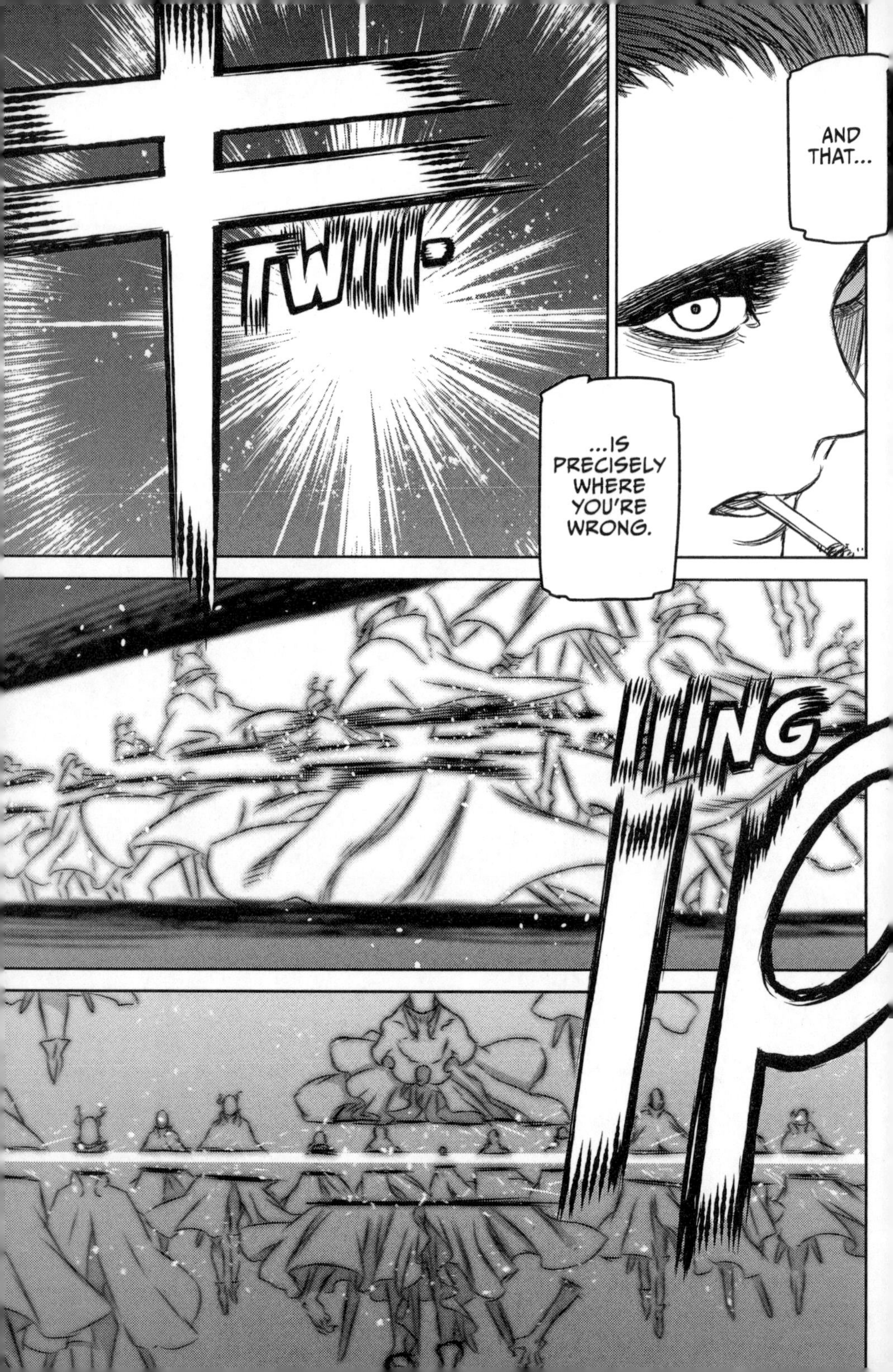
AND THAT...
...IS PRECISELY WHERE YOU'RE WRONG.
TWIIP
IIING

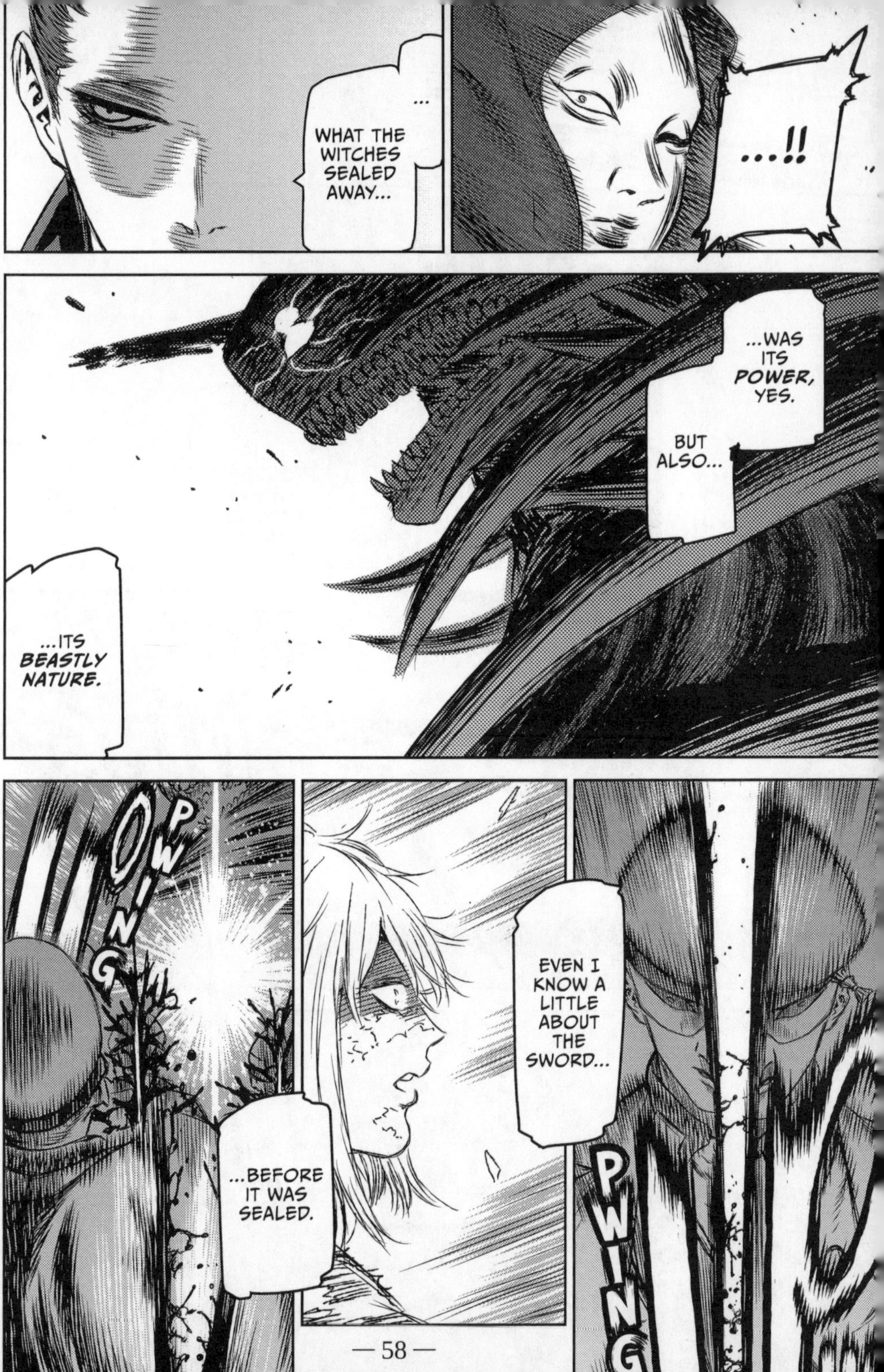
...!!
...
WHAT THE WITCHES SEALED AWAY...
...WAS ITS *POWER*, YES.
BUT ALSO...
...ITS *BEASTLY NATURE.*
PWING
EVEN I KNOW A LITTLE ABOUT THE SWORD...
...BEFORE IT WAS SEALED.
PWING

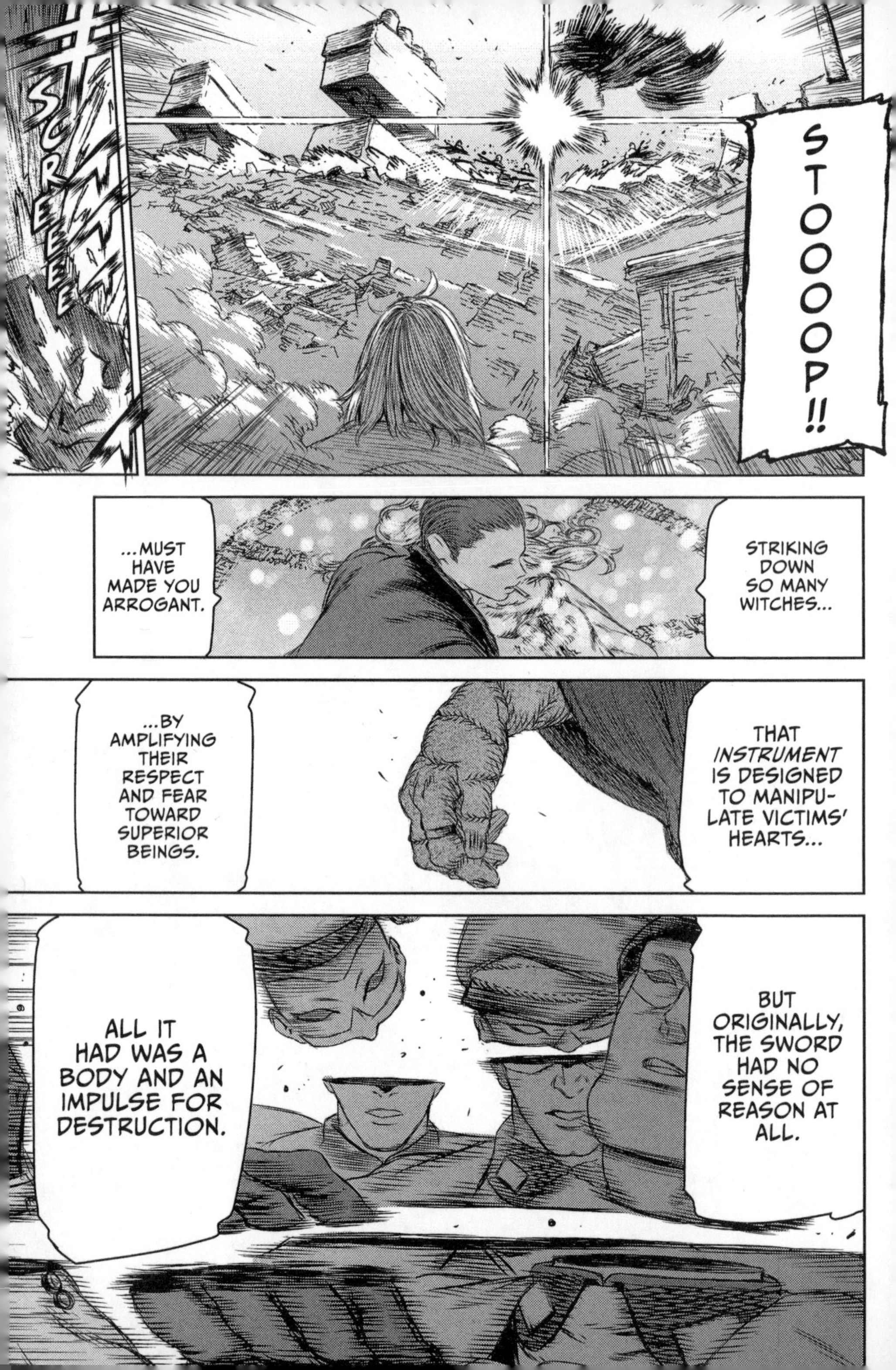
STOOOOP!!
SCREEEE
STRIKING DOWN SO MANY WITCHES...
...MUST HAVE MADE YOU ARROGANT.
THAT *INSTRUMENT* IS DESIGNED TO MANIPU-LATE VICTIMS' HEARTS...
...BY AMPLIFYING THEIR RESPECT AND FEAR TOWARD SUPERIOR BEINGS.
BUT ORIGINALLY, THE SWORD HAD NO SENSE OF REASON AT ALL.
ALL IT HAD WAS A BODY AND AN IMPULSE FOR DESTRUCTION.

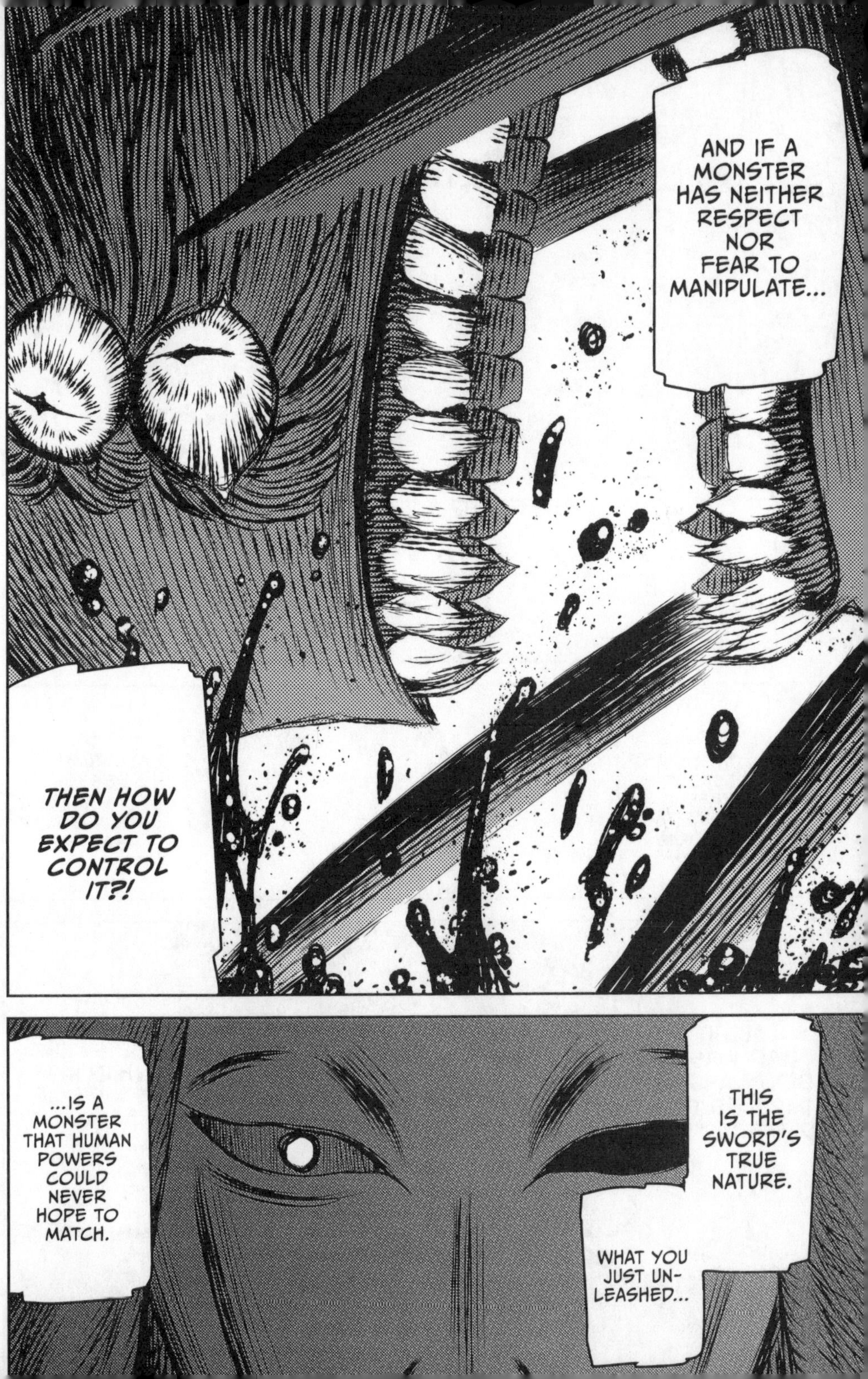
AND IF A MONSTER HAS NEITHER RESPECT NOR FEAR TO MANIPULATE...
THEN HOW DO YOU EXPECT TO CONTROL IT?!
THIS IS THE SWORD'S TRUE NATURE.
WHAT YOU JUST UN-LEASHED...
...IS A MONSTER THAT HUMAN POWERS COULD NEVER HOPE TO MATCH.

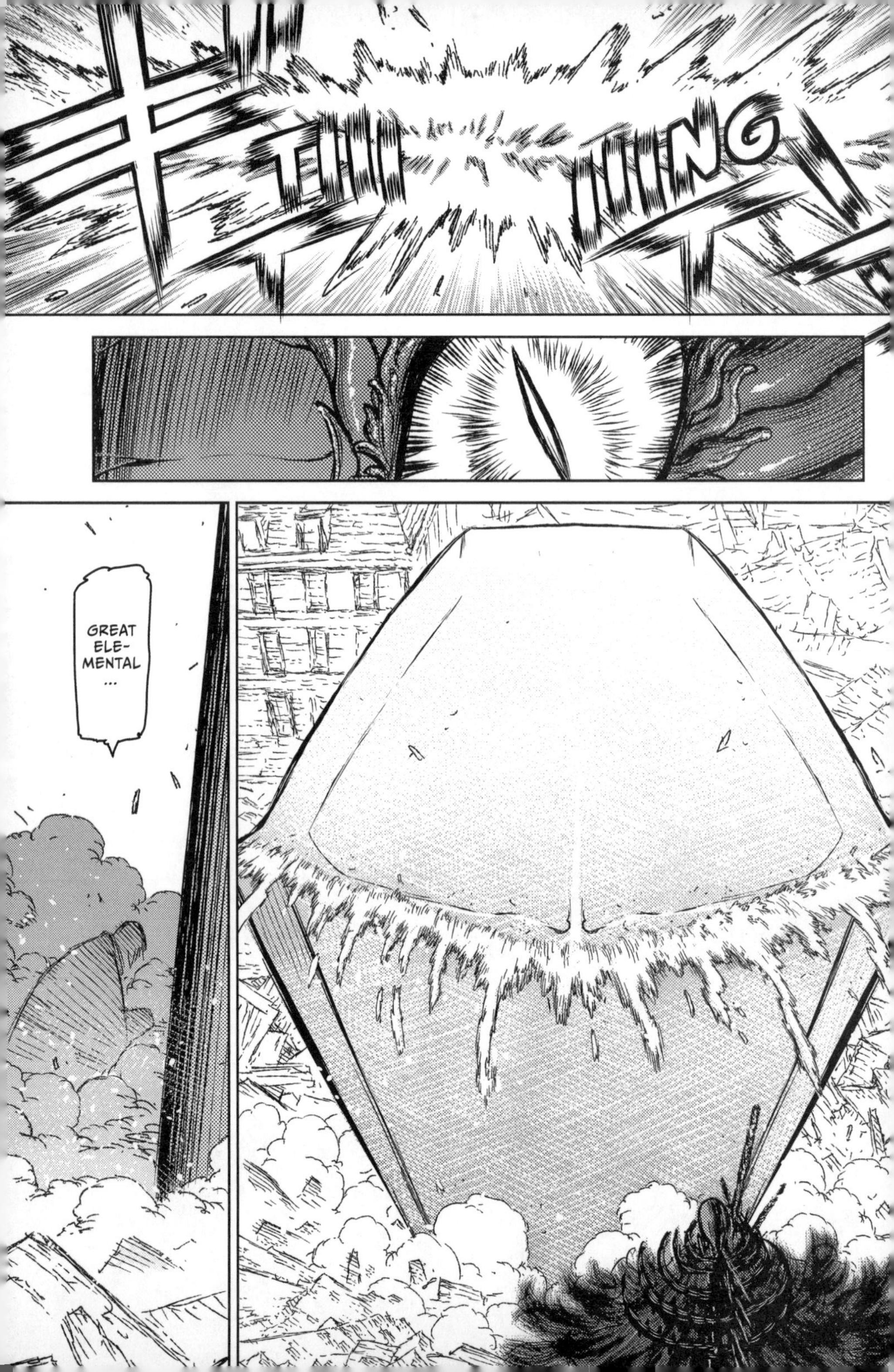
THIIIIIIIING
GREAT ELE-MENTAL ...

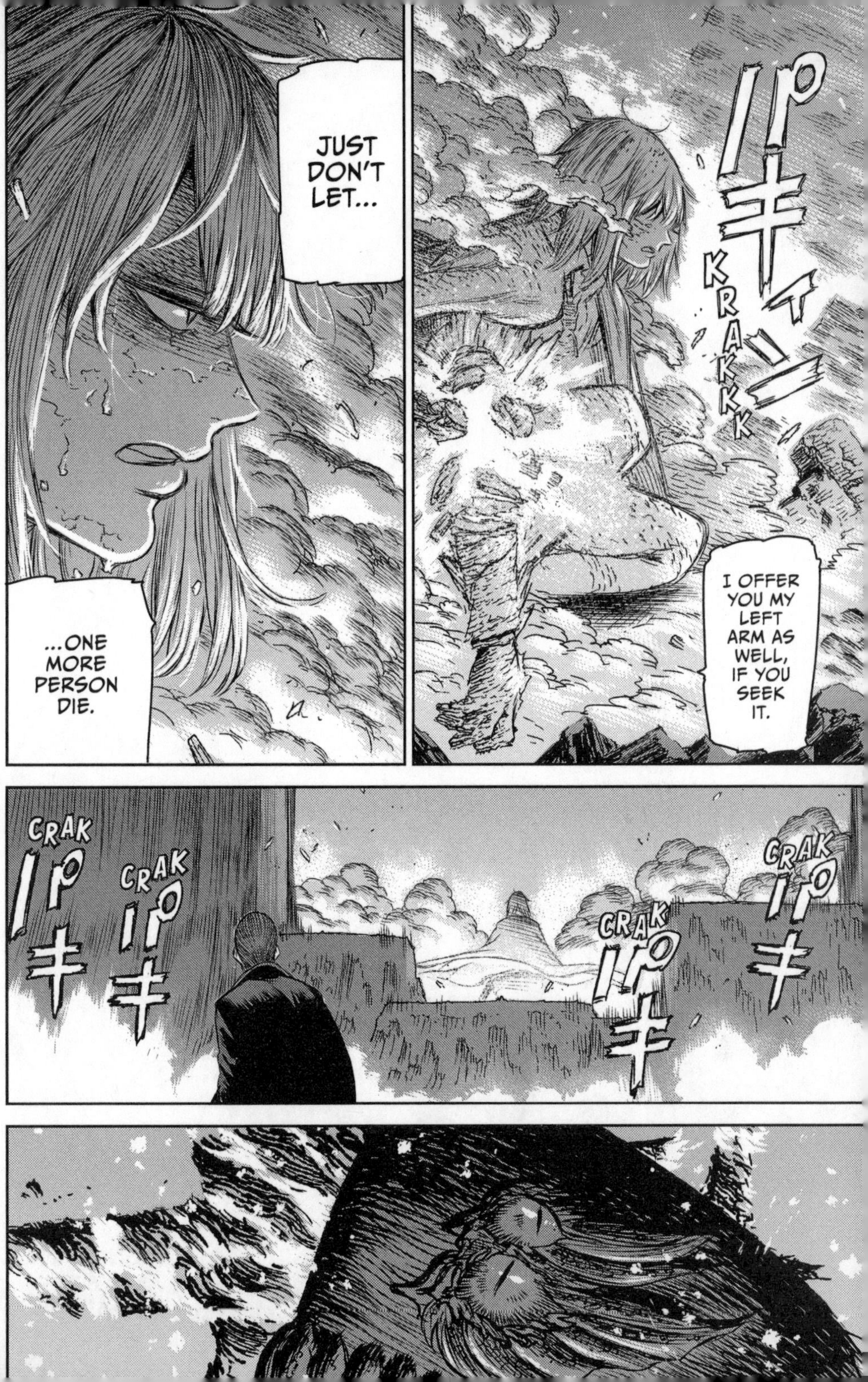
パキィン
KRAKKK
I OFFER YOU MY LEFT ARM AS WELL, IF YOU SEEK IT.
JUST DON'T LET...
...ONE MORE PERSON DIE.
CRAK
パキ
CRAK
パキ
CRAK
パキ
CRAK
パキ

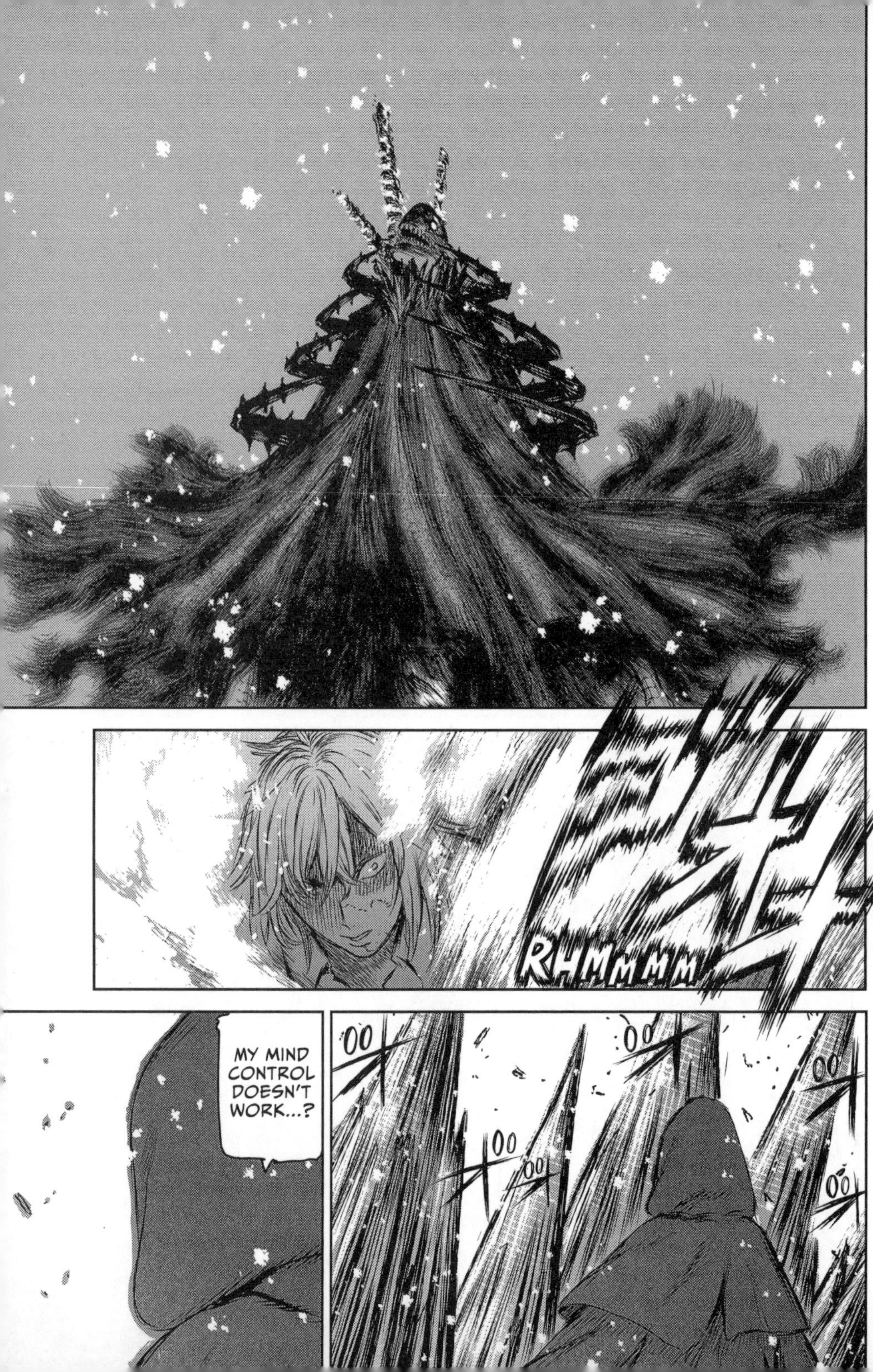
RHMMMM
MY MIND CONTROL DOESN'T WORK...?

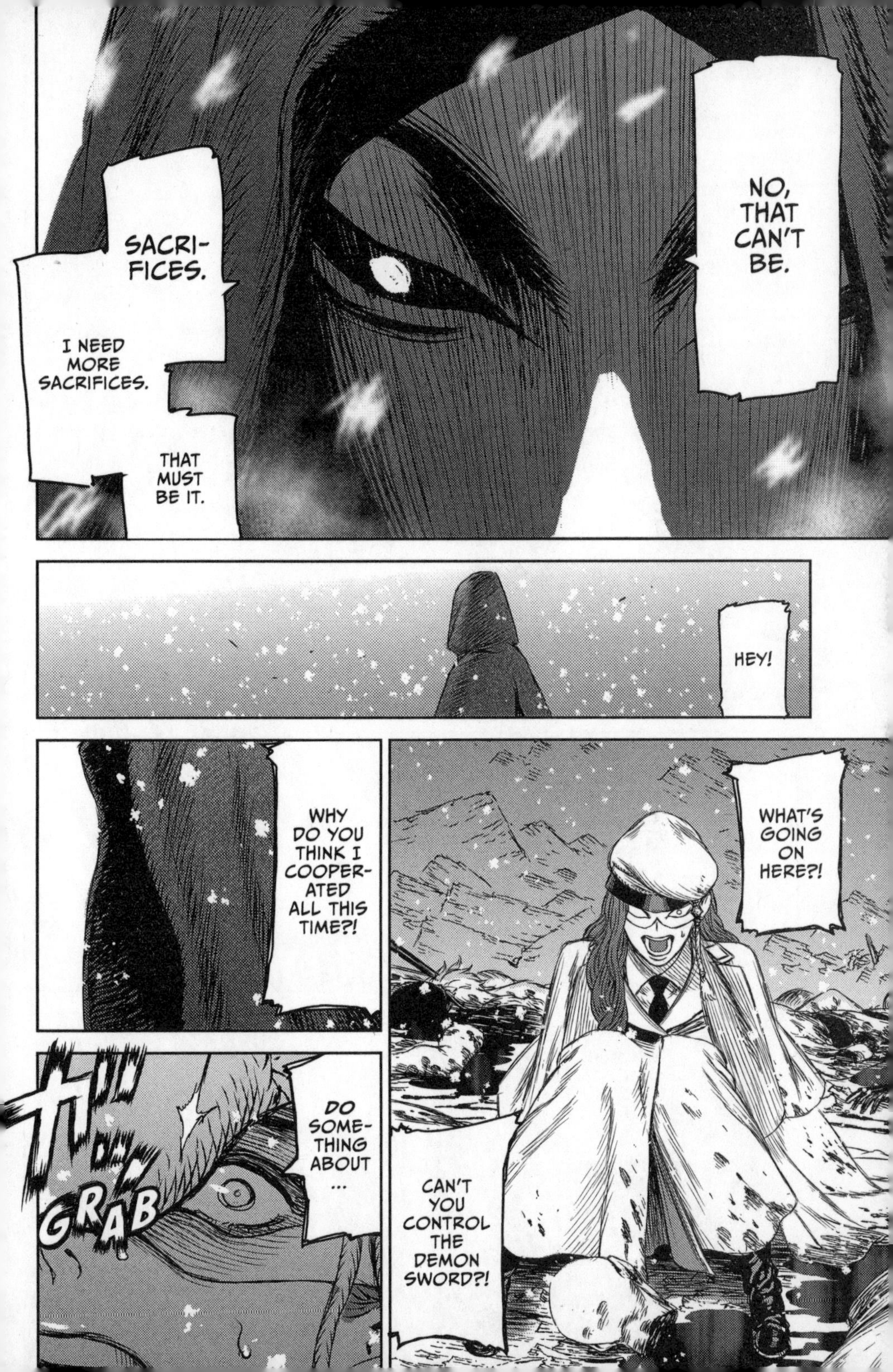
NO, THAT CAN'T BE.
SACRI-FICES.
I NEED MORE SACRIFICES.
THAT MUST BE IT.
HEY!
WHAT'S GOING ON HERE?!
CAN'T YOU CONTROL THE DEMON SWORD?!
WHY DO YOU THINK I COOPER-ATED ALL THIS TIME?!
DO SOME-THING ABOUT ...
GRAB

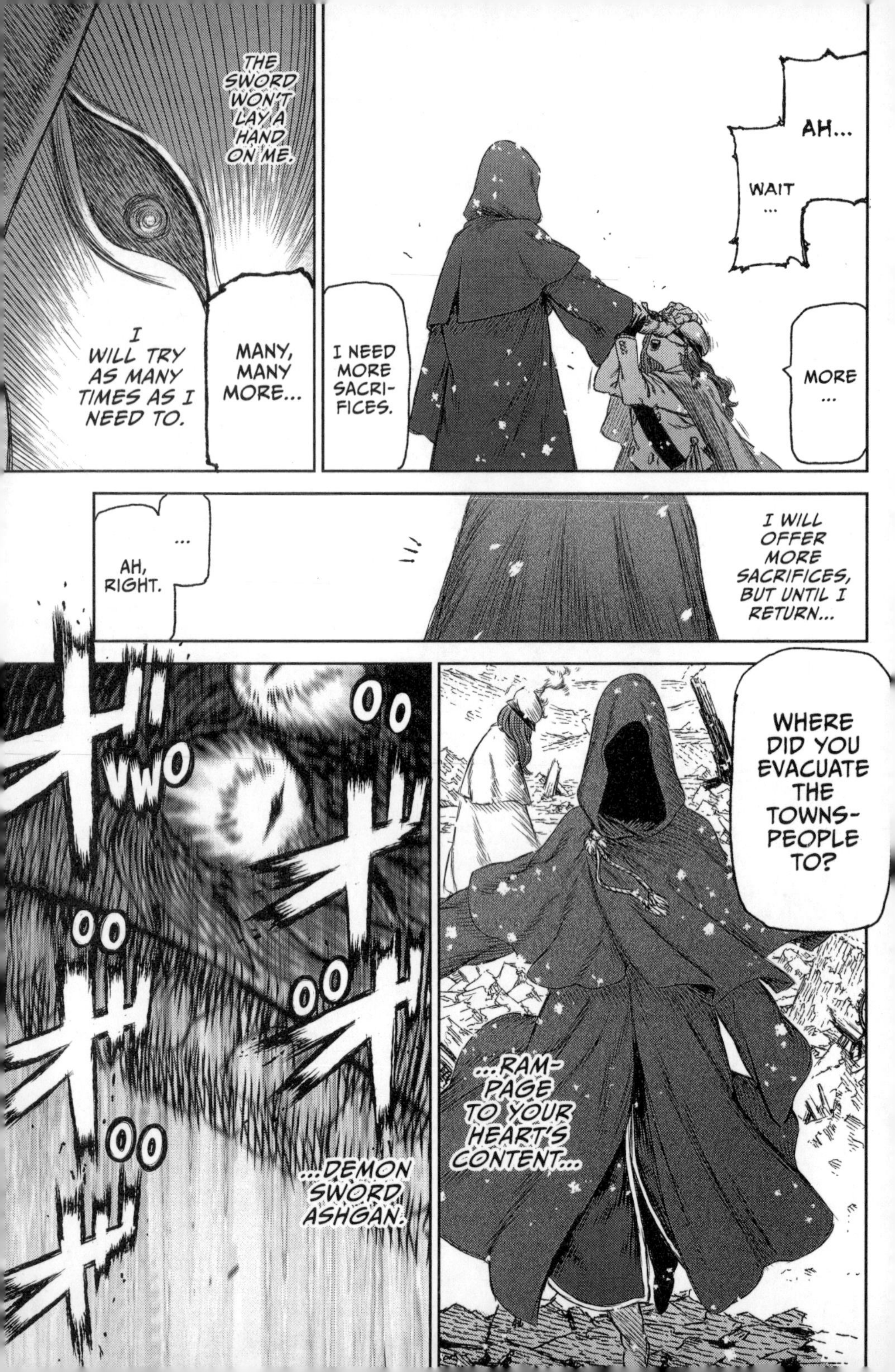
AH...
WAIT ...
MORE ...
I NEED MORE SACRIFICES.
THE SWORD WON'T LAY A HAND ON ME.
MANY, MANY MORE...
I WILL TRY AS MANY TIMES AS I NEED TO.
I WILL OFFER MORE SACRIFICES, BUT UNTIL I RETURN...
... AH, RIGHT.
WHERE DID YOU EVACUATE THE TOWNSPEOPLE TO?
...RAMPAGE TO YOUR HEART'S CONTENT...
VWO
OO
OO
OO
OO
OO
...DEMON SWORD ASHGAN.

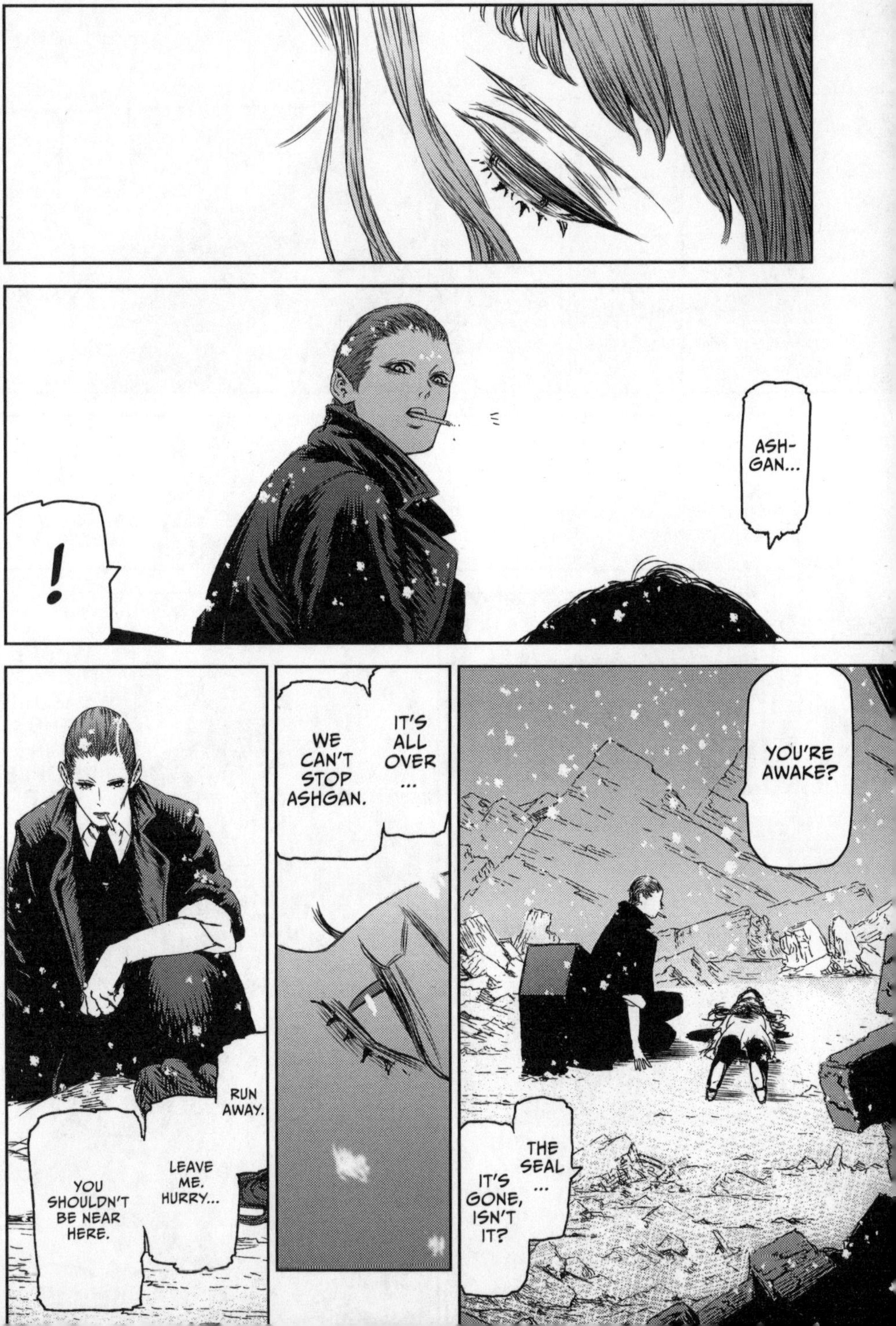
ASH-GAN...
!
YOU'RE AWAKE?
THE SEAL ...
IT'S GONE, ISN'T IT?
IT'S ALL OVER ...
WE CAN'T STOP ASHGAN.
RUN AWAY.
LEAVE ME. HURRY...
YOU SHOULDN'T BE NEAR HERE.

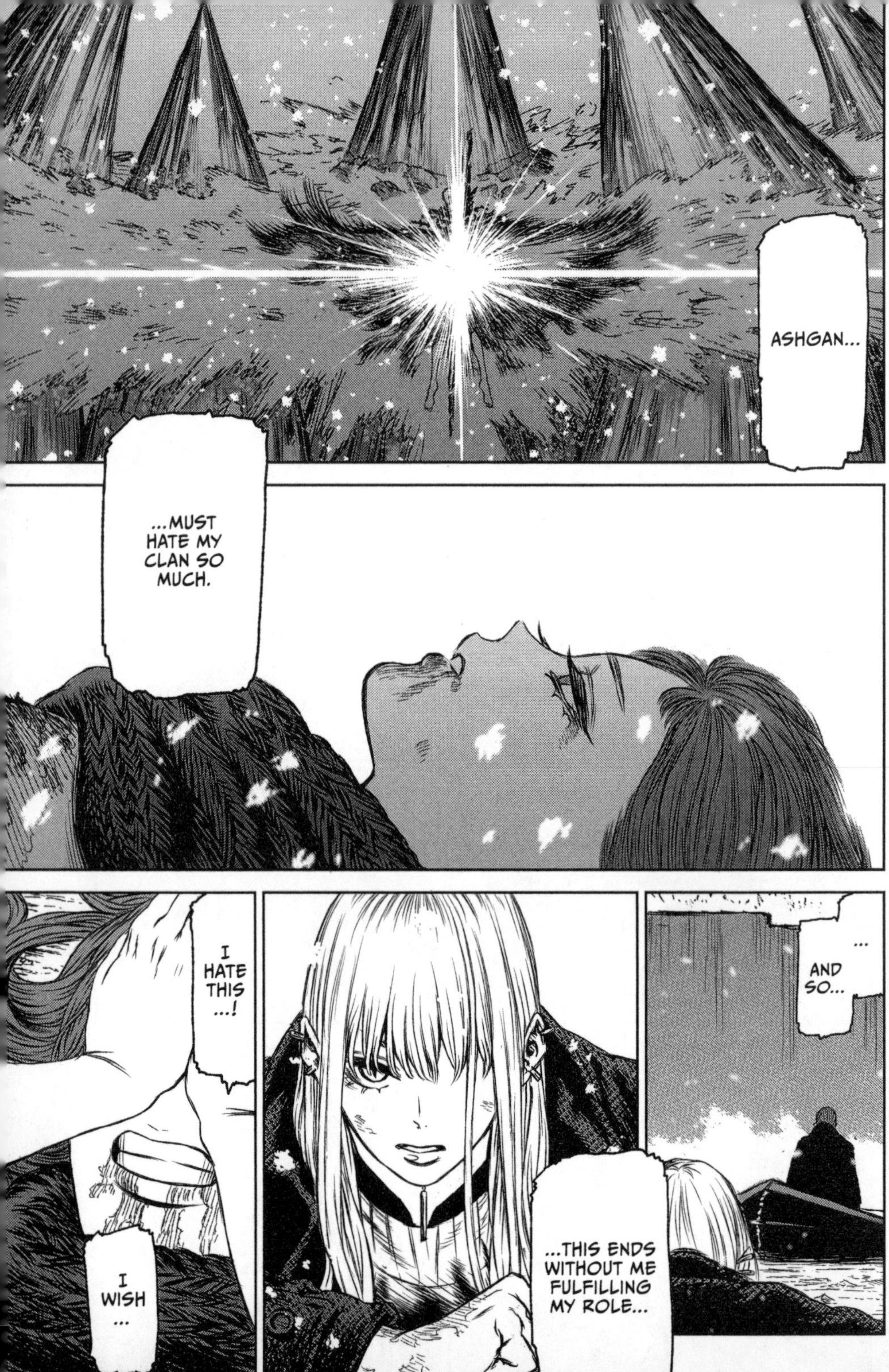
ASHGAN...
...MUST HATE MY CLAN SO MUCH.
... AND SO...
...THIS ENDS WITHOUT ME FULFILLING MY ROLE...
I HATE THIS ...!
I WISH ...

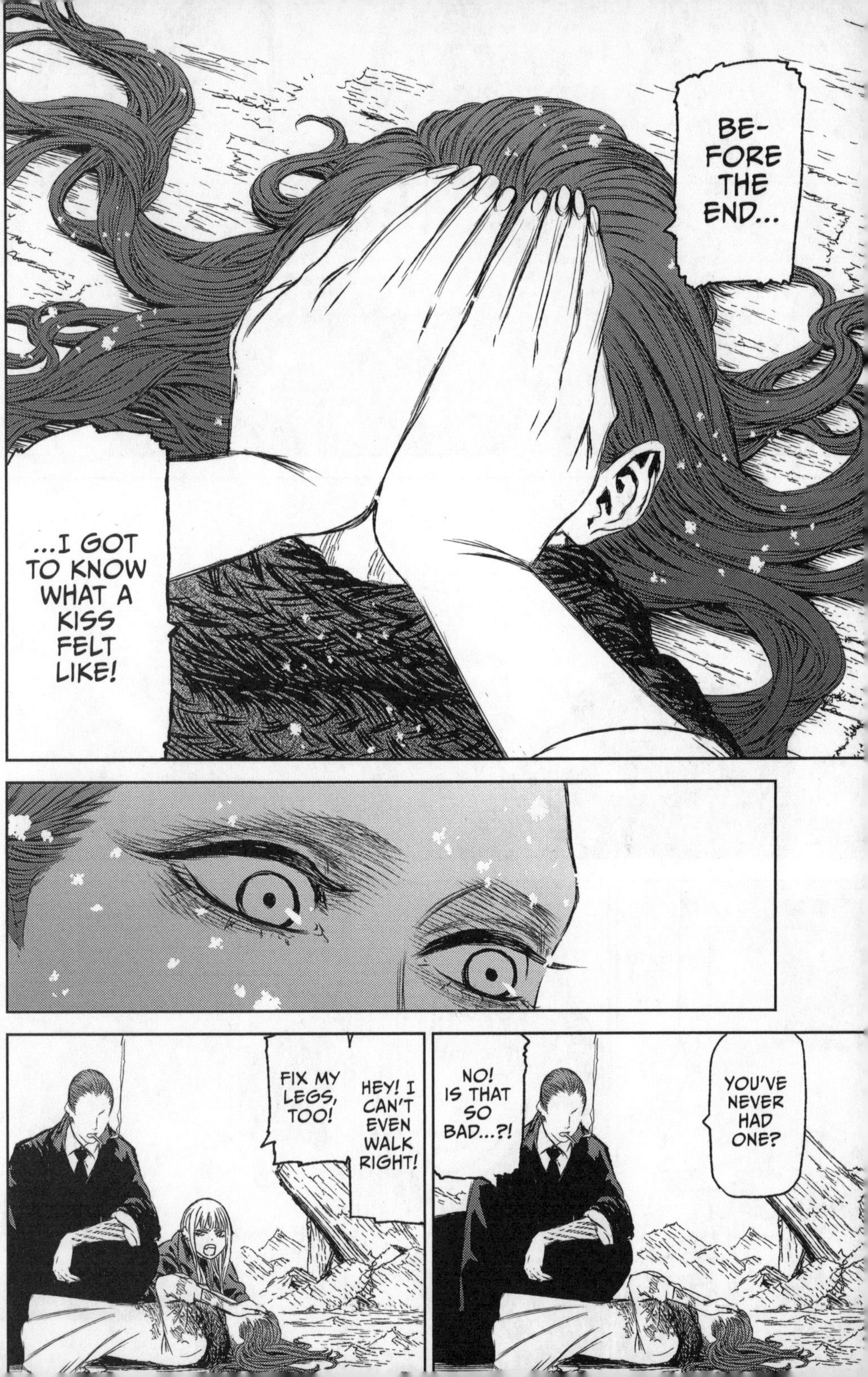
BE-FORE THE END...
...I GOT TO KNOW WHAT A KISS FELT LIKE!
YOU'VE NEVER HAD ONE?
NO! IS THAT SO BAD...?!
HEY! I CAN'T EVEN WALK RIGHT!
FIX MY LEGS, TOO!

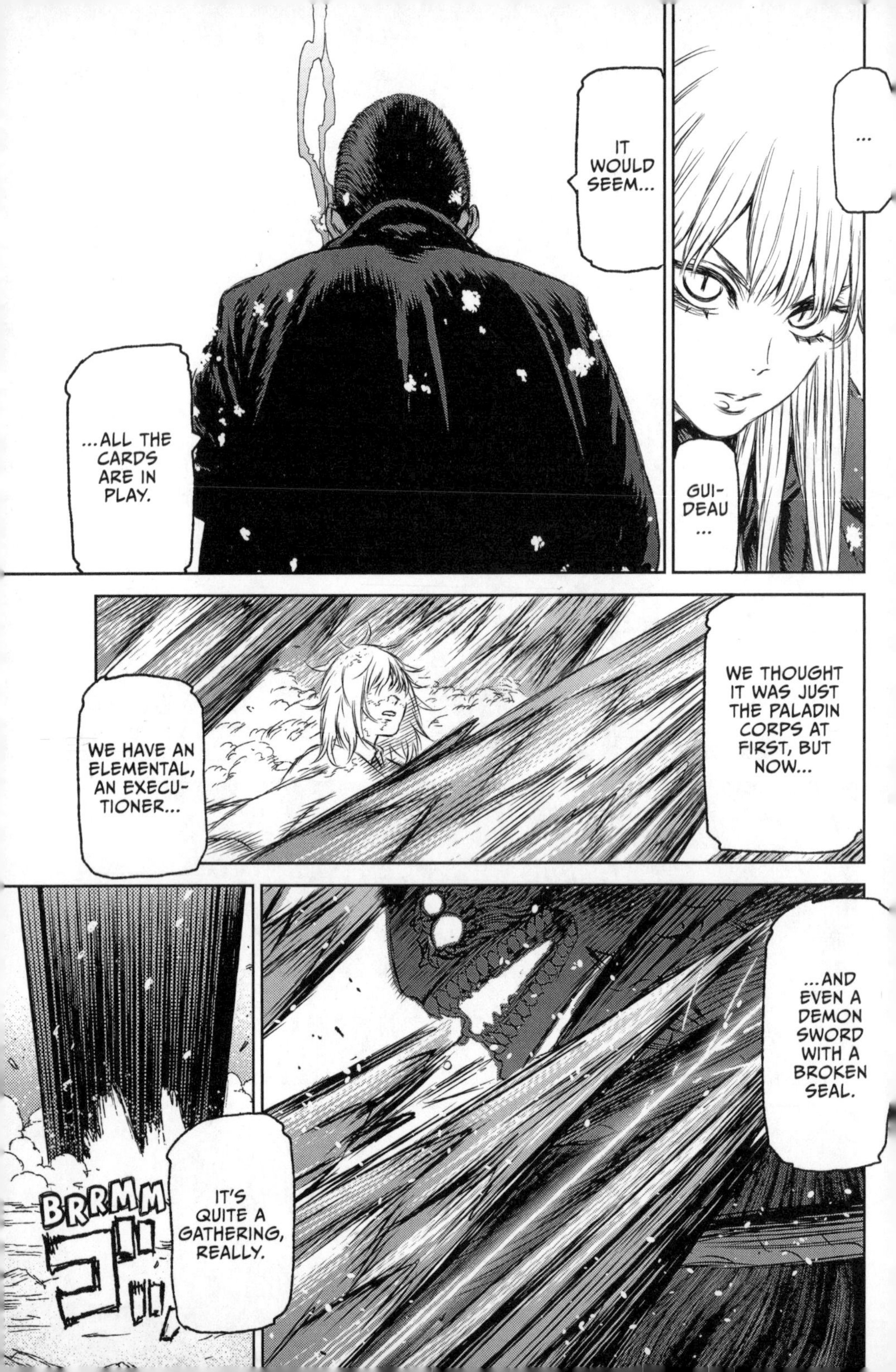
...
GUI-DEAU...
IT WOULD SEEM...
...ALL THE CARDS ARE IN PLAY.
WE THOUGHT IT WAS JUST THE PALADIN CORPS AT FIRST, BUT NOW...
WE HAVE AN ELEMENTAL, AN EXECUTIONER...
...AND EVEN A DEMON SWORD WITH A BROKEN SEAL.
IT'S QUITE A GATHERING, REALLY.
BRRMM

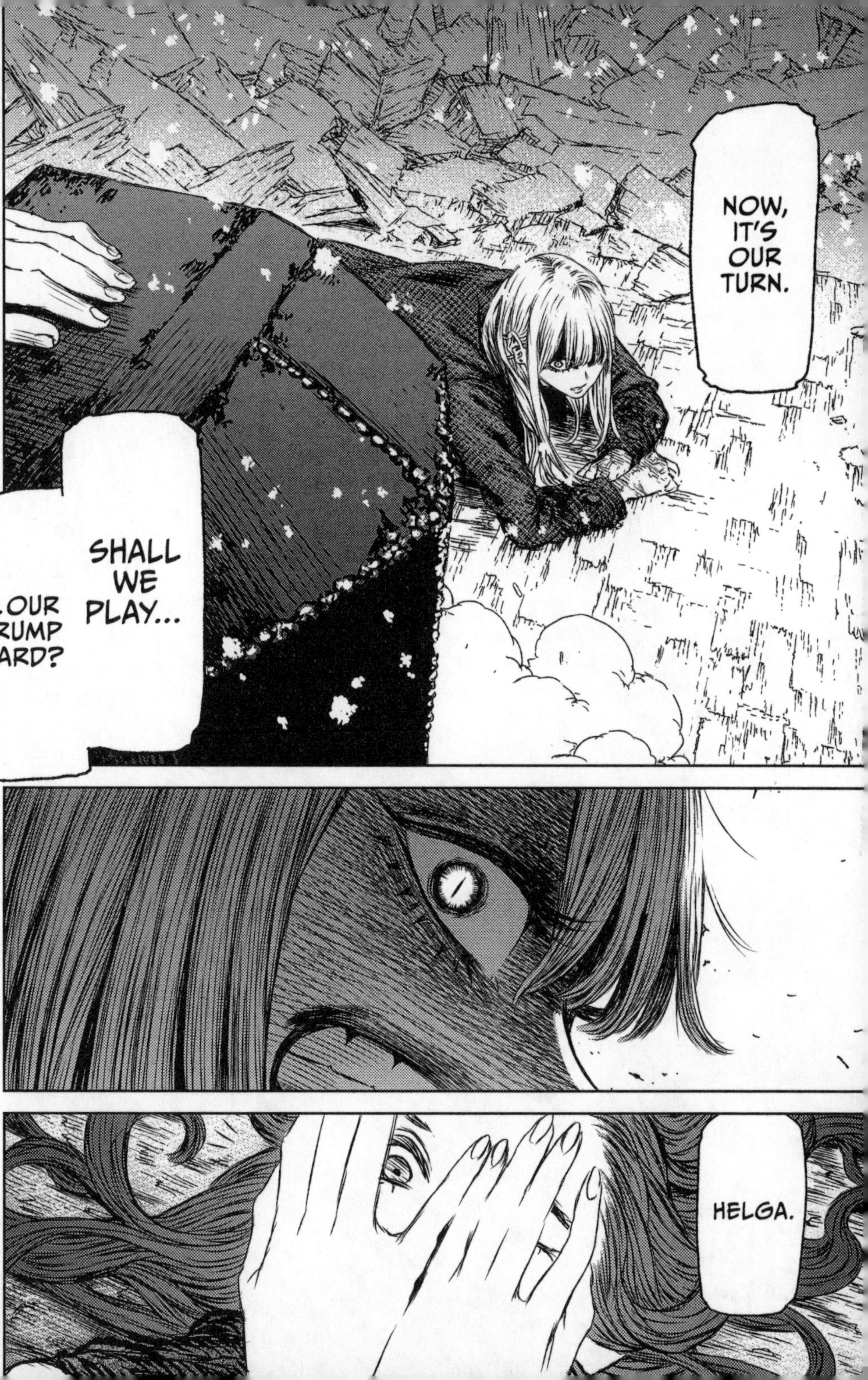
NOW, IT'S OUR TURN.
SHALL WE PLAY...
...OUR TRUMP CARD?
HELGA.

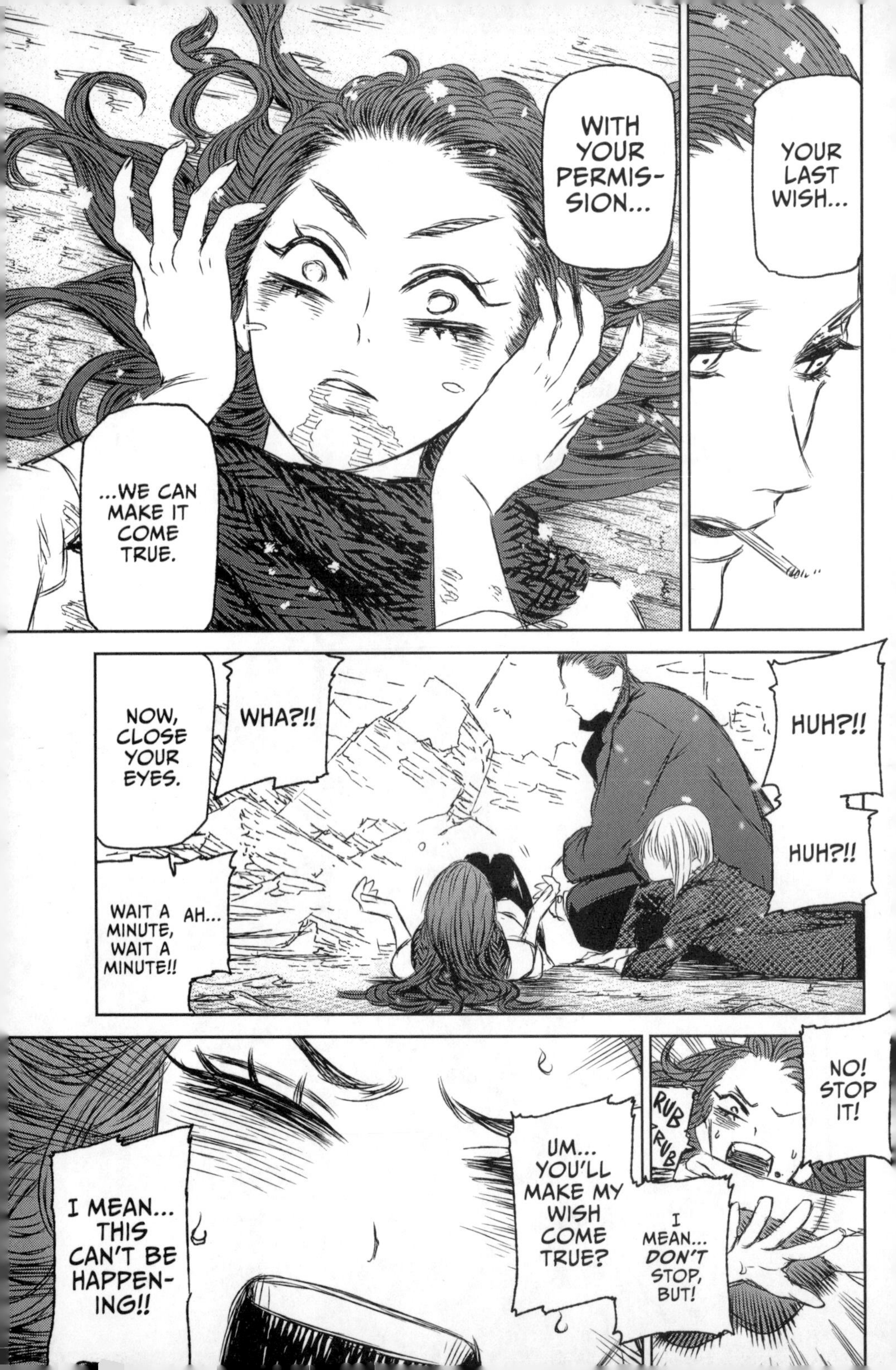
YOUR LAST WISH...
WITH YOUR PERMISSION...
...WE CAN MAKE IT COME TRUE.
HUH?!!
HUH?!!
WHA?!!
NOW, CLOSE YOUR EYES.
AH...
WAIT A MINUTE, WAIT A MINUTE!!
NO! STOP IT!
RUB RUB
I MEAN... DON'T STOP, BUT!
UM... YOU'LL MAKE MY WISH COME TRUE?
I MEAN... THIS CAN'T BE HAPPENING!!

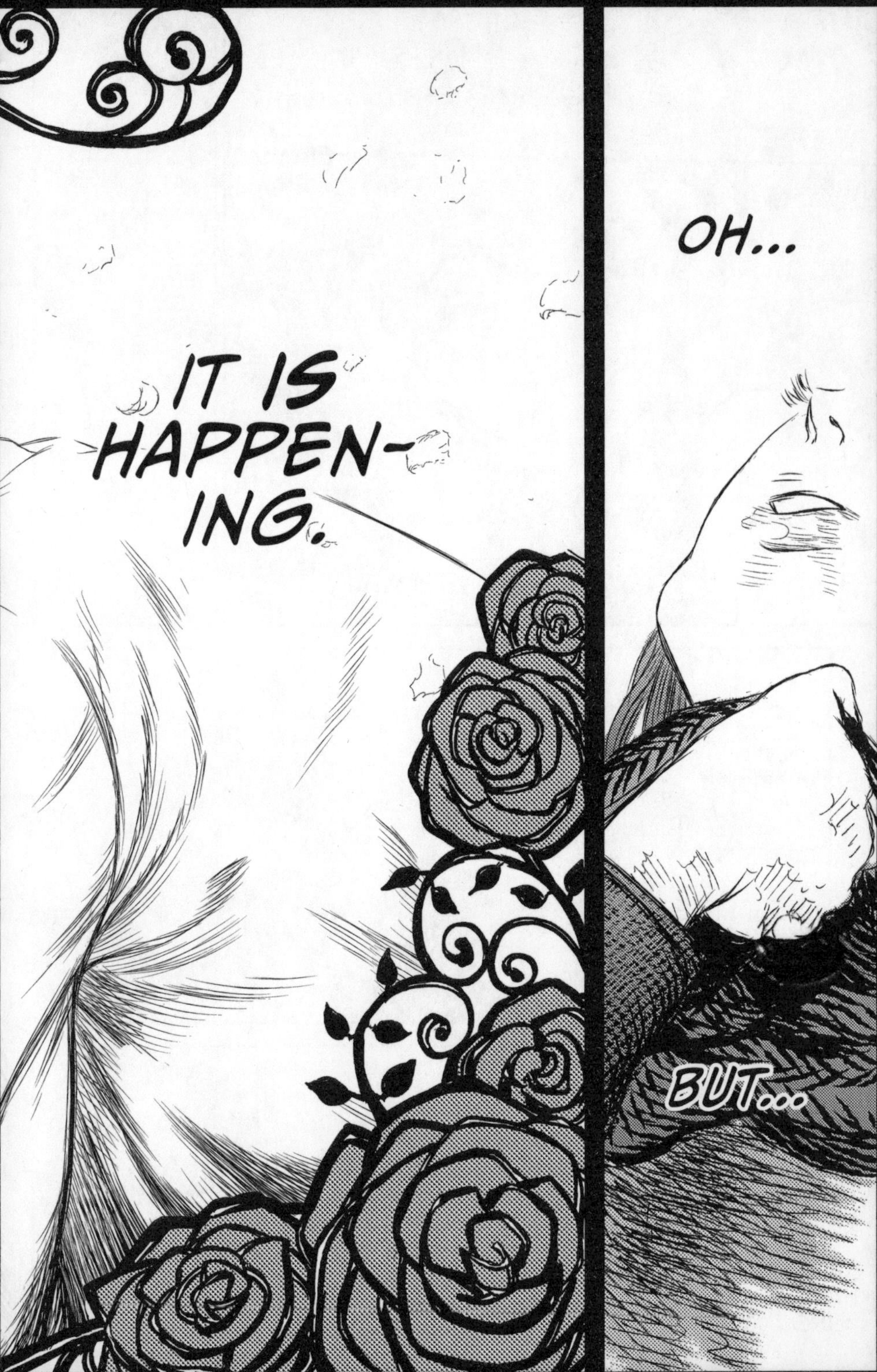
OH...
BUT...
IT IS HAPPEN-ING.

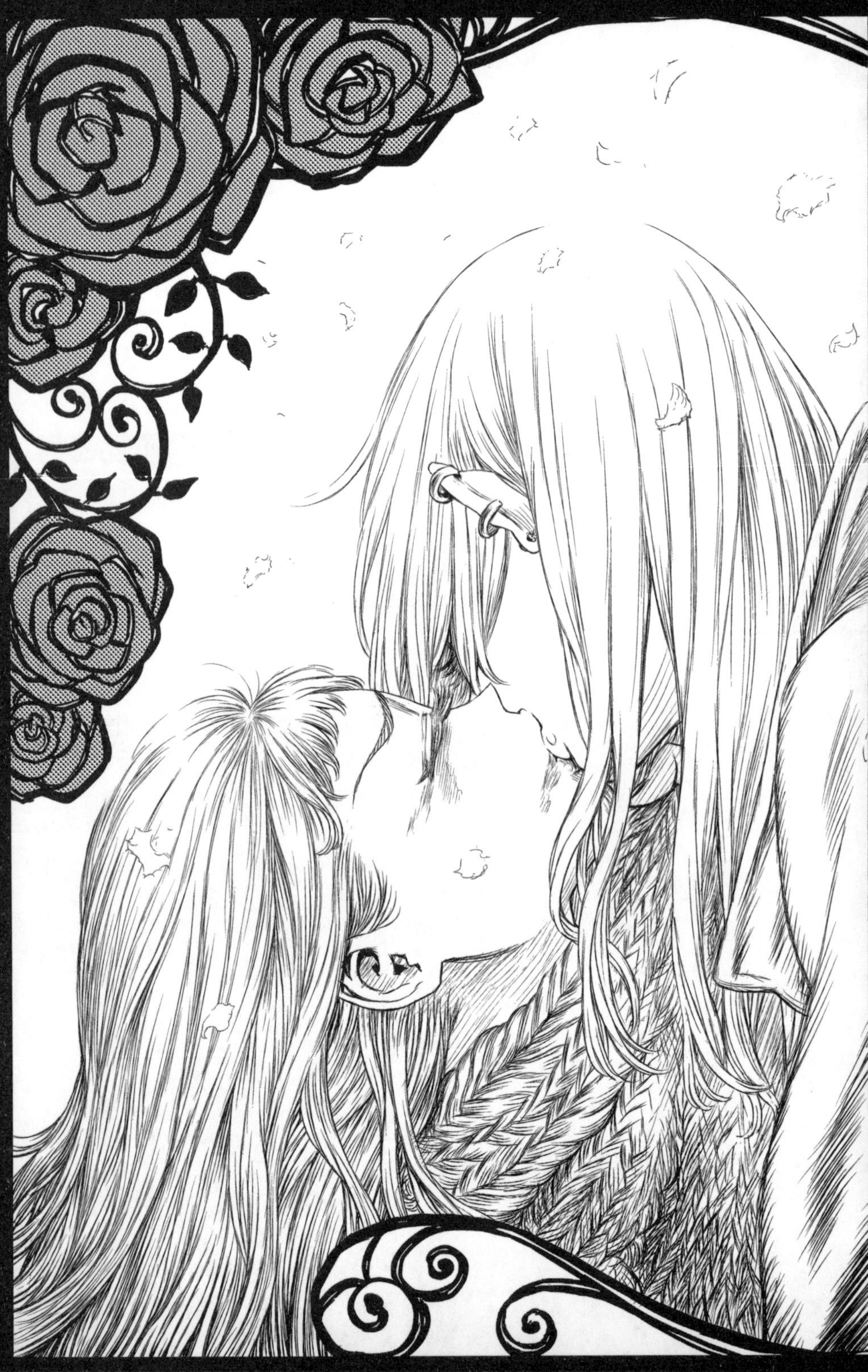

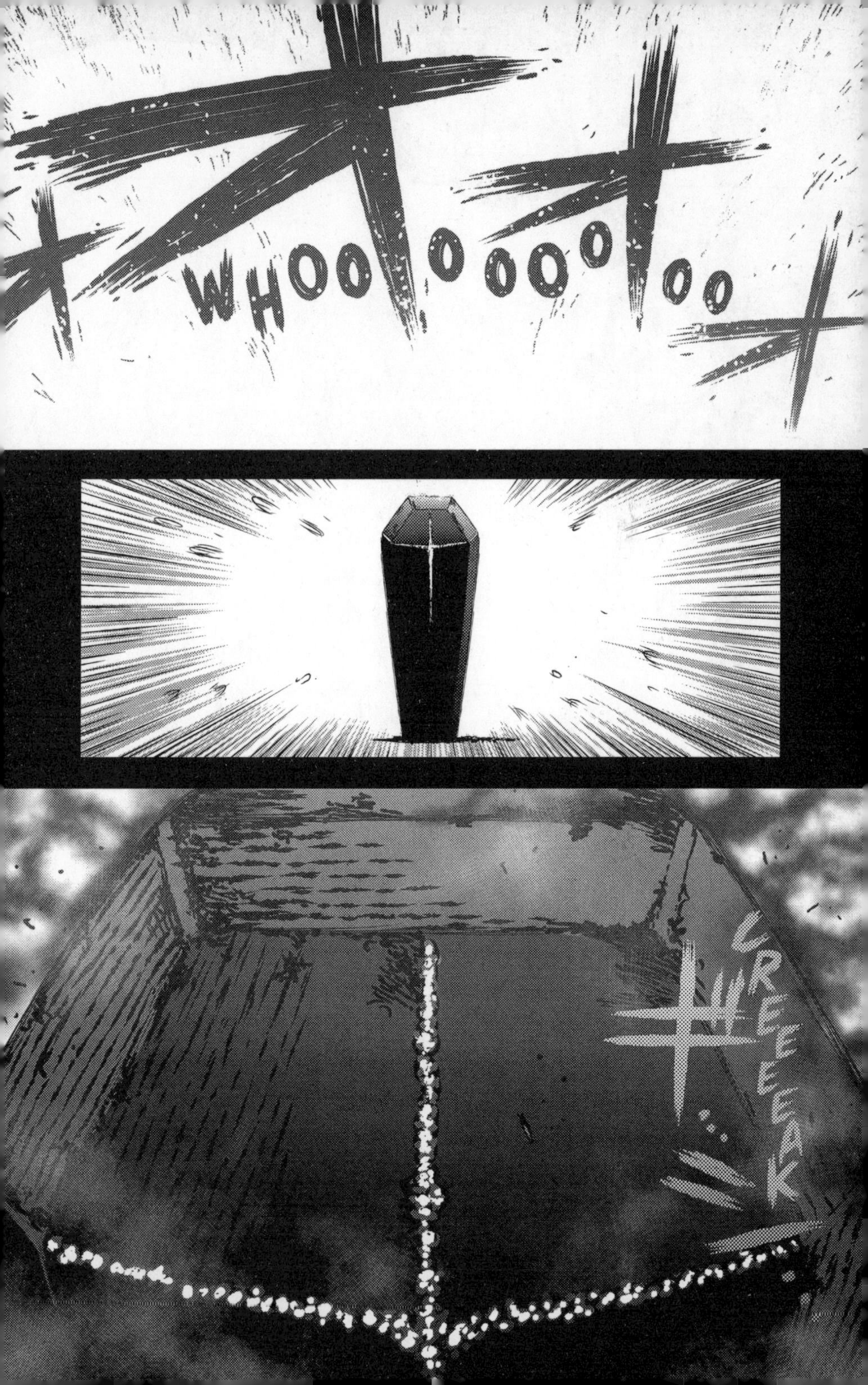
WHOOOOOOOOO
CREEEAK

THE WITCH AND THE BEAST

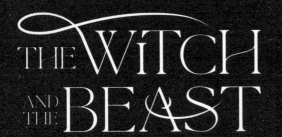

THE WITCH AND THE BEAST

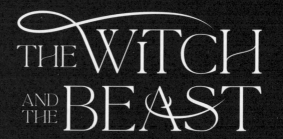

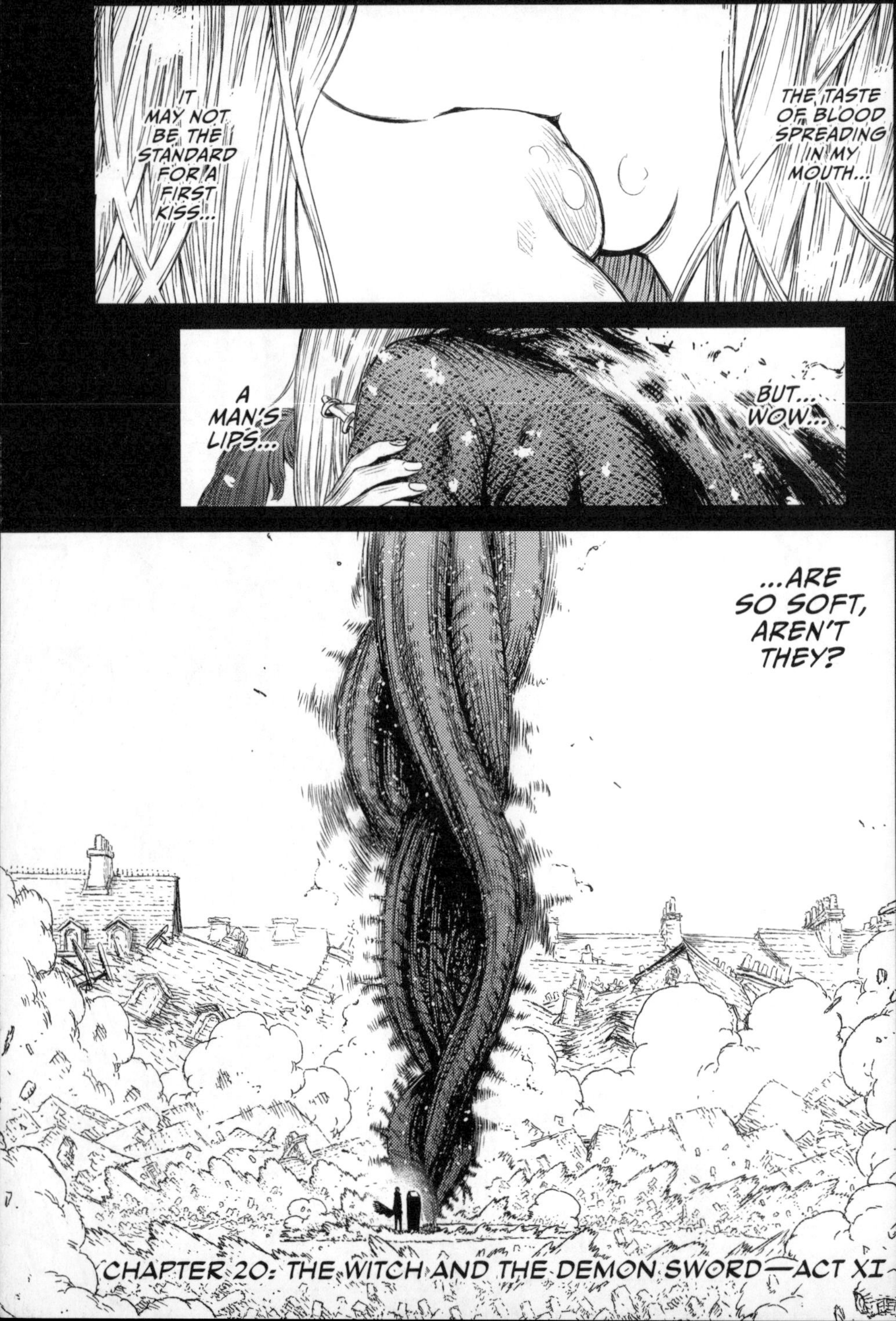
THE TASTE OF BLOOD SPREADING IN MY MOUTH...
IT MAY NOT BE THE STANDARD FOR A FIRST KISS...
BUT... WOW...
A MAN'S LIPS...
...ARE SO SOFT, AREN'T THEY?
CHAPTER 20: THE WITCH AND THE DEMON SWORD—ACT XI

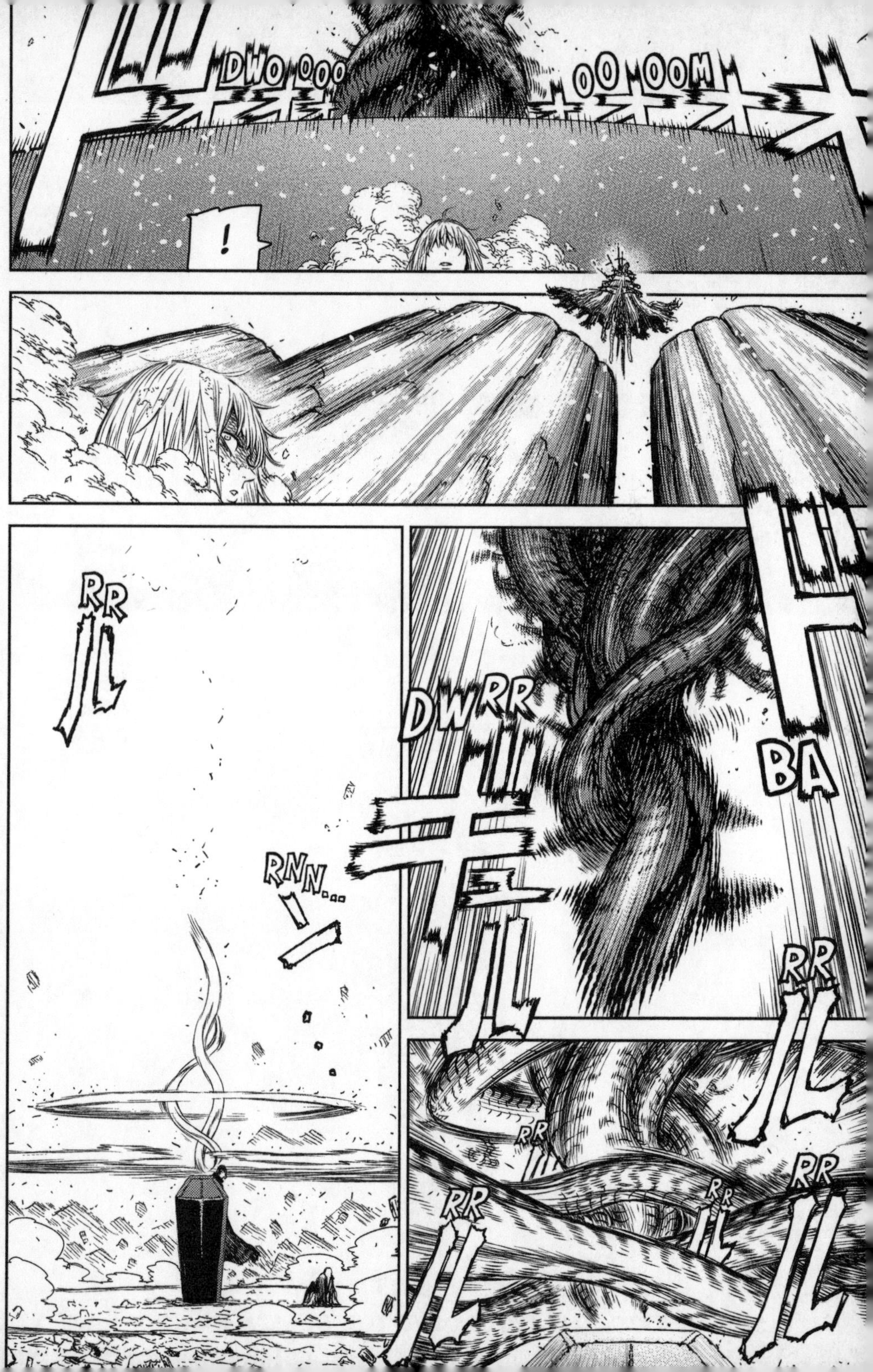
DWO OOO
OO OOM
!
BA
DWRR
RR
RR
RR
RR
RR
RR
RNN...

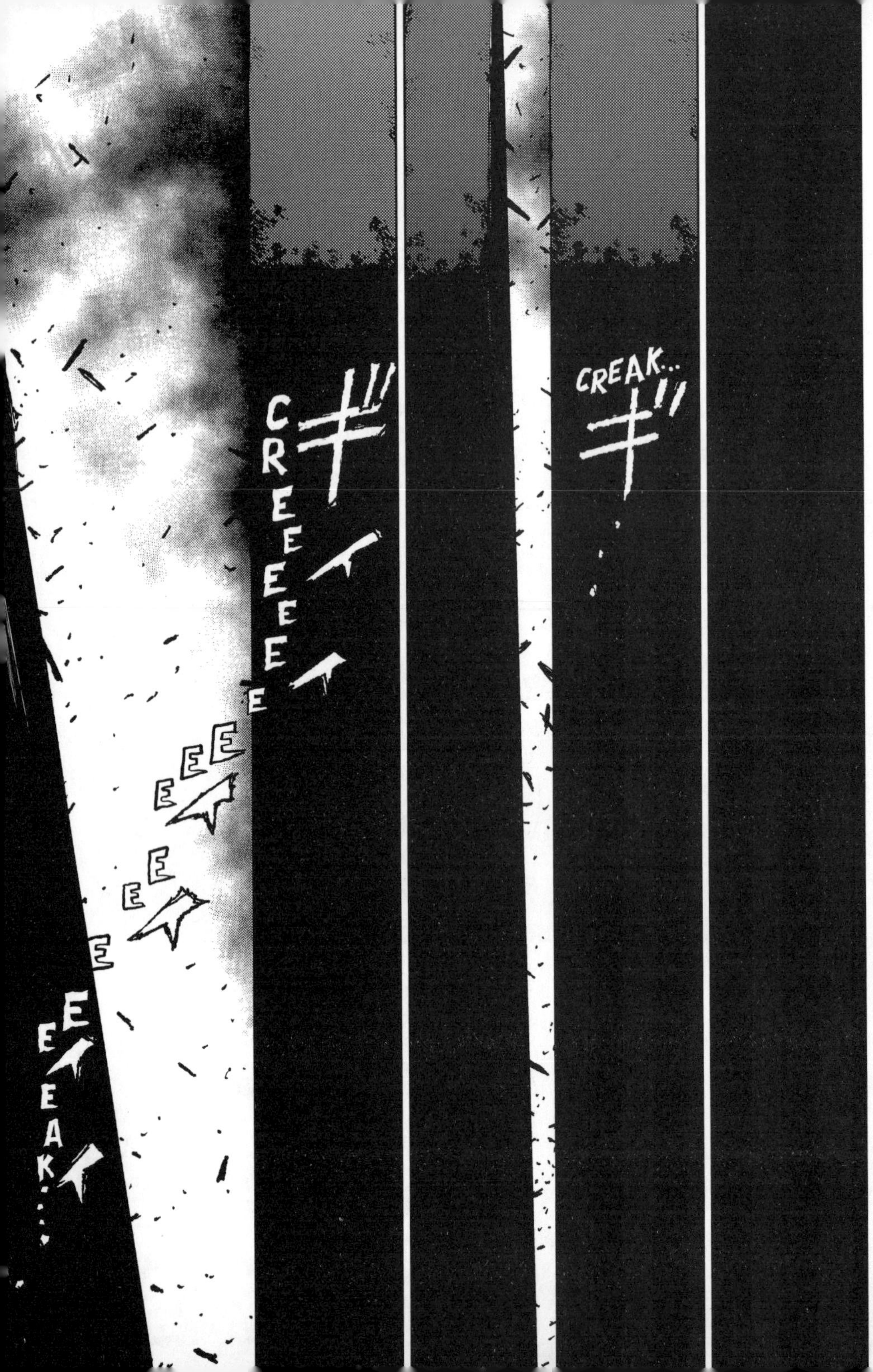

CREAK...
ギ
CREEEEEEEEEEEEEEEAK...
ギィィィ

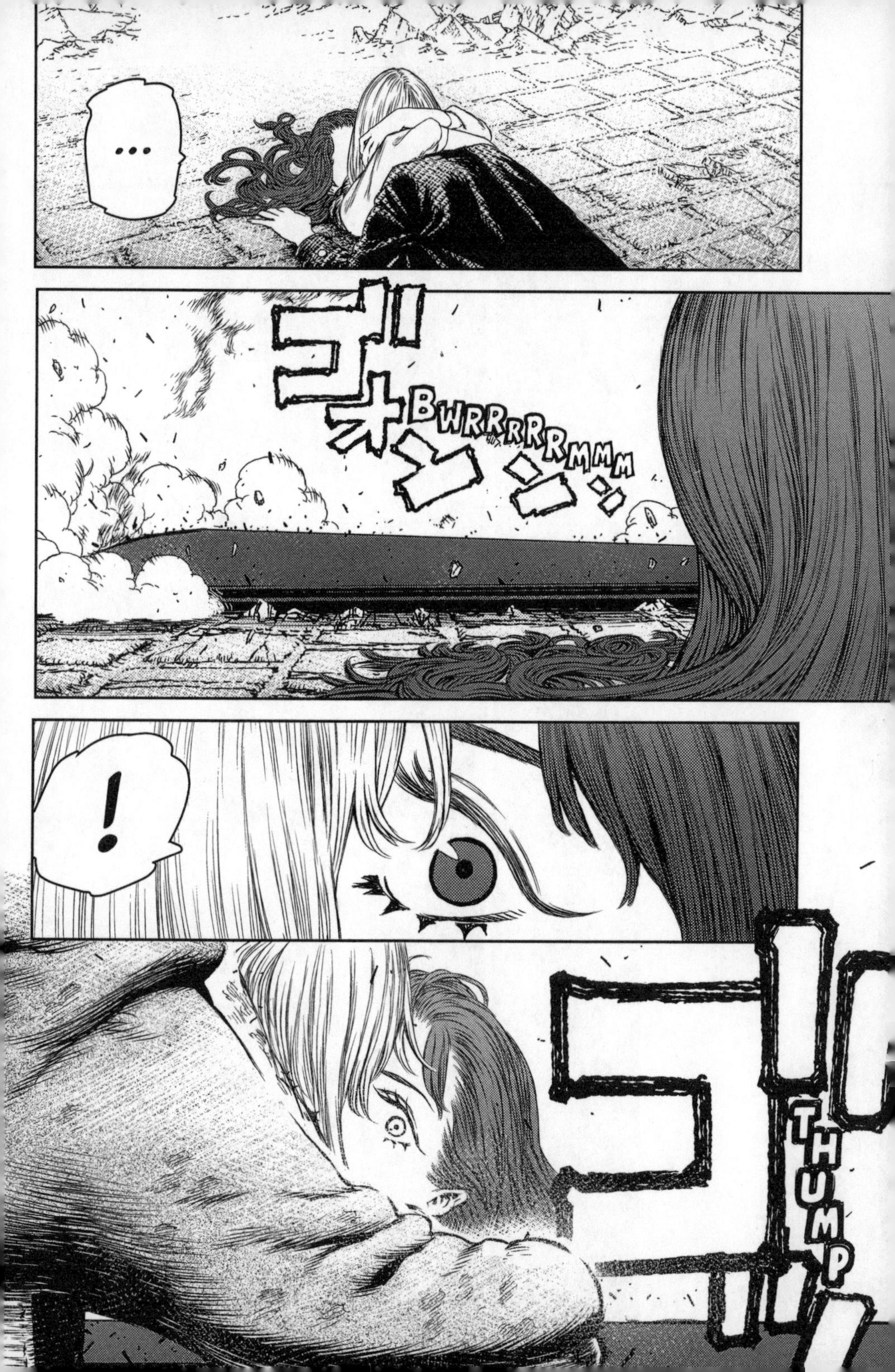
...
BWRRRRRRMMM
!
THUMP

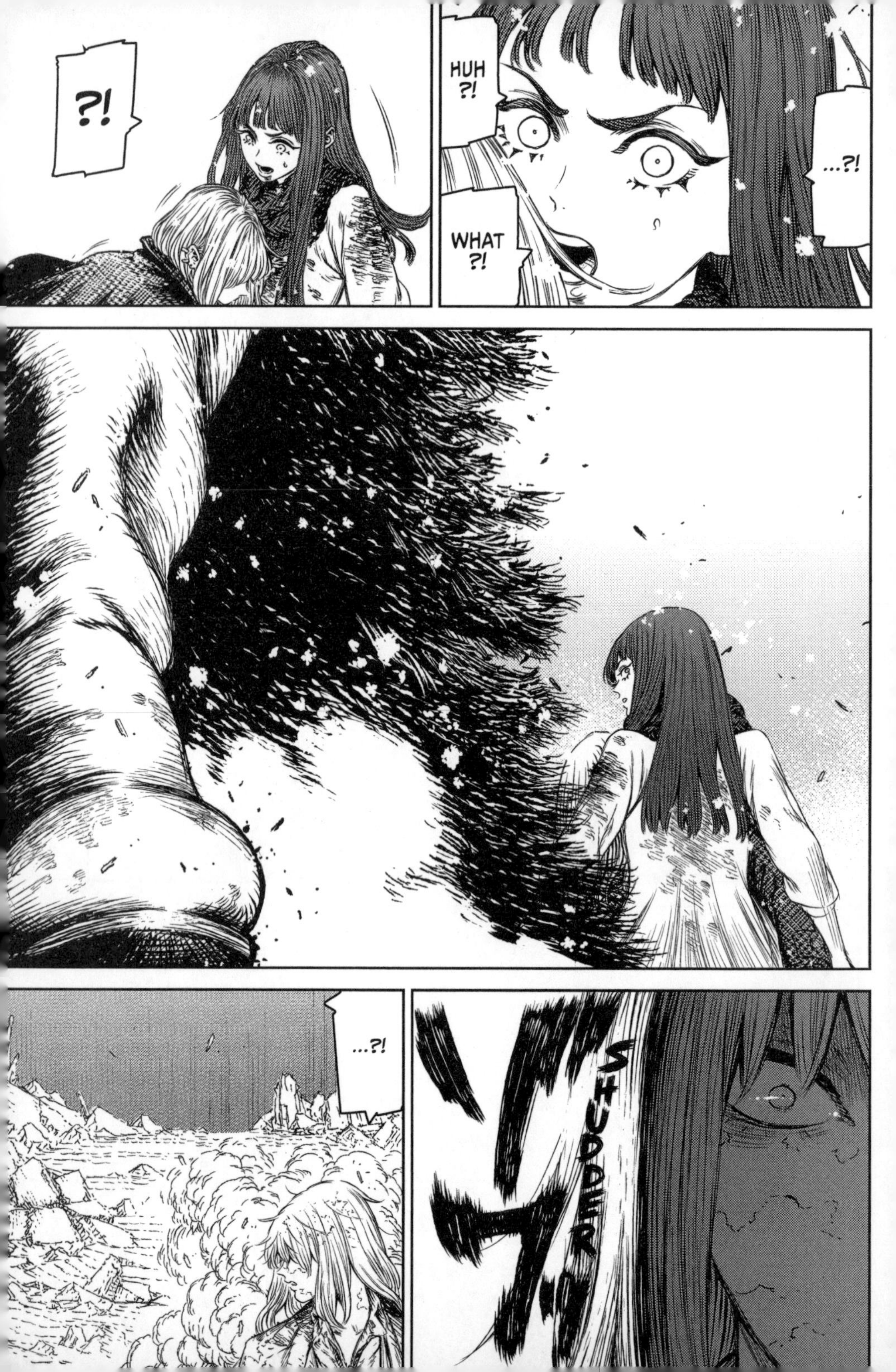
HUH ?!
...?!
WHAT ?!
?!
SHUDDER
...?!

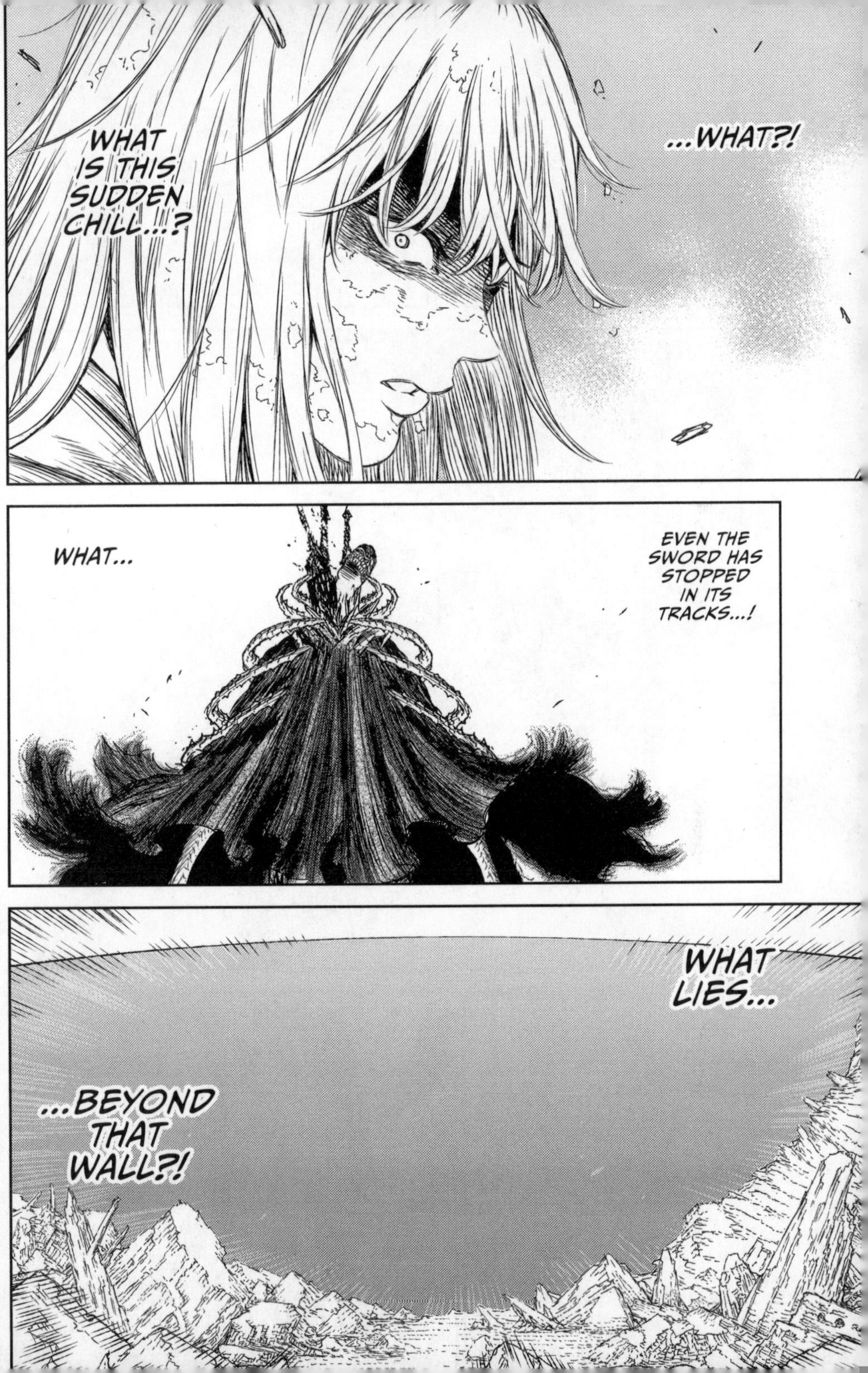
...WHAT?!
WHAT IS THIS SUDDEN CHILL...?
EVEN THE SWORD HAS STOPPED IN ITS TRACKS...!
WHAT...
WHAT LIES...
...BEYOND THAT WALL?!

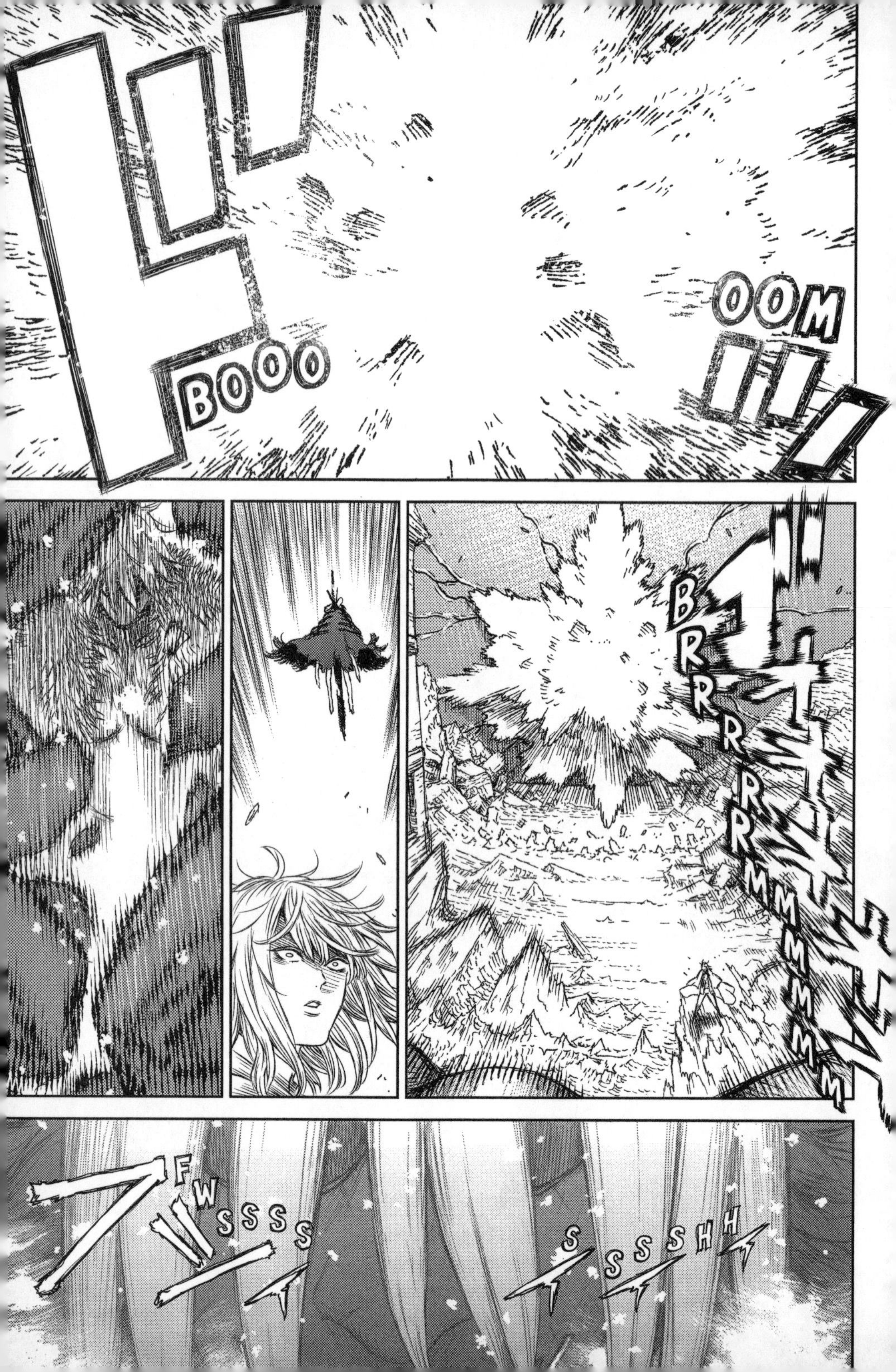
BOOOOOM
BRRRRRRMMMMMMM
FWSSSS
SSSSHH

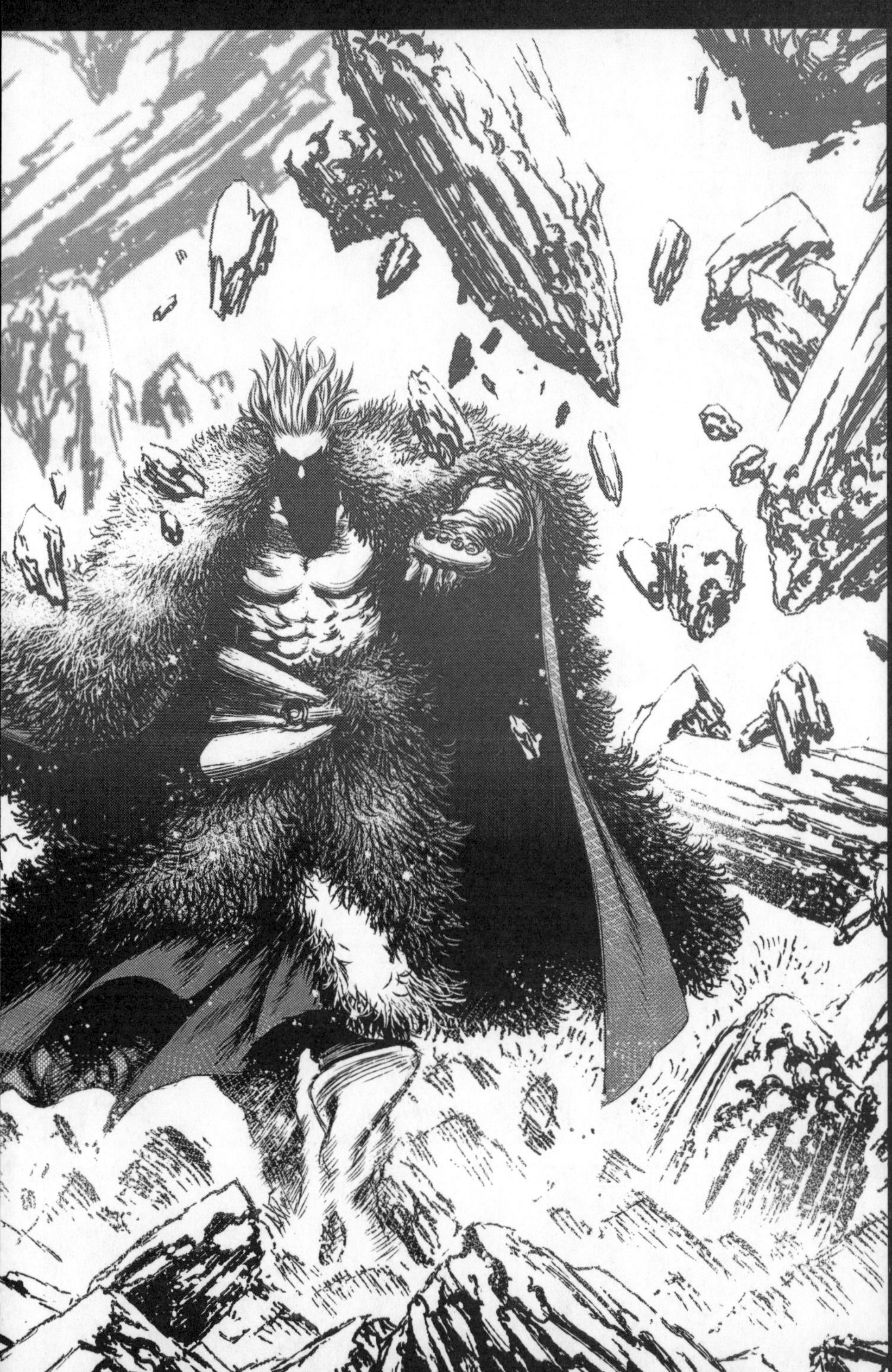

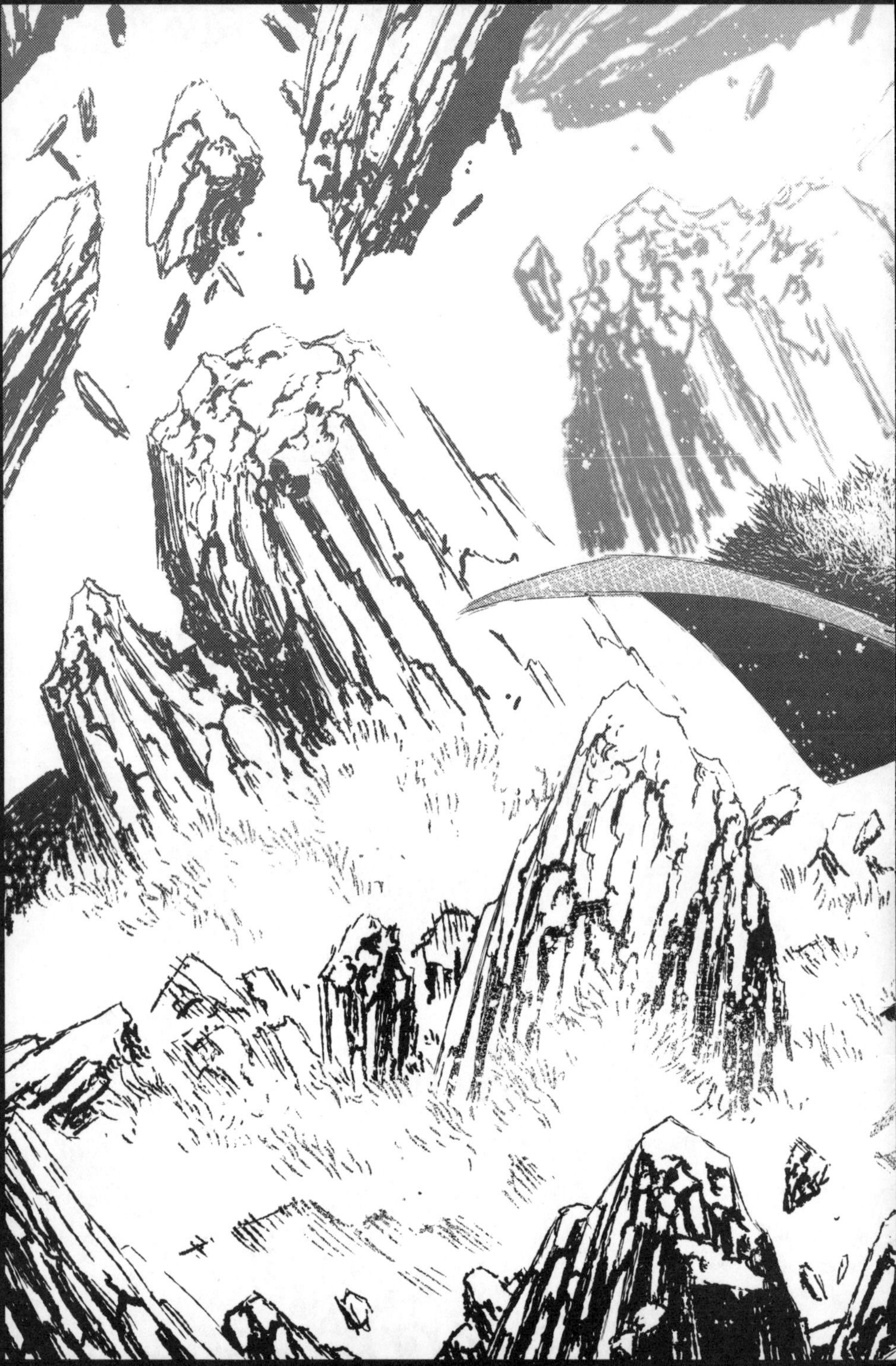

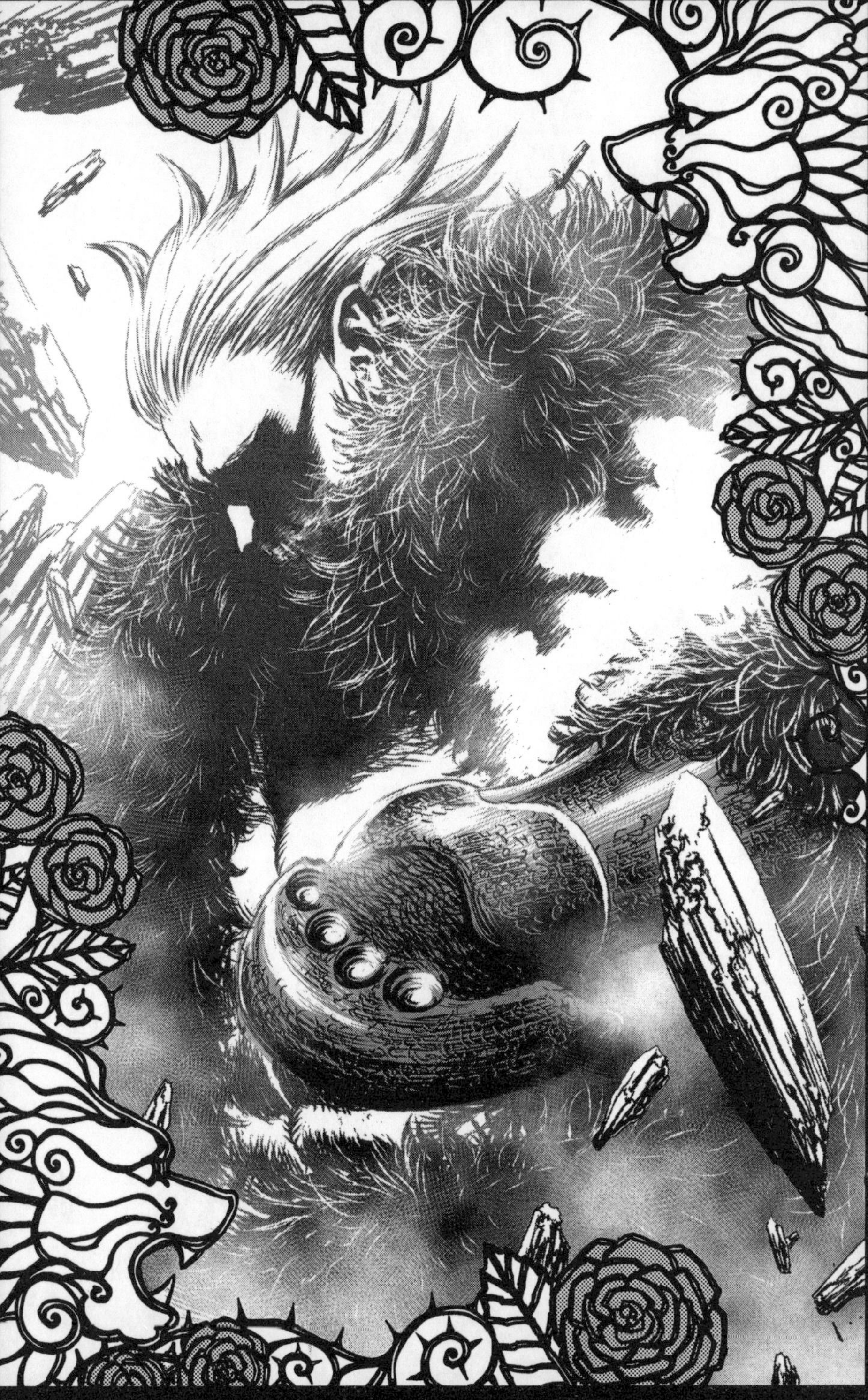

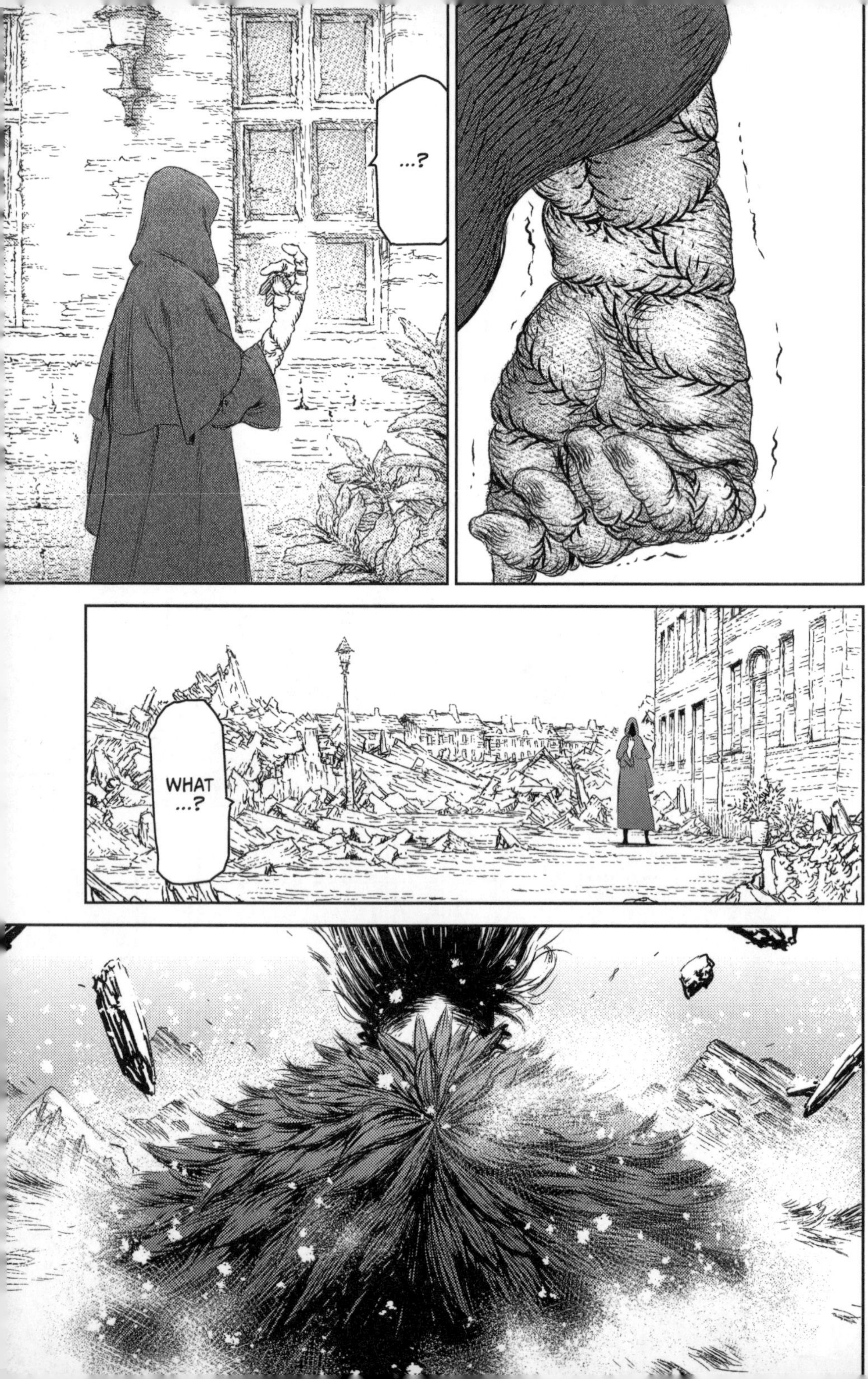
...?
WHAT ...?

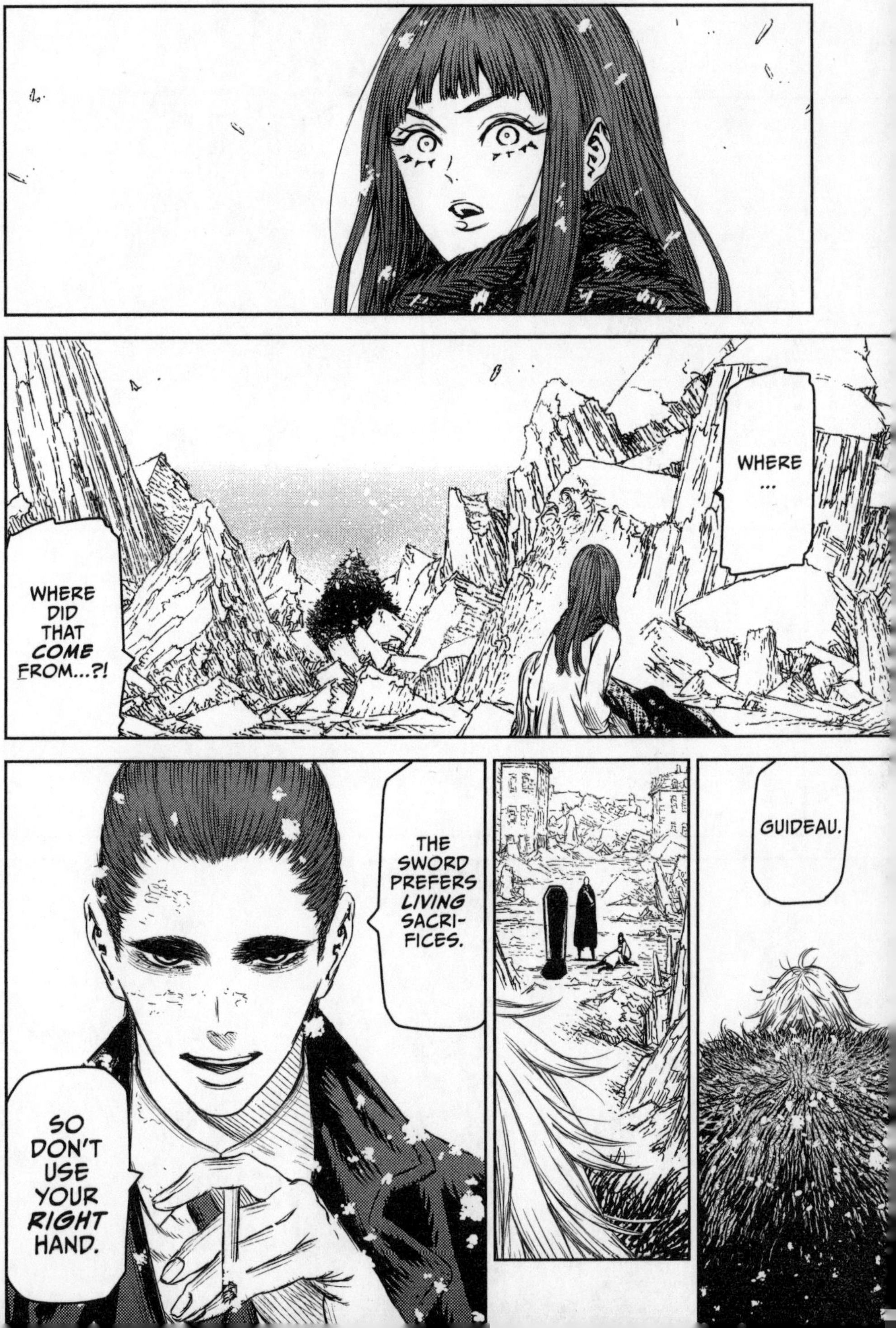
WHERE ...
WHERE DID THAT *COME* FROM...?!
GUIDEAU.
THE SWORD PREFERS *LIVING* SACRIFICES.
SO DON'T USE YOUR *RIGHT* HAND.

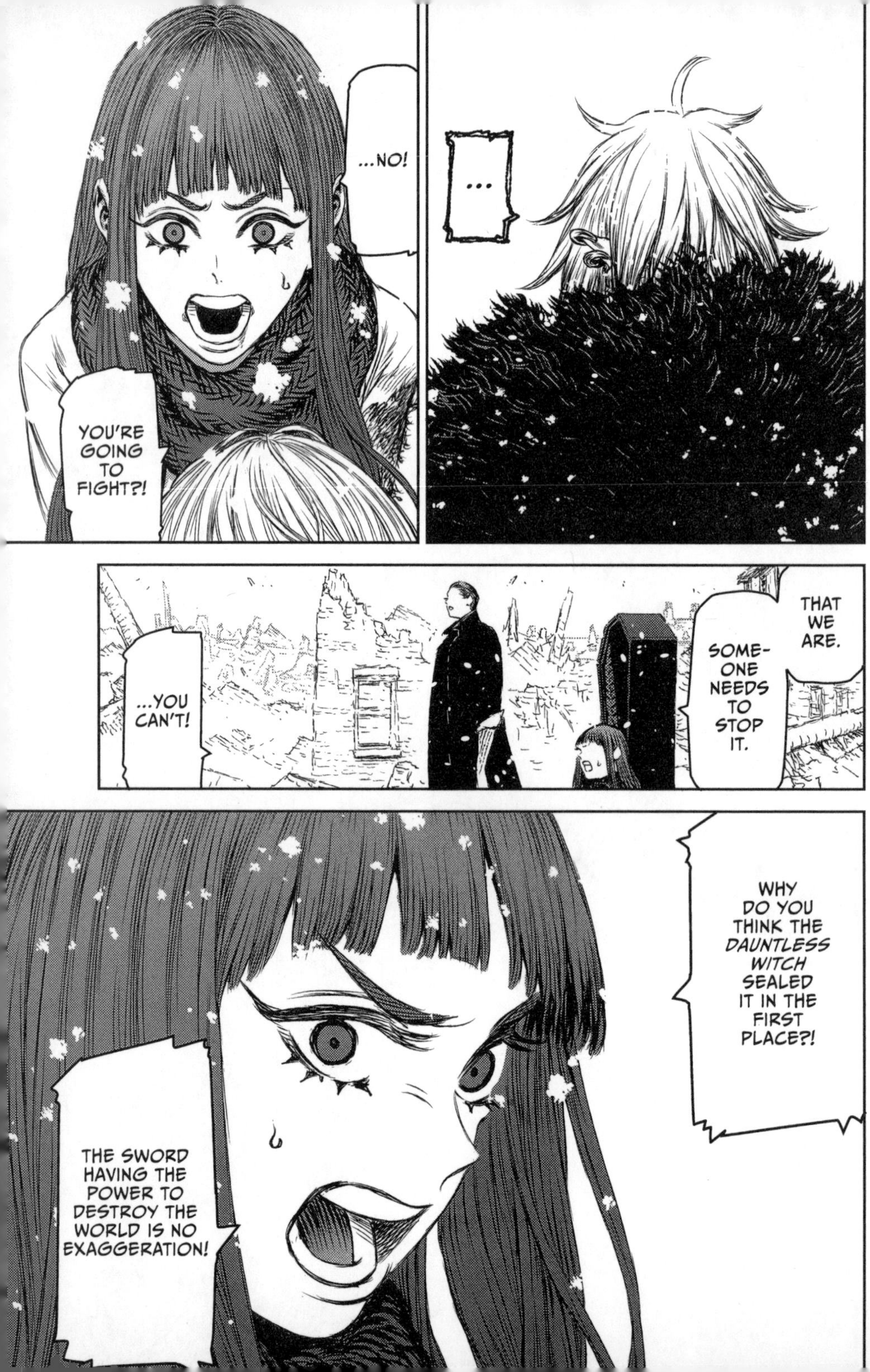
...
...NO!
YOU'RE GOING TO FIGHT?!
THAT WE ARE.
SOME-ONE NEEDS TO STOP IT.
...YOU CAN'T!
WHY DO YOU THINK THE *DAUNTLESS WITCH* SEALED IT IN THE FIRST PLACE?!
THE SWORD HAVING THE POWER TO DESTROY THE WORLD IS NO EXAGGERATION!

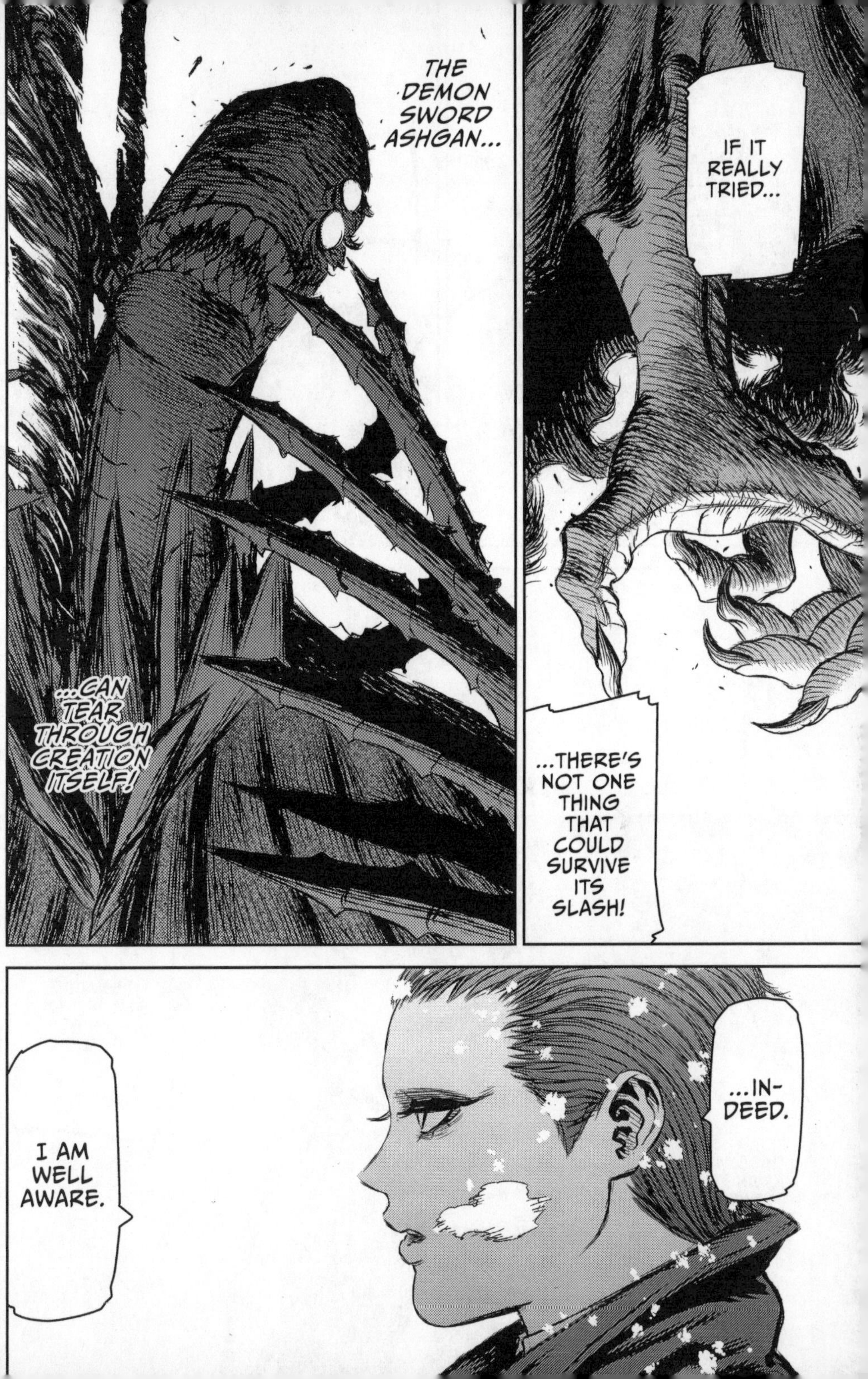
IF IT REALLY TRIED...
...THERE'S NOT ONE THING THAT COULD SURVIVE ITS SLASH!
THE DEMON SWORD ASHGAN...
...CAN TEAR THROUGH CREATION ITSELF!
...IN-DEED.
I AM WELL AWARE.

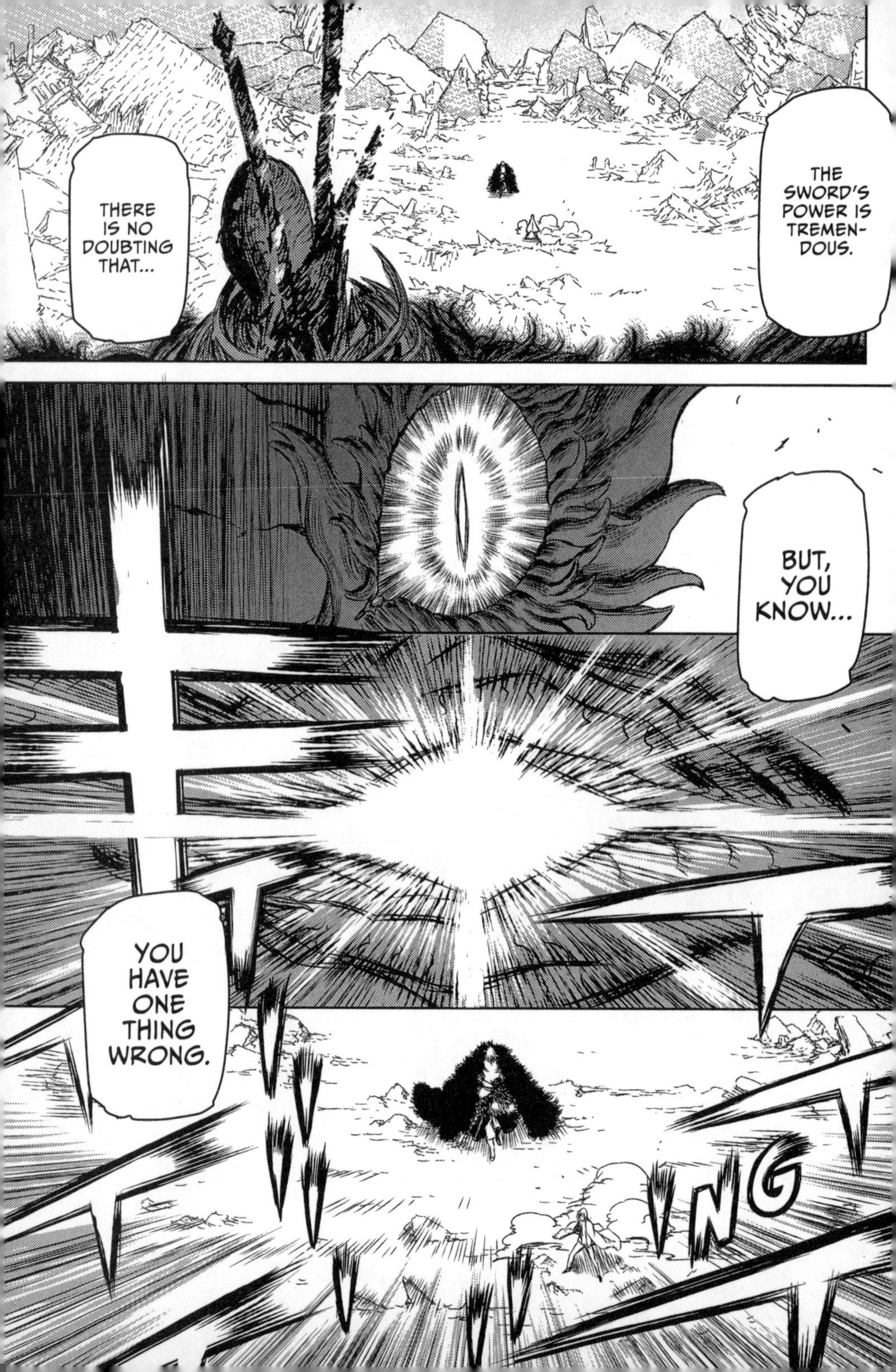
THE SWORD'S POWER IS TREMEN- DOUS.
THERE IS NO DOUBTING THAT...
BUT, YOU KNOW...
YOU HAVE ONE THING WRONG.
NG

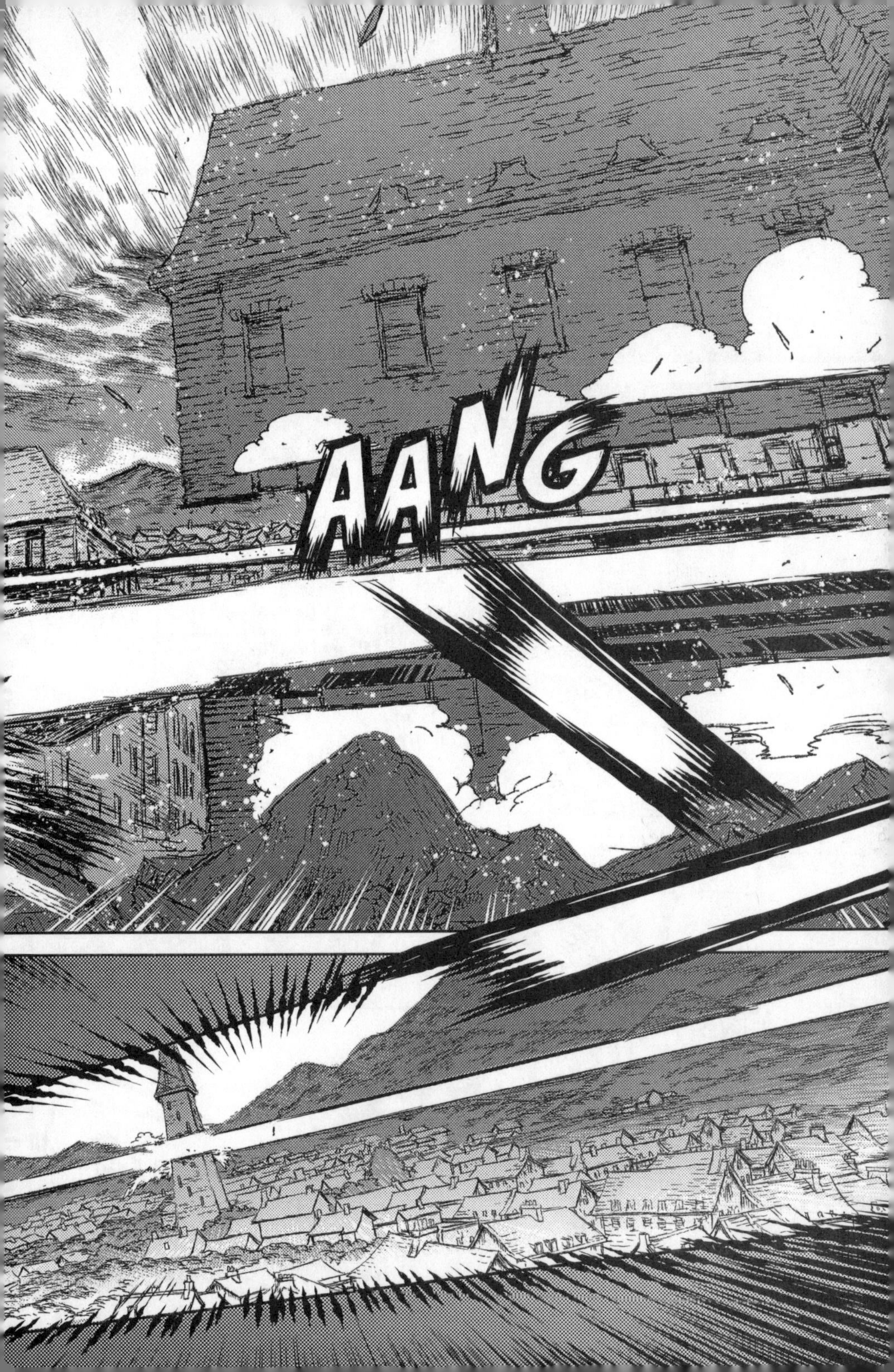
AANG

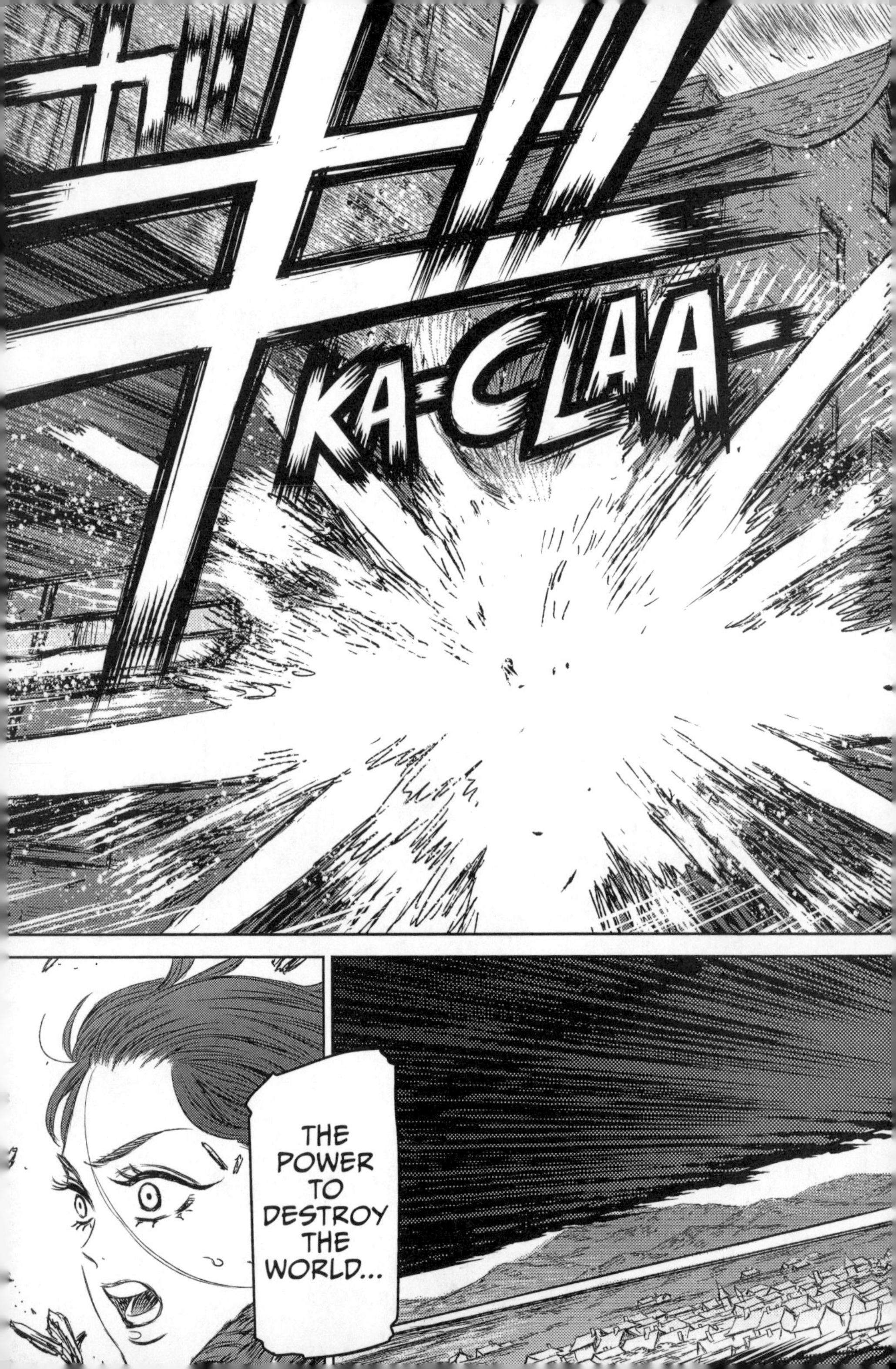
KA-CLAA
THE POWER TO DESTROY THE WORLD...

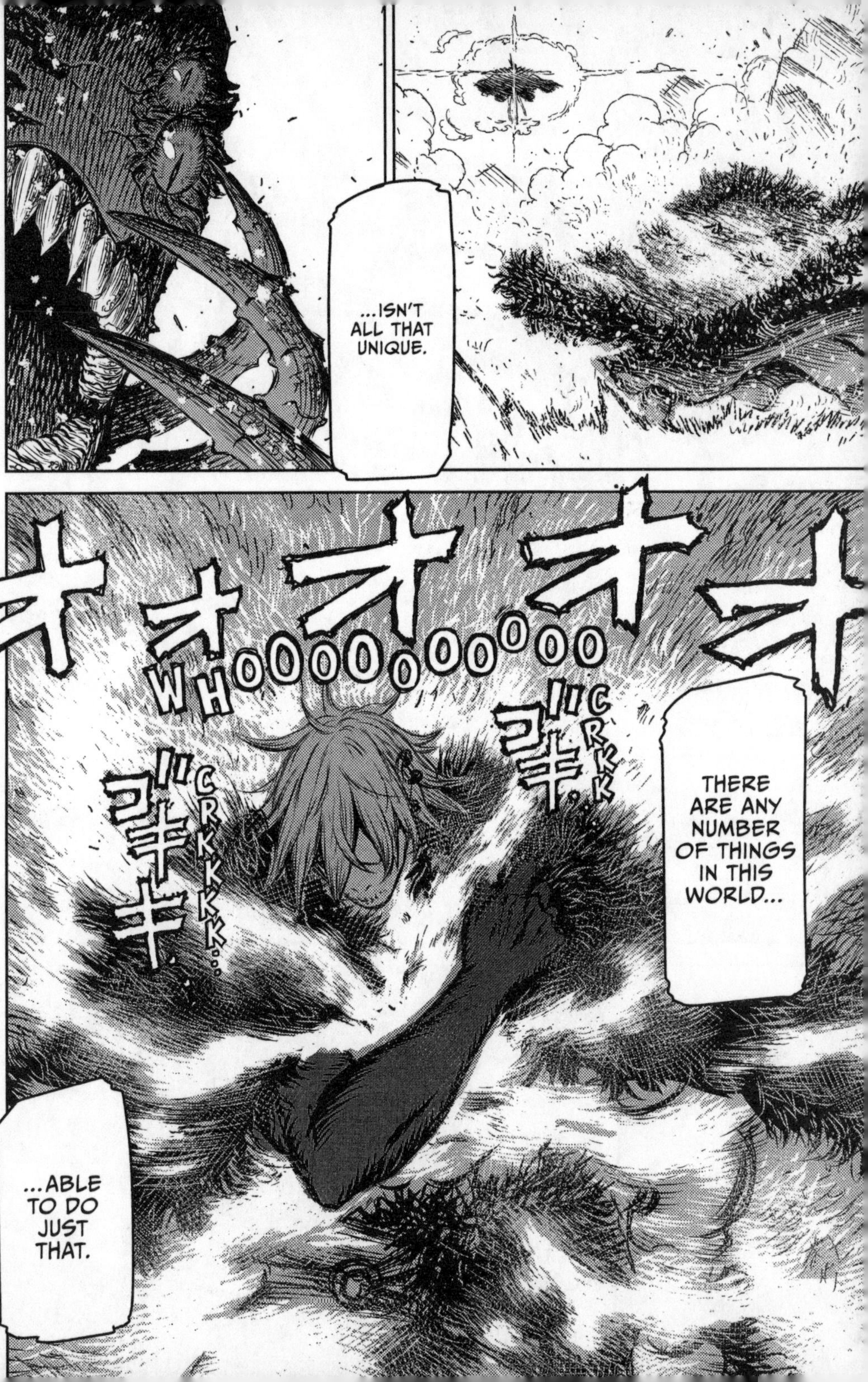

...ISN'T ALL THAT UNIQUE.
オオオオ
WHOOOOOOOOOO
ゴキ CRKK
THERE ARE ANY NUMBER OF THINGS IN THIS WORLD...
ゴキキ CRKKK...
...ABLE TO DO JUST THAT.

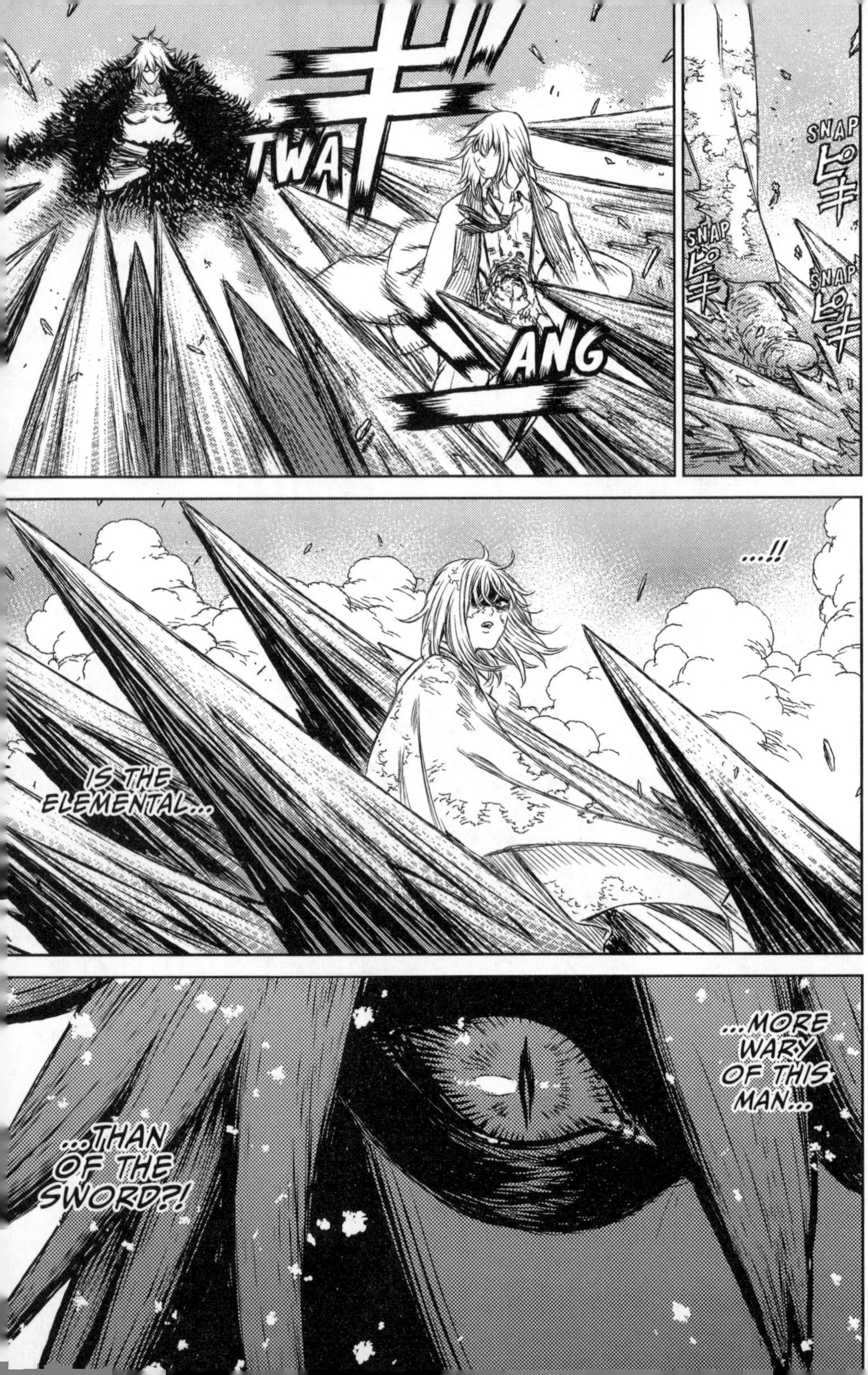
SNAP
ピキ
SNAP
ピキ
SNAP
ピキ
TWA
ANG
...!!
IS THE ELEMENTAL...
...MORE WARY OF THIS MAN...
...THAN OF THE SWORD?!

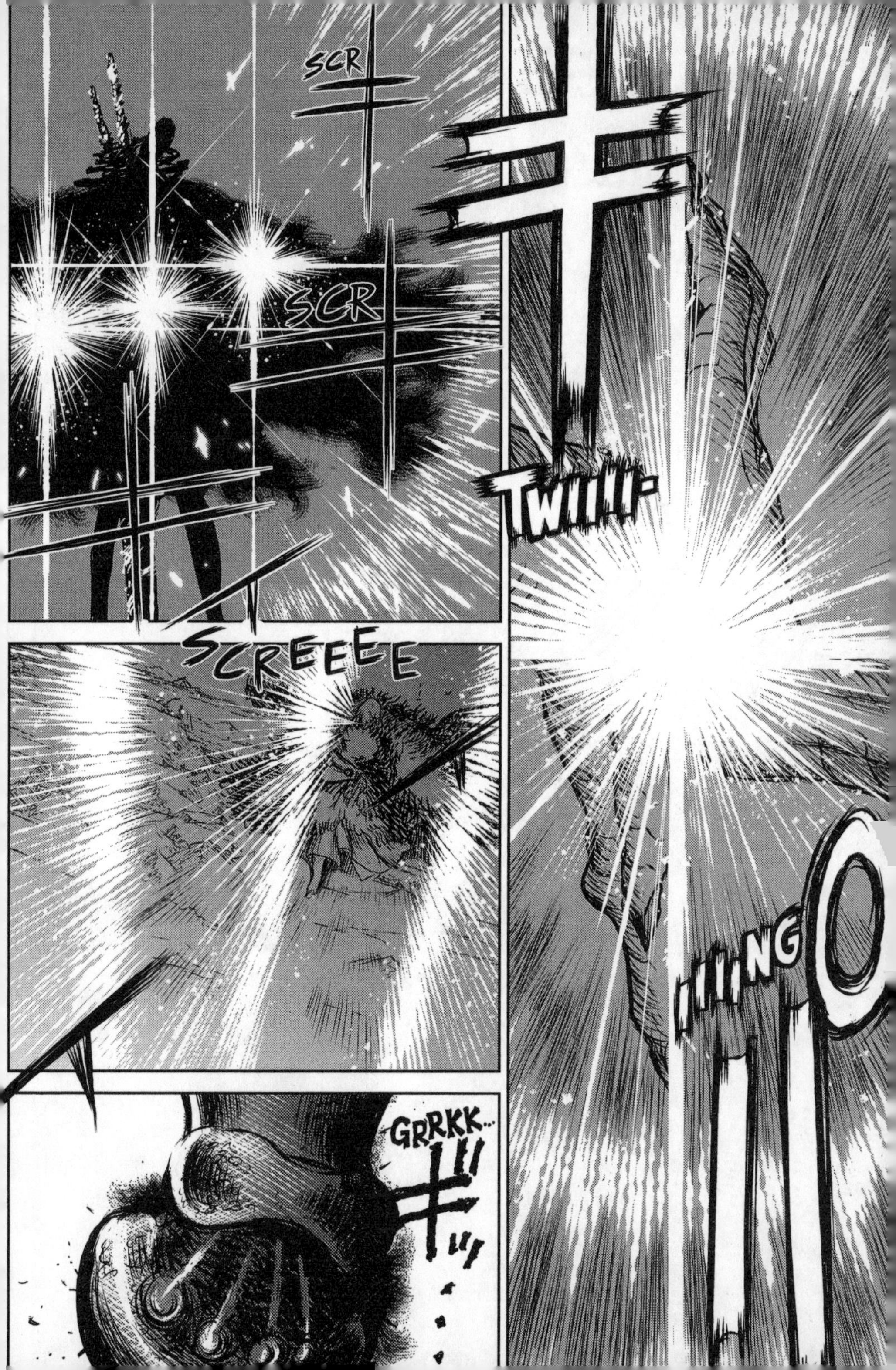
TWIIII-
IIIING
SCR
SCR
SCREEEE
GRRKK...

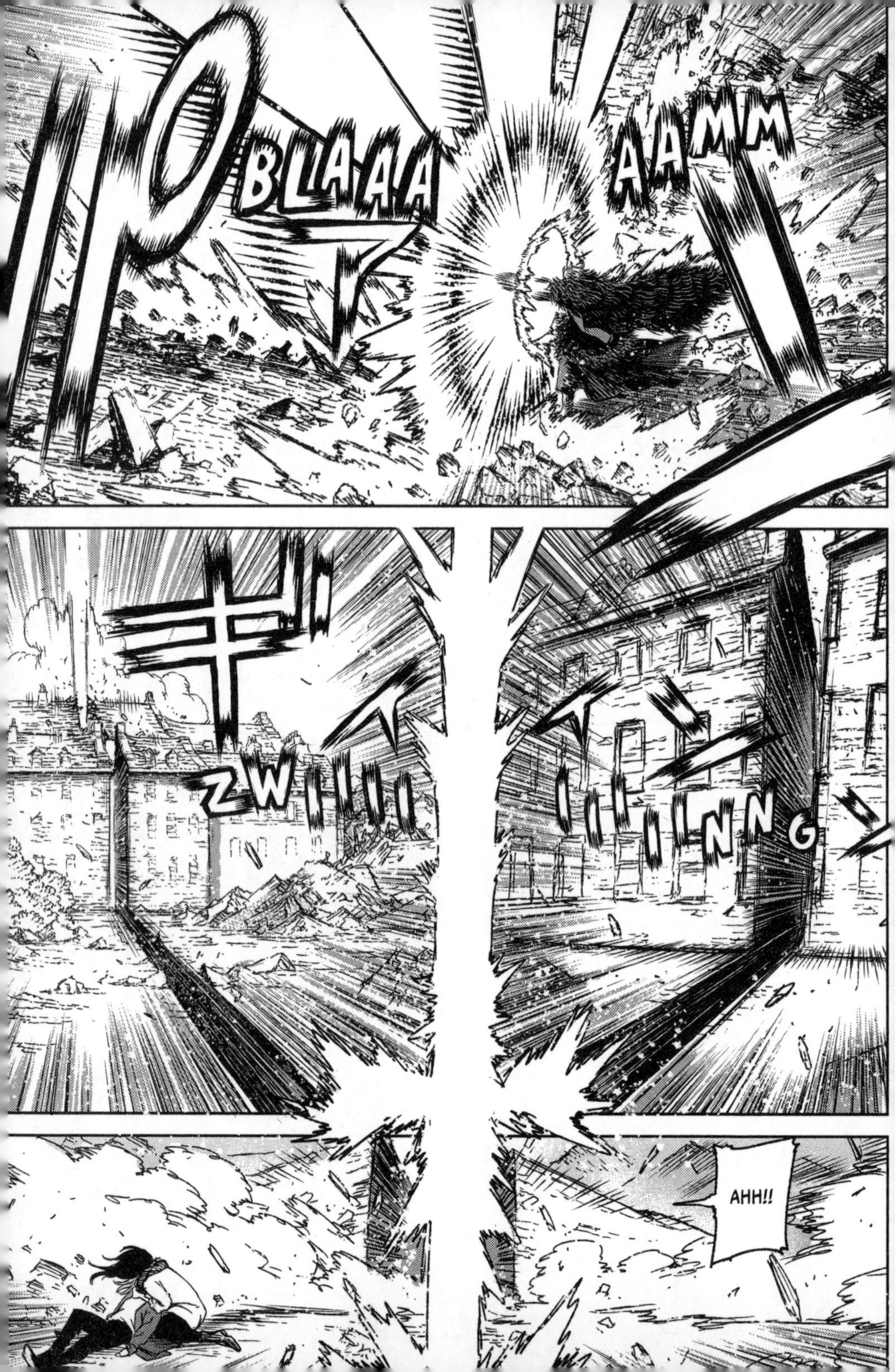
BLAAAAAMM
ZWIIIIIIIIINNG
AHH!!

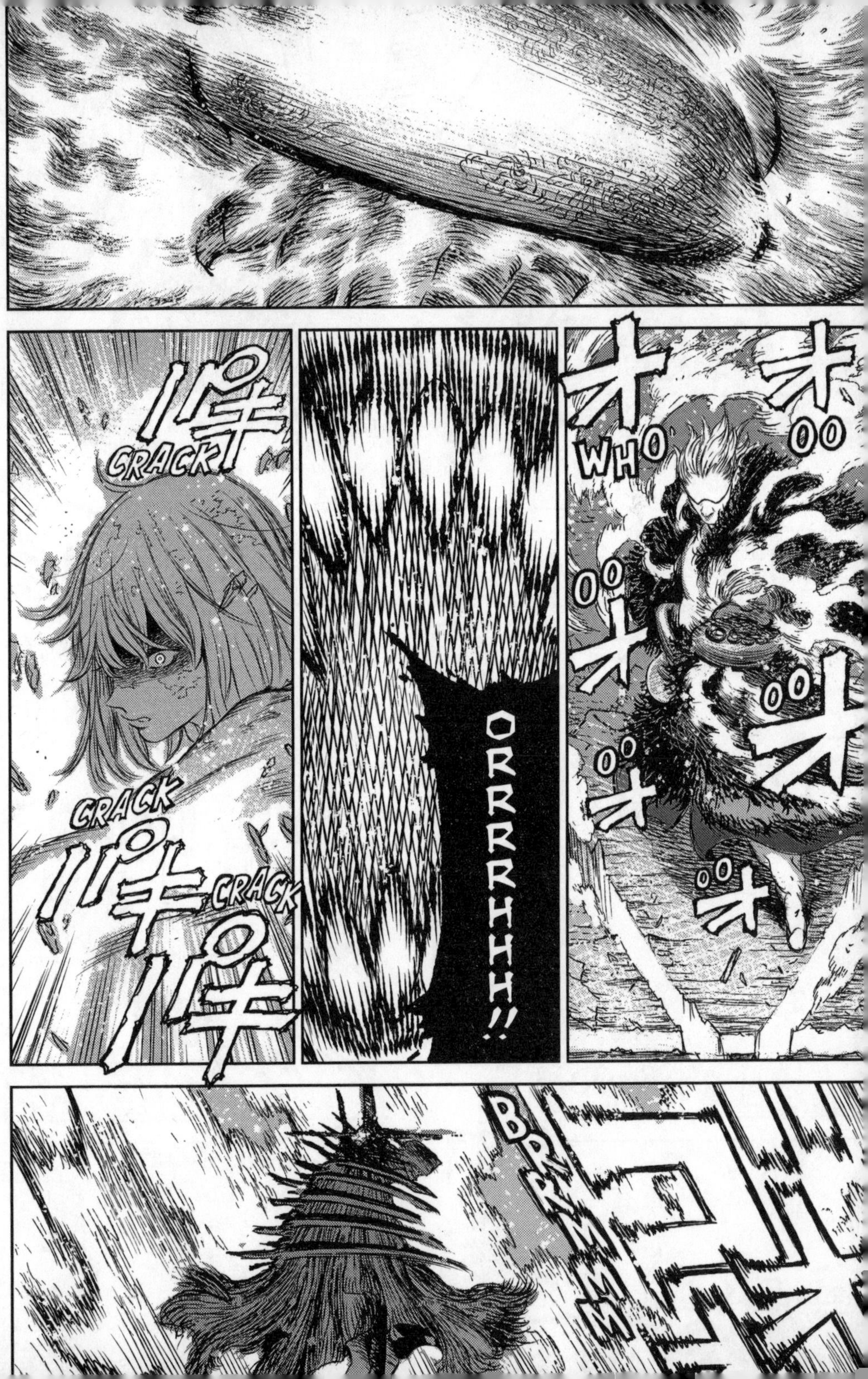
オ
OO
WHO
オ
OO
オ
OO
オ
OO
オ
OO
オ
ORRRRHHH!!
パキ
CRACK
CRACK
パキ
CRACK
パキ
BRRMMMM

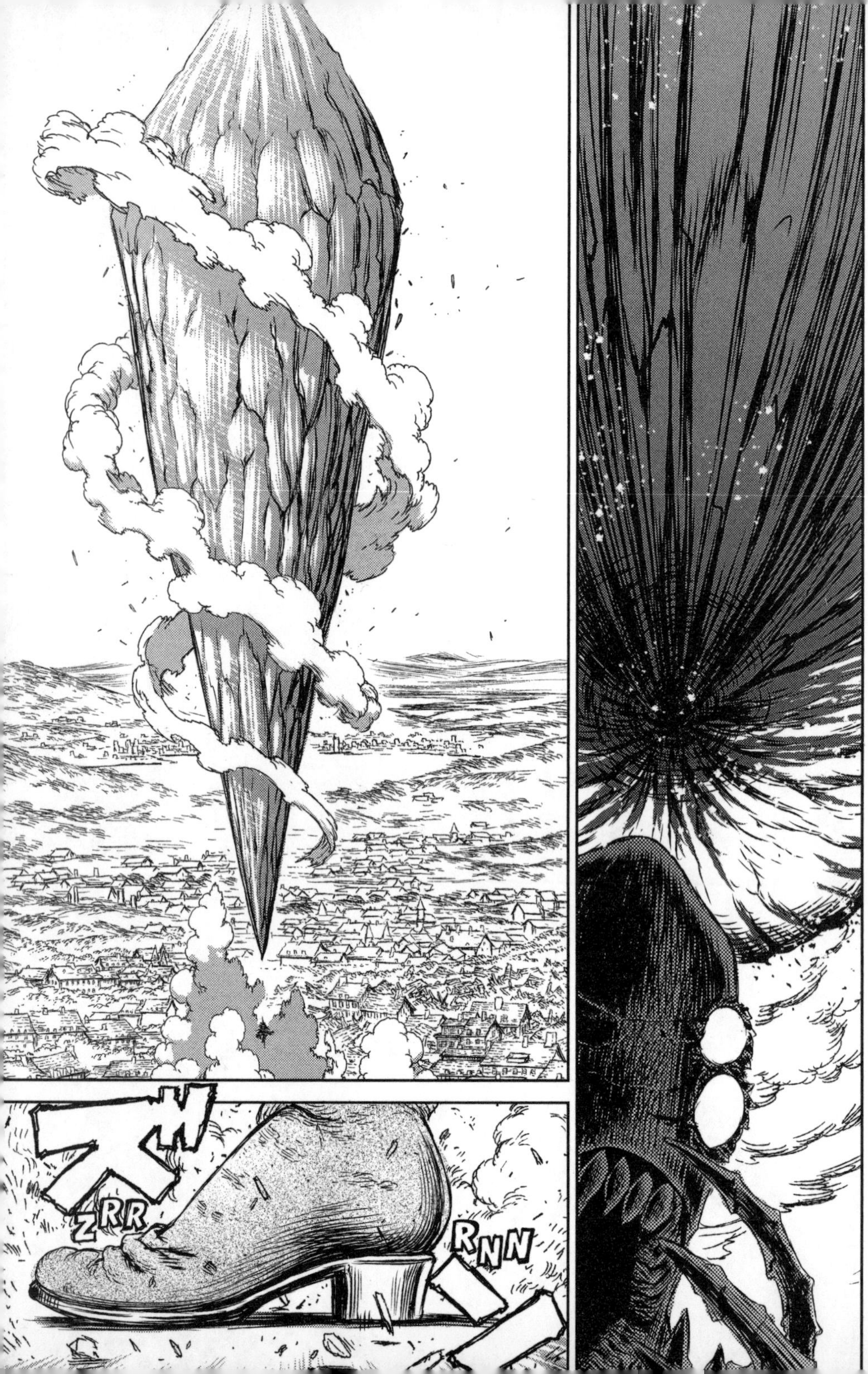
ZRRR
RNN

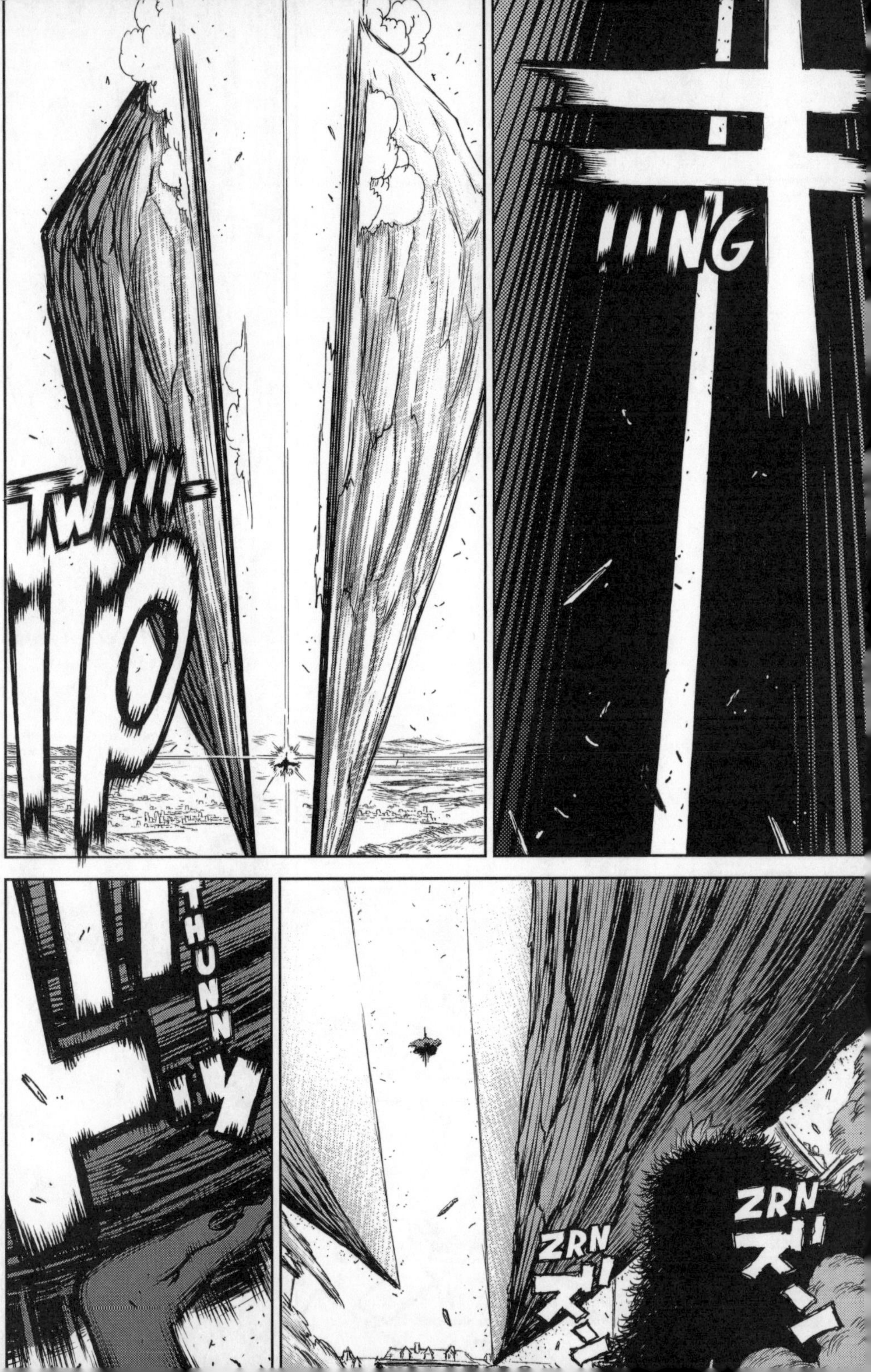
IIING
TWIIII-
ZRN
ZRN
THUNN

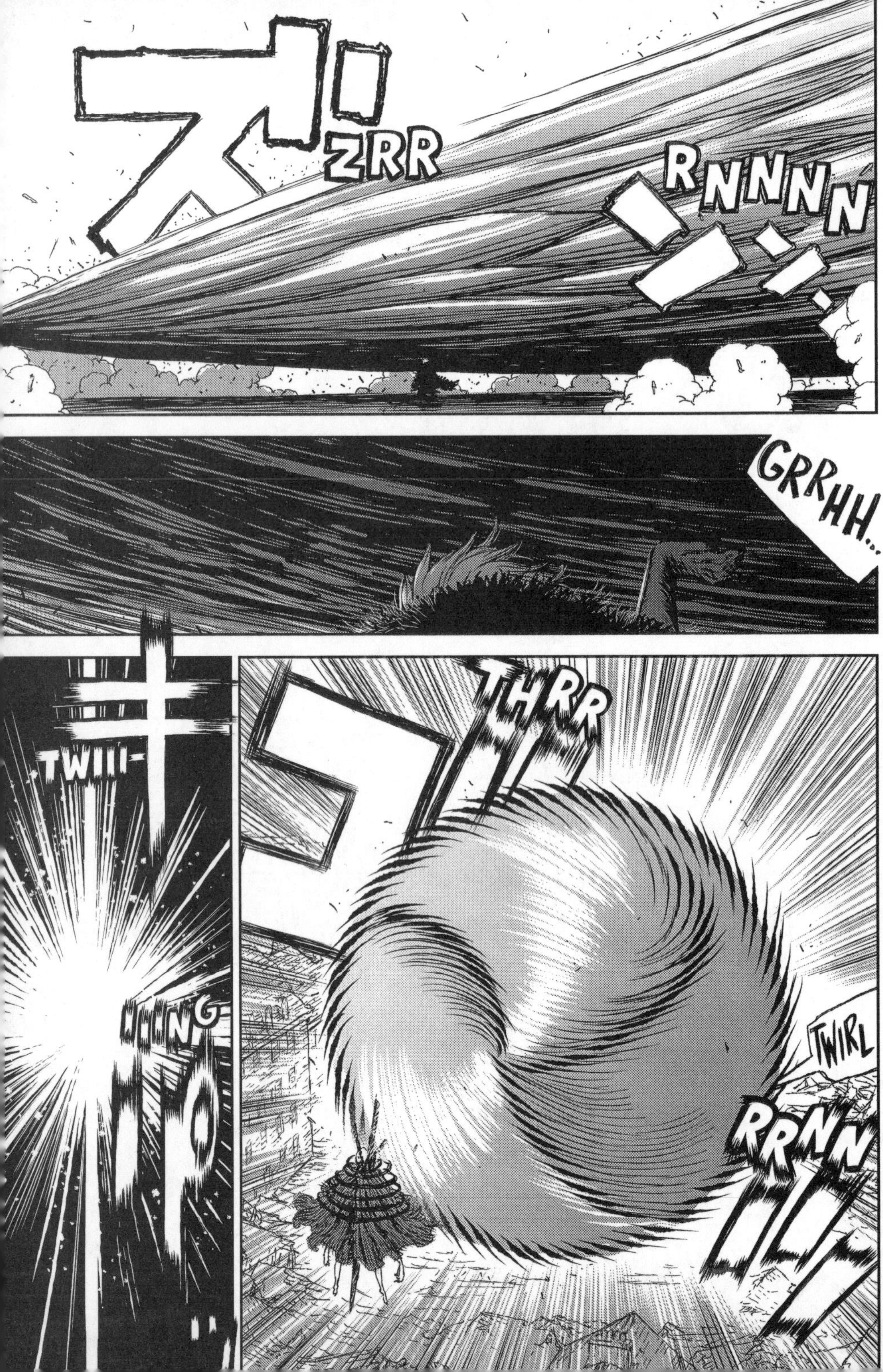
RNNNNN
ZRR
GRRHH...
THRR
TWIRL
RRNN
TWIII-

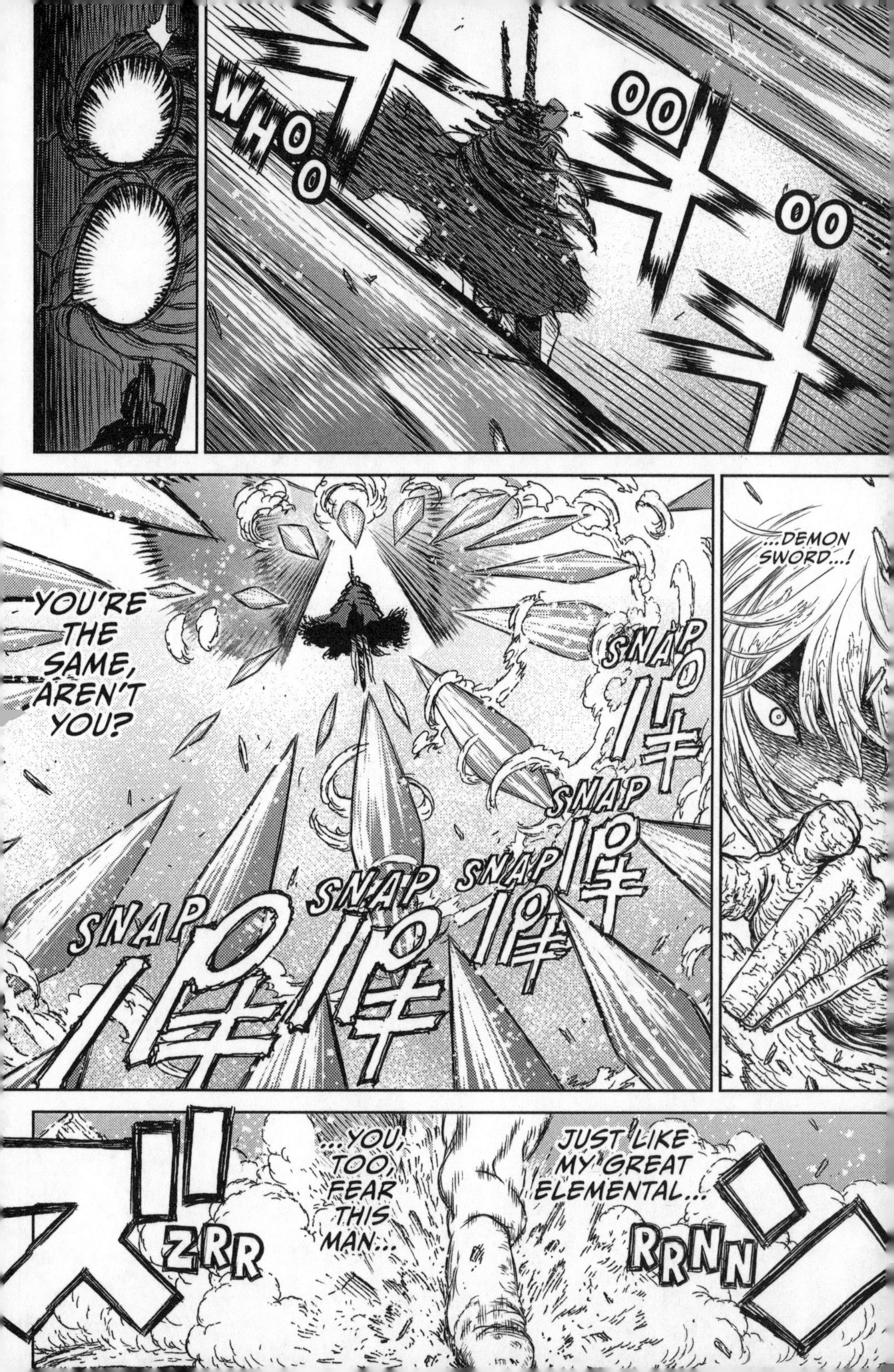
WHOO
OO
OO
...DEMON SWORD...!
SNAP
SNAP
SNAP
SNAP
SNAP
YOU'RE THE SAME, AREN'T YOU?
JUST LIKE MY GREAT ELEMENTAL...
...YOU, TOO, FEAR THIS MAN...
RRNN
ZRR

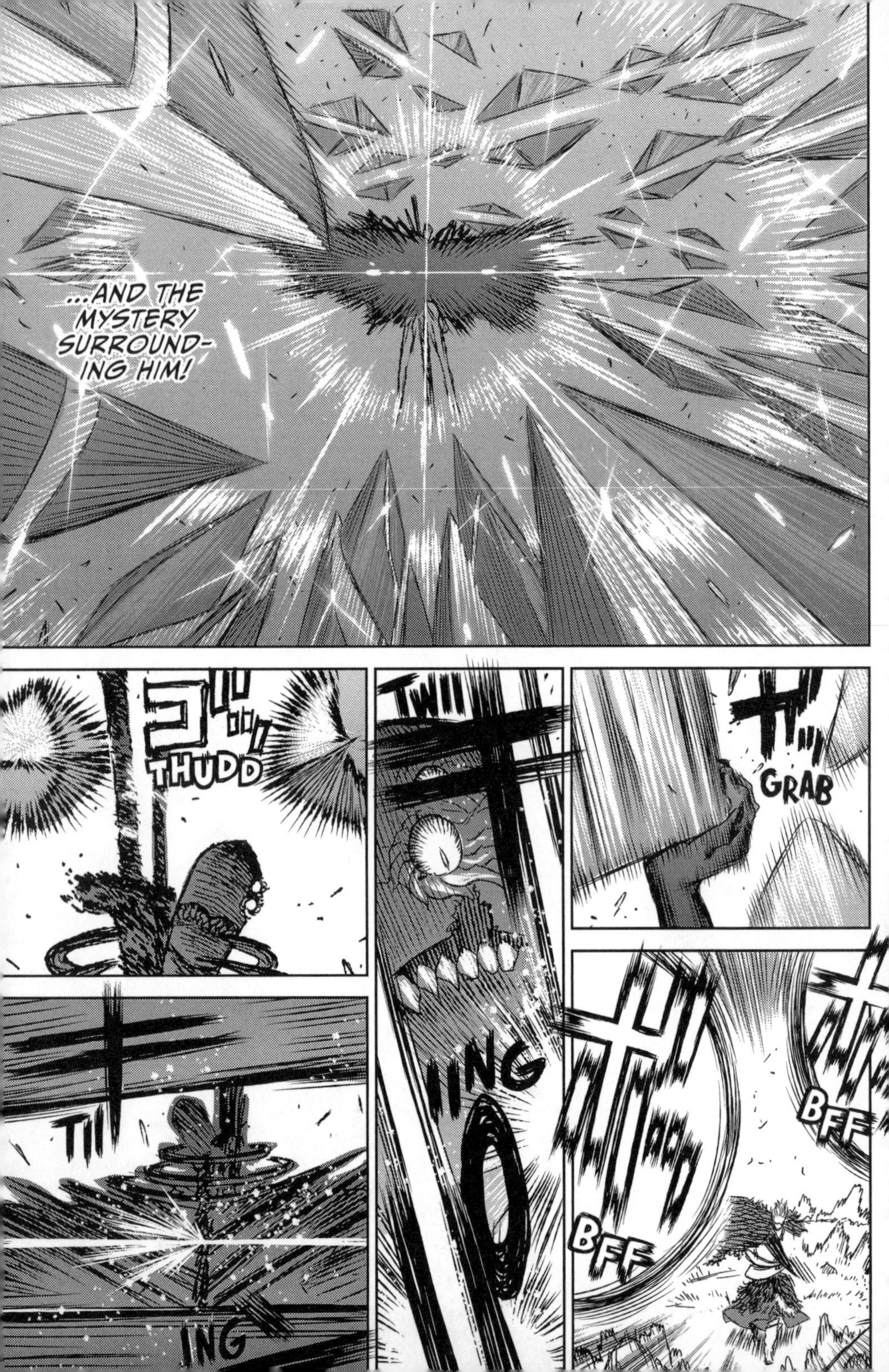
...AND THE MYSTERY SURROUNDING HIM!
GRAB
BFF
BFF
TWII
IING
THUDD
TII
ING

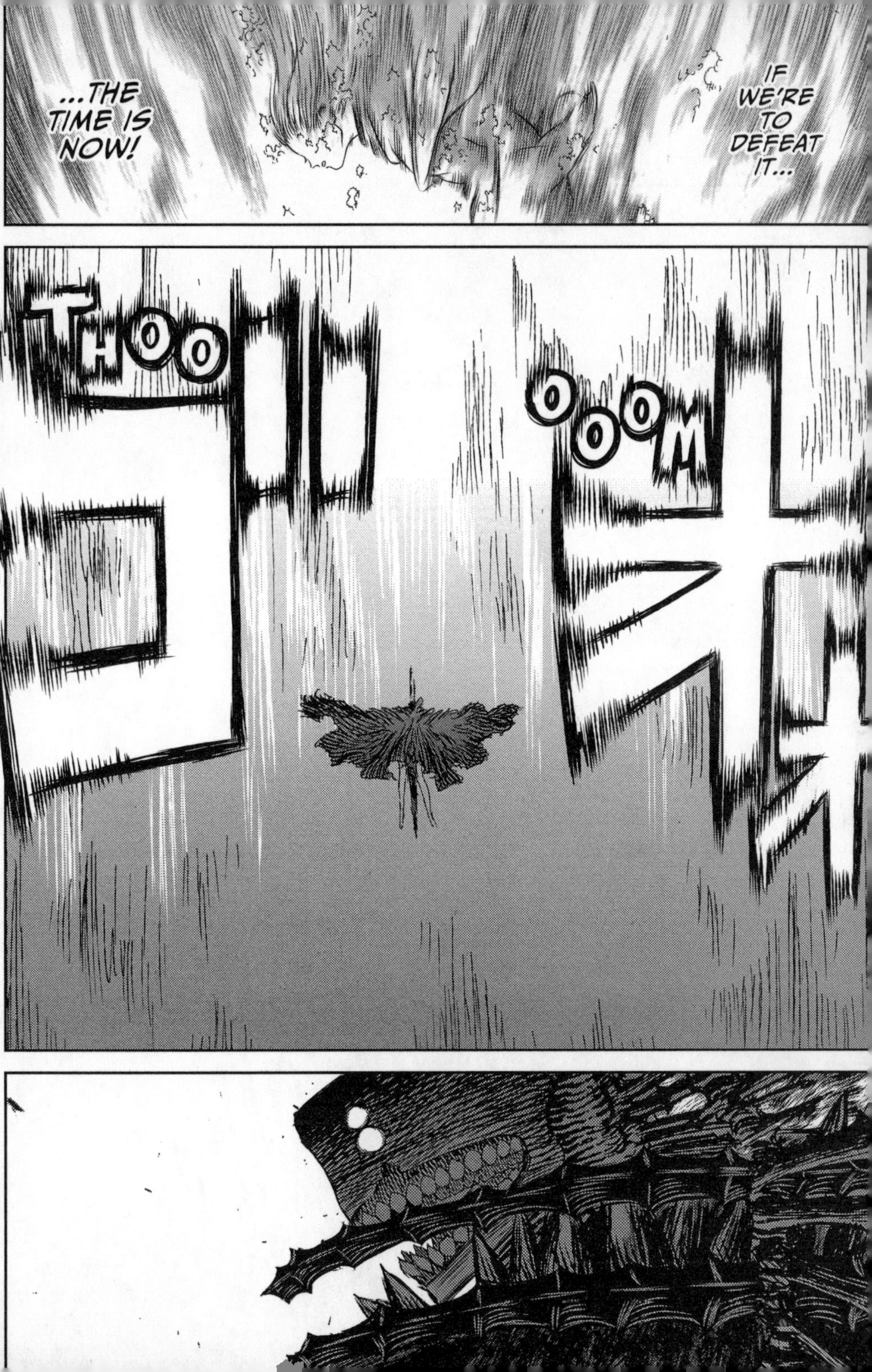
IF WE'RE TO DEFEAT IT...
...THE TIME IS NOW!
THOOOOOOM

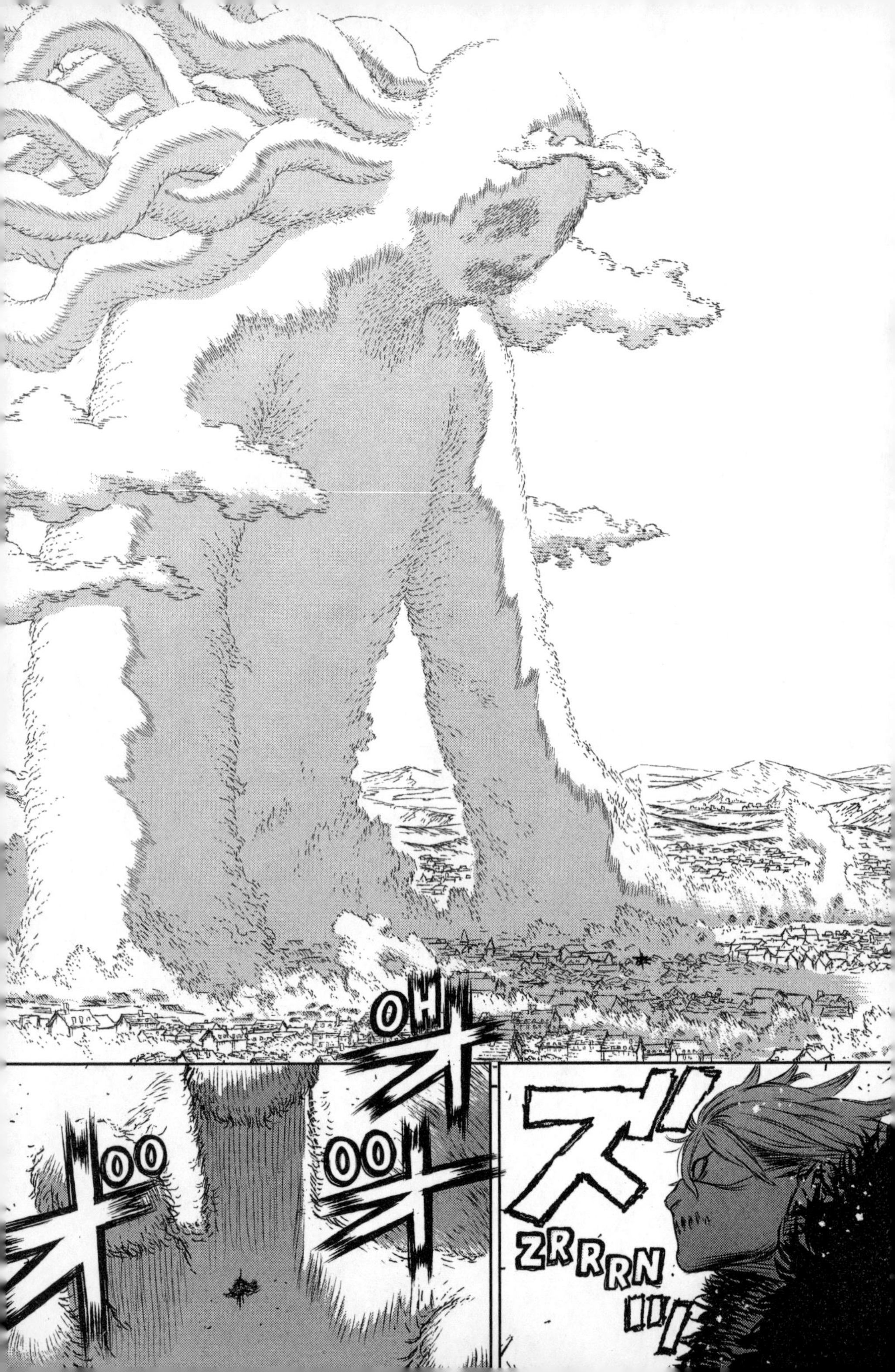

オ
OH
ズ
ZRRRN!!
オ
OO
オ
OO

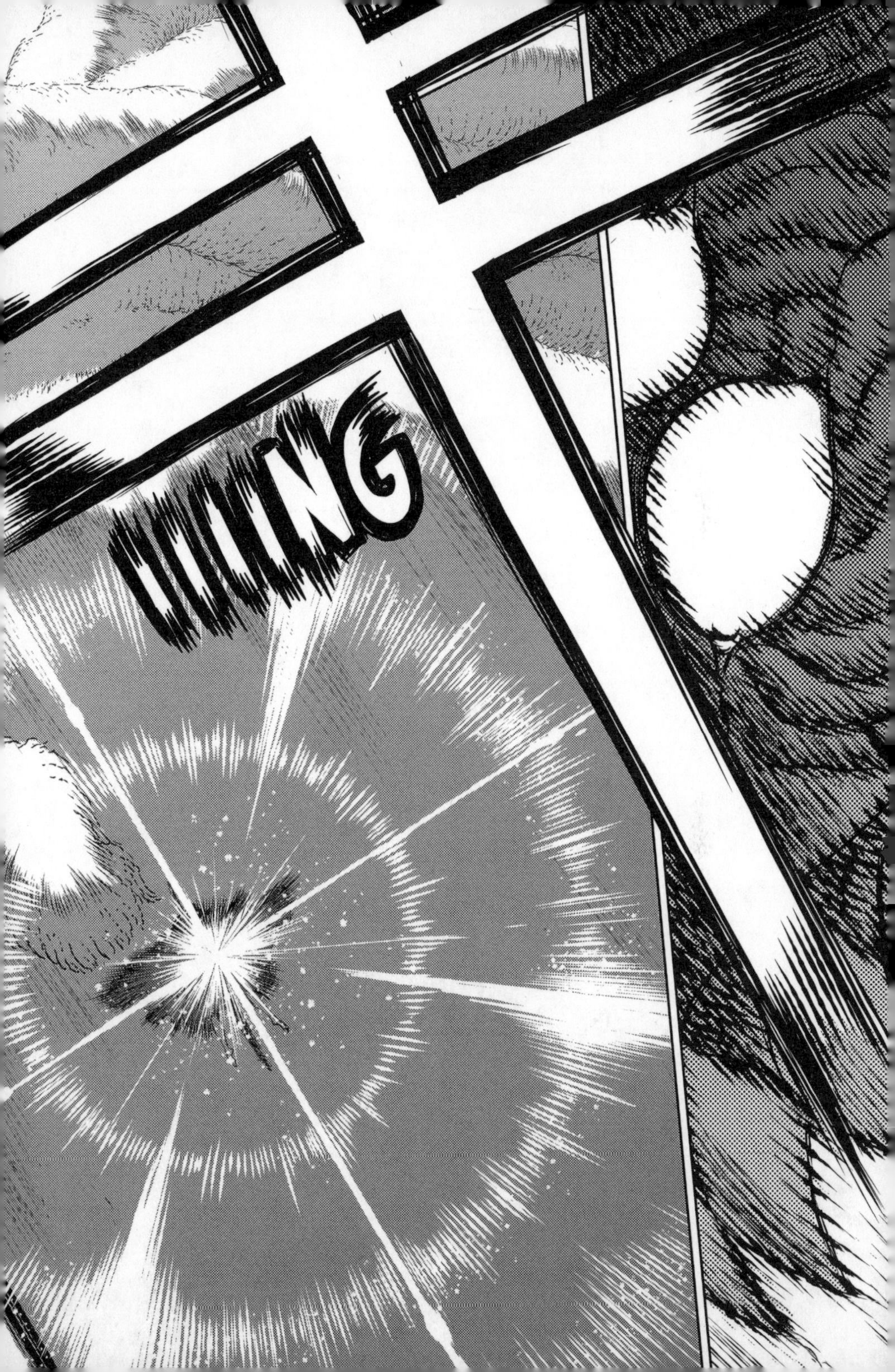
WWING

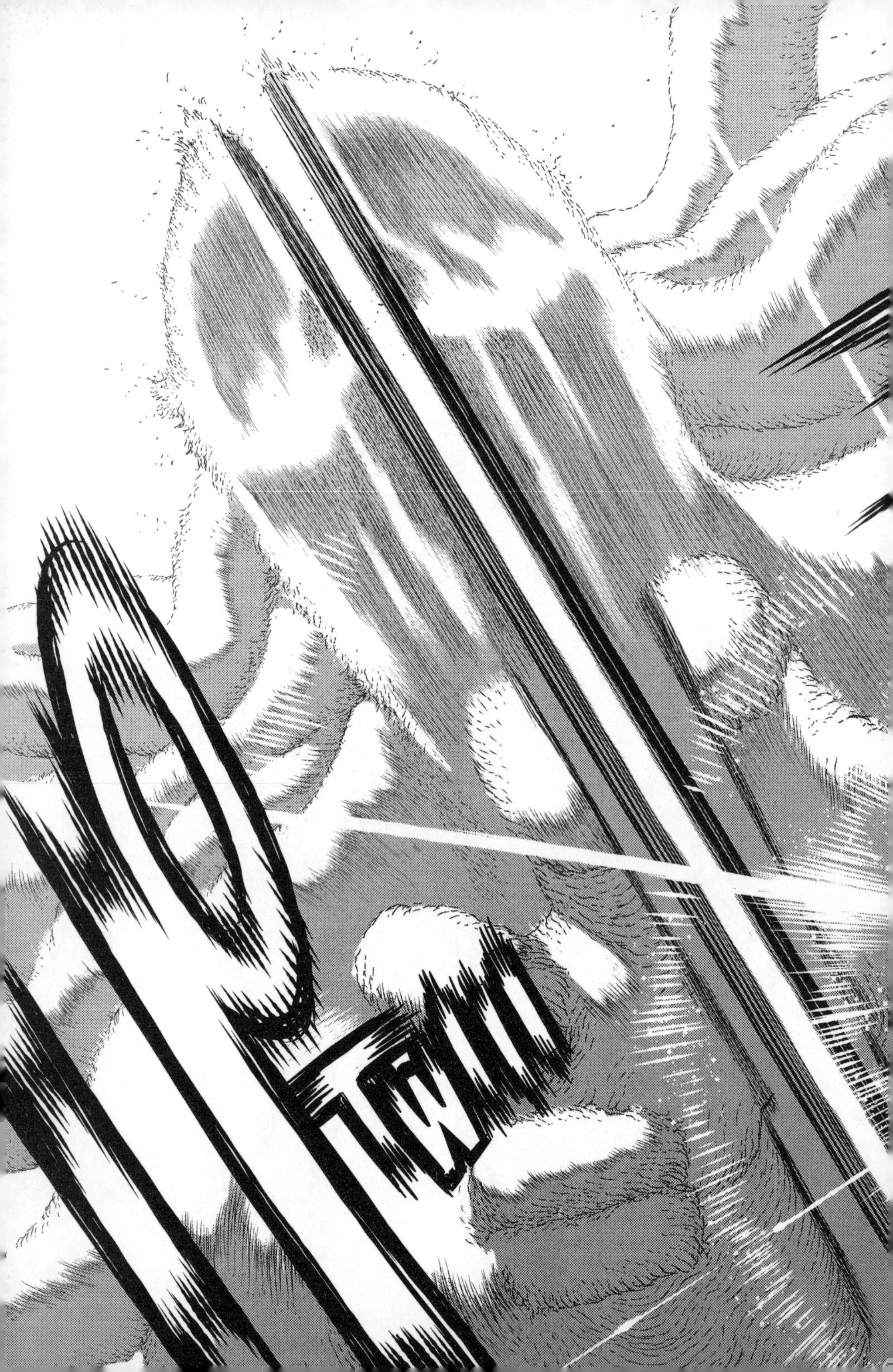

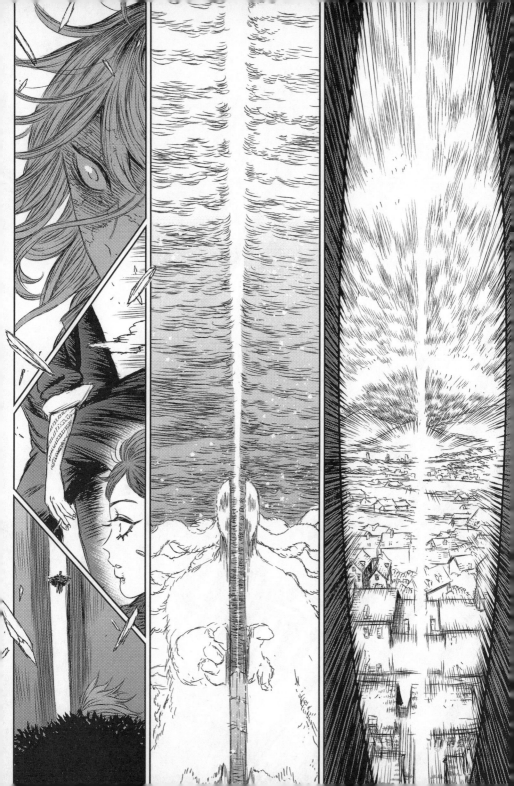

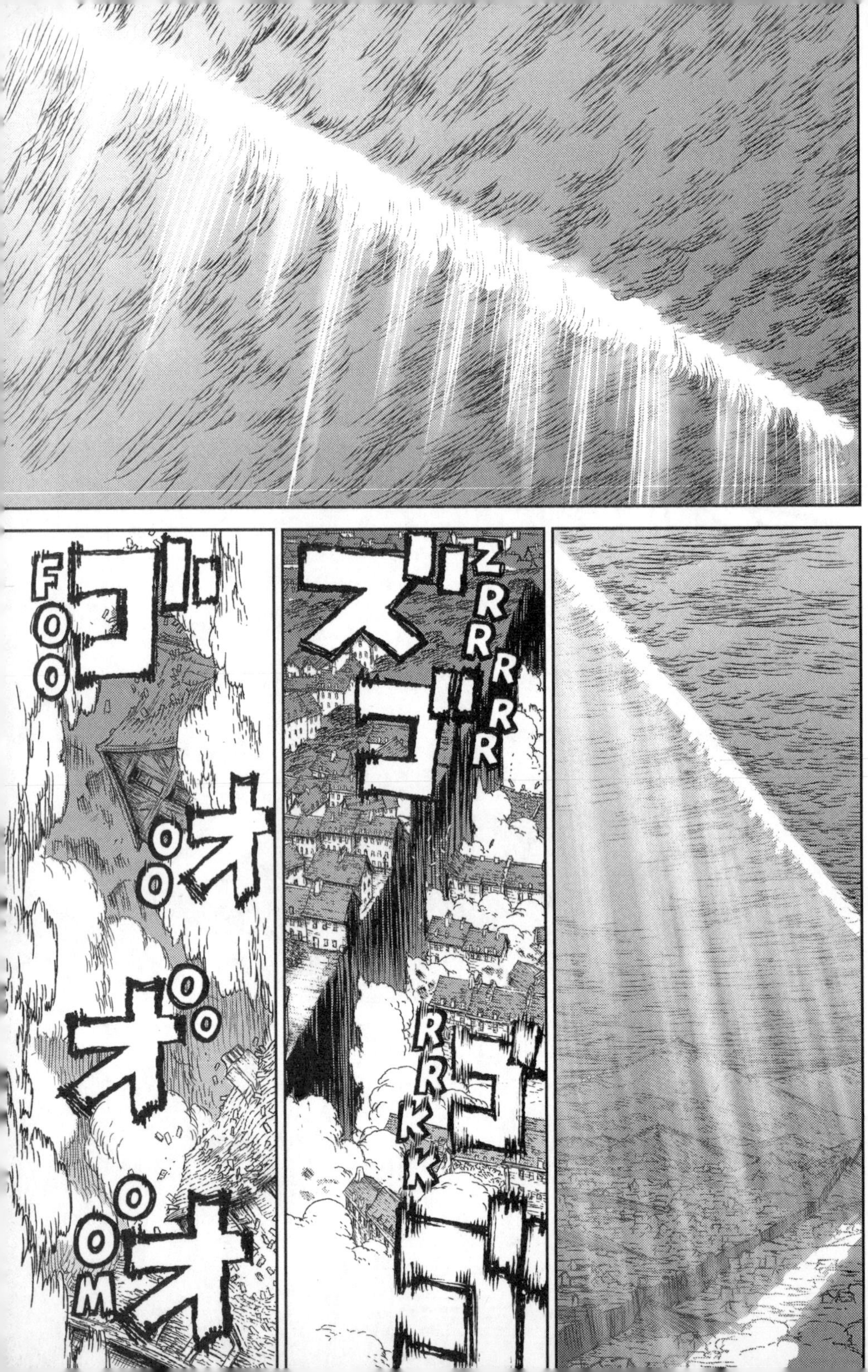
ズゴ
ZRRRRR
ゴゴ
RRKK
ゴオオオ
FOO
OO
OO
OOM

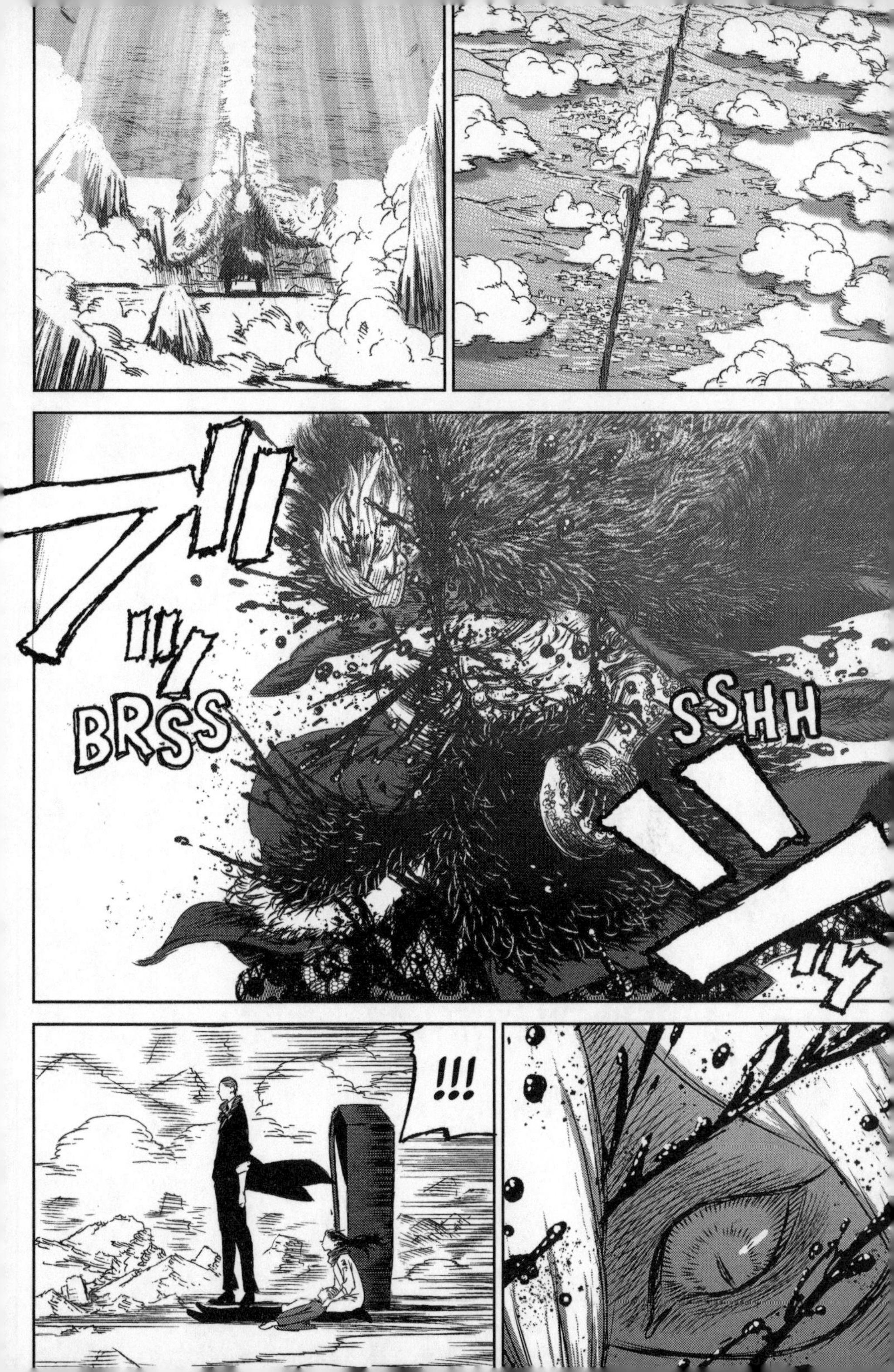
SSHH
BRSS
!!!

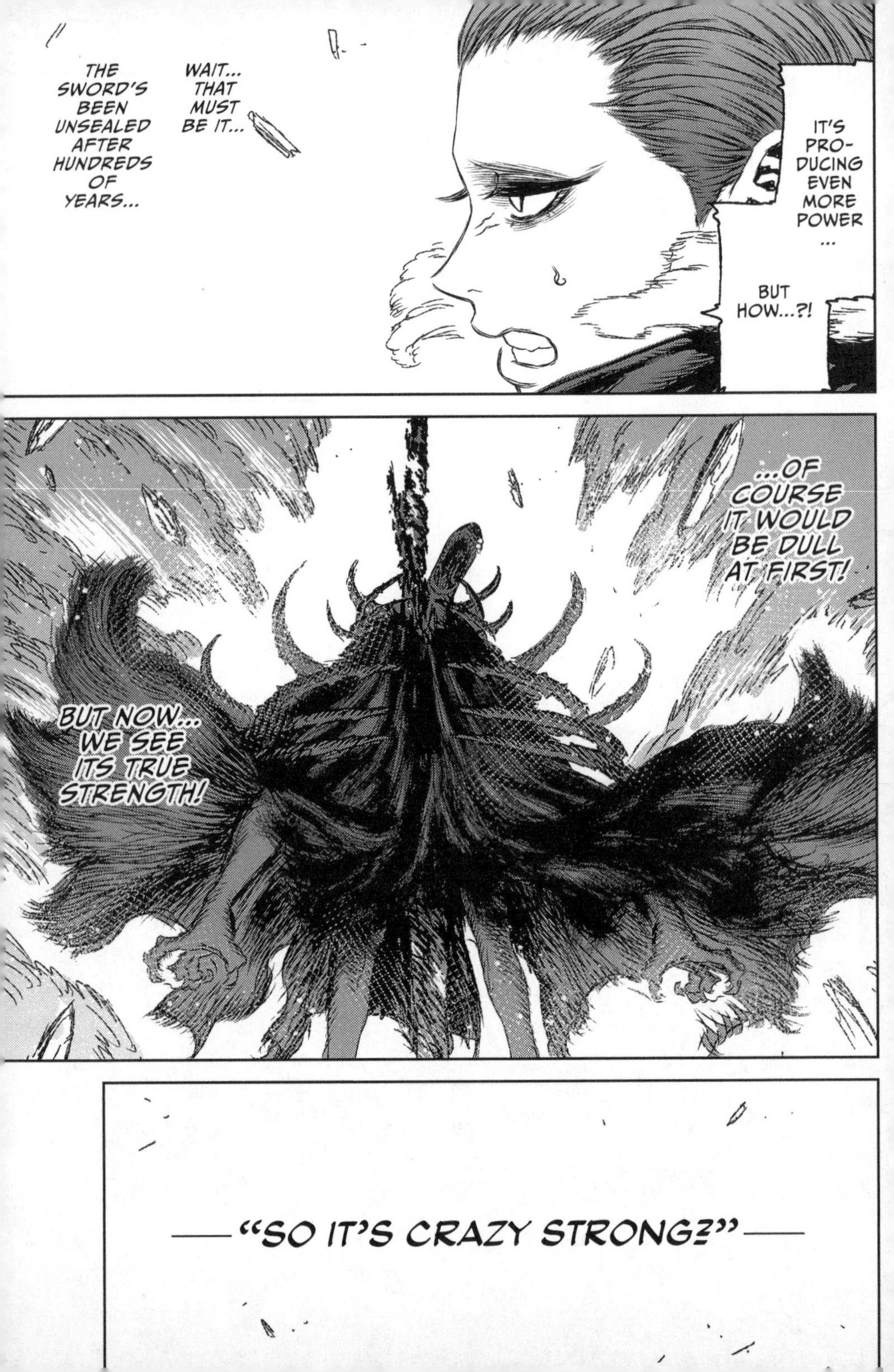
IT'S PRO-DUCING EVEN MORE POWER...
BUT HOW...?!
WAIT... THAT MUST BE IT...
THE SWORD'S BEEN UNSEALED AFTER HUNDREDS OF YEARS...
...OF COURSE IT WOULD BE DULL AT FIRST!
BUT NOW... WE SEE ITS TRUE STRENGTH!
—"SO IT'S CRAZY STRONG?"—

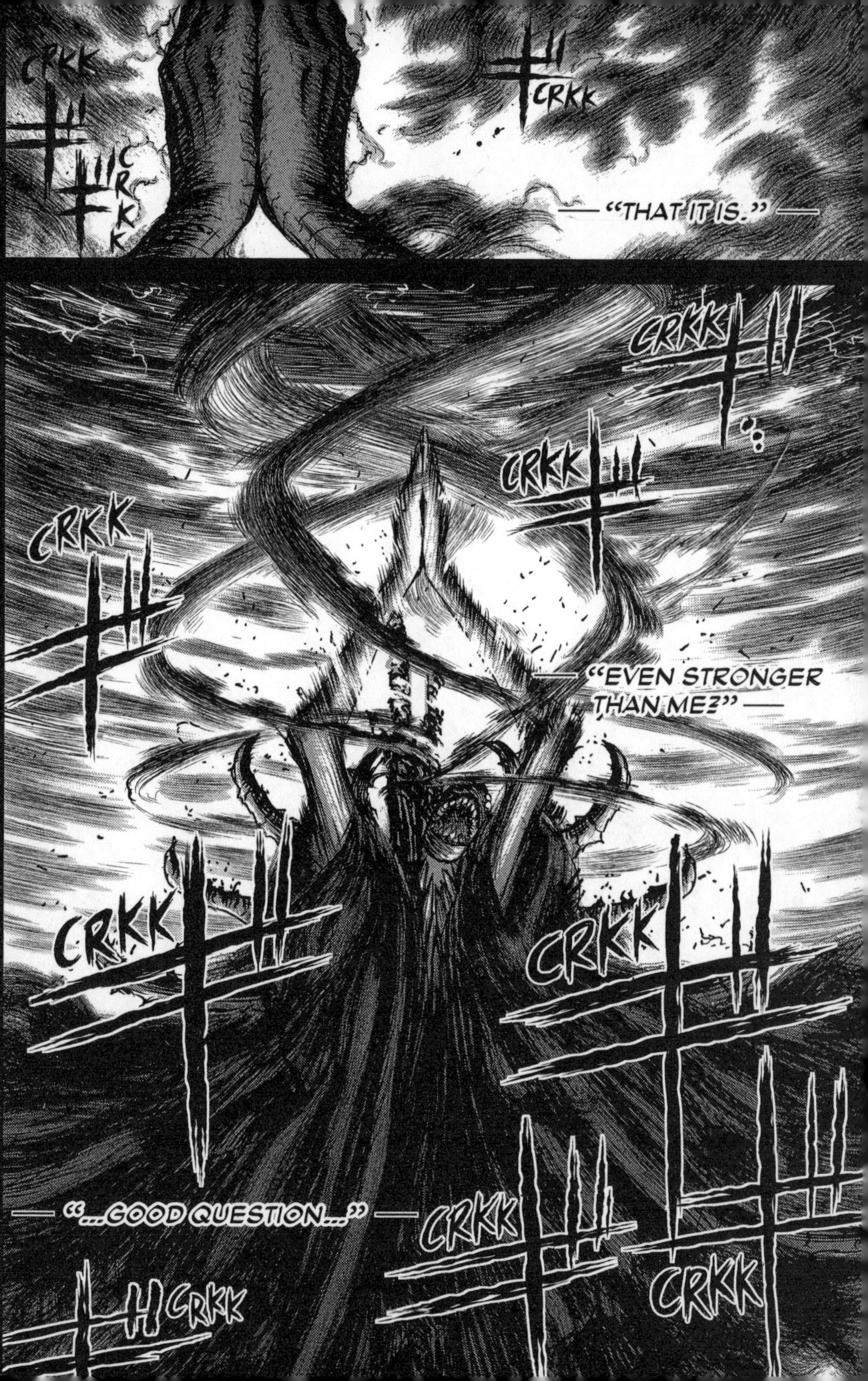
CRKK
CRKK
CRKK
—"THAT IT IS."—
CRKK
CRKK
CRKK
—"EVEN STRONGER THAN ME?"—
CRKK
CRKK
CRKK
—"...GOOD QUESTION..."—
CRKK
CRKK

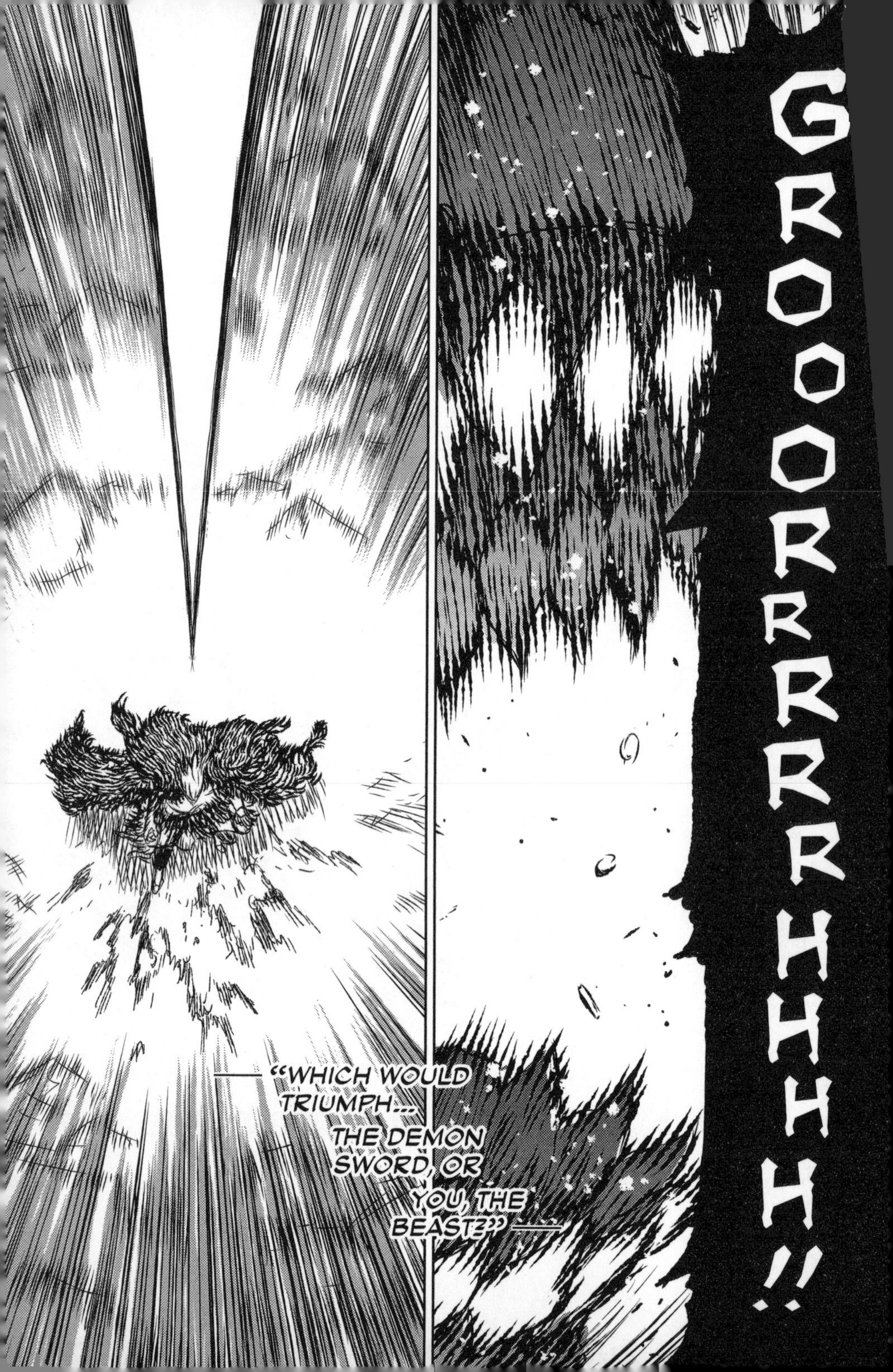
GROOORRRRRHHHH!!
——"WHICH WOULD TRIUMPH... THE DEMON SWORD, OR YOU, THE BEAST?"——

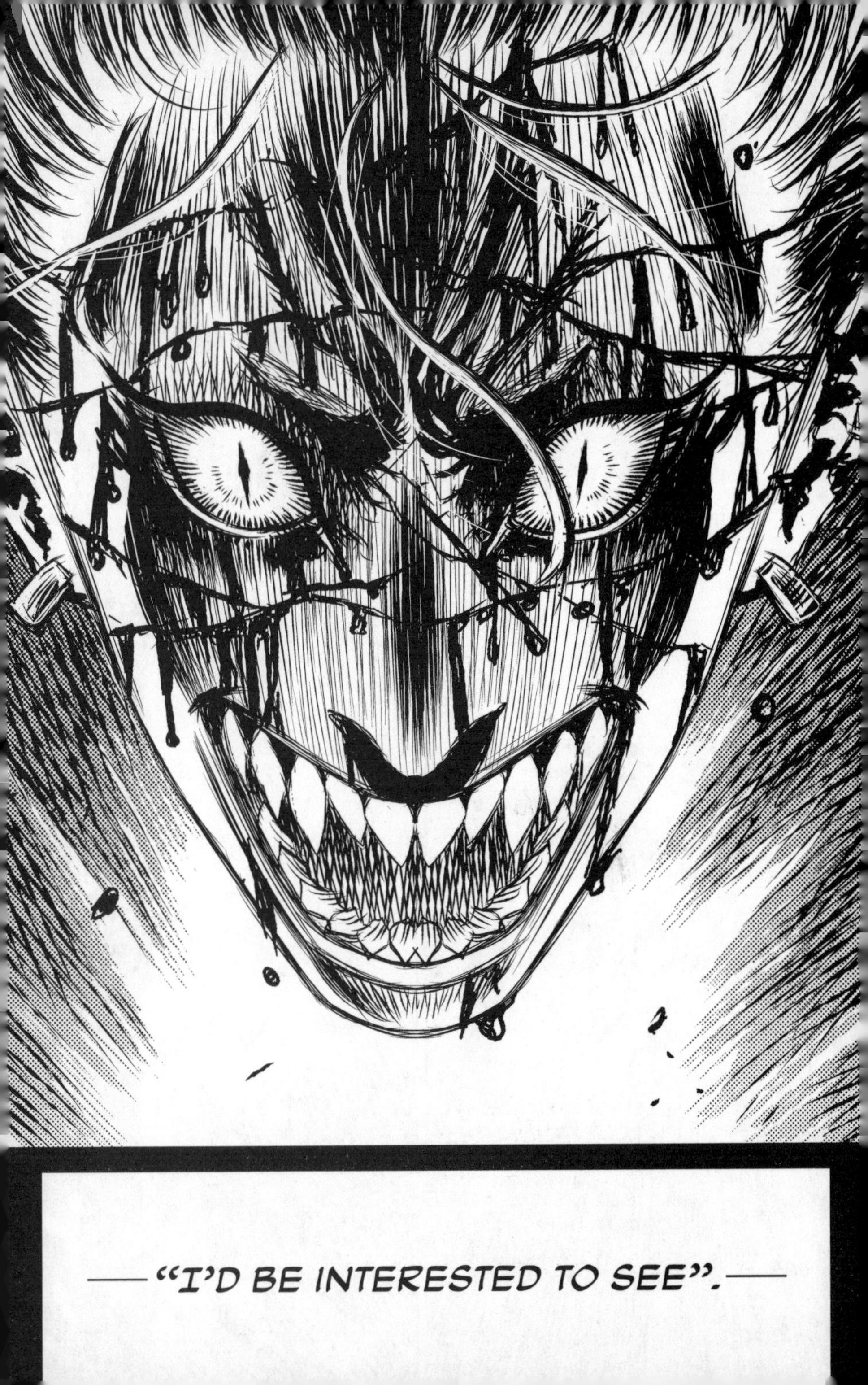
—"I'D BE INTERESTED TO SEE".—

THE WITCH AND THE BEAST

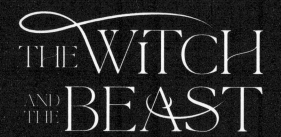

THE WITCH AND THE BEAST

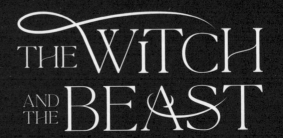

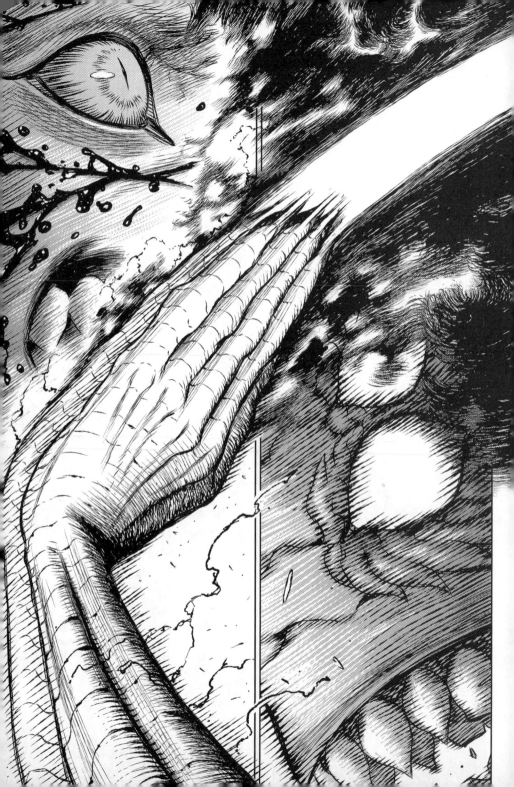

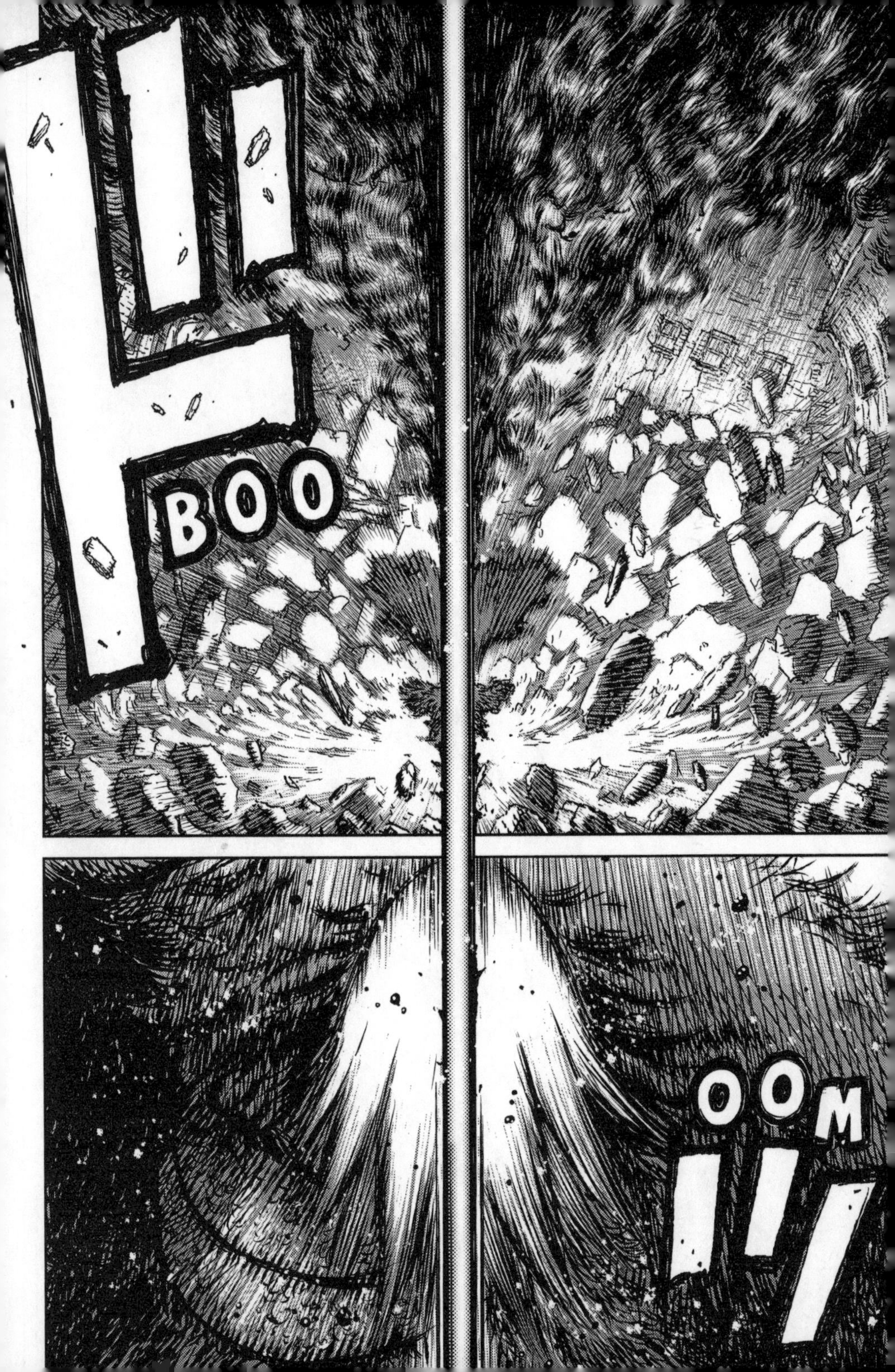
BOO
OOM

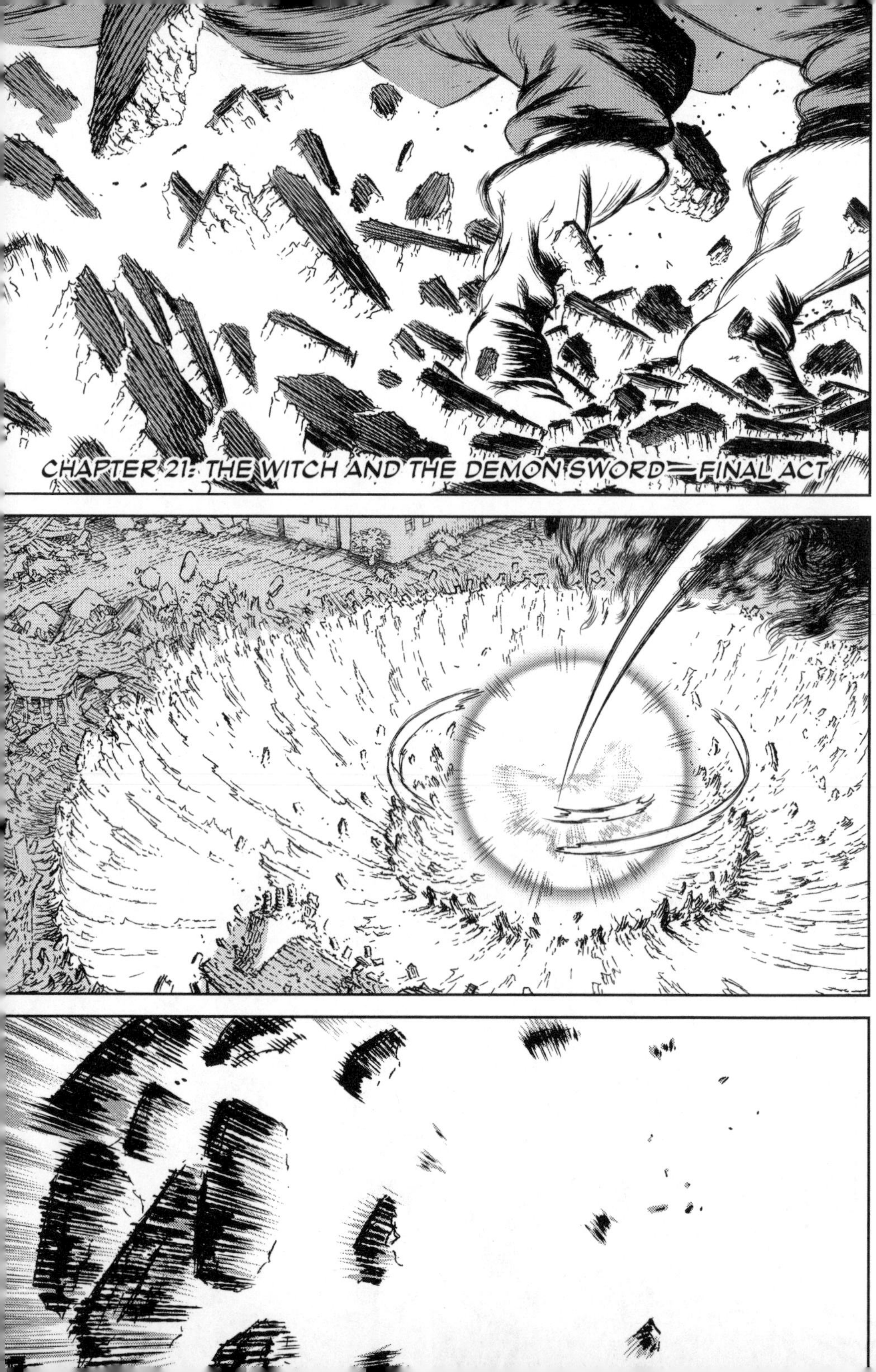
CHAPTER 21: THE WITCH AND THE DEMON SWORD—FINAL ACT

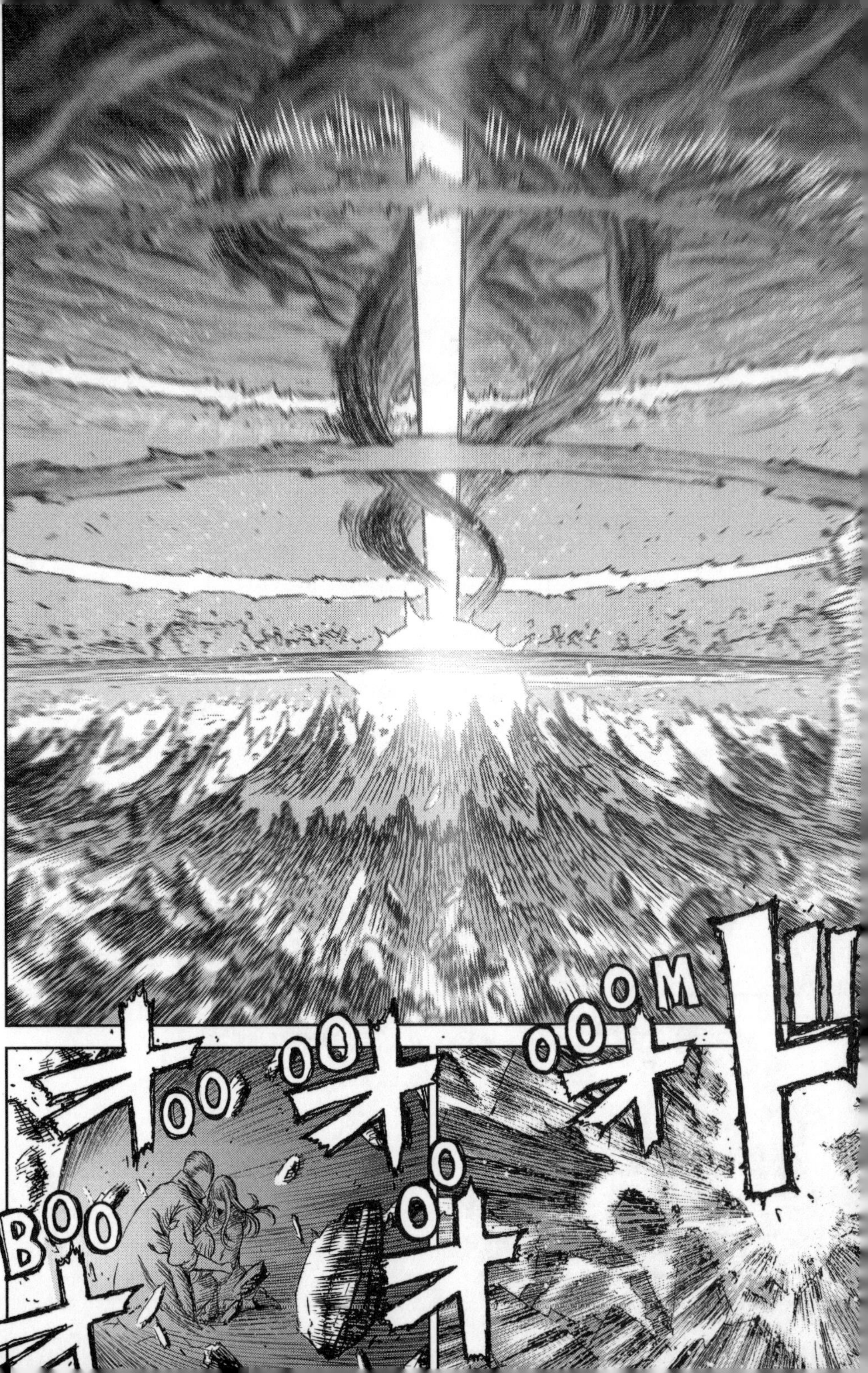
ドオオオオオ
BOOOOOOOOOOOM

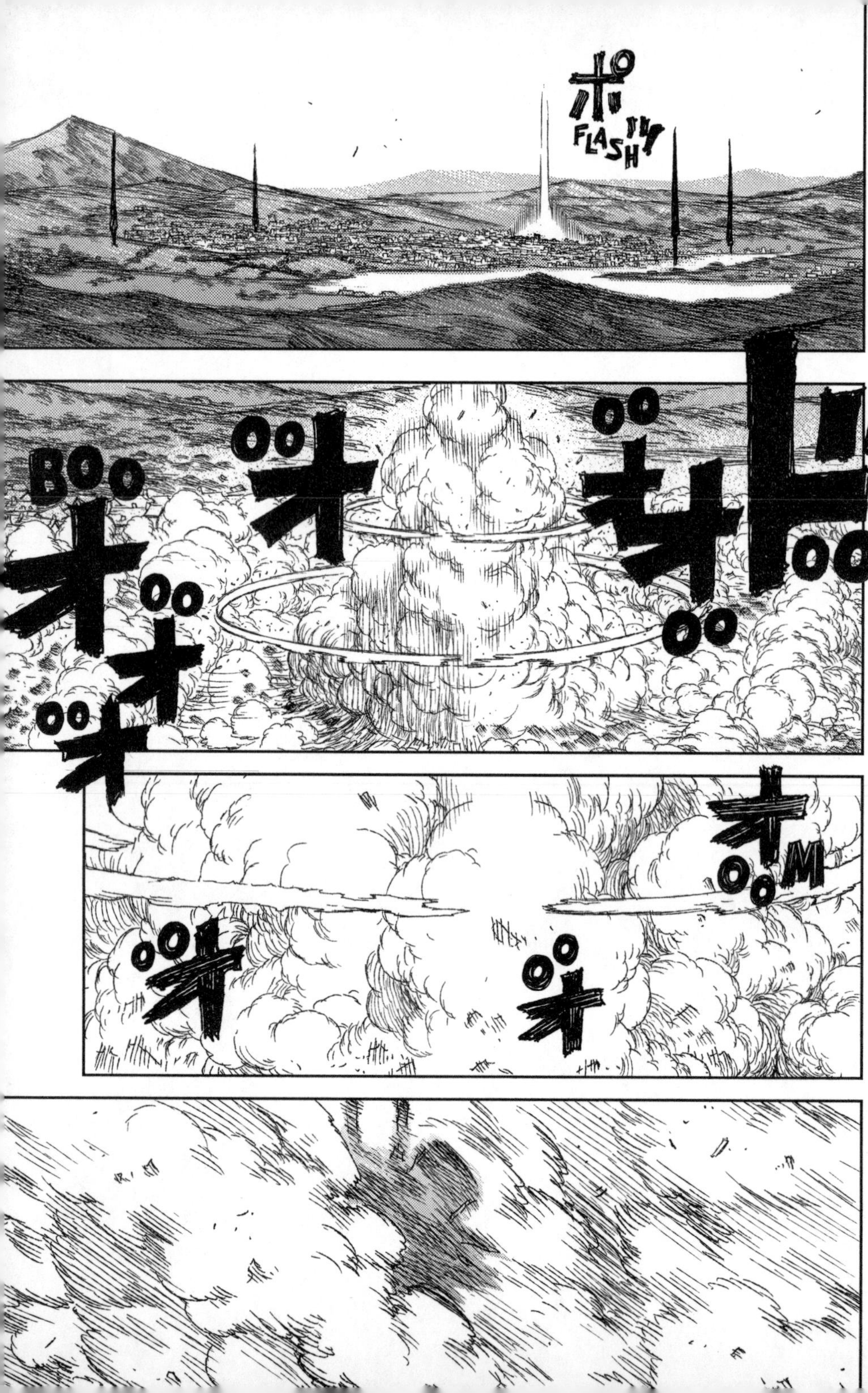
ポ
FLASH
BOO
M

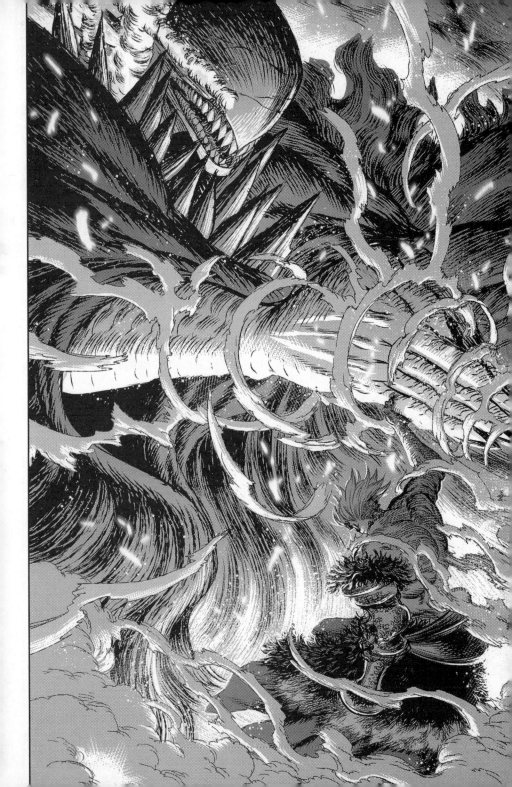

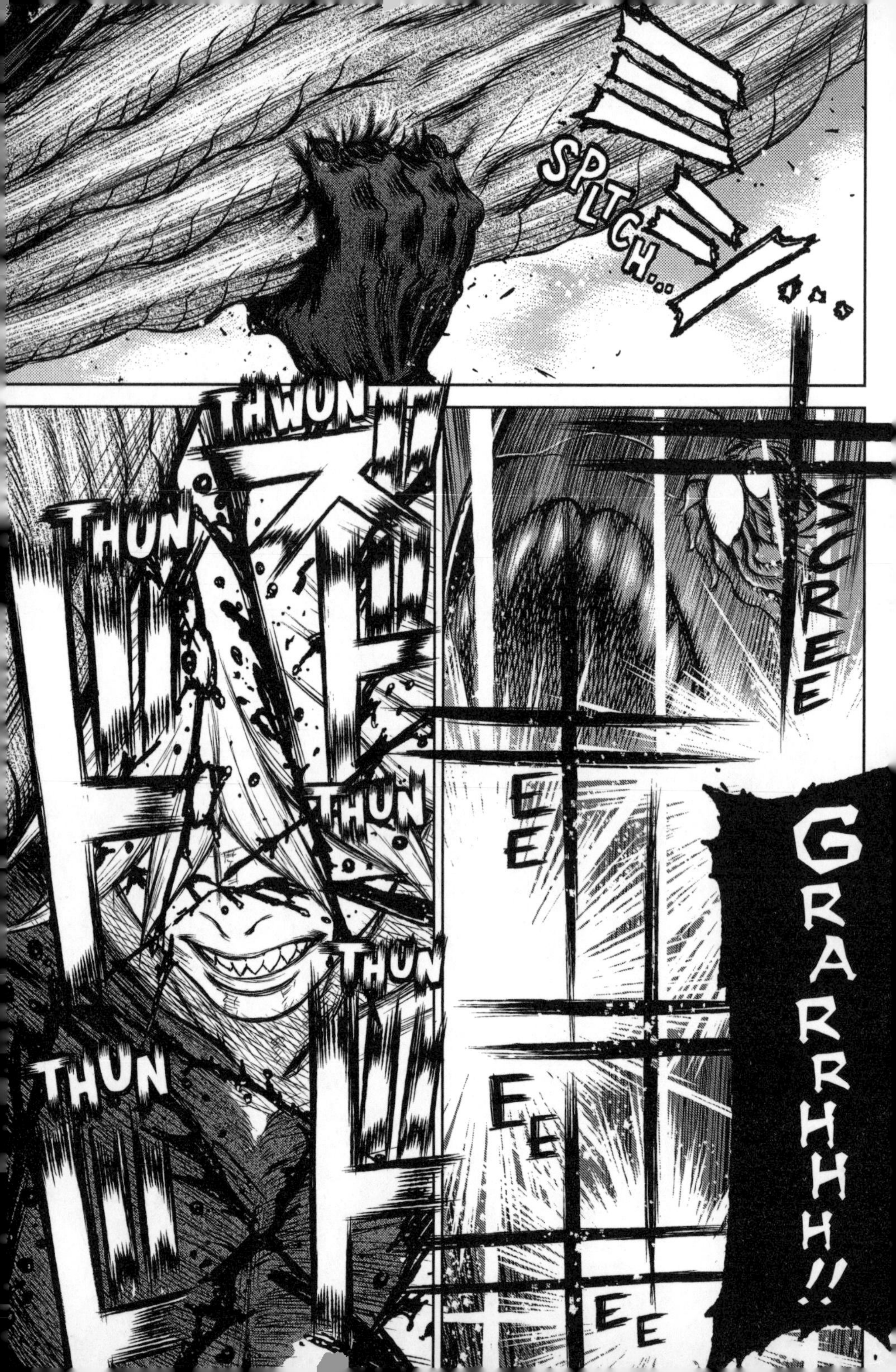
SPLTCH...
SCREE
EE
EE
EE
GRARRHH!!
THWONK
THUN
THUN
THUN
THUN

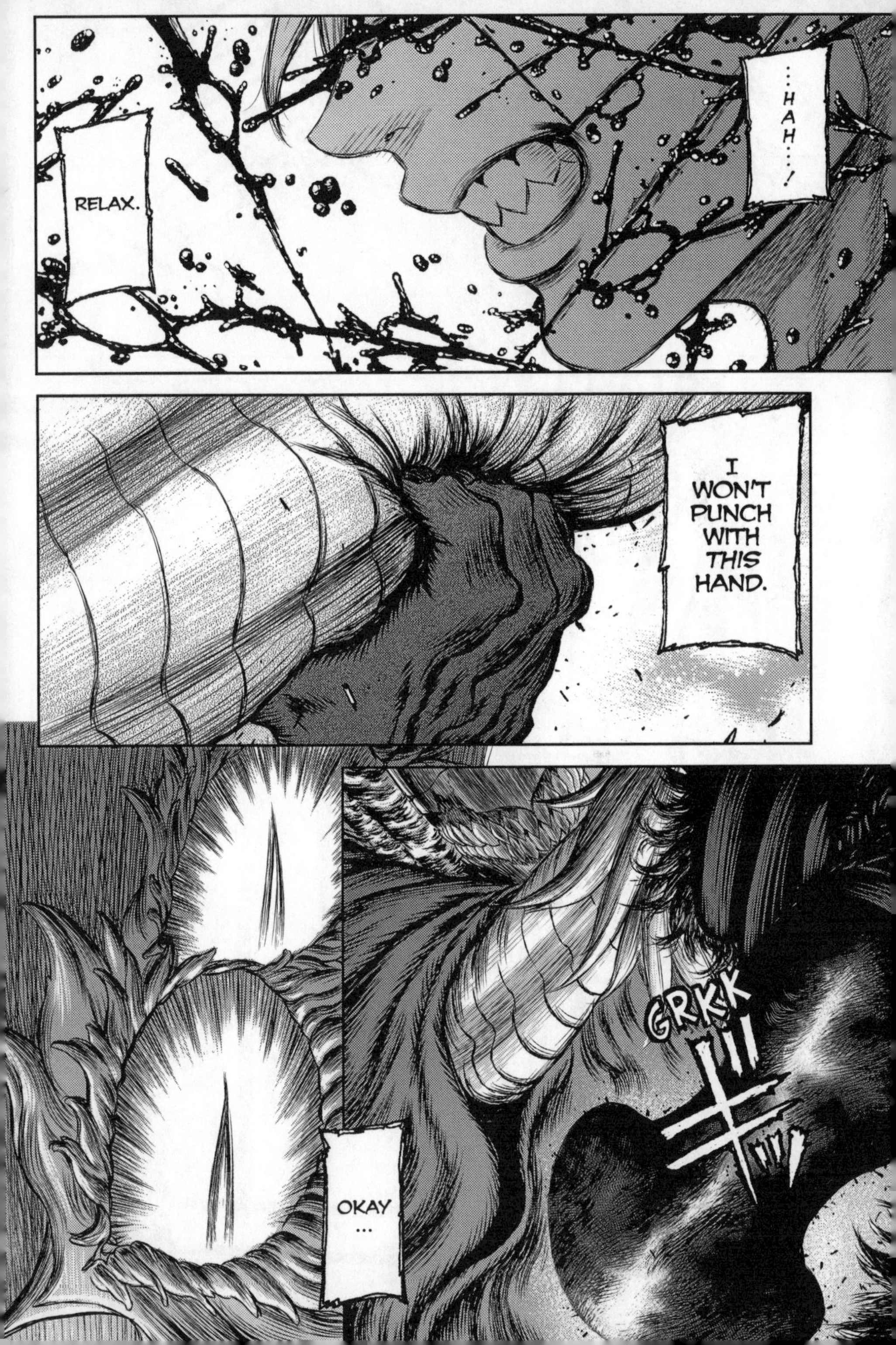
...HAH...!
RELAX.
I WON'T PUNCH WITH *THIS* HAND.
GRKK
OKAY ...

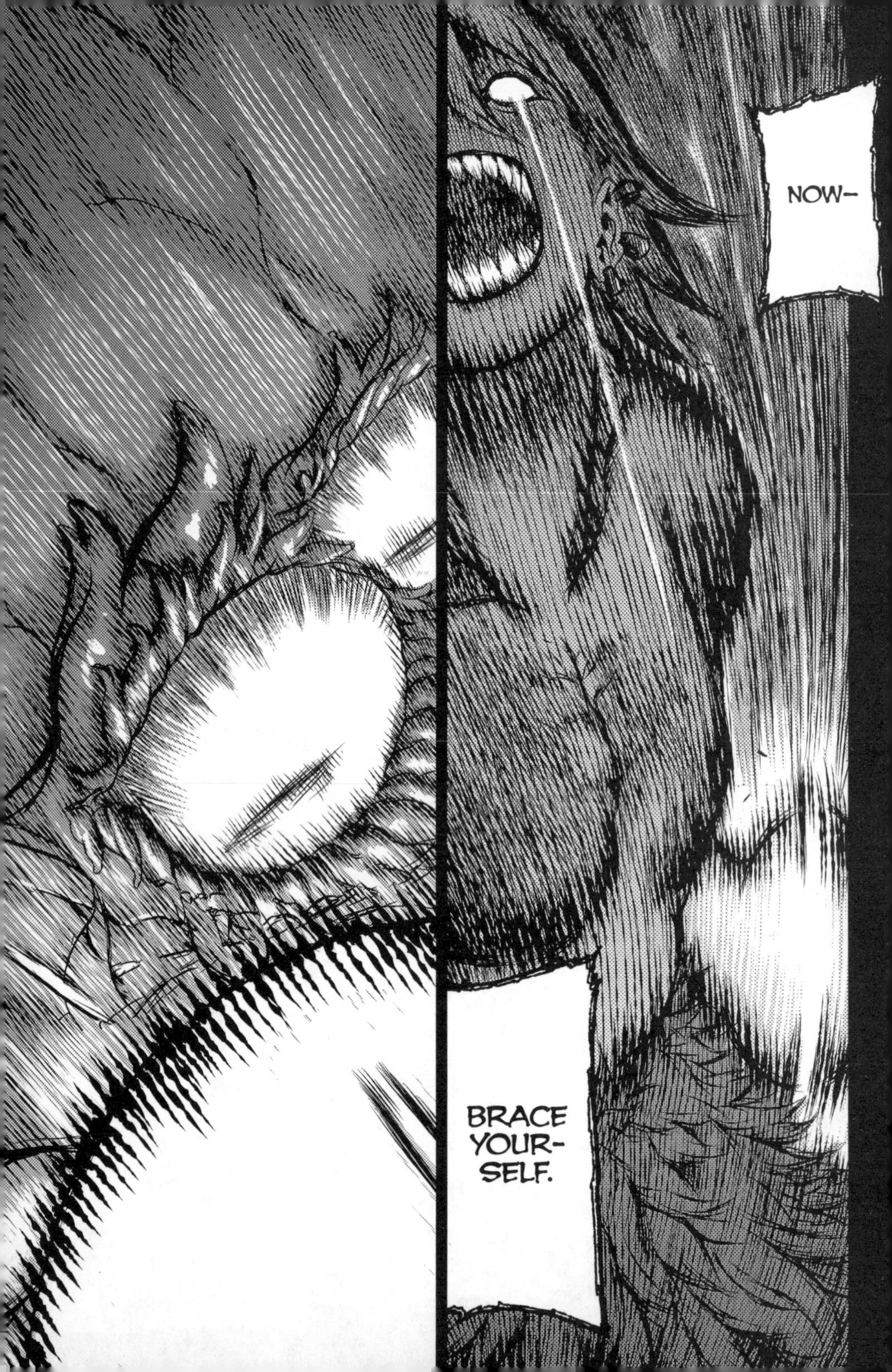
NOW-
BRACE YOUR-SELF.

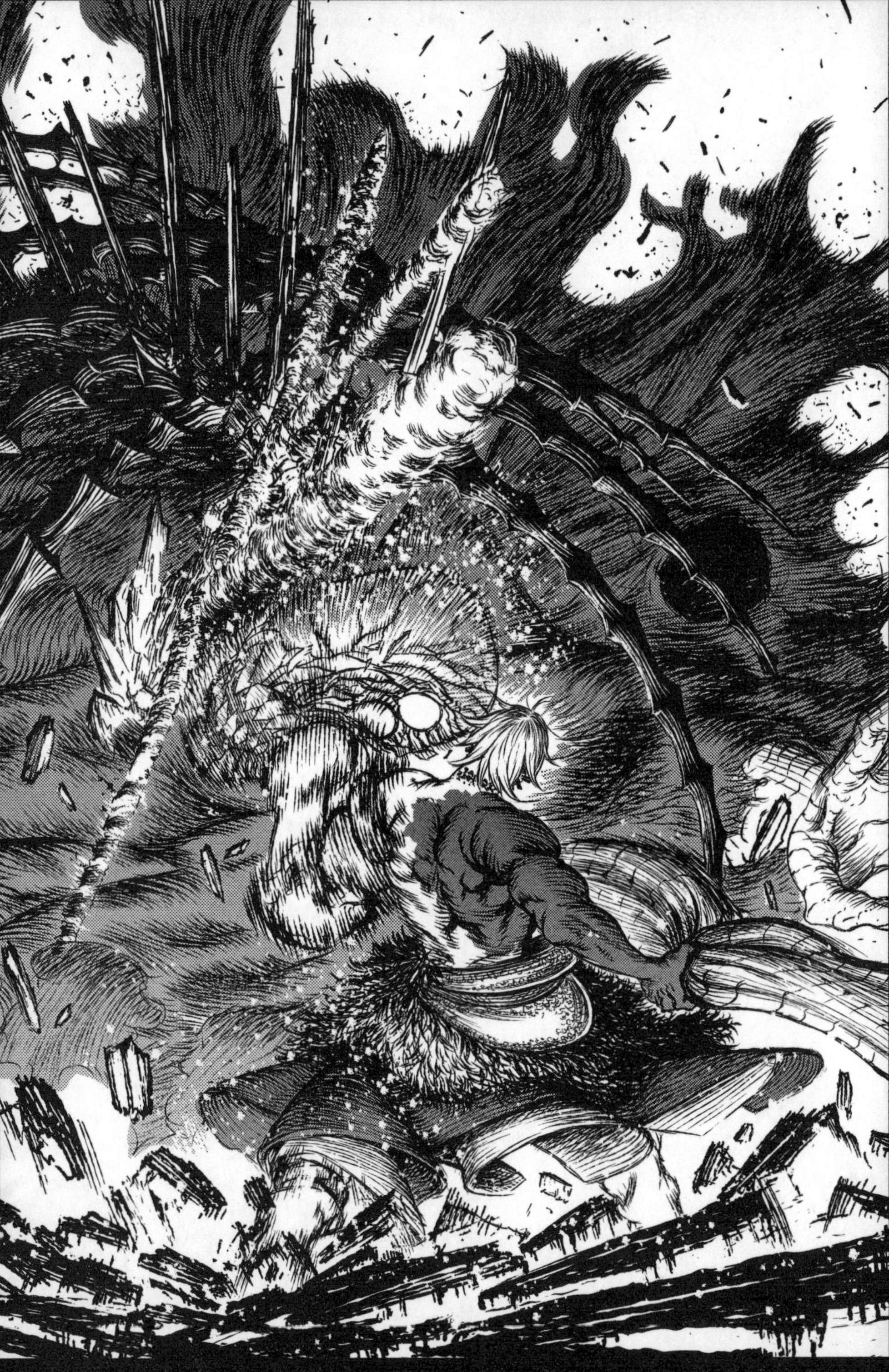

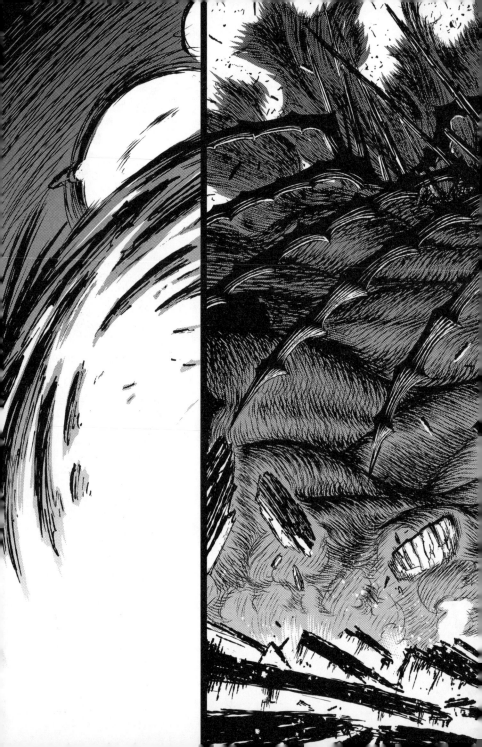

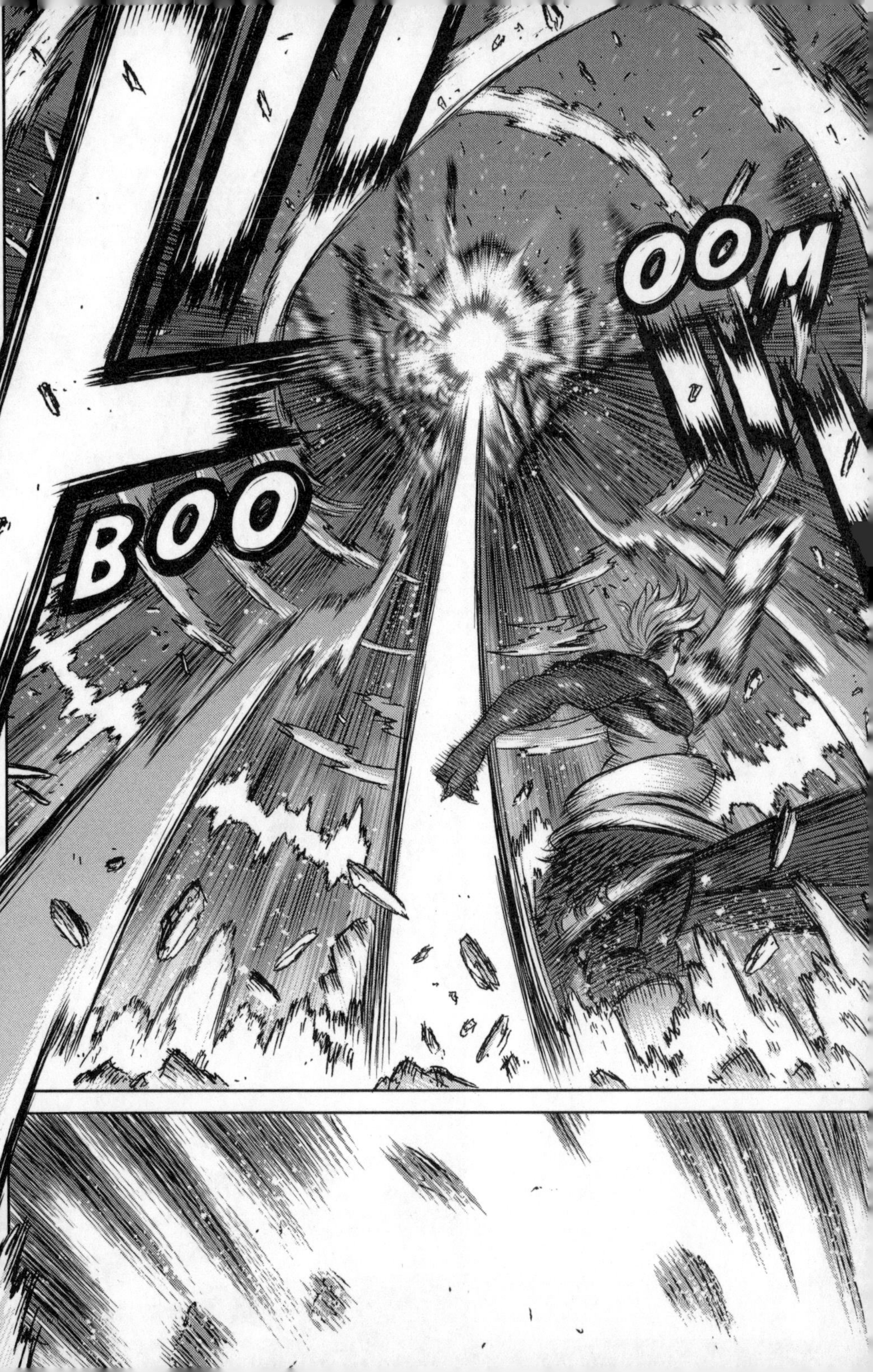
BOO
OOM

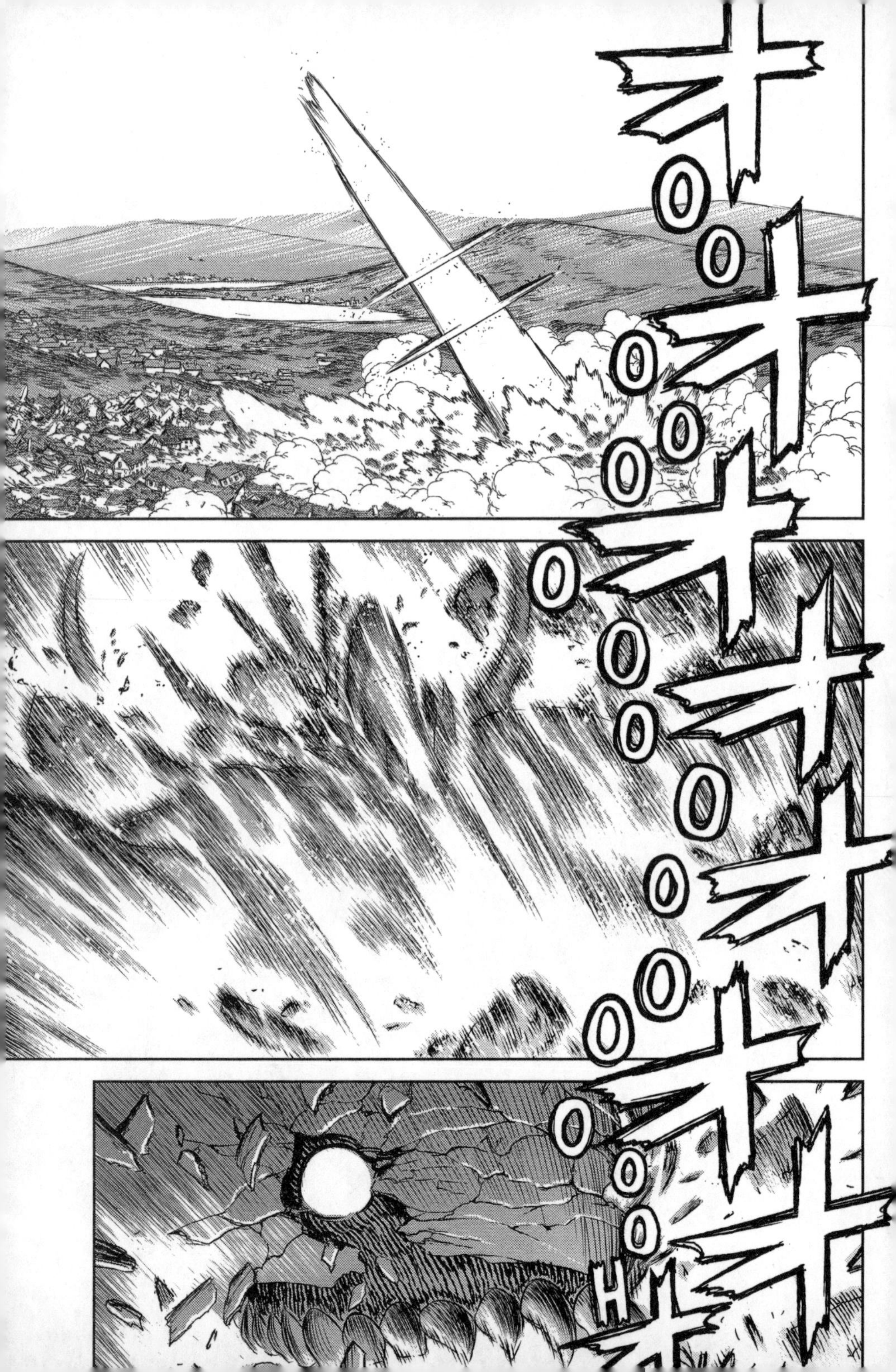

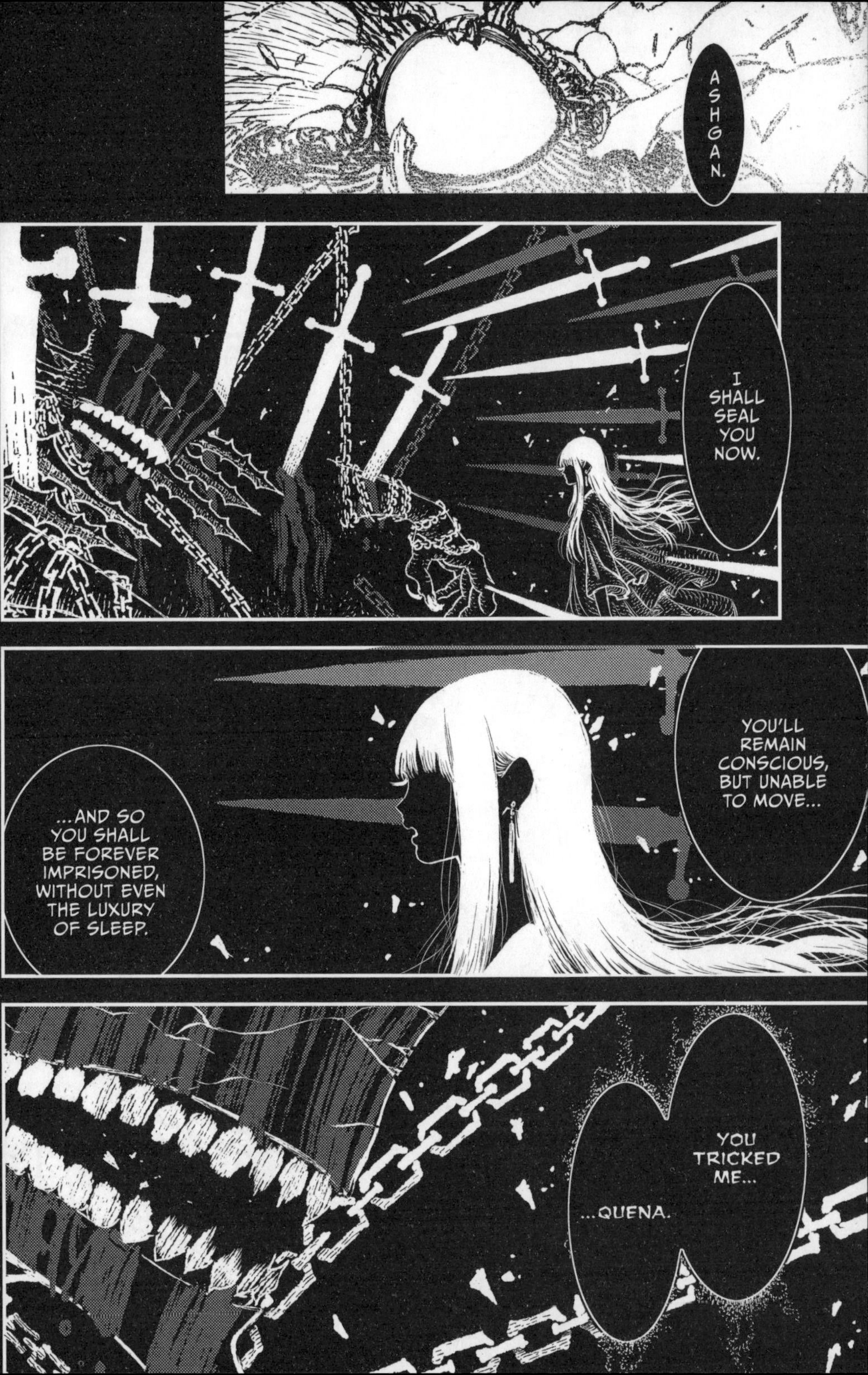
ASHGAN.
I SHALL SEAL YOU NOW.
YOU'LL REMAIN CONSCIOUS, BUT UNABLE TO MOVE...
...AND SO YOU SHALL BE FOREVER IMPRISONED, WITHOUT EVEN THE LUXURY OF SLEEP.
YOU TRICKED ME...
...QUENA.

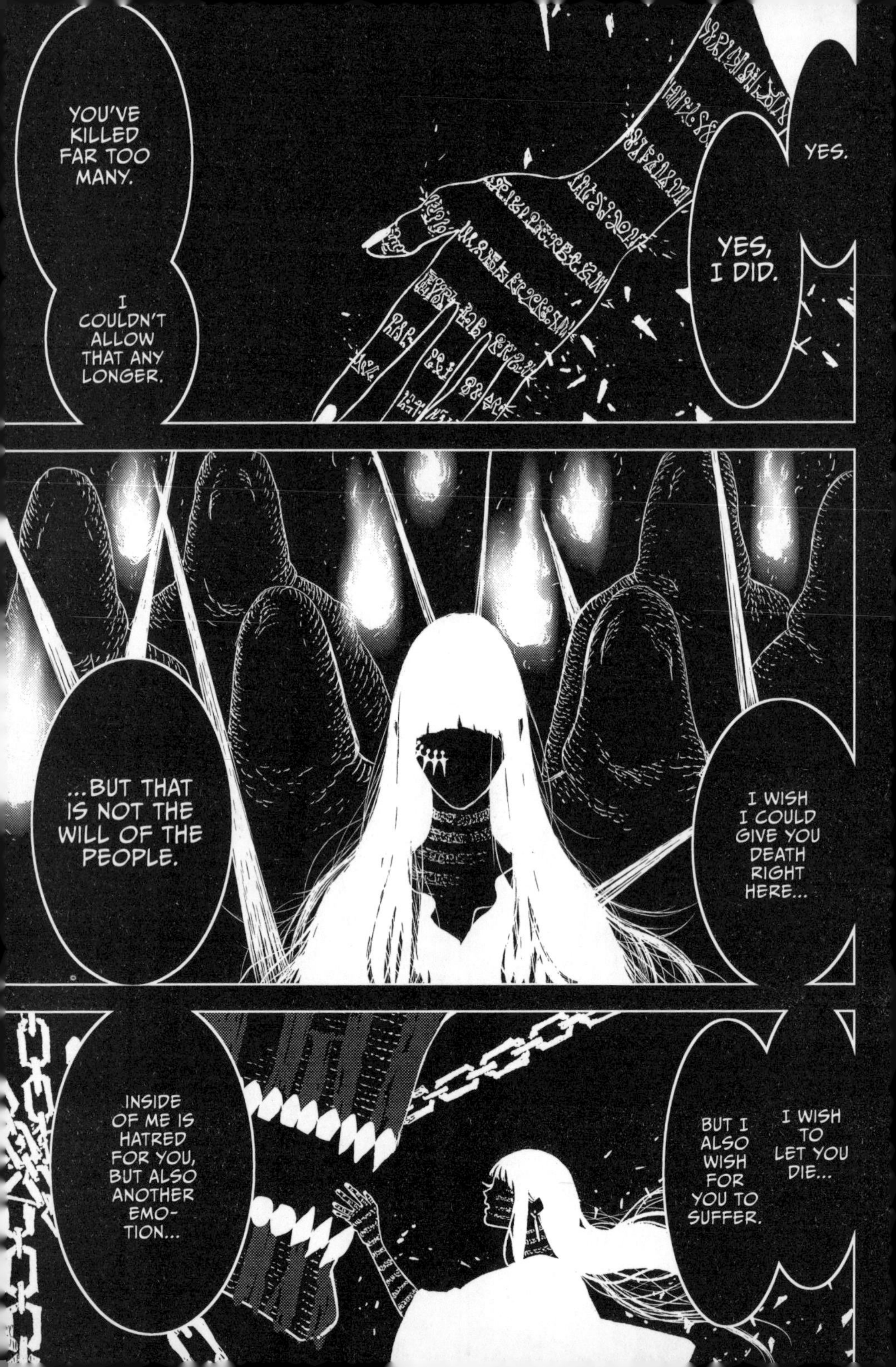
YES.
YES, I DID.
YOU'VE KILLED FAR TOO MANY.
I COULDN'T ALLOW THAT ANY LONGER.
I WISH I COULD GIVE YOU DEATH RIGHT HERE...
...BUT THAT IS NOT THE WILL OF THE PEOPLE.
I WISH TO LET YOU DIE...
BUT I ALSO WISH FOR YOU TO SUFFER.
INSIDE OF ME IS HATRED FOR YOU, BUT ALSO ANOTHER EMO-TION...

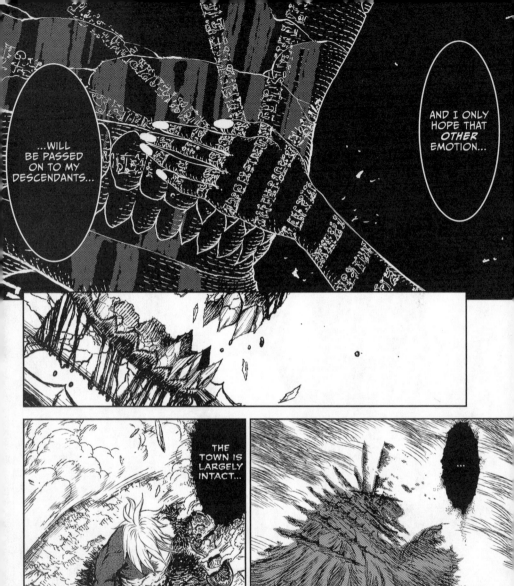

AND I ONLY HOPE THAT OTHER EMOTION...
...WILL BE PASSED ON TO MY DESCENDANTS...
...
WHAT A SHOCK ...
THE TOWN IS LARGELY INTACT...
TO THINK THERE WAS A BEING THAT COULD STOP ME THIS QUICKLY.

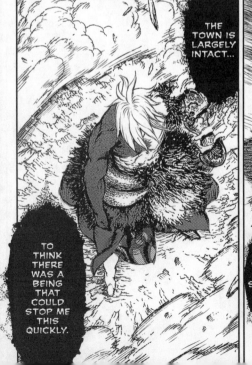

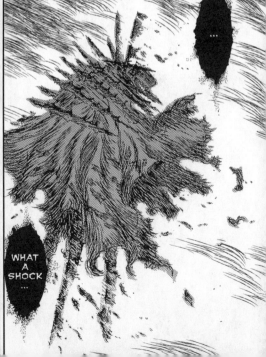

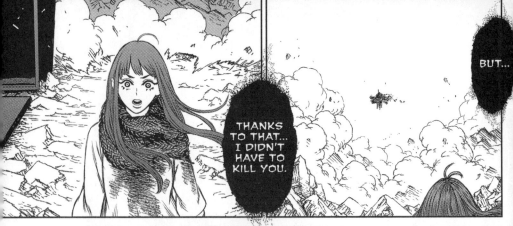

BUT...
THANKS TO THAT... I DIDN'T HAVE TO KILL YOU.
GAH...
NO MATTER HOW MUCH DANGER I INVITED UPON YOU...
YOU NEVER DID UNSHEATH ME.
I... JUST COULDN'T HAVE MY WAY...
HELGA...
WHAT...AN INCREDIBLY... STUBBORN GIRL...

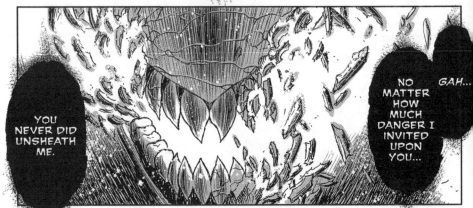

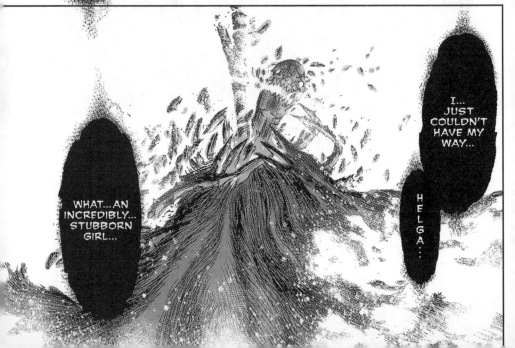

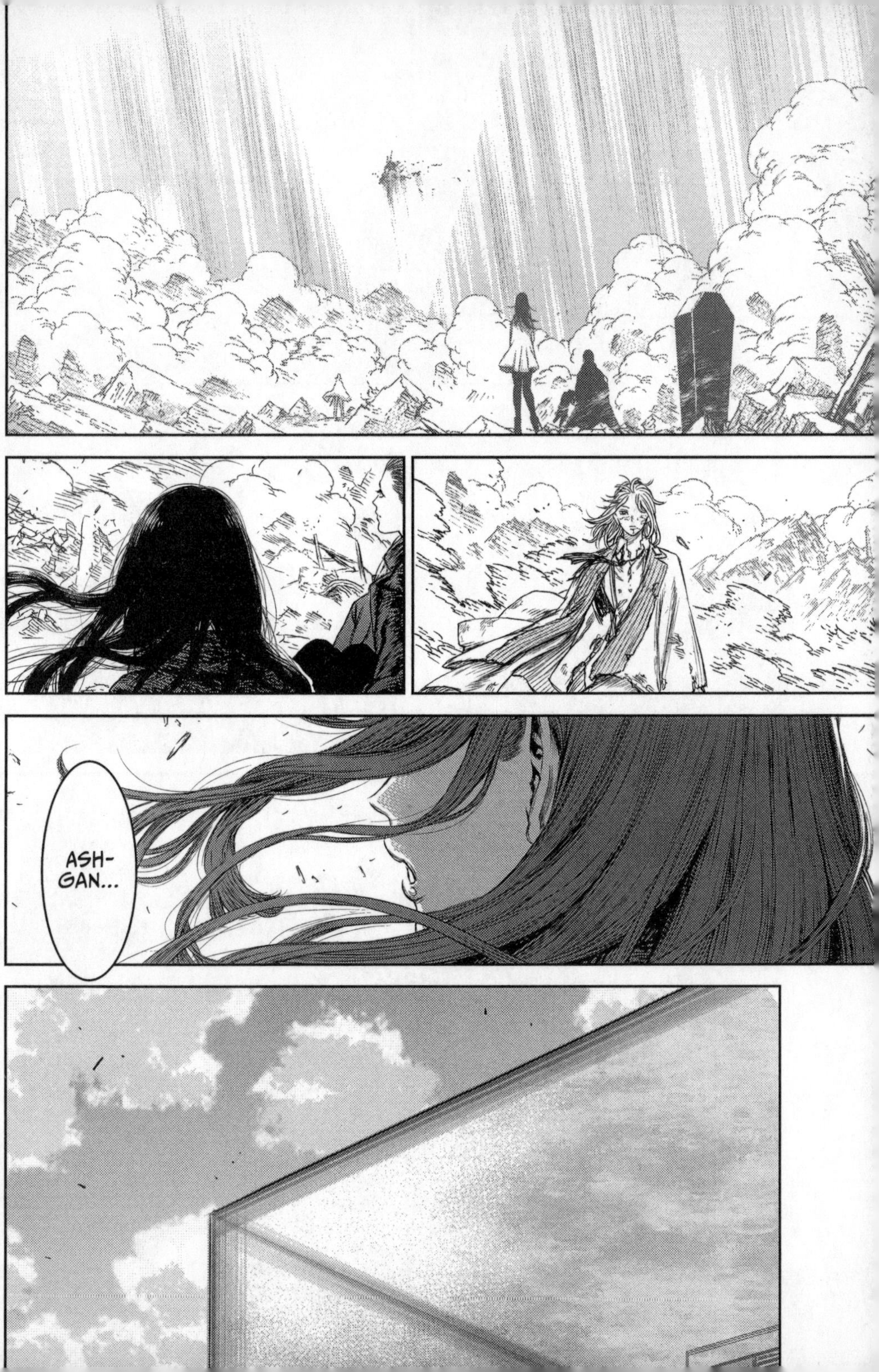
ASH-
GAN...

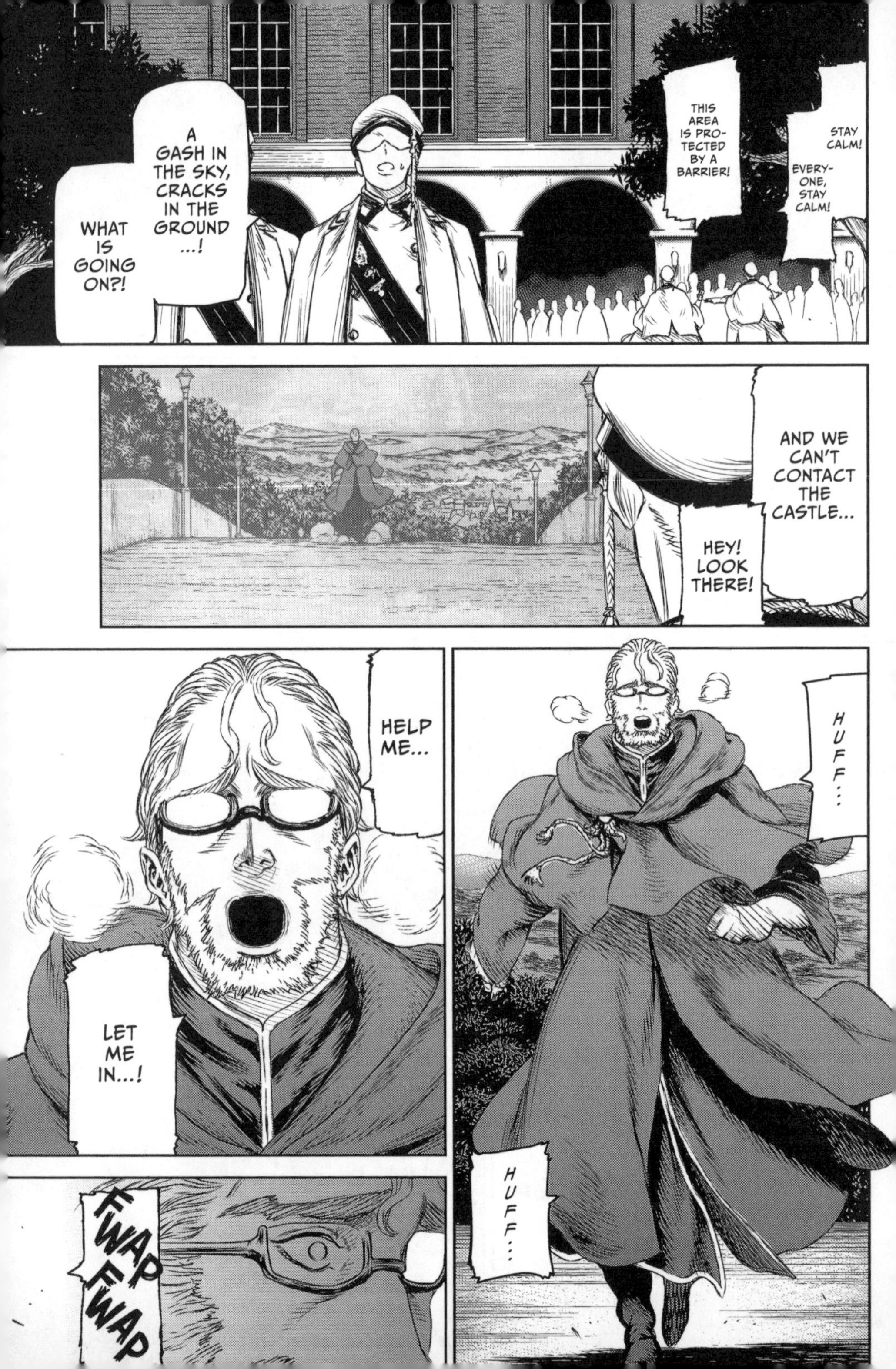
STAY CALM!
EVERY-ONE, STAY CALM!
THIS AREA IS PRO-TECTED BY A BARRIER!
A GASH IN THE SKY, CRACKS IN THE GROUND ...!
WHAT IS GOING ON?!
AND WE CAN'T CONTACT THE CASTLE...
HEY! LOOK THERE!
HUFF...
HUFF...
HELP ME...
LET ME IN...!
FWAP FWAP

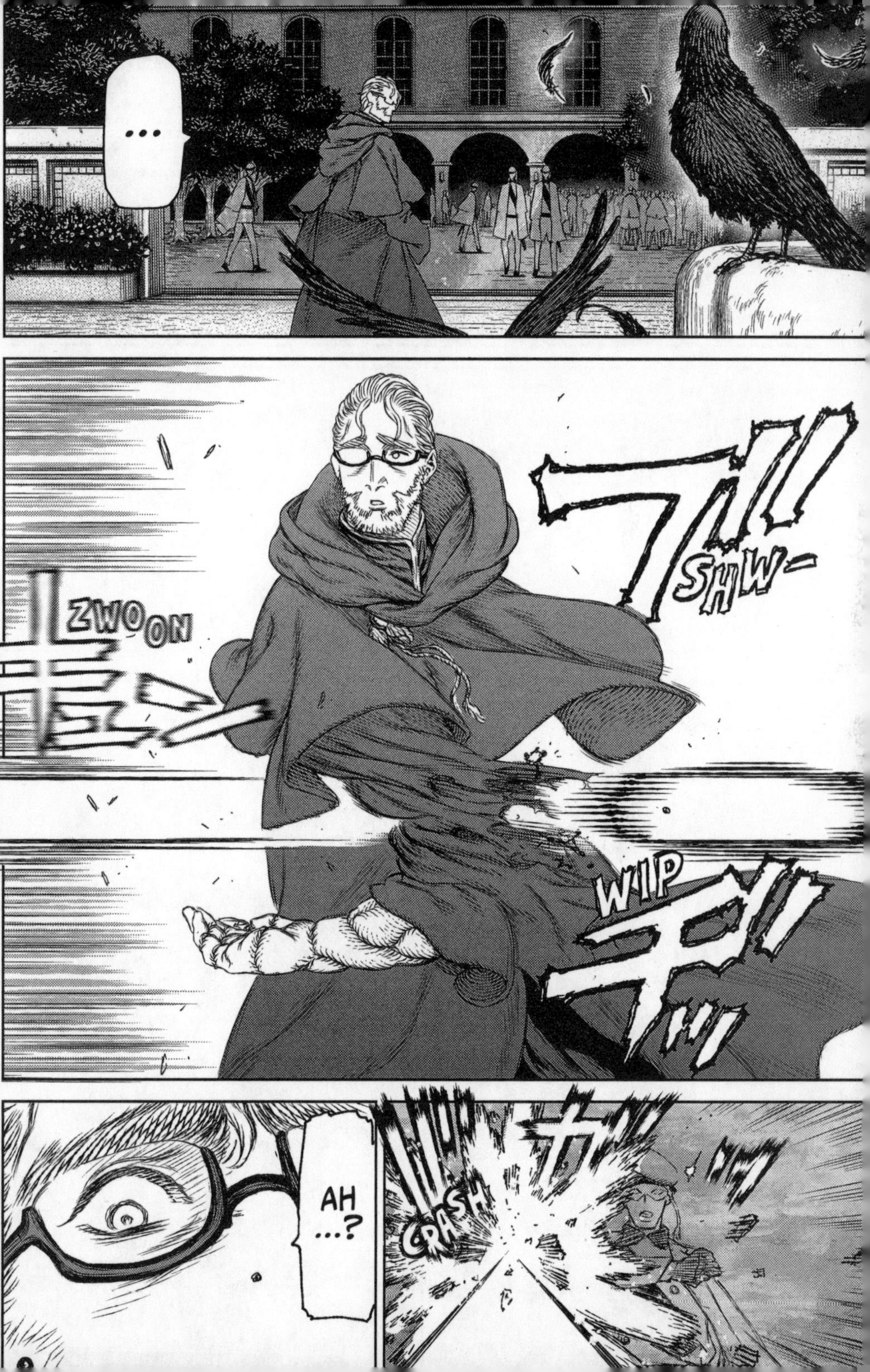

...
SHW-
ZWOON
WIP
CRASH
AH ...?

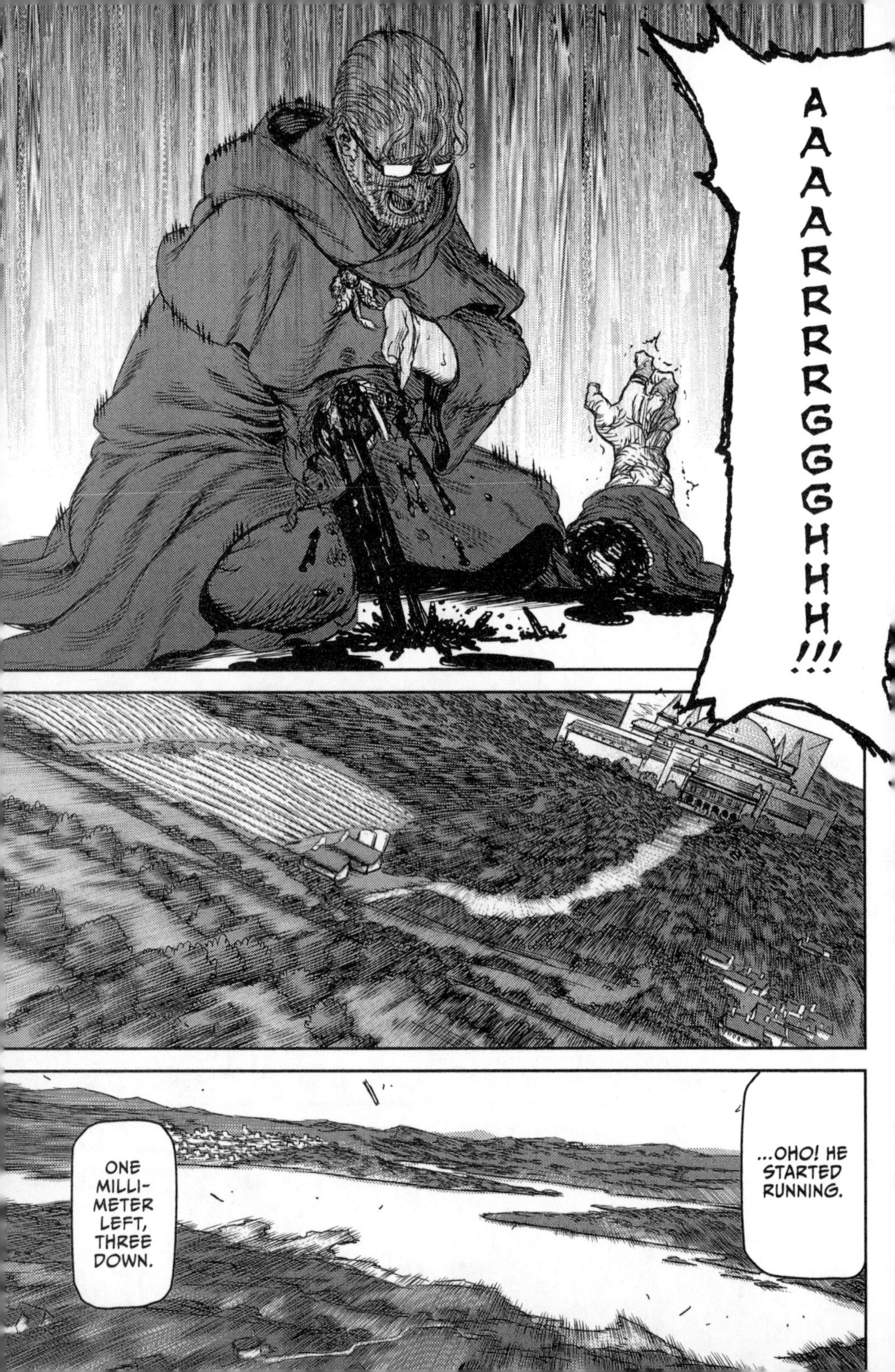
AAAARRRRGGGHHHH!!!
...OHO! HE STARTED RUNNING.
ONE MILLI-METER LEFT, THREE DOWN.

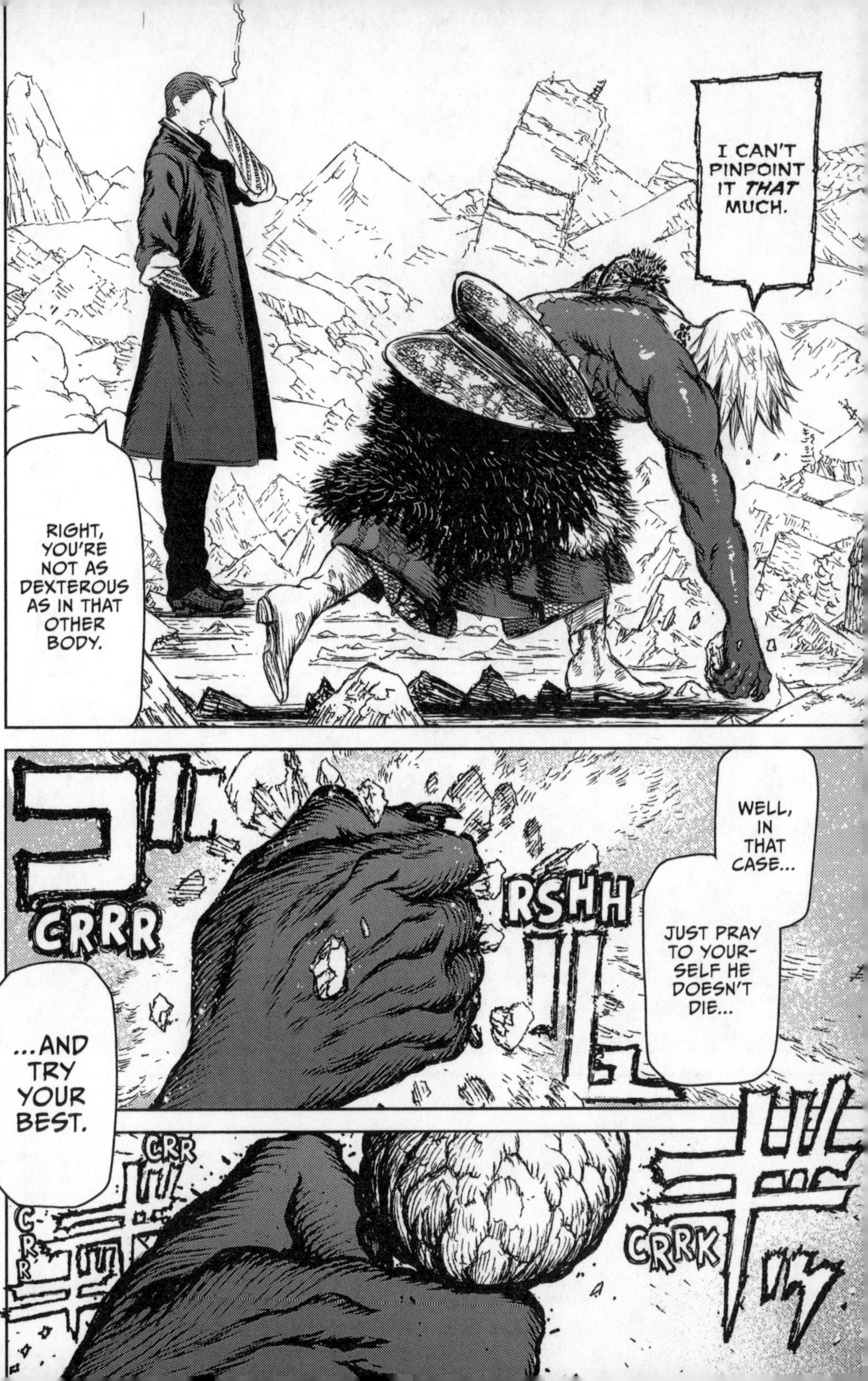
I CAN'T PINPOINT IT *THAT* MUCH.
RIGHT, YOU'RE NOT AS DEXTEROUS AS IN THAT OTHER BODY.
WELL, IN THAT CASE...
JUST PRAY TO YOUR-SELF HE DOESN'T DIE...
RSHH
CRRR
...AND TRY YOUR BEST.
CRRK
CRR
C-R-R

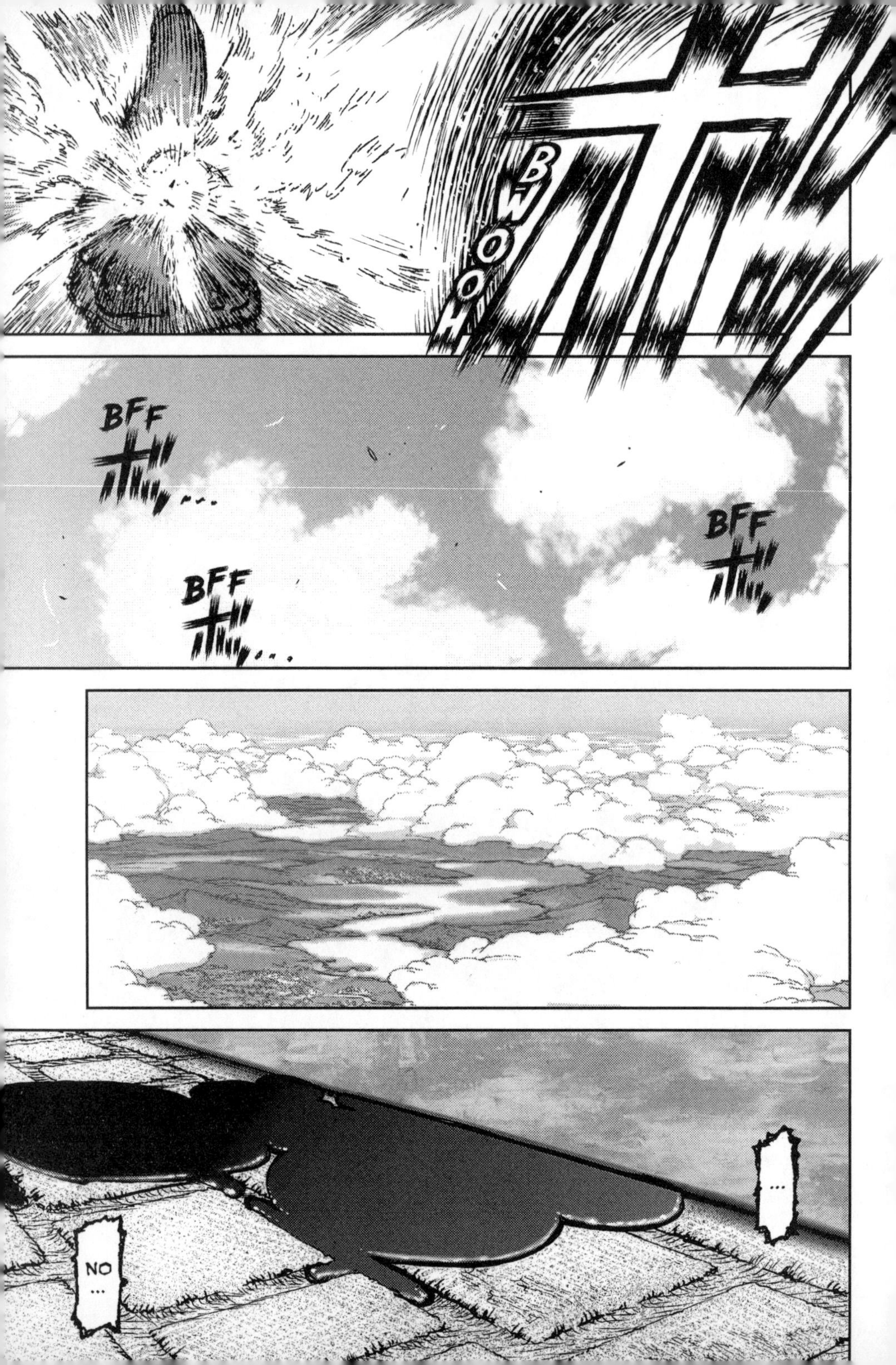

BWOOOH
BFF
BFF
BFF
...
NO ...

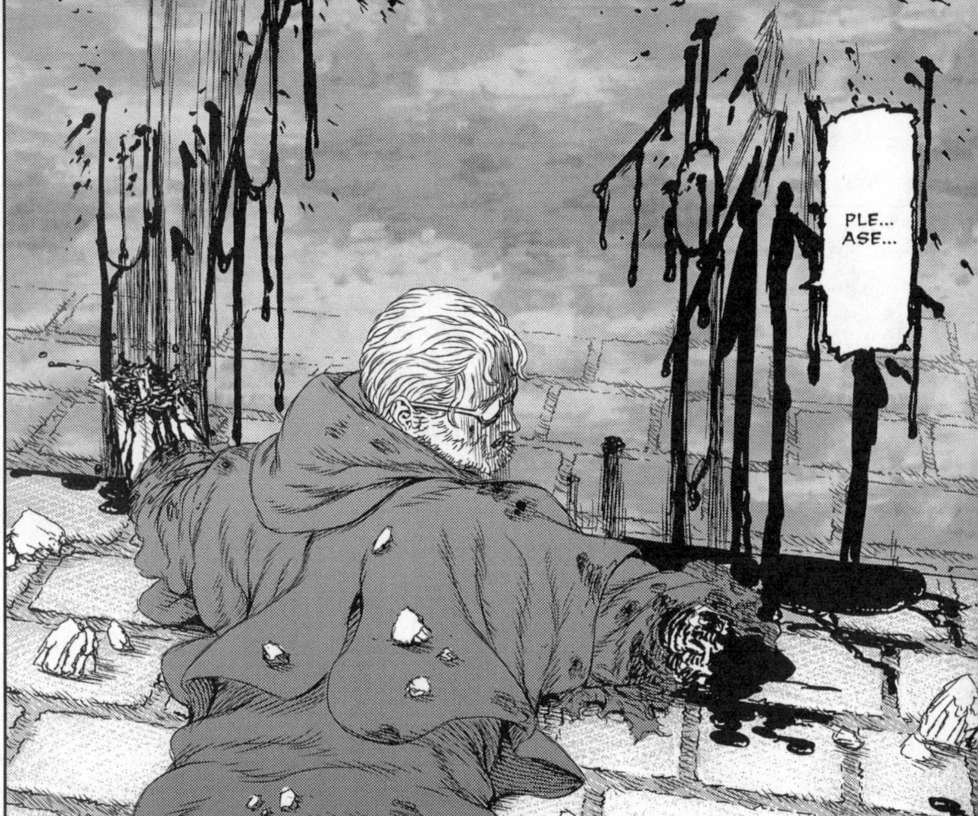
PLE... ASE...
NO...
NO MORE ...

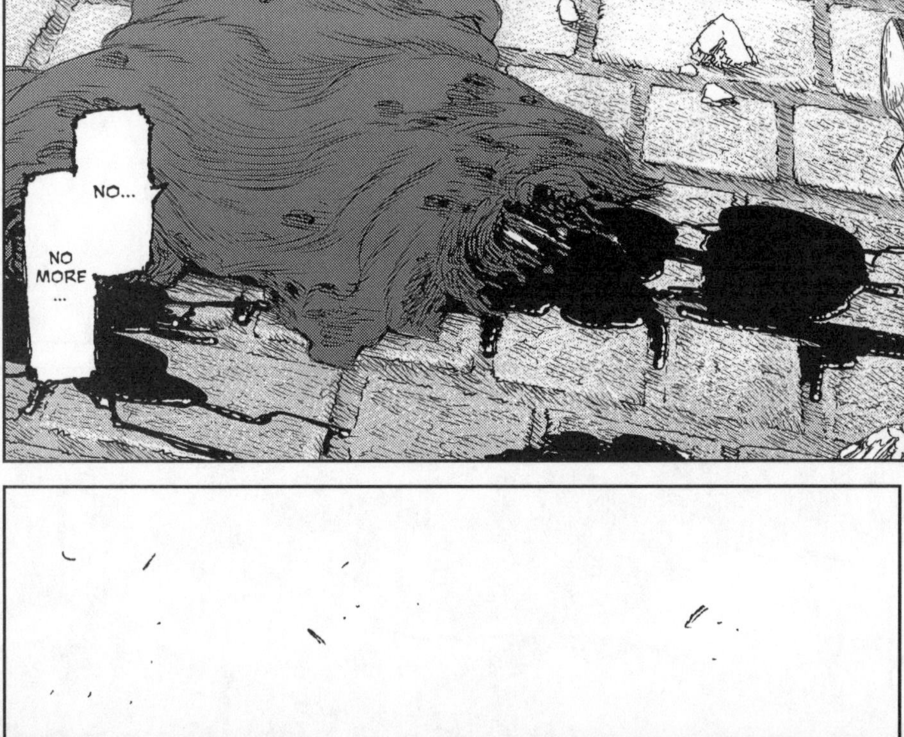

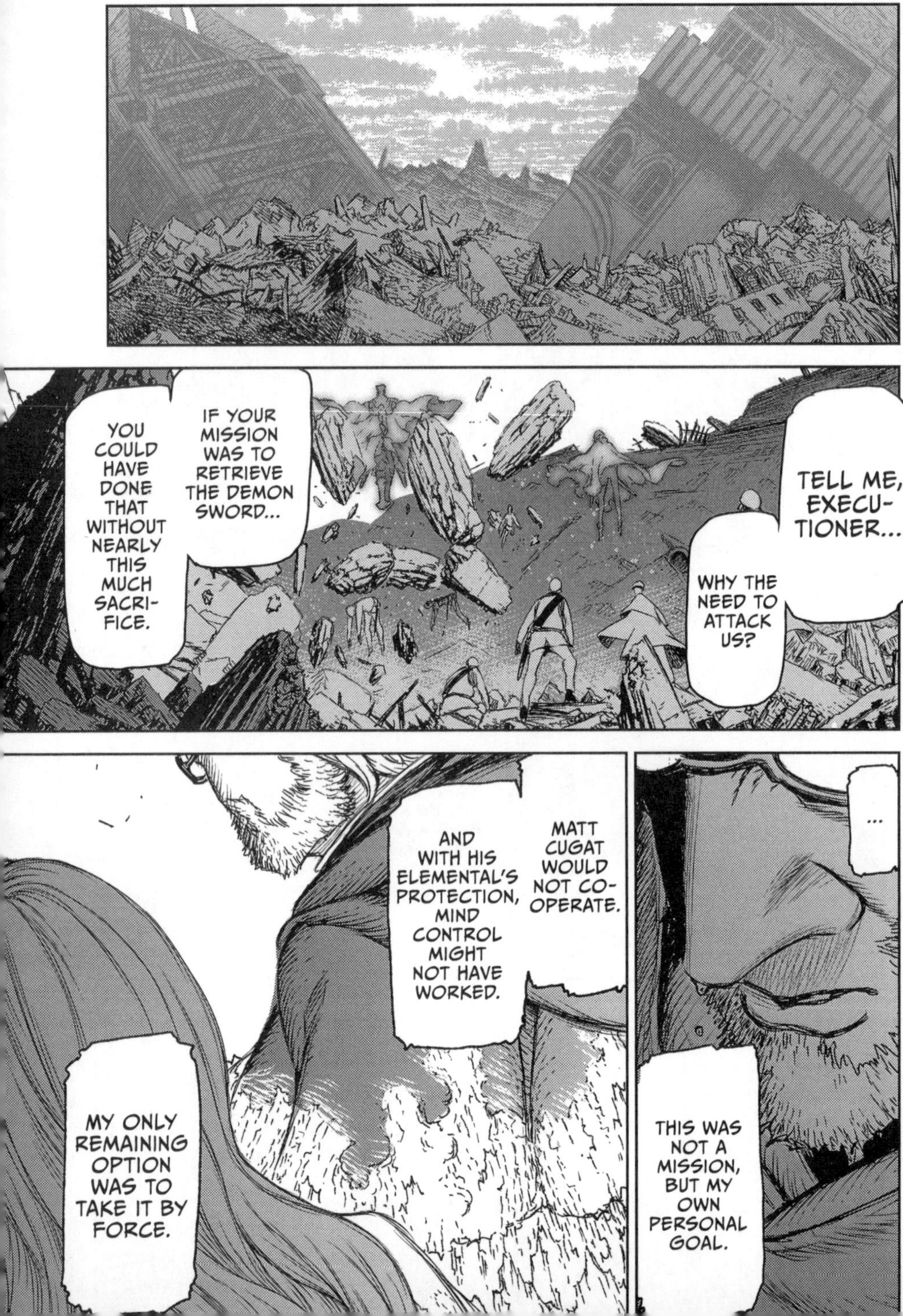
TELL ME, EXECUTIONER...
WHY THE NEED TO ATTACK US?
IF YOUR MISSION WAS TO RETRIEVE THE DEMON SWORD...
YOU COULD HAVE DONE THAT WITHOUT NEARLY THIS MUCH SACRIFICE.
...
THIS WAS NOT A MISSION, BUT MY OWN PERSONAL GOAL.
MATT CUGAT WOULD NOT CO-OPERATE.
AND WITH HIS ELEMENTAL'S PROTECTION, MIND CONTROL MIGHT NOT HAVE WORKED.
MY ONLY REMAINING OPTION WAS TO TAKE IT BY FORCE.

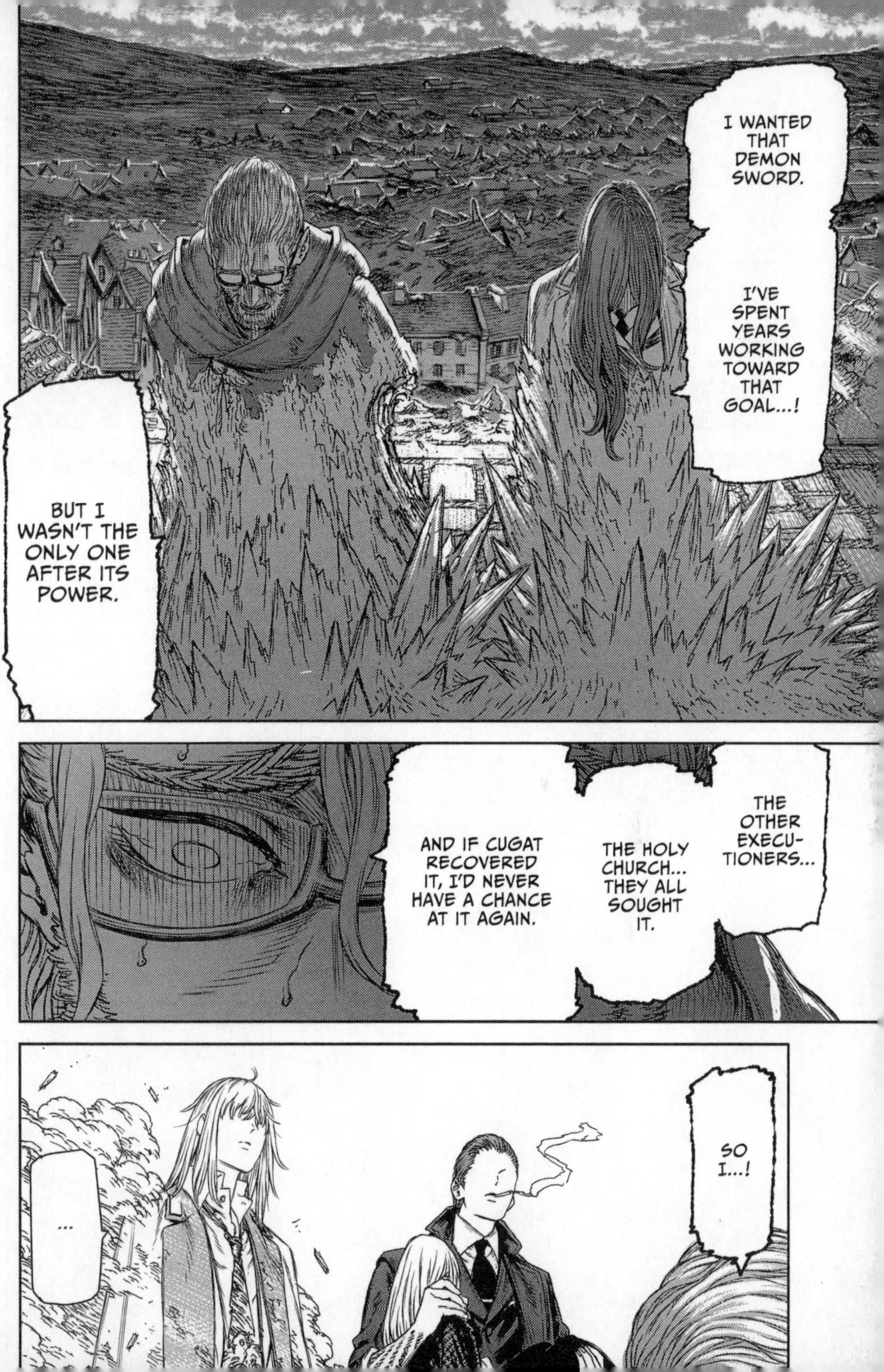
I WANTED THAT DEMON SWORD.
I'VE SPENT YEARS WORKING TOWARD THAT GOAL...!
BUT I WASN'T THE ONLY ONE AFTER ITS POWER.
THE OTHER EXECU-TIONERS...
THE HOLY CHURCH... THEY ALL SOUGHT IT.
AND IF CUGAT RECOVERED IT, I'D NEVER HAVE A CHANCE AT IT AGAIN.
SO I...!
...

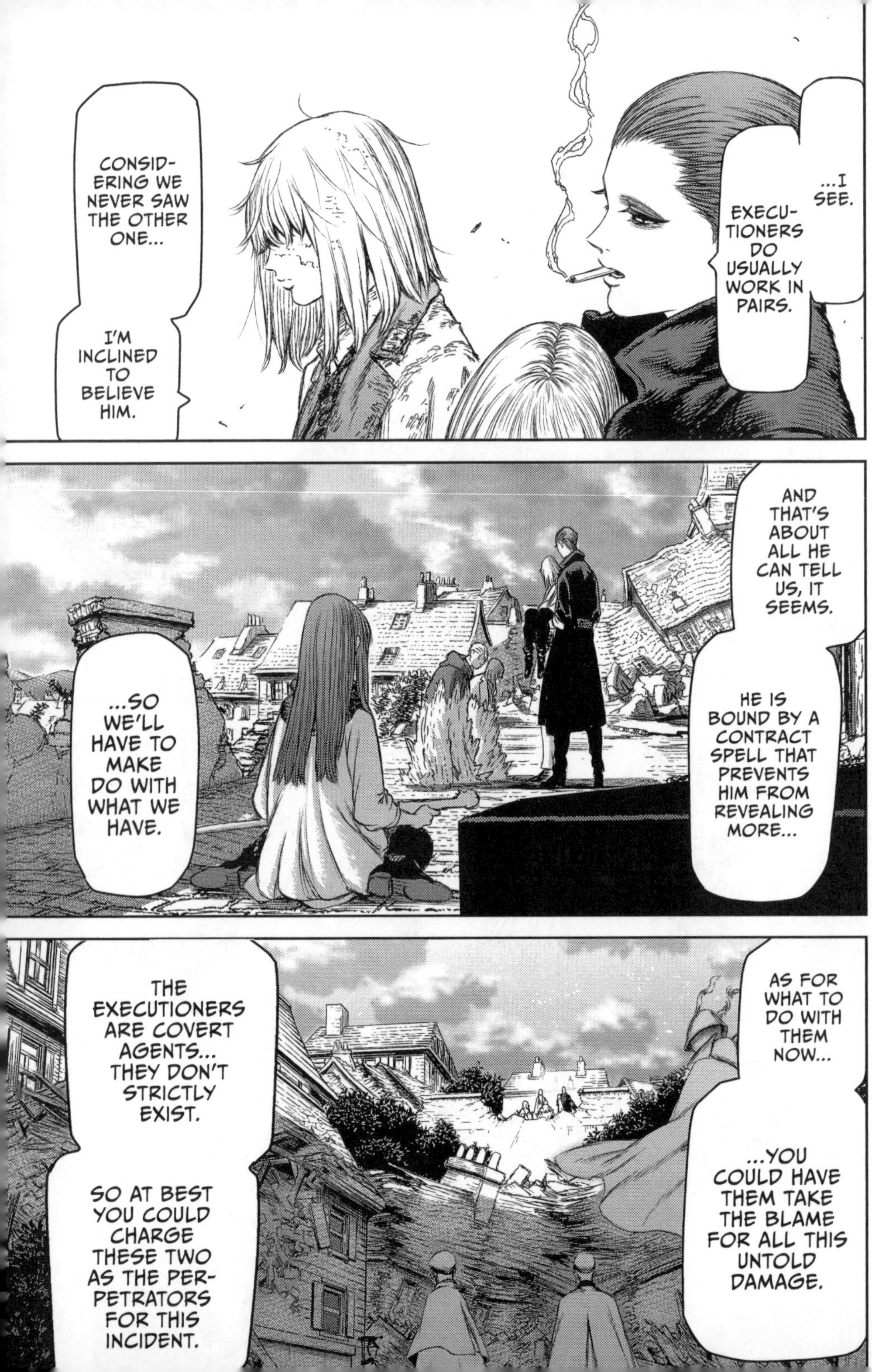
...I SEE.
EXECUTIONERS DO USUALLY WORK IN PAIRS.
CONSIDERING WE NEVER SAW THE OTHER ONE...
I'M INCLINED TO BELIEVE HIM.
AND THAT'S ABOUT ALL HE CAN TELL US, IT SEEMS.
HE IS BOUND BY A CONTRACT SPELL THAT PREVENTS HIM FROM REVEALING MORE...
...SO WE'LL HAVE TO MAKE DO WITH WHAT WE HAVE.
AS FOR WHAT TO DO WITH THEM NOW...
...YOU COULD HAVE THEM TAKE THE BLAME FOR ALL THIS UNTOLD DAMAGE.
THE EXECUTIONERS ARE COVERT AGENTS... THEY DON'T STRICTLY EXIST.
SO AT BEST YOU COULD CHARGE THESE TWO AS THE PERPETRATORS FOR THIS INCIDENT.

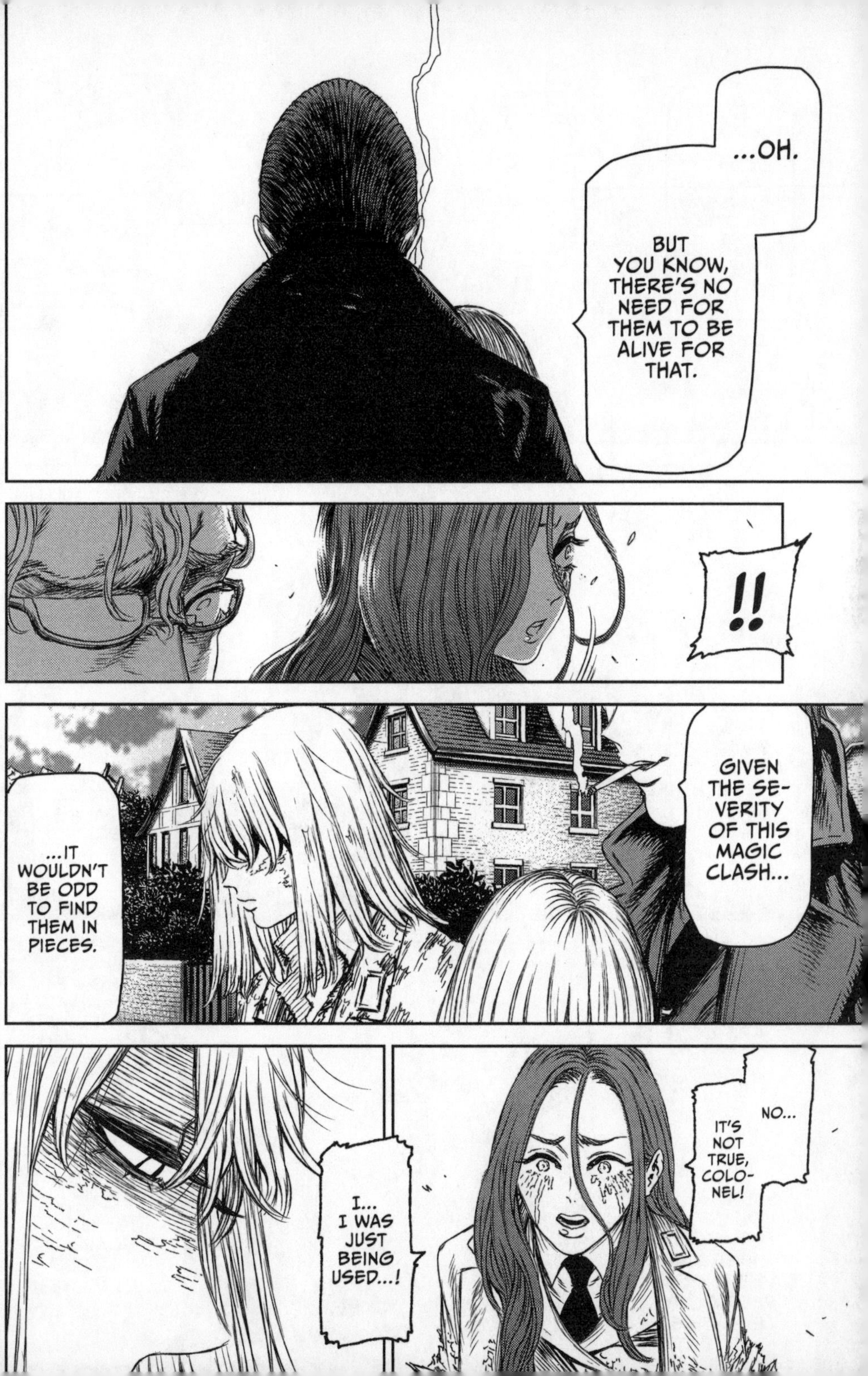
...OH.
BUT YOU KNOW, THERE'S NO NEED FOR THEM TO BE ALIVE FOR THAT.
!!
GIVEN THE SE-VERITY OF THIS MAGIC CLASH...
...IT WOULDN'T BE ODD TO FIND THEM IN PIECES.
NO...
IT'S NOT TRUE, COLO-NEL!
I... I WAS JUST BEING USED...!

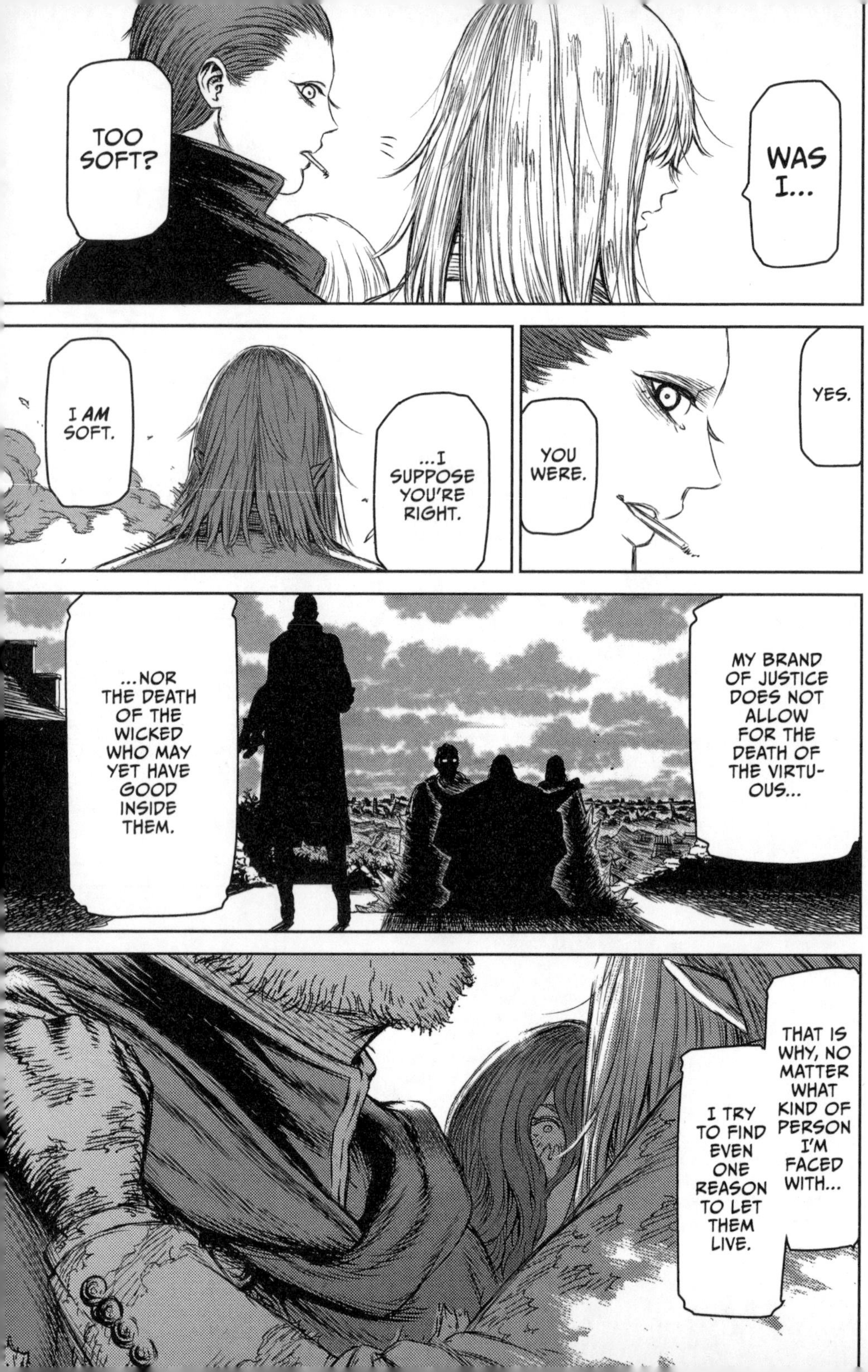
WAS I...
TOO SOFT?
YES.
YOU WERE.
...I SUPPOSE YOU'RE RIGHT.
I AM SOFT.
MY BRAND OF JUSTICE DOES NOT ALLOW FOR THE DEATH OF THE VIRTUOUS...
...NOR THE DEATH OF THE WICKED WHO MAY YET HAVE GOOD INSIDE THEM.
THAT IS WHY, NO MATTER WHAT KIND OF PERSON I'M FACED WITH...
I TRY TO FIND EVEN ONE REASON TO LET THEM LIVE.

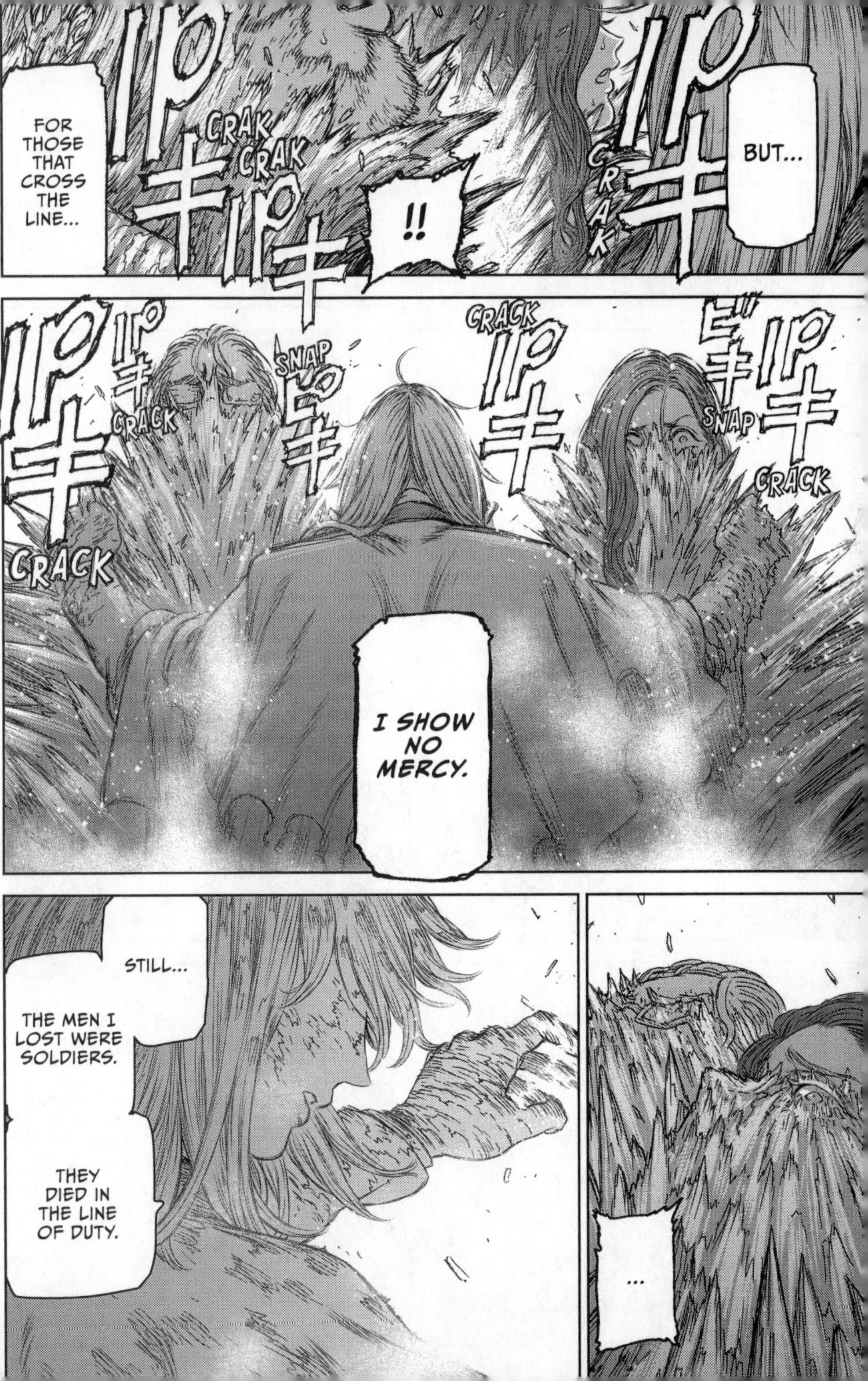
BUT...
CRAK
!!
CRAK CRAK
FOR THOSE THAT CROSS THE LINE...
CRACK
SNAP
CRACK
SNAP
CRACK
CRACK
I SHOW NO MERCY.
...
STILL...
THE MEN I LOST WERE SOLDIERS.
THEY DIED IN THE LINE OF DUTY.

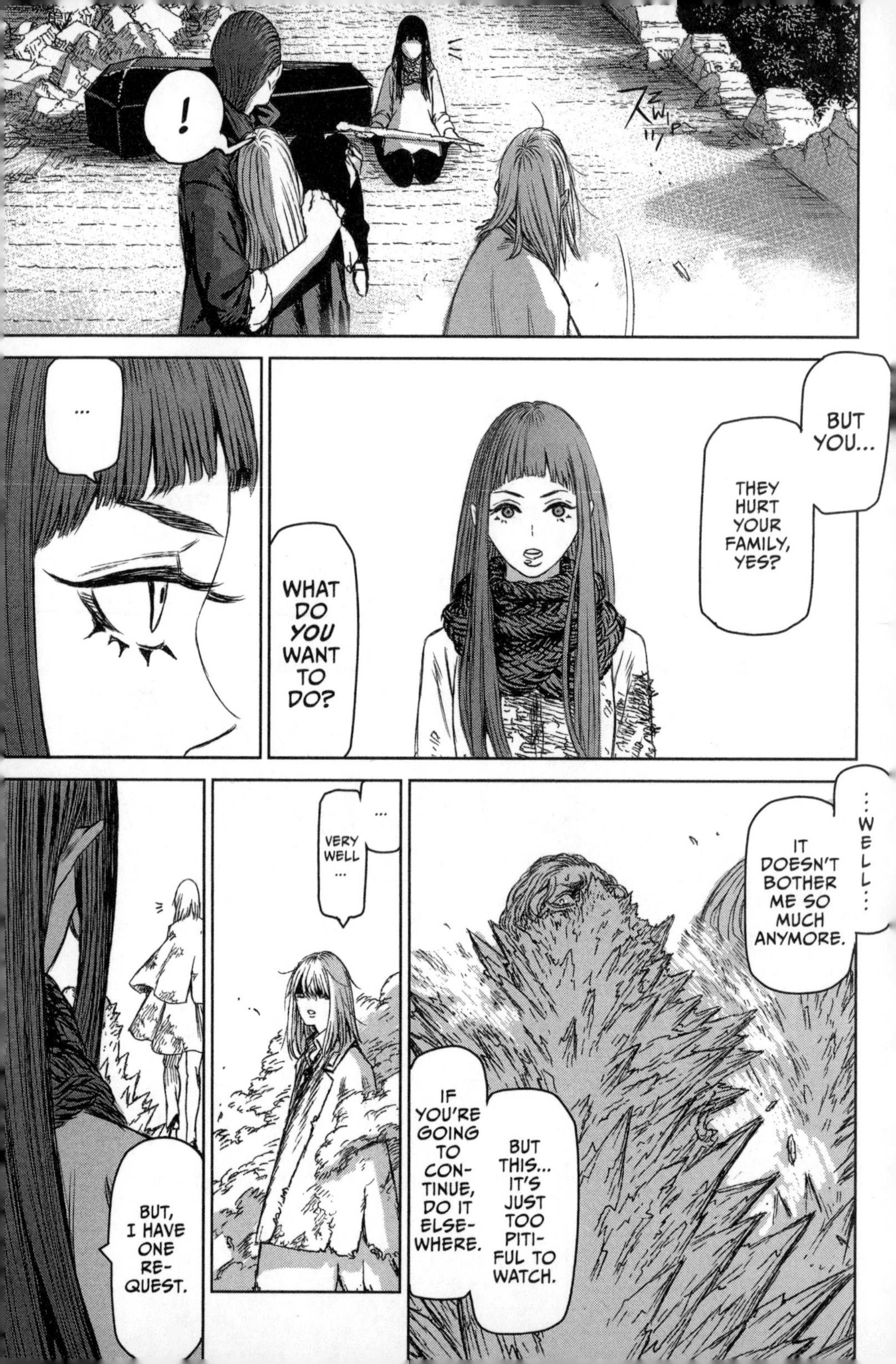
ZWIP
!
BUT YOU...
THEY HURT YOUR FAMILY, YES?
WHAT DO *YOU* WANT TO DO?
...
...WELL...
IT DOESN'T BOTHER ME SO MUCH ANYMORE.
BUT THIS... IT'S JUST TOO PITIFUL TO WATCH.
IF YOU'RE GOING TO CONTINUE, DO IT ELSEWHERE.
...
VERY WELL ...
BUT, I HAVE ONE REQUEST.

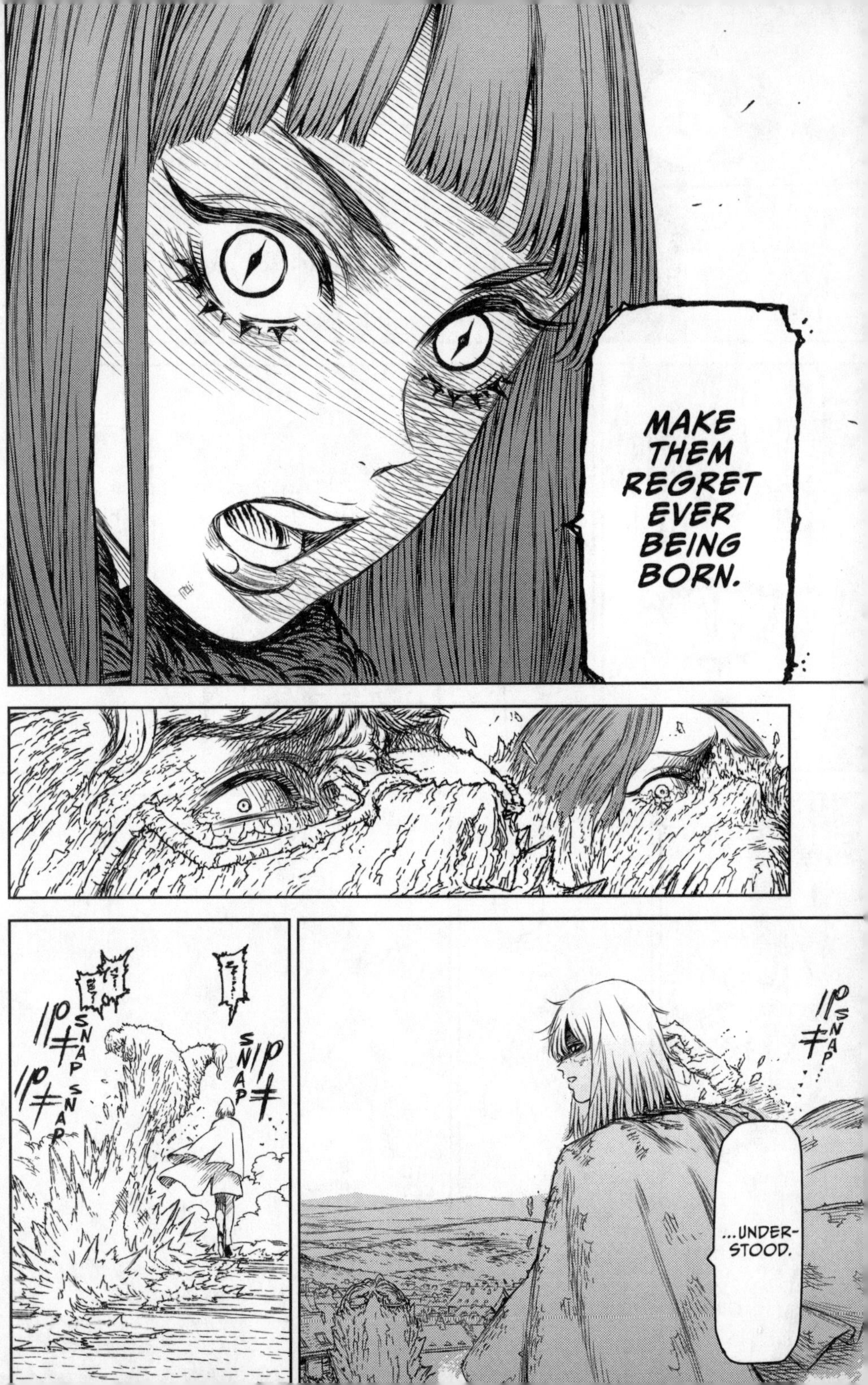
MAKE THEM REGRET EVER BEING BORN.
SNAP...
...UNDER-STOOD.
SNAP
SNAP SNAP
SNAP

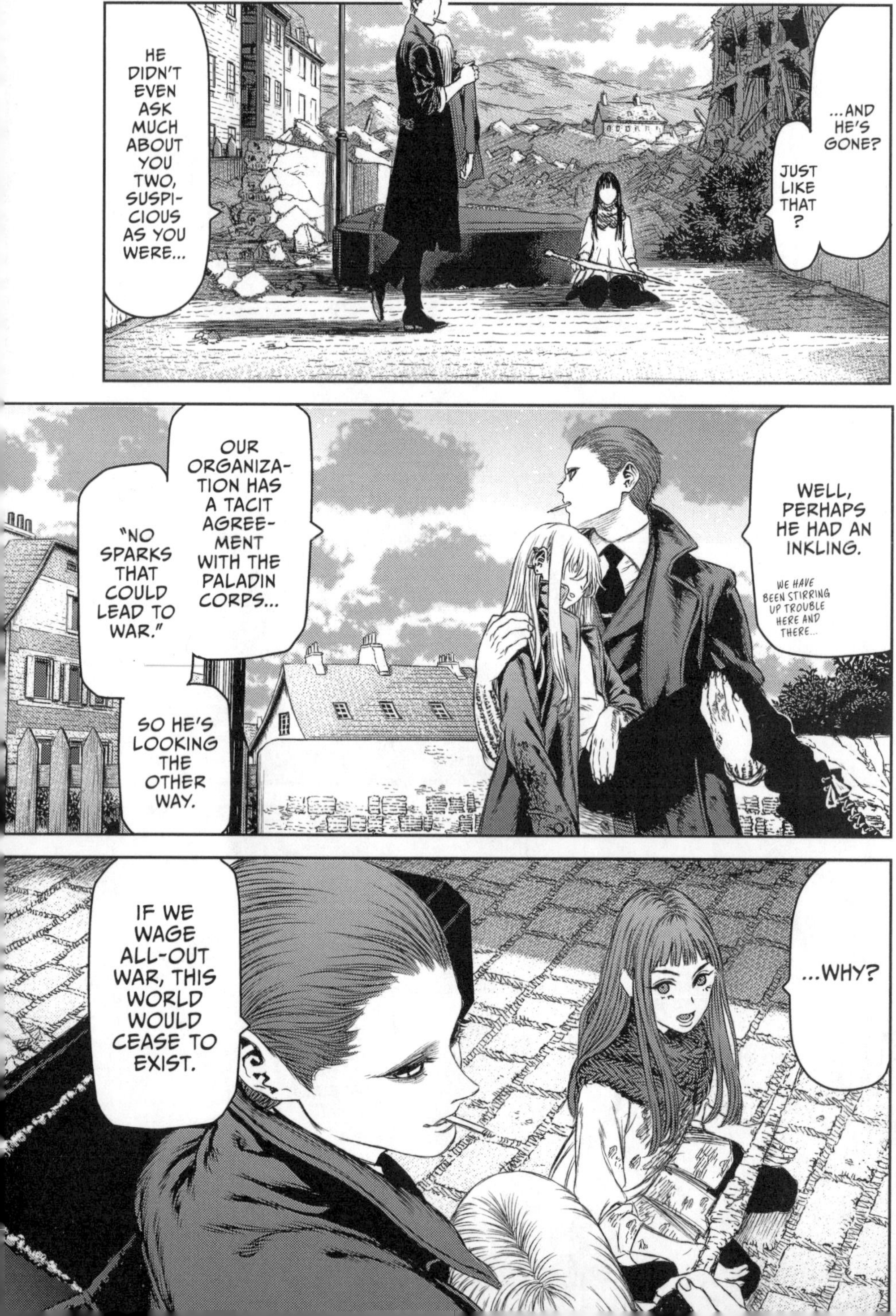
...AND HE'S GONE?
JUST LIKE THAT?
HE DIDN'T EVEN ASK MUCH ABOUT YOU TWO, SUSPICIOUS AS YOU WERE...
WELL, PERHAPS HE HAD AN INKLING.
WE HAVE BEEN STIRRING UP TROUBLE HERE AND THERE...
OUR ORGANIZATION HAS A TACIT AGREEMENT WITH THE PALADIN CORPS...
"NO SPARKS THAT COULD LEAD TO WAR."
SO HE'S LOOKING THE OTHER WAY.
...WHY?
IF WE WAGE ALL-OUT WAR, THIS WORLD WOULD CEASE TO EXIST.

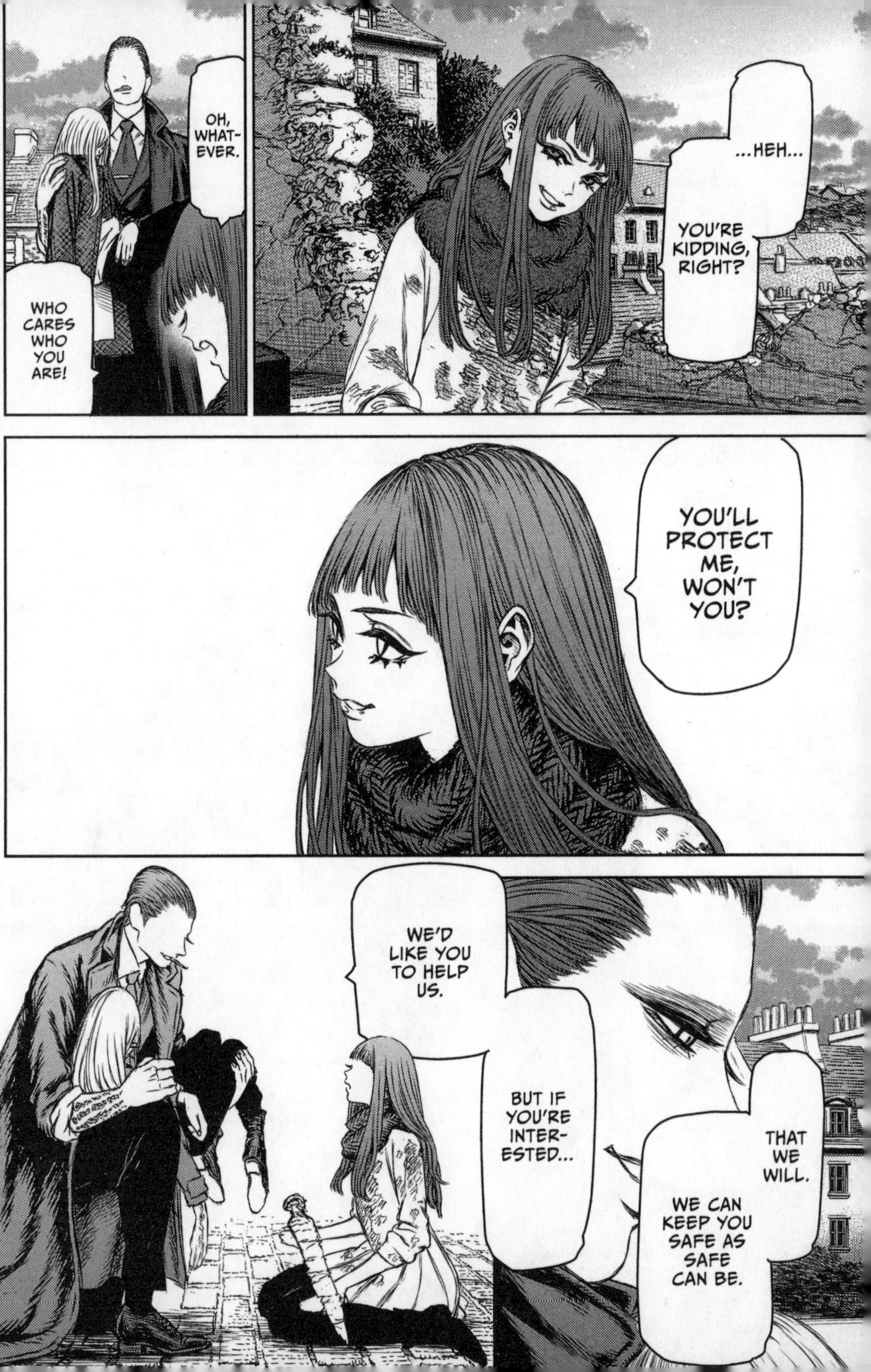
...HEH...
YOU'RE KIDDING, RIGHT?
OH, WHAT-EVER.
WHO CARES WHO YOU ARE!
YOU'LL PROTECT ME, WON'T YOU?
THAT WE WILL.
WE CAN KEEP YOU SAFE AS SAFE CAN BE.
WE'D LIKE YOU TO HELP US.
BUT IF YOU'RE INTER-ESTED...

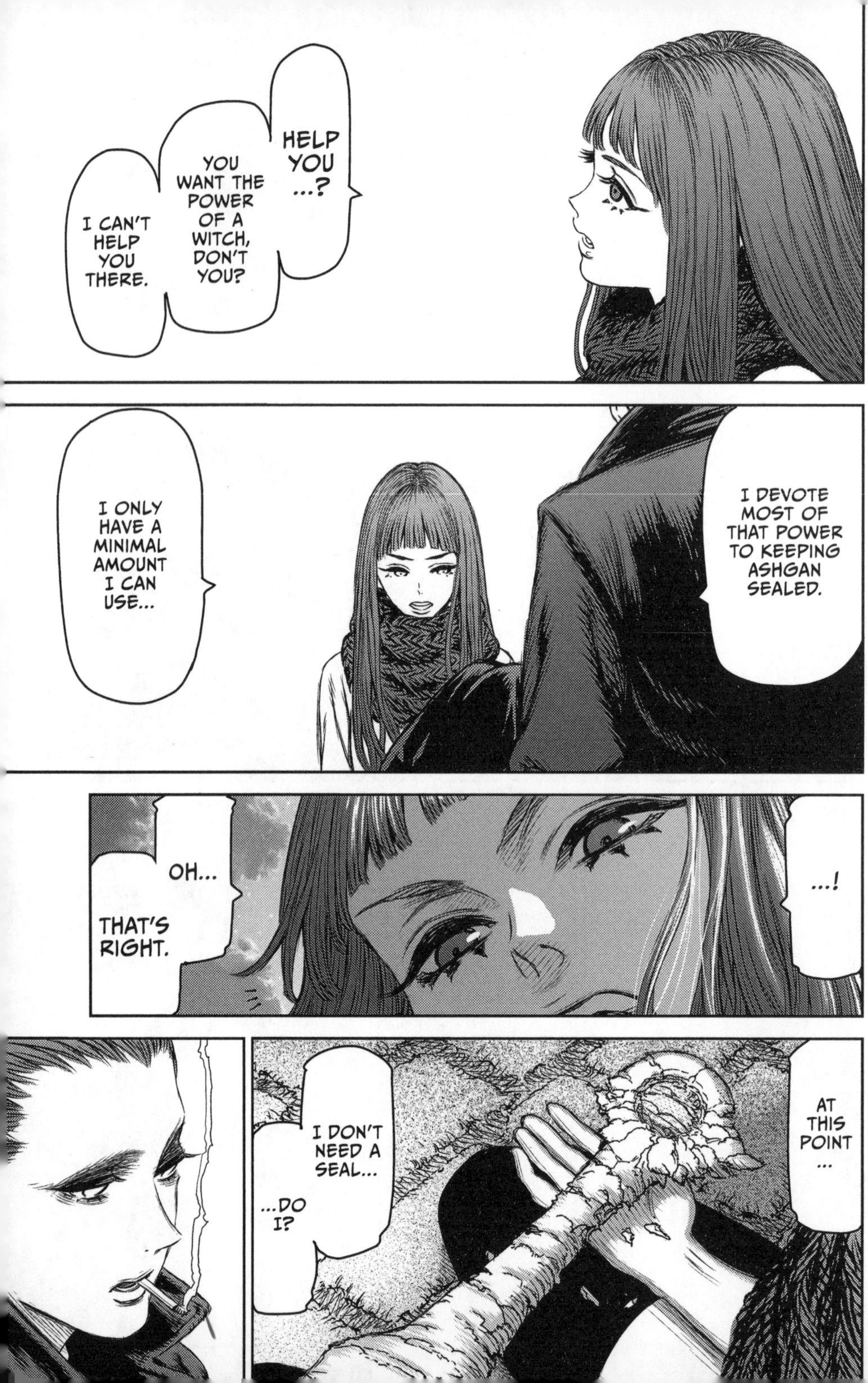
HELP YOU ...?
YOU WANT THE POWER OF A WITCH, DON'T YOU?
I CAN'T HELP YOU THERE.
I DEVOTE MOST OF THAT POWER TO KEEPING ASHGAN SEALED.
I ONLY HAVE A MINIMAL AMOUNT I CAN USE...
...!
OH...
THAT'S RIGHT.
AT THIS POINT ...
I DON'T NEED A SEAL...
...DO I?

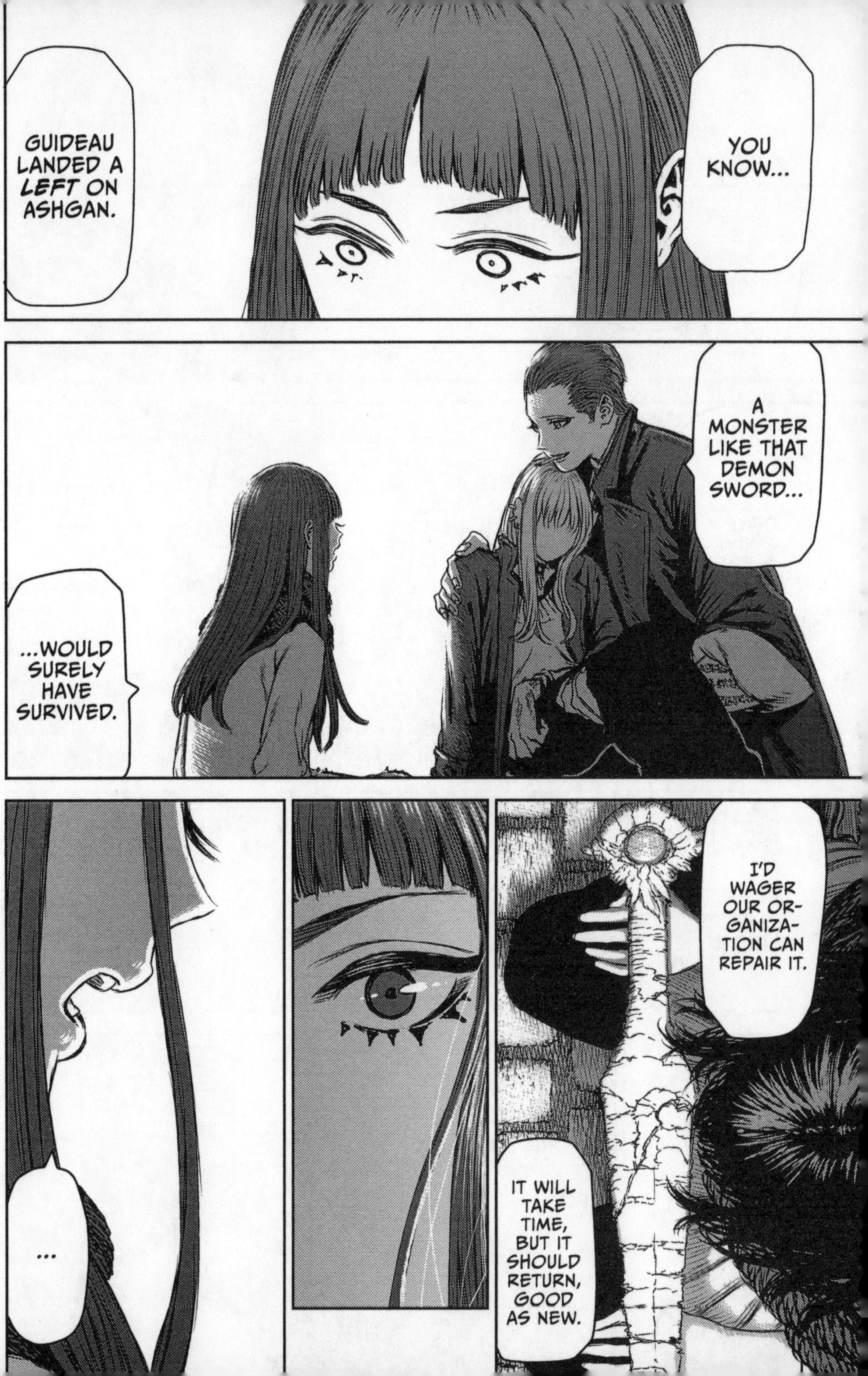
YOU KNOW...
GUIDEAU LANDED A *LEFT* ON ASHGAN.
A MONSTER LIKE THAT DEMON SWORD...
...WOULD SURELY HAVE SURVIVED.
I'D WAGER OUR ORGANIZATION CAN REPAIR IT.
IT WILL TAKE TIME, BUT IT SHOULD RETURN, GOOD AS NEW.
...

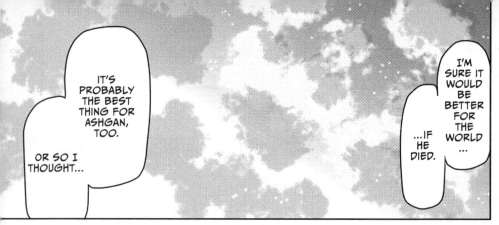

I'M SURE IT WOULD BE BETTER FOR THE WORLD ...
...IF HE DIED.
IT'S PROBABLY THE BEST THING FOR ASHGAN, TOO.
OR SO I THOUGHT...
BUT... HMM...
HE'S ALIVE, HUH...?
WOULD YOU LOOK AT THAT...

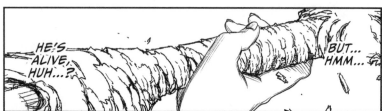

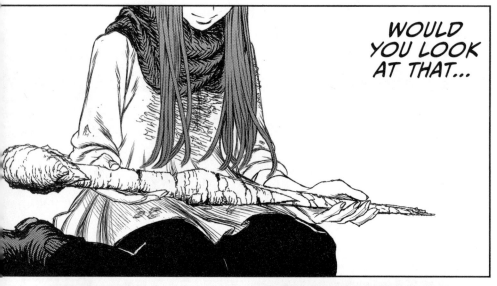

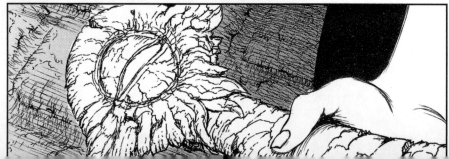

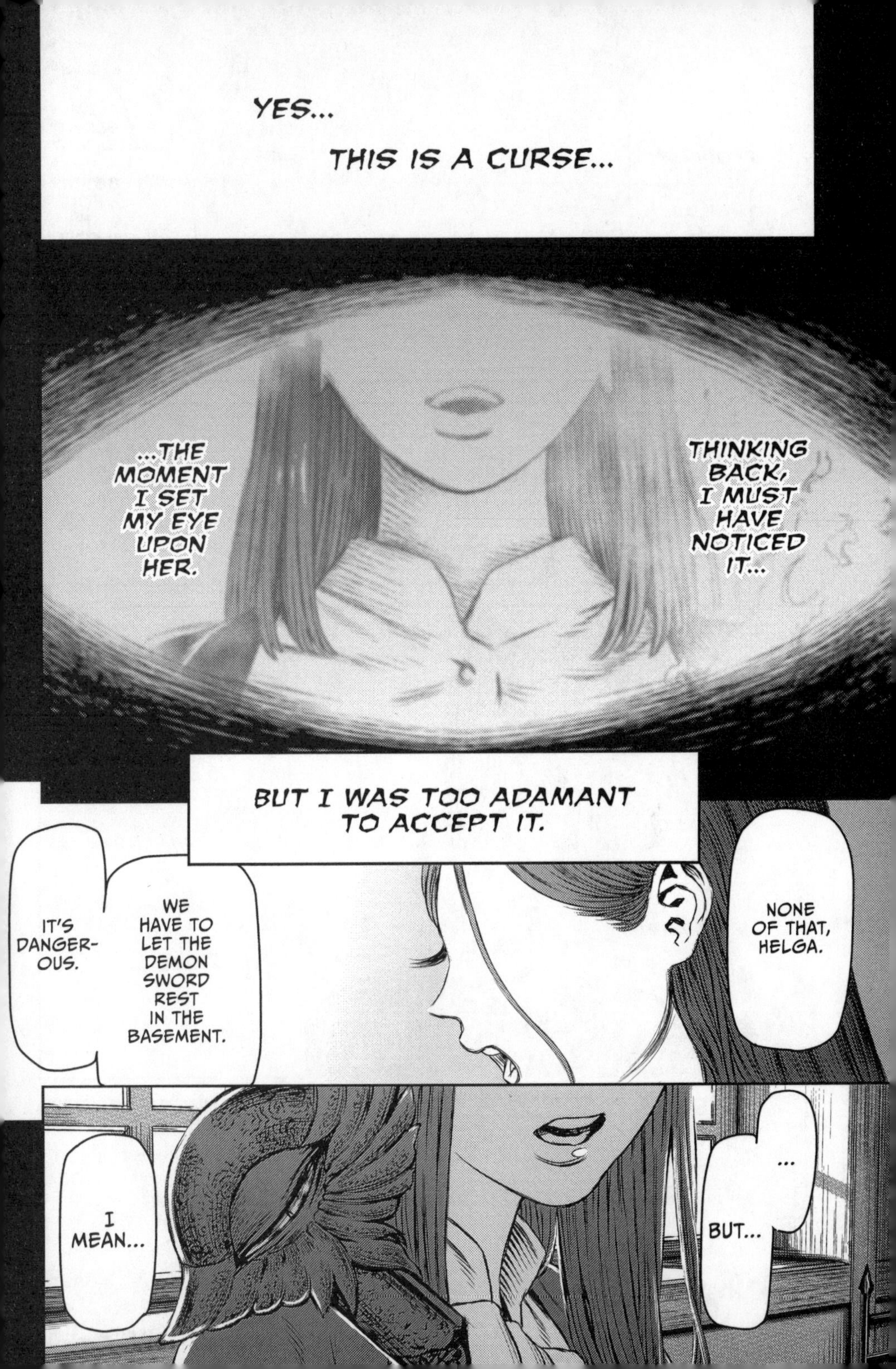
YES...
THIS IS A CURSE...
THINKING BACK, I MUST HAVE NOTICED IT...
...THE MOMENT I SET MY EYE UPON HER.
BUT I WAS TOO ADAMANT TO ACCEPT IT.
NONE OF THAT, HELGA.
WE HAVE TO LET THE DEMON SWORD REST IN THE BASEMENT.
IT'S DANGER-OUS.
...
BUT...
I MEAN...

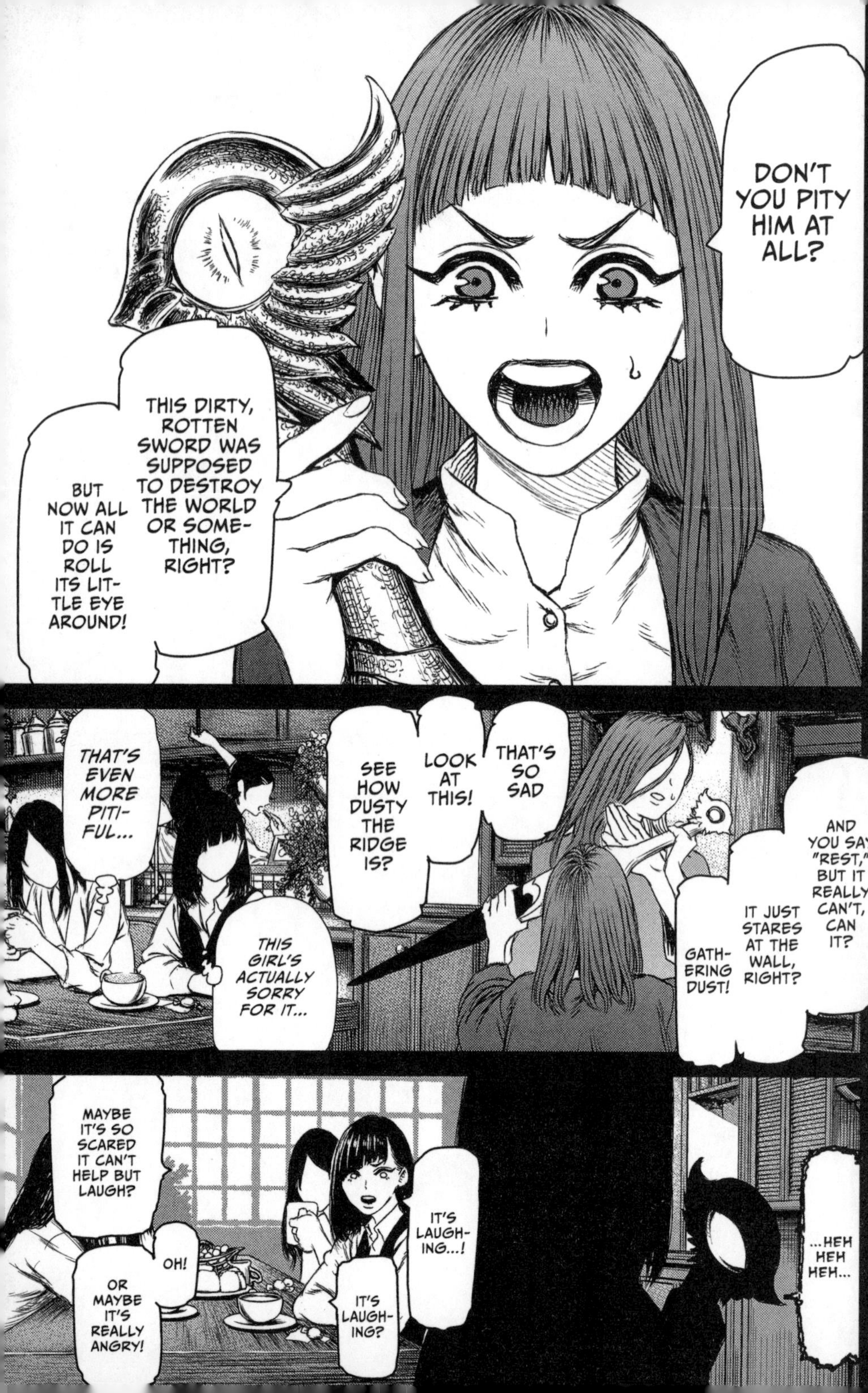
DON'T YOU PITY HIM AT ALL?
THIS DIRTY, ROTTEN SWORD WAS SUPPOSED TO DESTROY THE WORLD OR SOMETHING, RIGHT?
BUT NOW ALL IT CAN DO IS ROLL ITS LITTLE EYE AROUND!
AND YOU SAY "REST," BUT IT REALLY CAN'T, CAN IT?
IT JUST STARES AT THE WALL, RIGHT?
GATHERING DUST!
THAT'S SO SAD
LOOK AT THIS!
SEE HOW DUSTY THE RIDGE IS?
THIS GIRL'S ACTUALLY SORRY FOR IT...
THAT'S EVEN MORE PITIFUL...
...HEH HEH HEH...
IT'S LAUGHING...!
IT'S LAUGHING?
MAYBE IT'S SO SCARED IT CAN'T HELP BUT LAUGH?
OH!
OR MAYBE IT'S REALLY ANGRY!

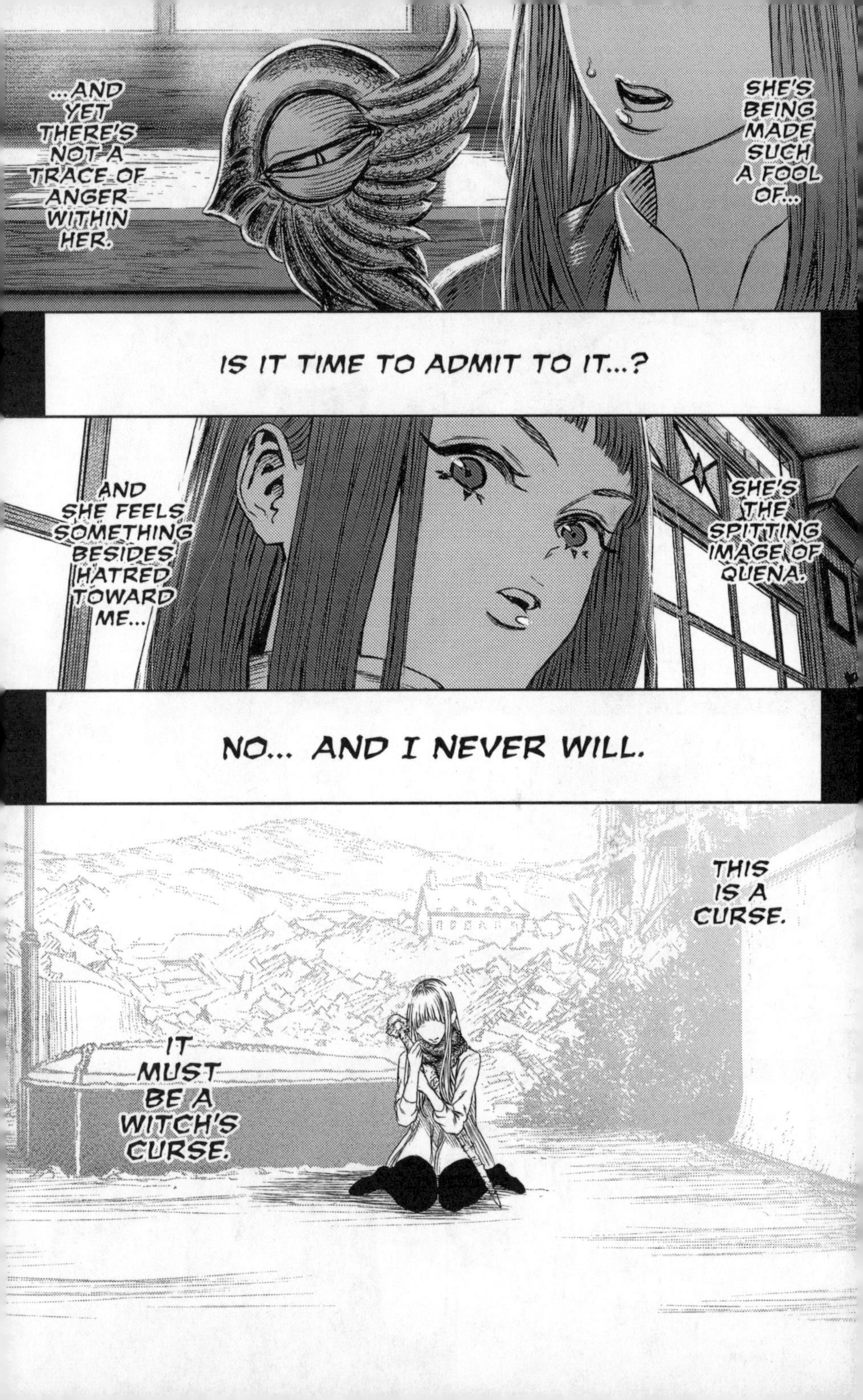
SHE'S BEING MADE SUCH A FOOL OF...
...AND YET THERE'S NOT A TRACE OF ANGER WITHIN HER.
IS IT TIME TO ADMIT TO IT...?
SHE'S THE SPITTING IMAGE OF QUENA.
AND SHE FEELS SOMETHING BESIDES HATRED TOWARD ME...
NO... AND I NEVER WILL.
THIS IS A CURSE.
IT MUST BE A WITCH'S CURSE.

THE WITCH AND THE BEAST

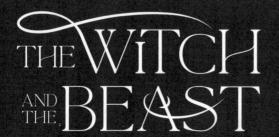

THE WITCH AND THE BEAST

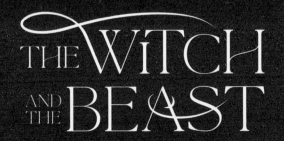

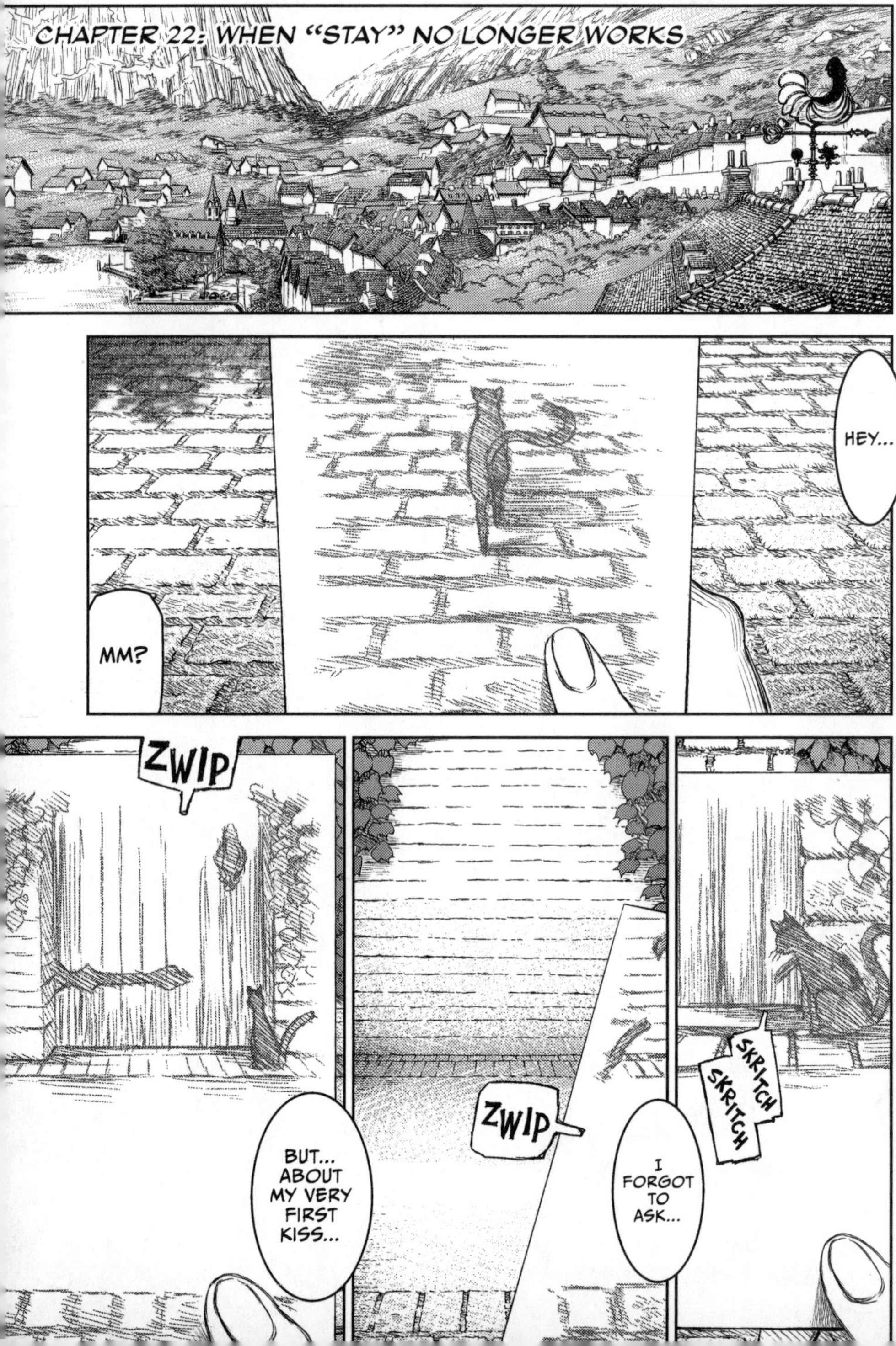
CHAPTER 22: WHEN "STAY" NO LONGER WORKS
HEY...
MM?
SKRITCH SKRITCH
I FORGOT TO ASK...
ZWIP
ZWIP
BUT... ABOUT MY VERY FIRST KISS...

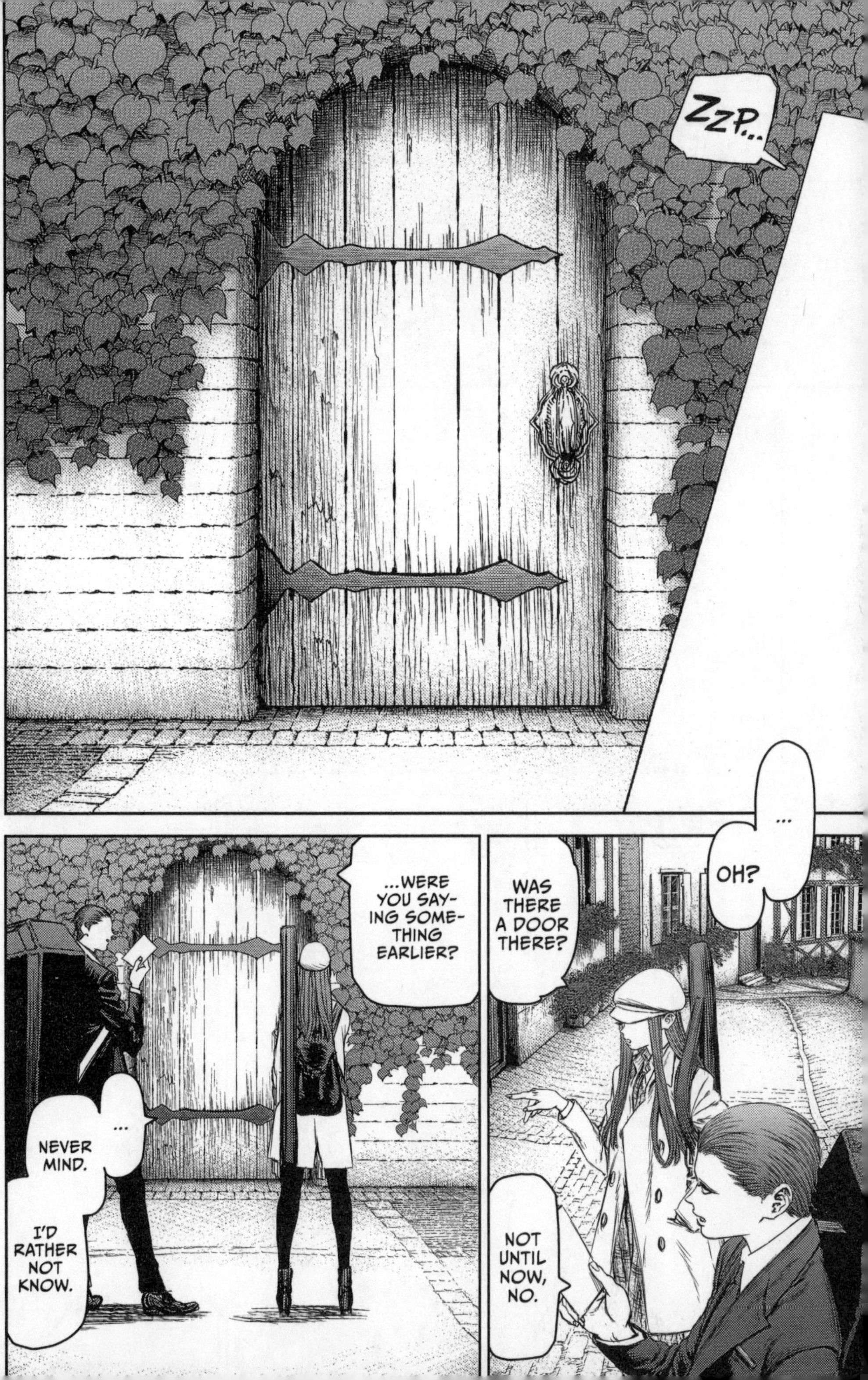
ZZP...
...
OH?
WAS THERE A DOOR THERE?
NOT UNTIL NOW, NO.
...WERE YOU SAYING SOMETHING EARLIER?
...
NEVER MIND.
I'D RATHER NOT KNOW.

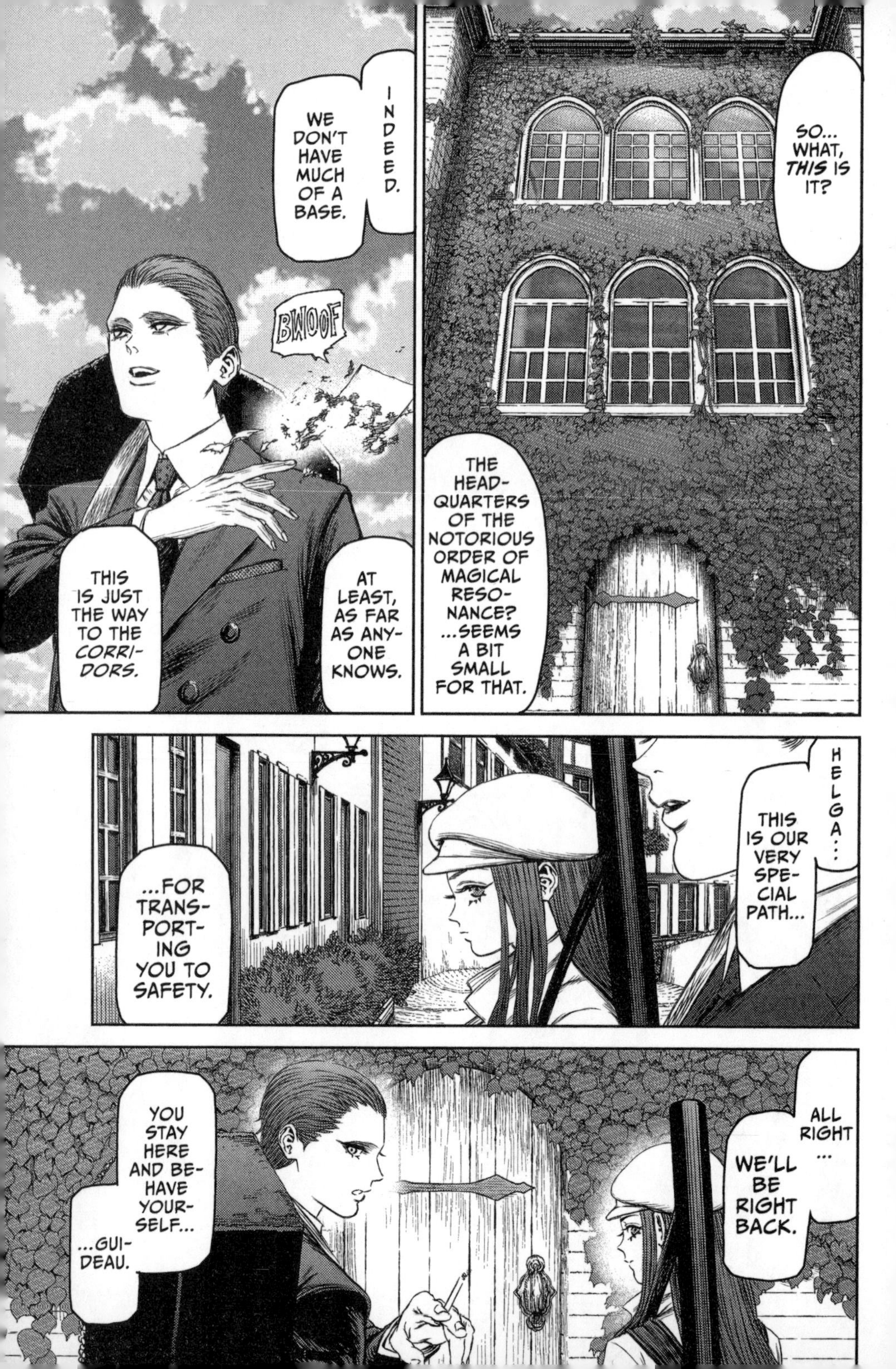
SO... WHAT, *THIS* IS IT?
THE HEAD-QUARTERS OF THE NOTORIOUS ORDER OF MAGICAL RESO-NANCE? ...SEEMS A BIT SMALL FOR THAT.
INDEED.
WE DON'T HAVE MUCH OF A BASE.
BWOOF
AT LEAST, AS FAR AS ANY-ONE KNOWS.
THIS IS JUST THE WAY TO THE *CORRI-DORS.*
HELGA...
THIS IS OUR VERY SPE-CIAL PATH...
...FOR TRANS-PORT-ING YOU TO SAFETY.
ALL RIGHT...
WE'LL BE RIGHT BACK.
YOU STAY HERE AND BE-HAVE YOUR-SELF...
...GUI-DEAU.

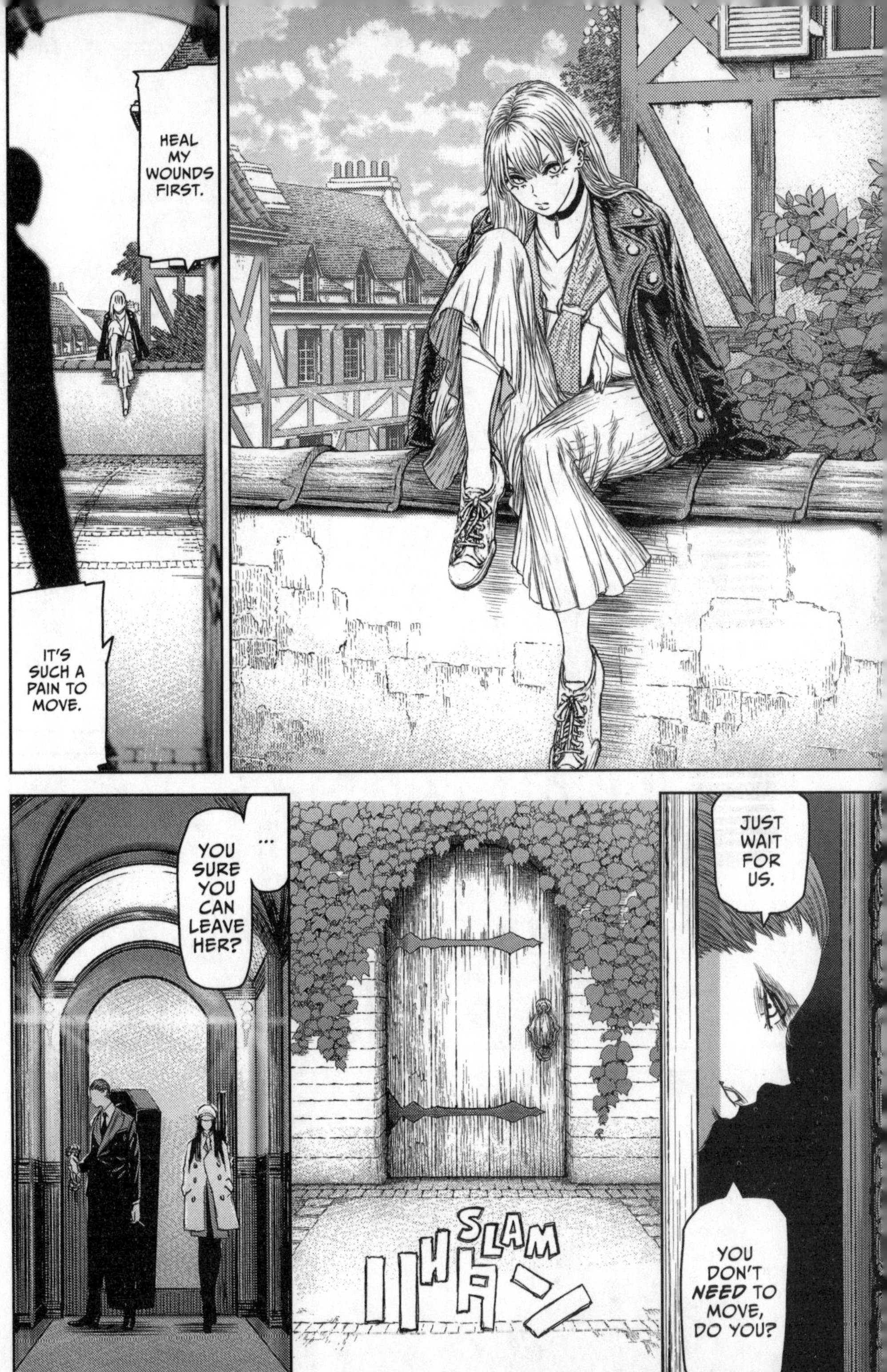
HEAL MY WOUNDS FIRST.
IT'S SUCH A PAIN TO MOVE.
JUST WAIT FOR US.
YOU DON'T *NEED* TO MOVE, DO YOU?
SLAM
...
YOU SURE YOU CAN LEAVE HER?

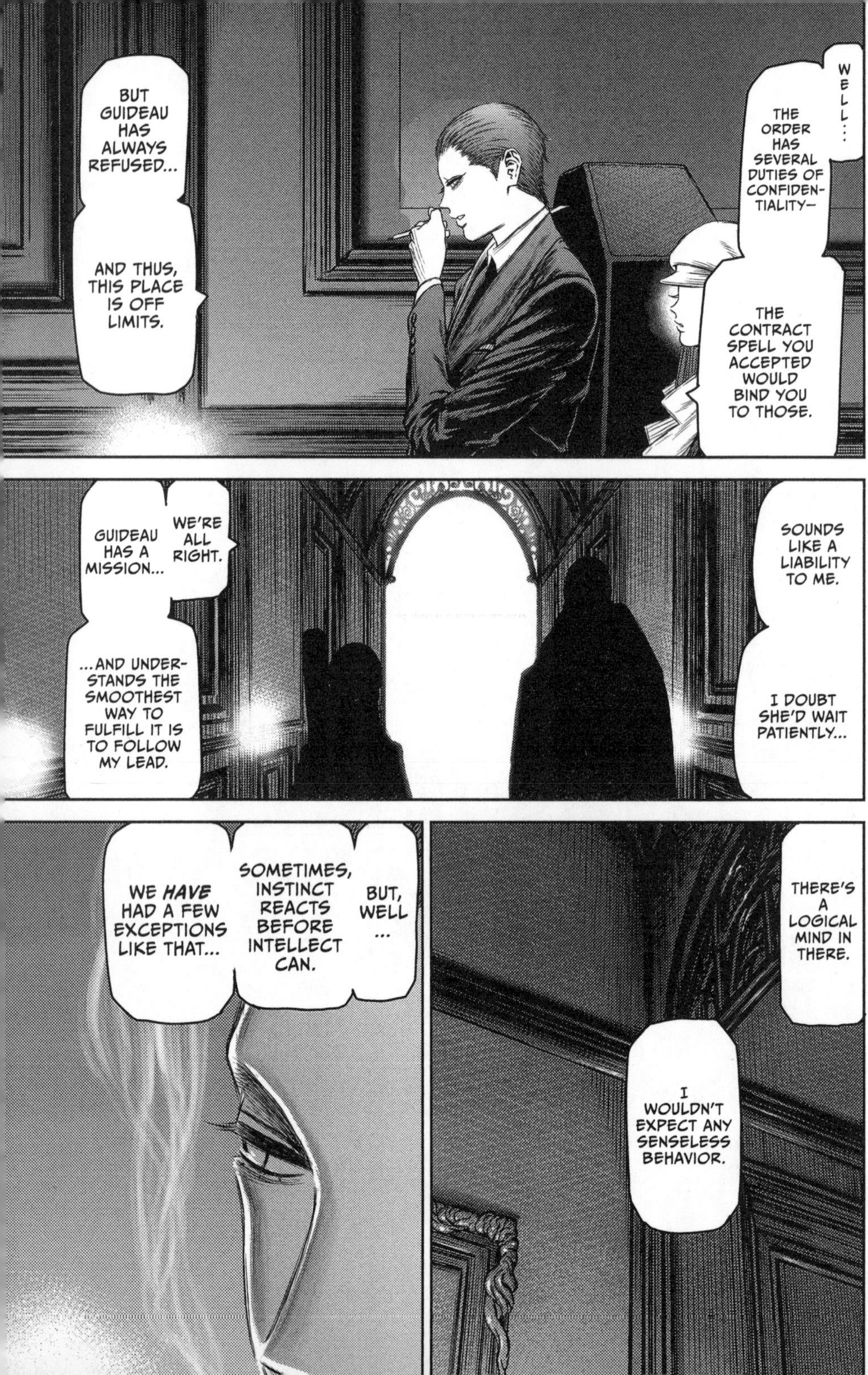
WELL...
THE ORDER HAS SEVERAL DUTIES OF CONFIDENTIALITY—
THE CONTRACT SPELL YOU ACCEPTED WOULD BIND YOU TO THOSE.
BUT GUIDEAU HAS ALWAYS REFUSED...
AND THUS, THIS PLACE IS OFF LIMITS.
SOUNDS LIKE A LIABILITY TO ME.
I DOUBT SHE'D WAIT PATIENTLY...
WE'RE ALL RIGHT.
GUIDEAU HAS A MISSION...
...AND UNDERSTANDS THE SMOOTHEST WAY TO FULFILL IT IS TO FOLLOW MY LEAD.
THERE'S A LOGICAL MIND IN THERE.
I WOULDN'T EXPECT ANY SENSELESS BEHAVIOR.
BUT, WELL...
SOMETIMES, INSTINCT REACTS BEFORE INTELLECT CAN.
WE *HAVE* HAD A FEW EXCEPTIONS LIKE THAT...

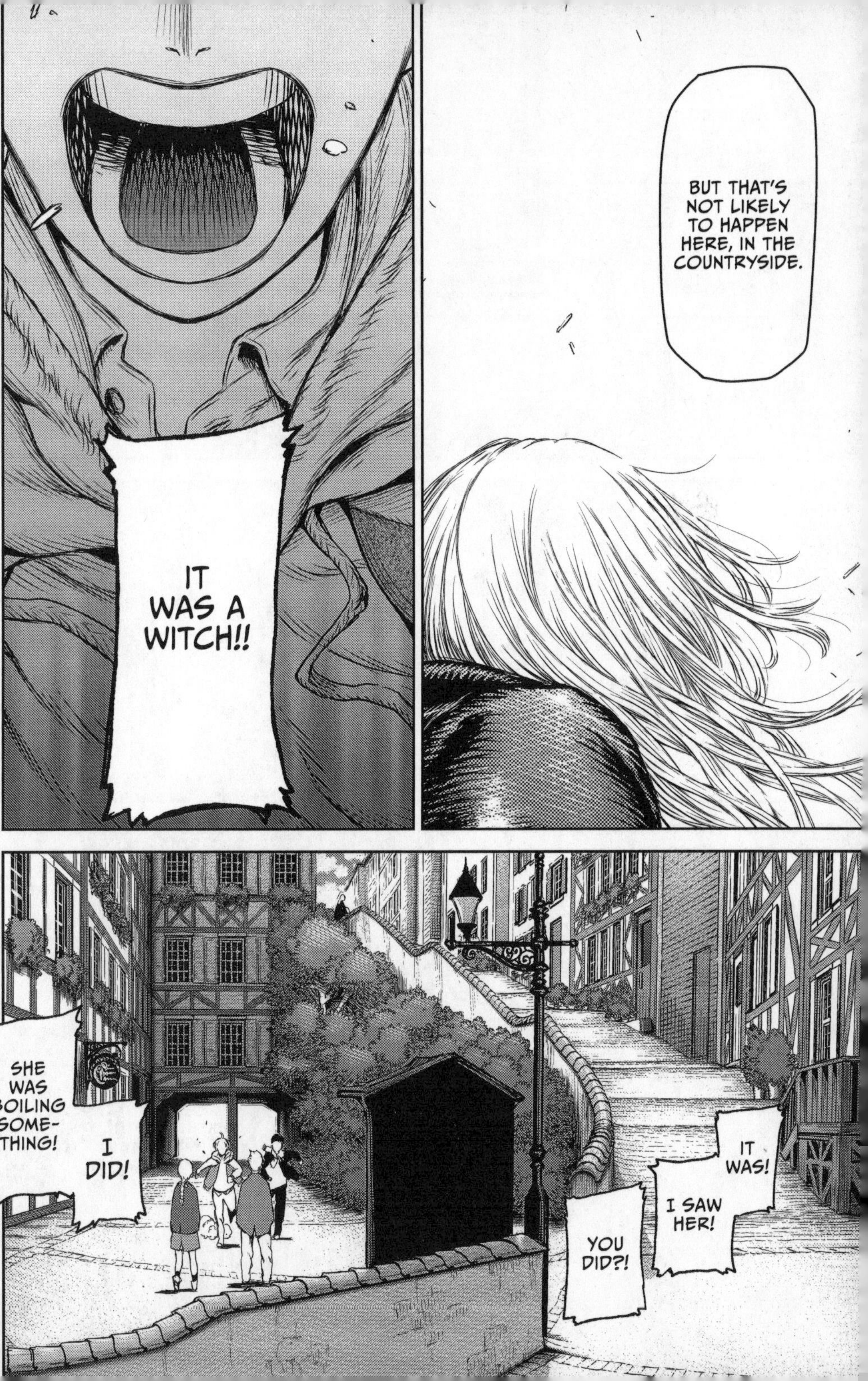
BUT THAT'S NOT LIKELY TO HAPPEN HERE, IN THE COUNTRYSIDE.
IT WAS A WITCH!!
IT WAS!
I SAW HER!
YOU DID?!
I DID!
SHE WAS BOILING SOME-THING!

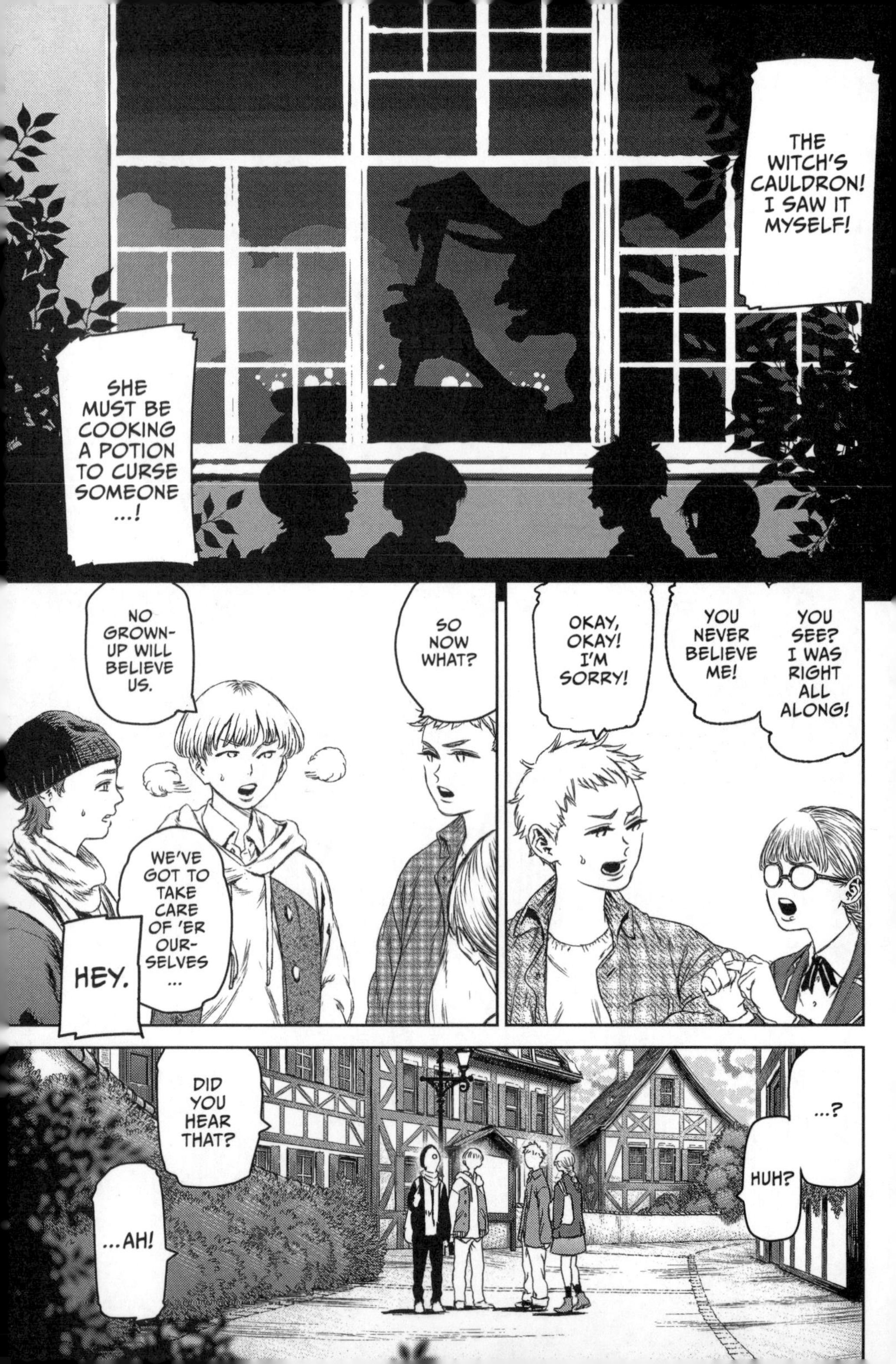
THE WITCH'S CAULDRON! I SAW IT MYSELF!
SHE MUST BE COOKING A POTION TO CURSE SOMEONE ...!
YOU SEE? I WAS RIGHT ALL ALONG!
YOU NEVER BELIEVE ME!
OKAY, OKAY! I'M SORRY!
SO NOW WHAT?
NO GROWN-UP WILL BELIEVE US.
WE'VE GOT TO TAKE CARE OF 'ER OUR-SELVES ...
HEY.
...?
HUH?
DID YOU HEAR THAT?
...AH!

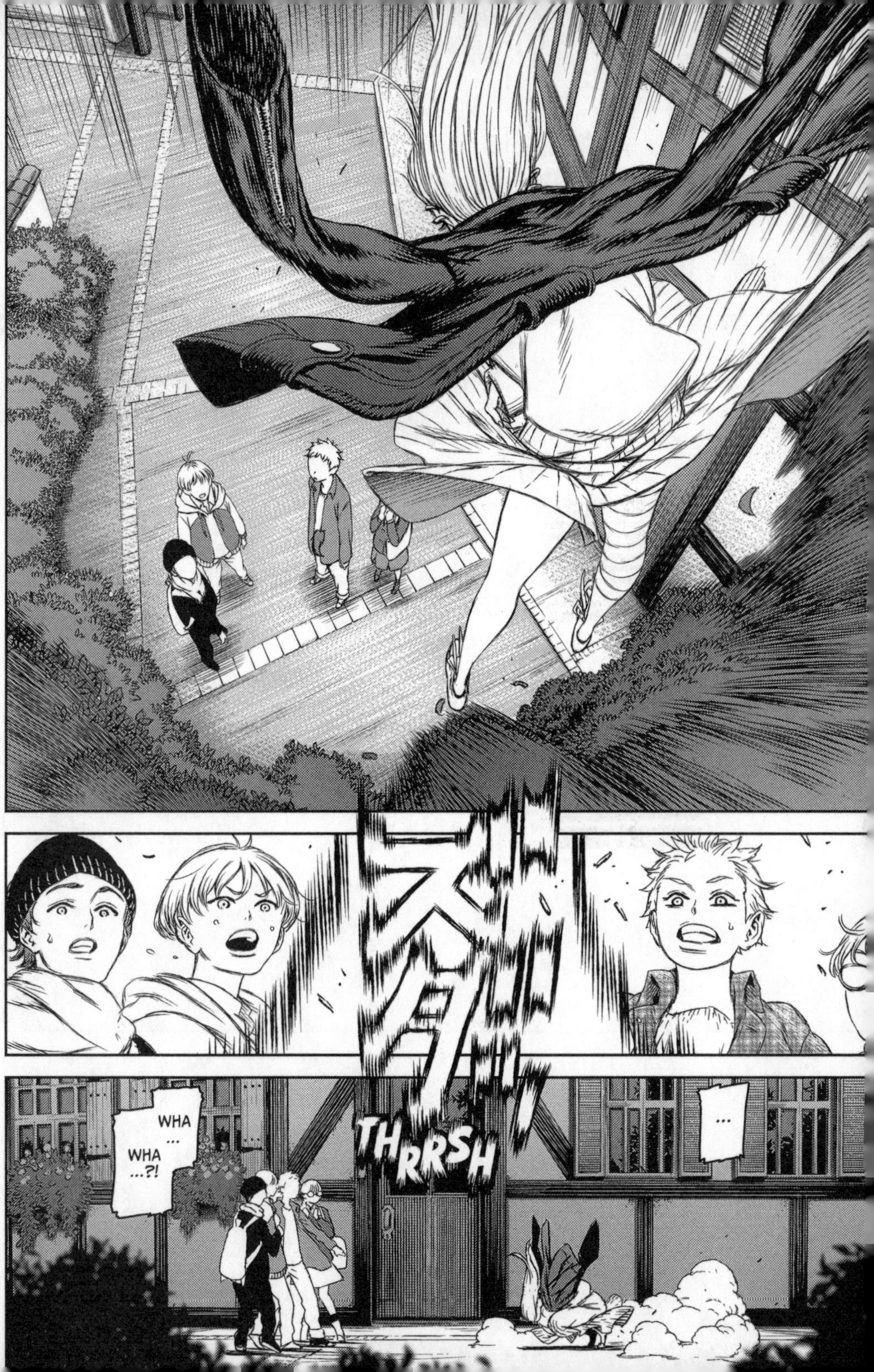
...
THRRSH
WHA ... WHA ...?!

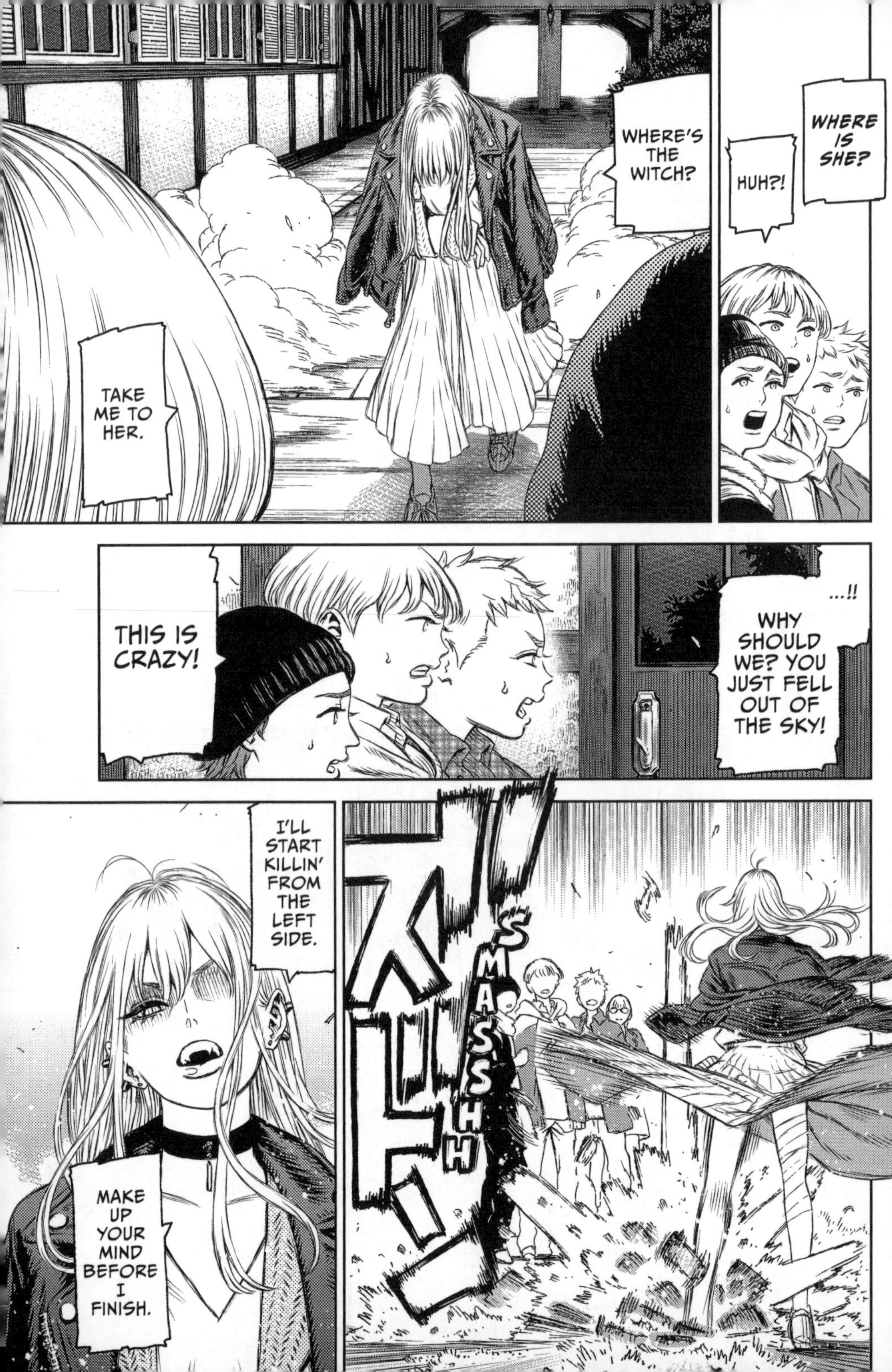
WHERE IS SHE?
HUH?!
WHERE'S THE WITCH?
TAKE ME TO HER.
...!!
WHY SHOULD WE? YOU JUST FELL OUT OF THE SKY!
THIS IS CRAZY!
SMASSHH
I'LL START KILLIN' FROM THE LEFT SIDE.
MAKE UP YOUR MIND BEFORE I FINISH.

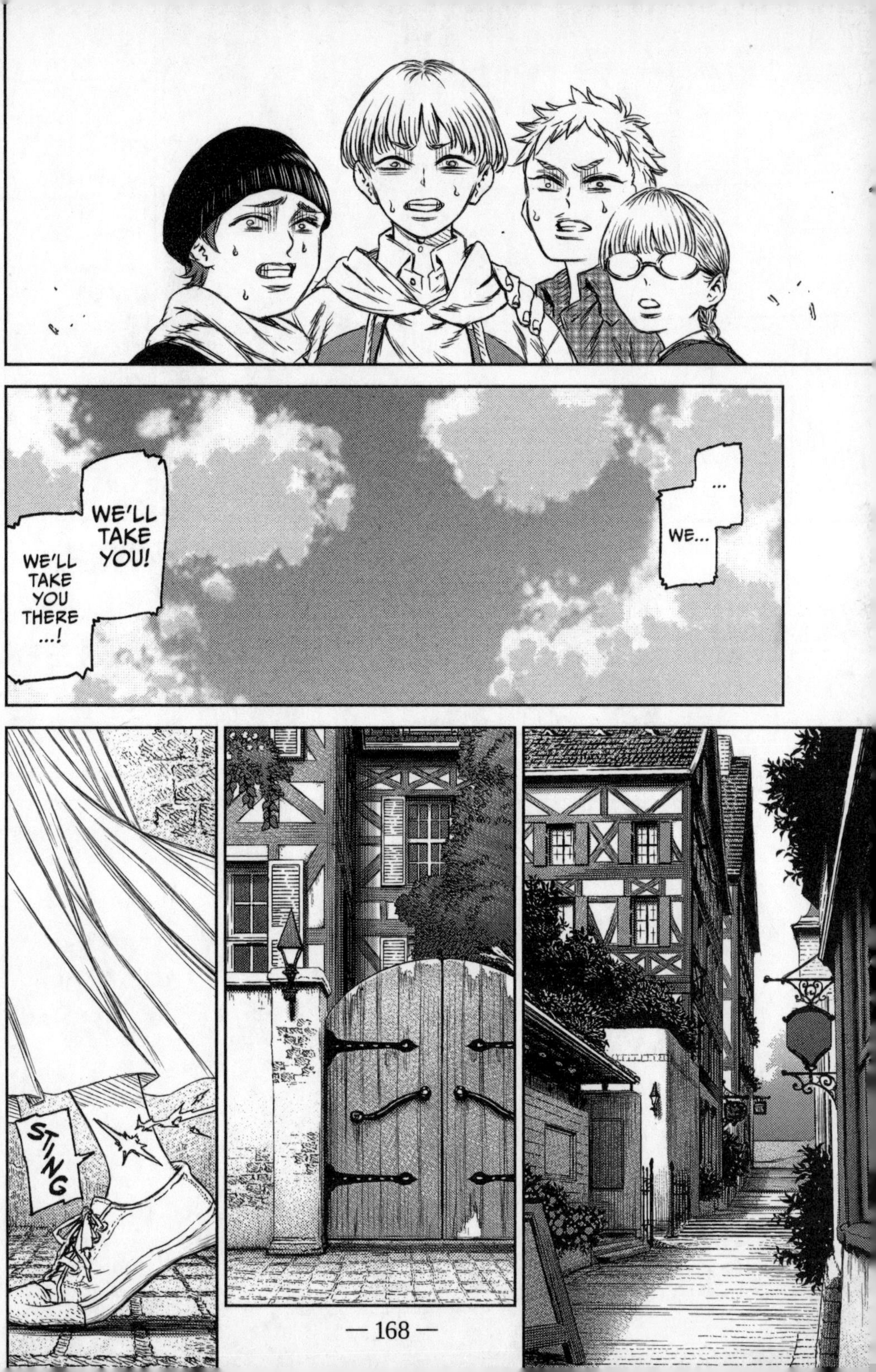

...
WE...
WE'LL TAKE YOU!
WE'LL TAKE YOU THERE ...!
STING

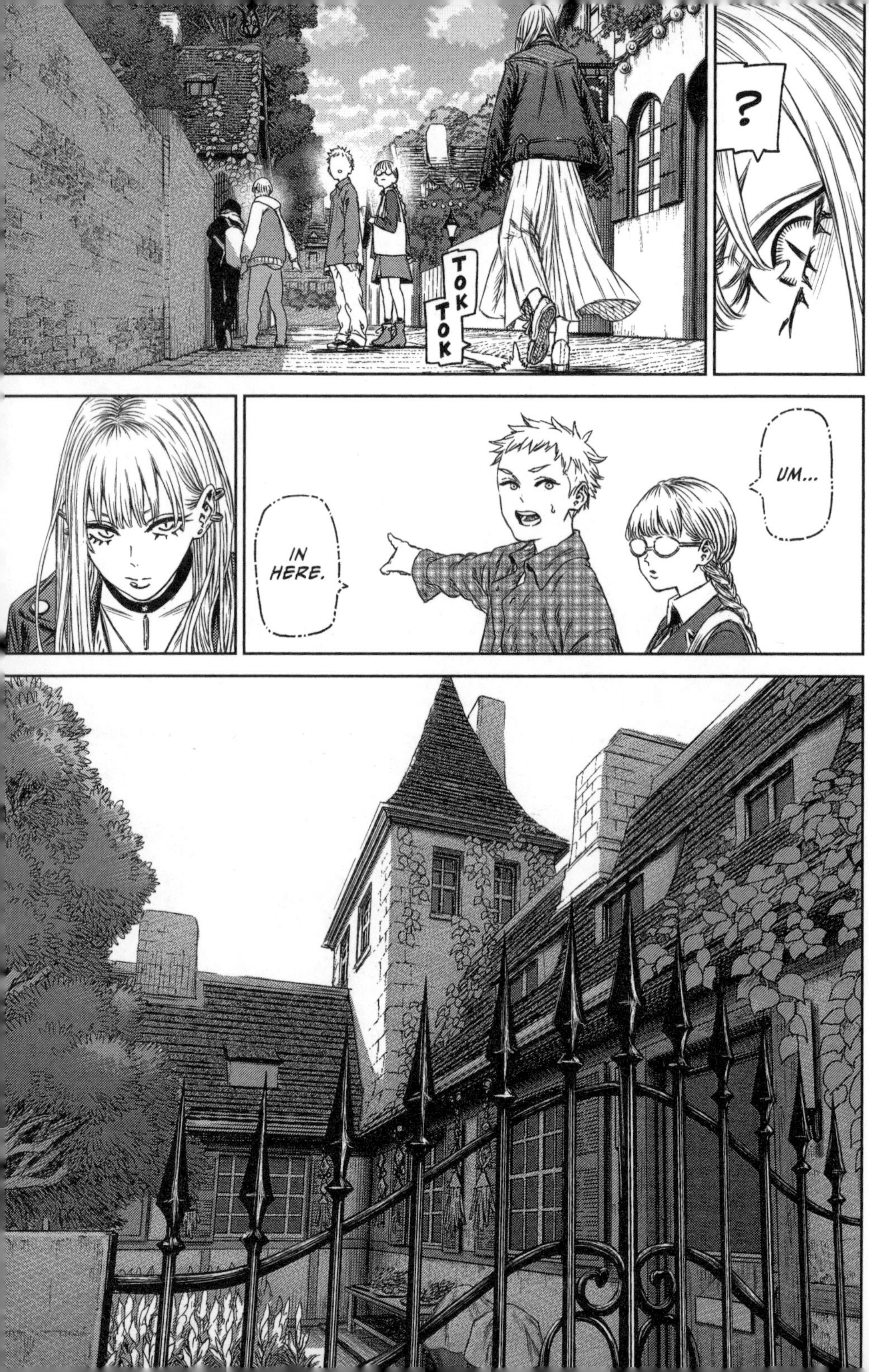
?
TOK TOK
UM...
IN HERE.

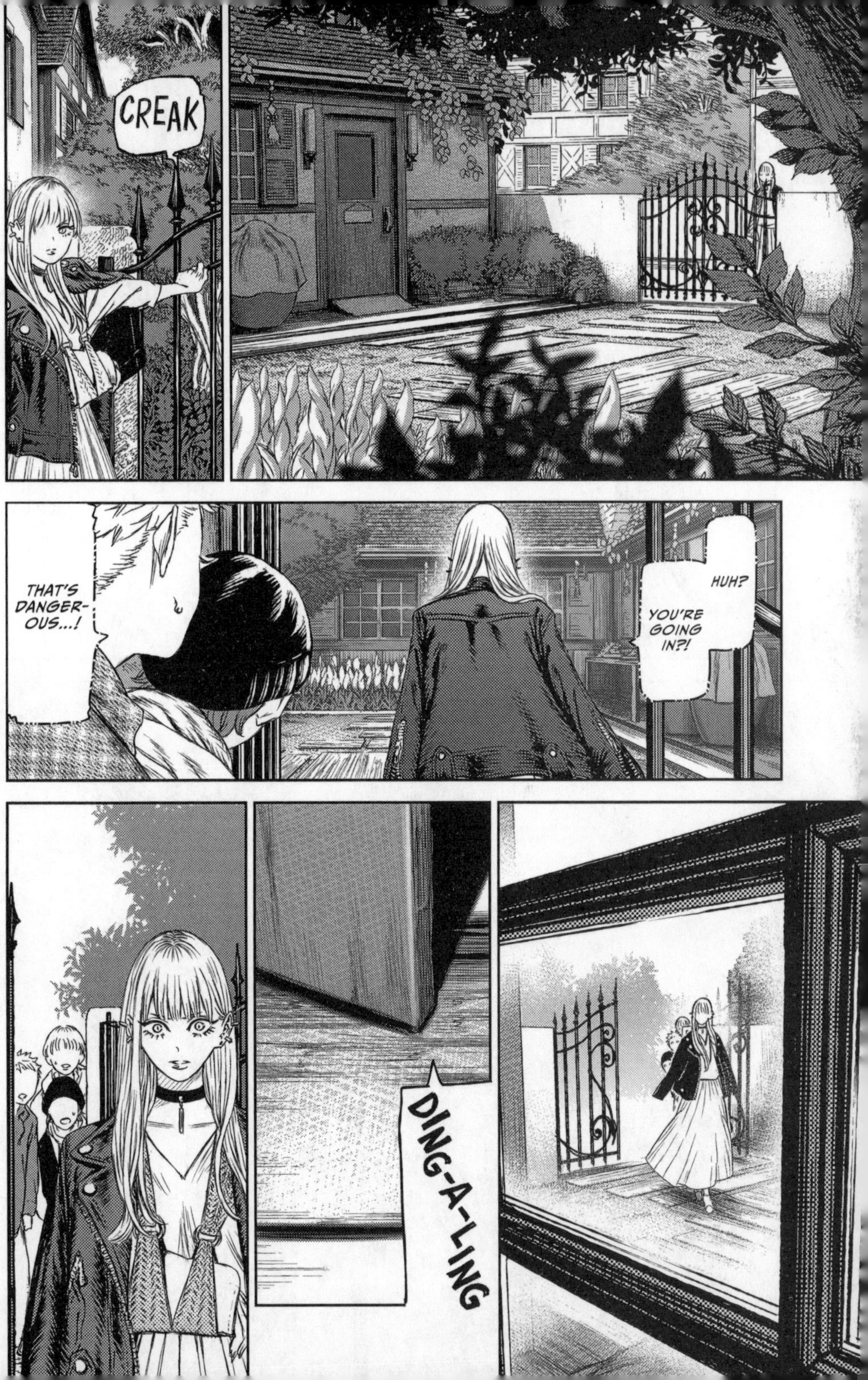
CREAK
HUH?
YOU'RE GOING IN?!
THAT'S DANGER-OUS...!
DING-A-LING

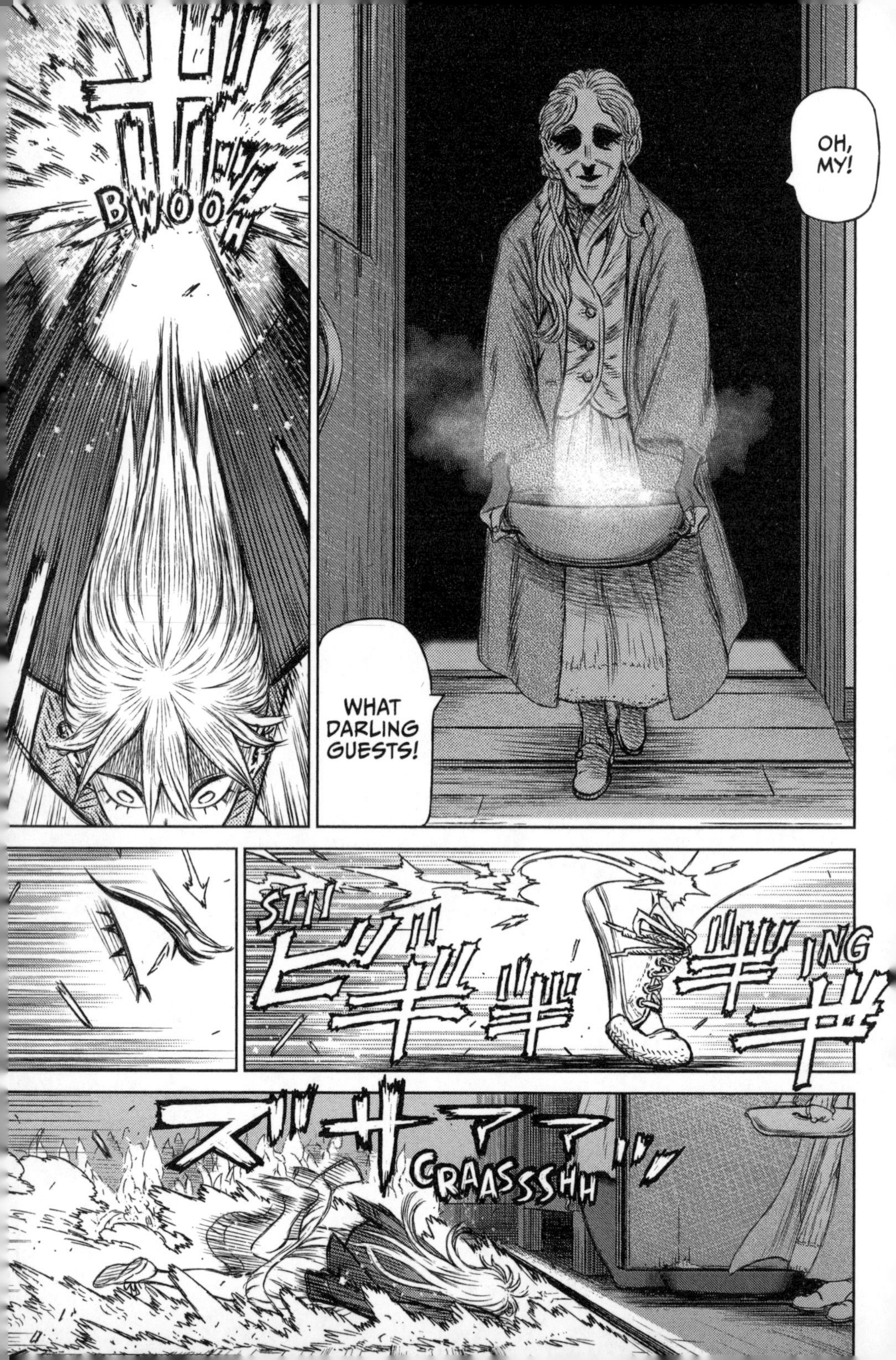
OH, MY!
WHAT DARLING GUESTS!
BWOOH
STIIING
CRAASSSHH

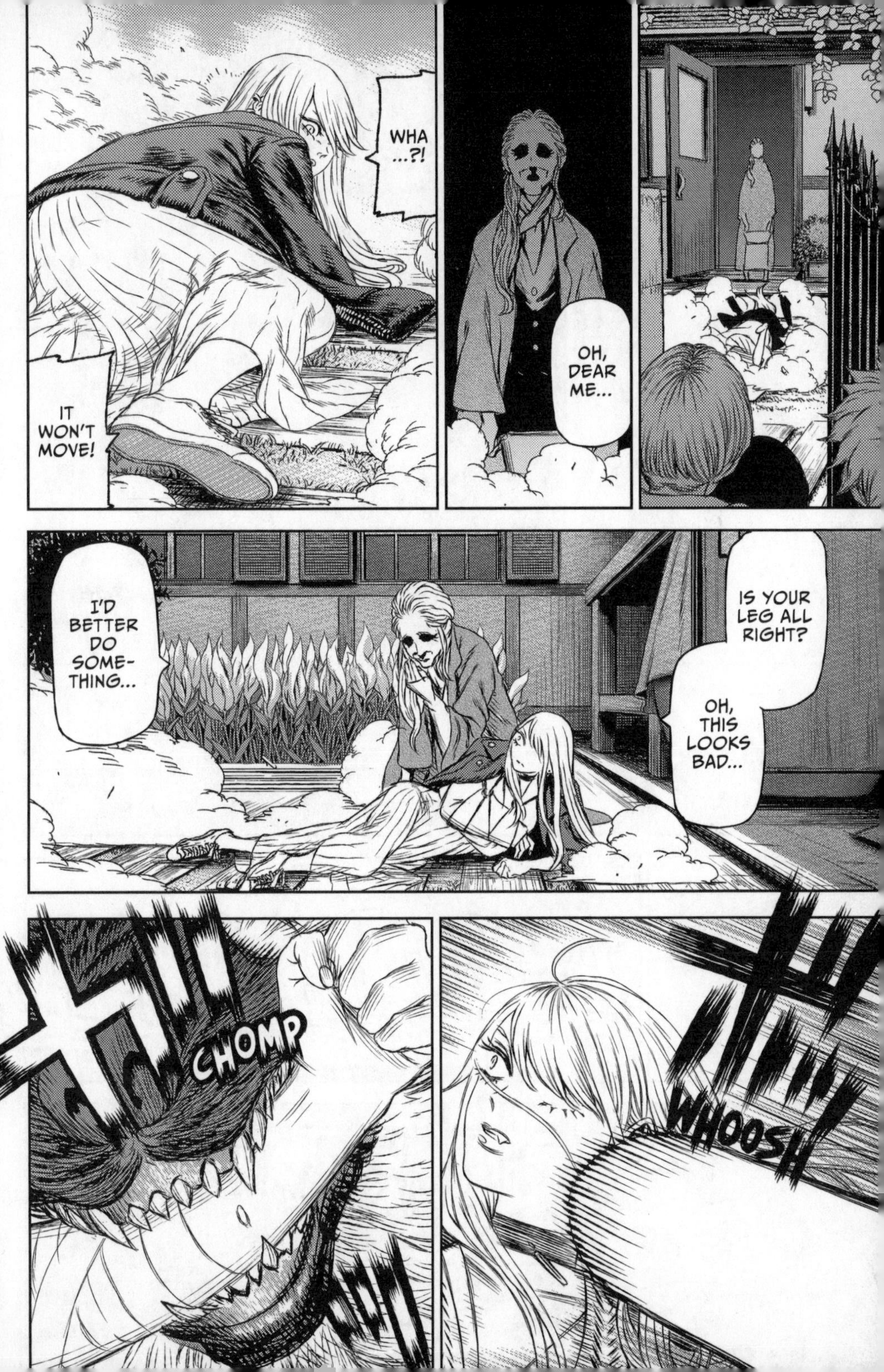
OH, DEAR ME...
WHA ...?!
IT WON'T MOVE!
IS YOUR LEG ALL RIGHT?
OH, THIS LOOKS BAD...
I'D BETTER DO SOME-THING...
WHOOSH
CHOMP

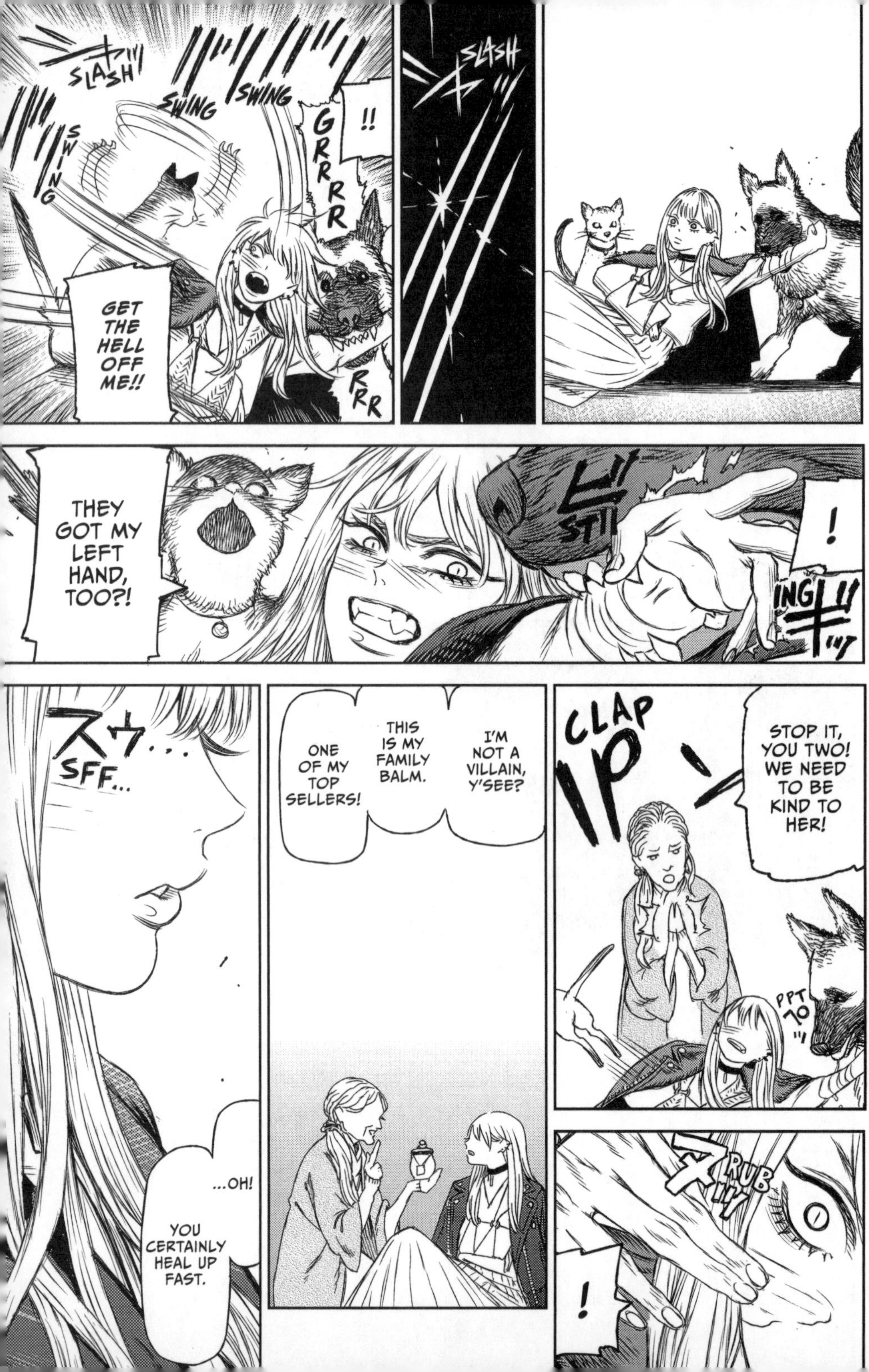
SLASH
SLASH
SWING
SWING
SWING
GRRRR
!!
GET THE HELL OFF ME!!
RRR
!
ING!!
STI
THEY GOT MY LEFT HAND, TOO?!
CLAP
STOP IT, YOU TWO! WE NEED TO BE KIND TO HER!
PPT
RUB
!
I'M NOT A VILLAIN, Y'SEE?
THIS IS MY FAMILY BALM.
ONE OF MY TOP SELLERS!
スゥ...
SFF...
...OH!
YOU CERTAINLY HEAL UP FAST.

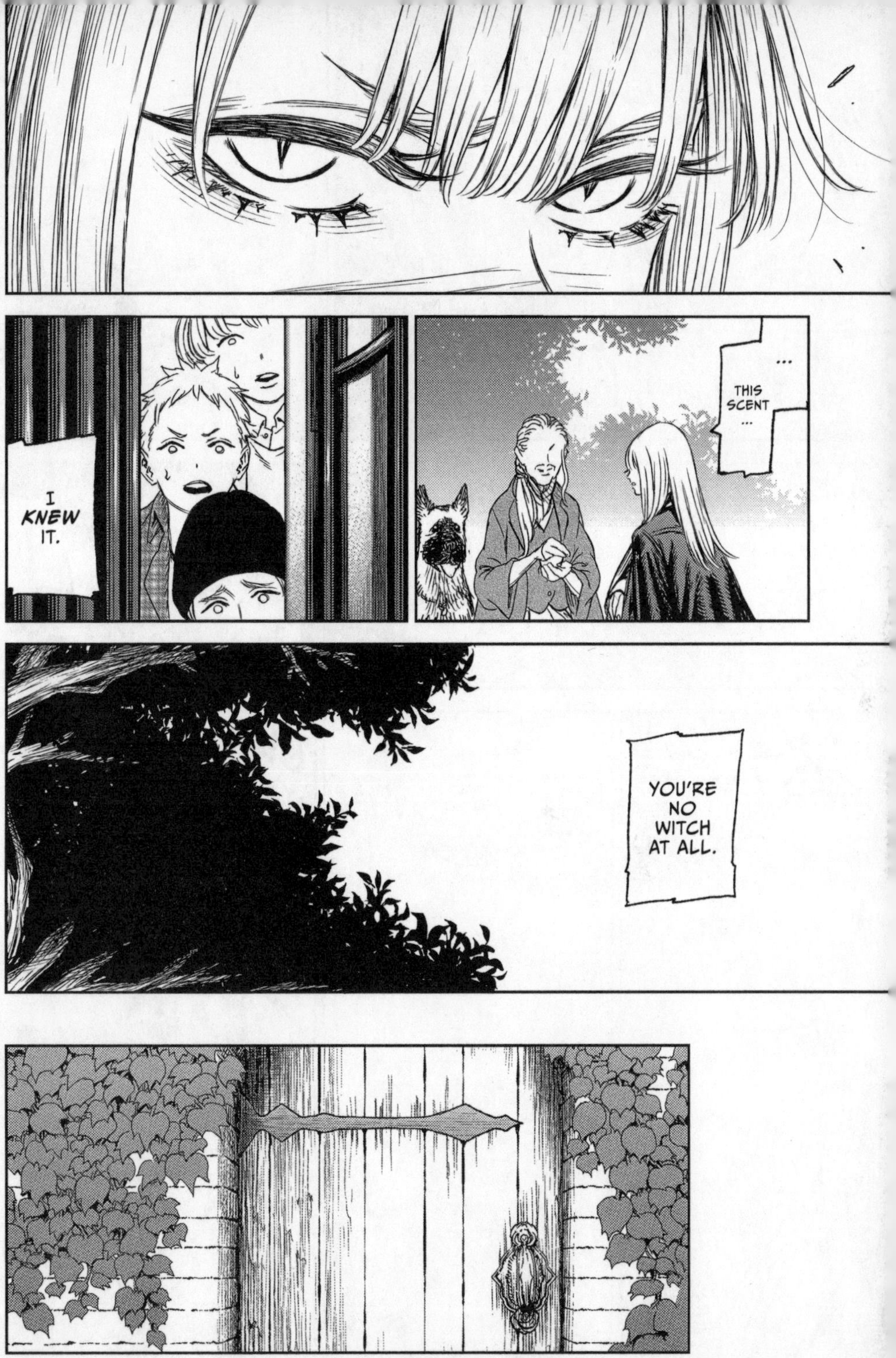
... THIS SCENT ...
I KNEW IT.
YOU'RE NO WITCH AT ALL.

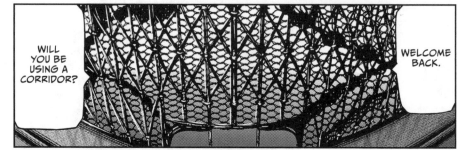

WELCOME
BACK.

WILL
YOU BE
USING A
CORRIDOR?

YES,
WE'D
LIKE
ACCESS,
PLEASE.

WHERE
DO
THESE
ONES
HERE
LEAD
TO?

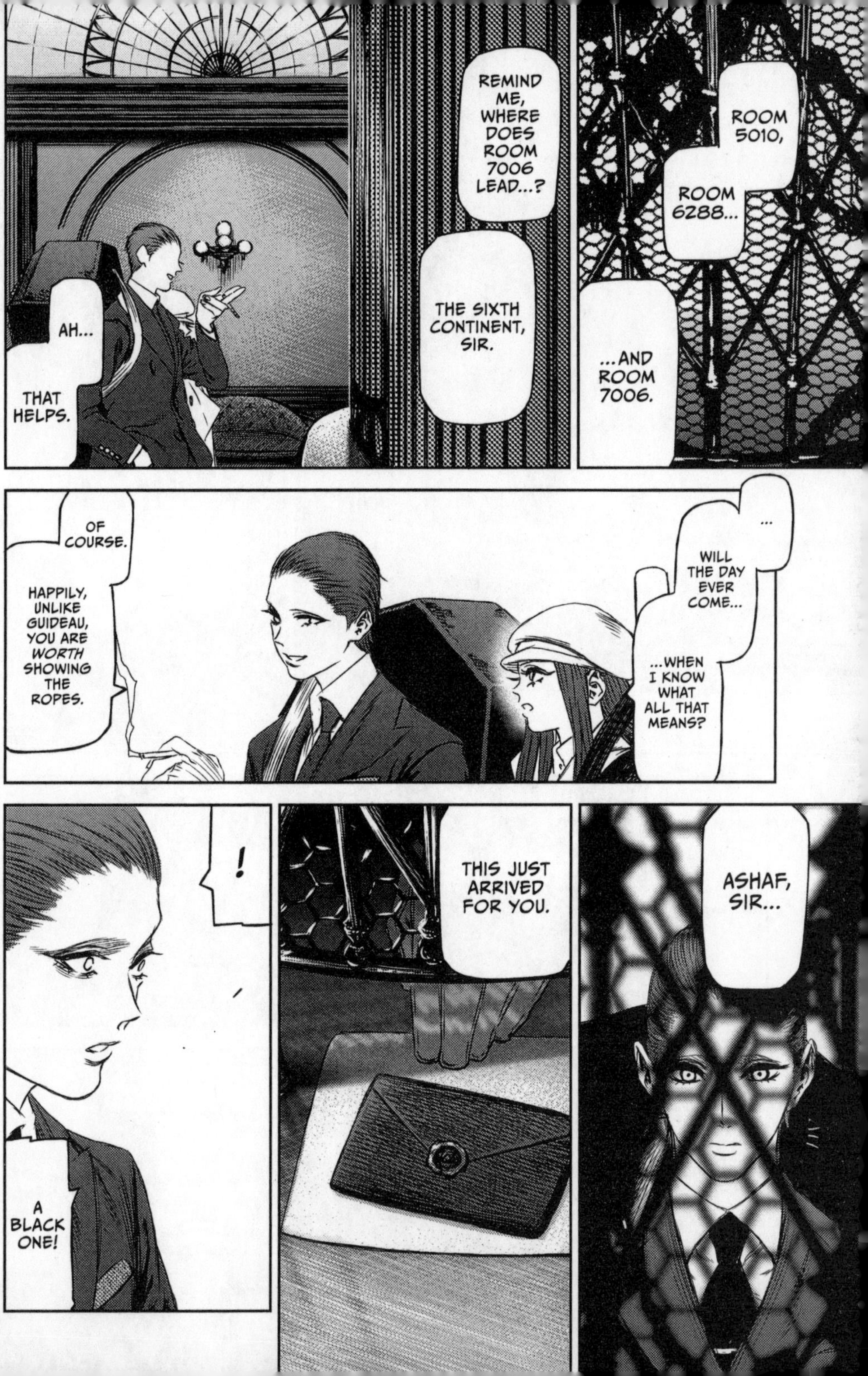
ROOM 5010,
ROOM 6288...
...AND ROOM 7006.
REMIND ME, WHERE DOES ROOM 7006 LEAD...?
THE SIXTH CONTINENT, SIR.
AH...
THAT HELPS.
...
WILL THE DAY EVER COME...
...WHEN I KNOW WHAT ALL THAT MEANS?
OF COURSE.
HAPPILY, UNLIKE GUIDEAU, YOU ARE *WORTH* SHOWING THE ROPES.
ASHAF, SIR...
THIS JUST ARRIVED FOR YOU.
!
A BLACK ONE!

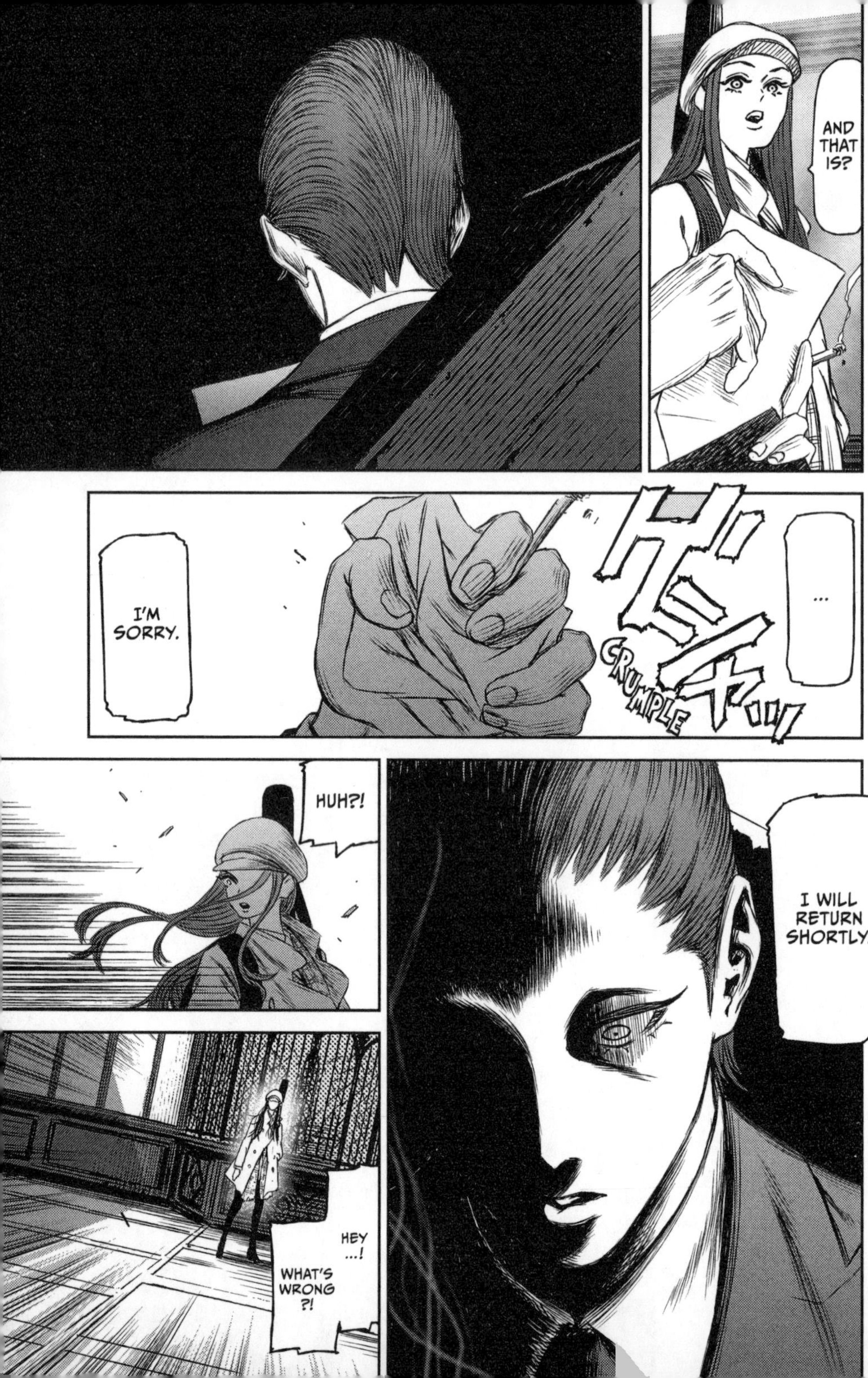
AND THAT IS?
...
CRUMPLE
I'M SORRY.
I WILL RETURN SHORTLY.
HUH?!
HEY ...!
WHAT'S WRONG ?!

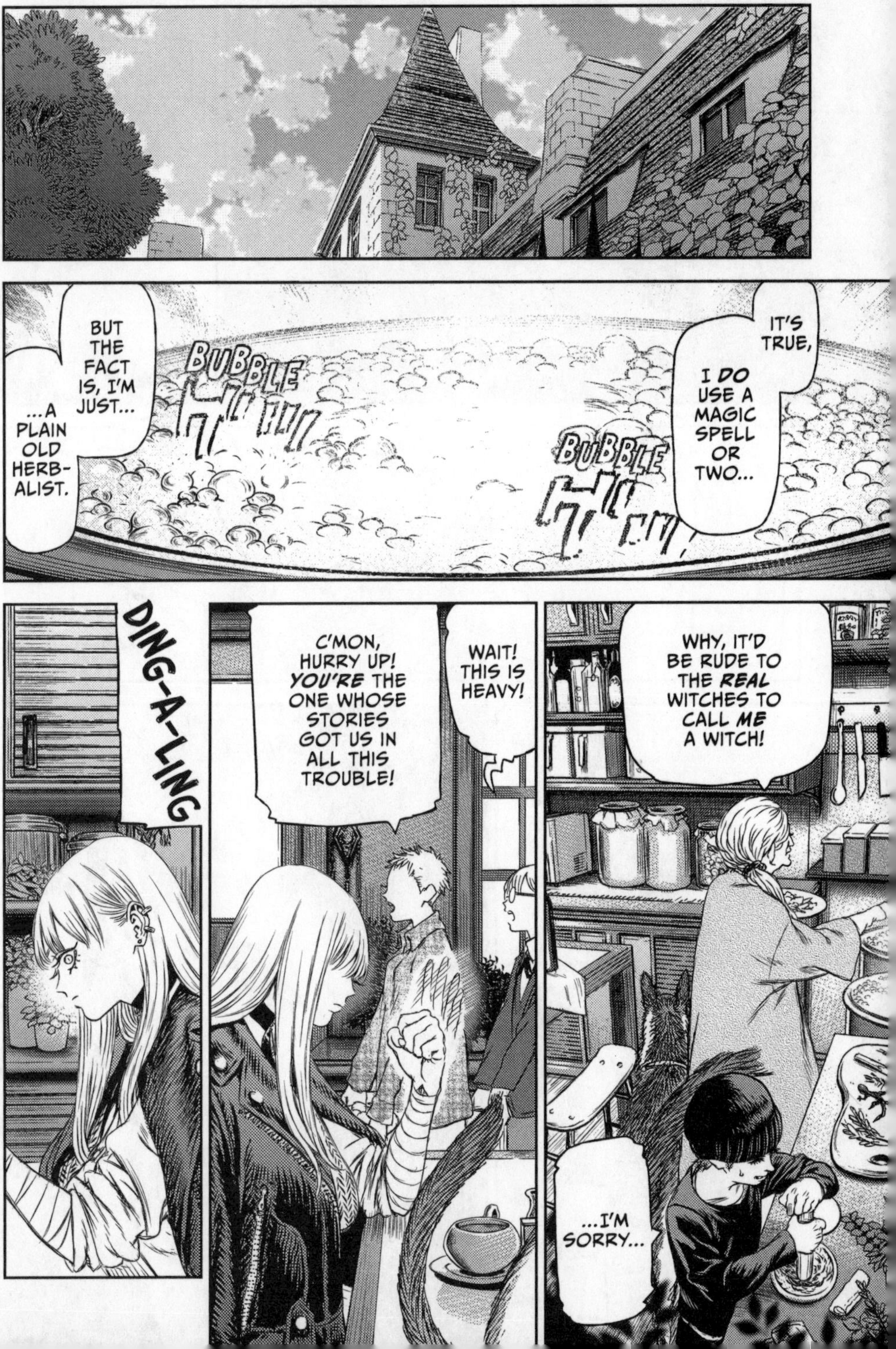
IT'S TRUE,
I *DO* USE A MAGIC SPELL OR TWO...
BUBBLE
BUBBLE
BUT THE FACT IS, I'M JUST...
...A PLAIN OLD HERBALIST.
WHY, IT'D BE RUDE TO THE *REAL* WITCHES TO CALL *ME* A WITCH!
...I'M SORRY...
WAIT! THIS IS HEAVY!
C'MON, HURRY UP! *YOU'RE* THE ONE WHOSE STORIES GOT US IN ALL THIS TROUBLE!
DING-A-LING

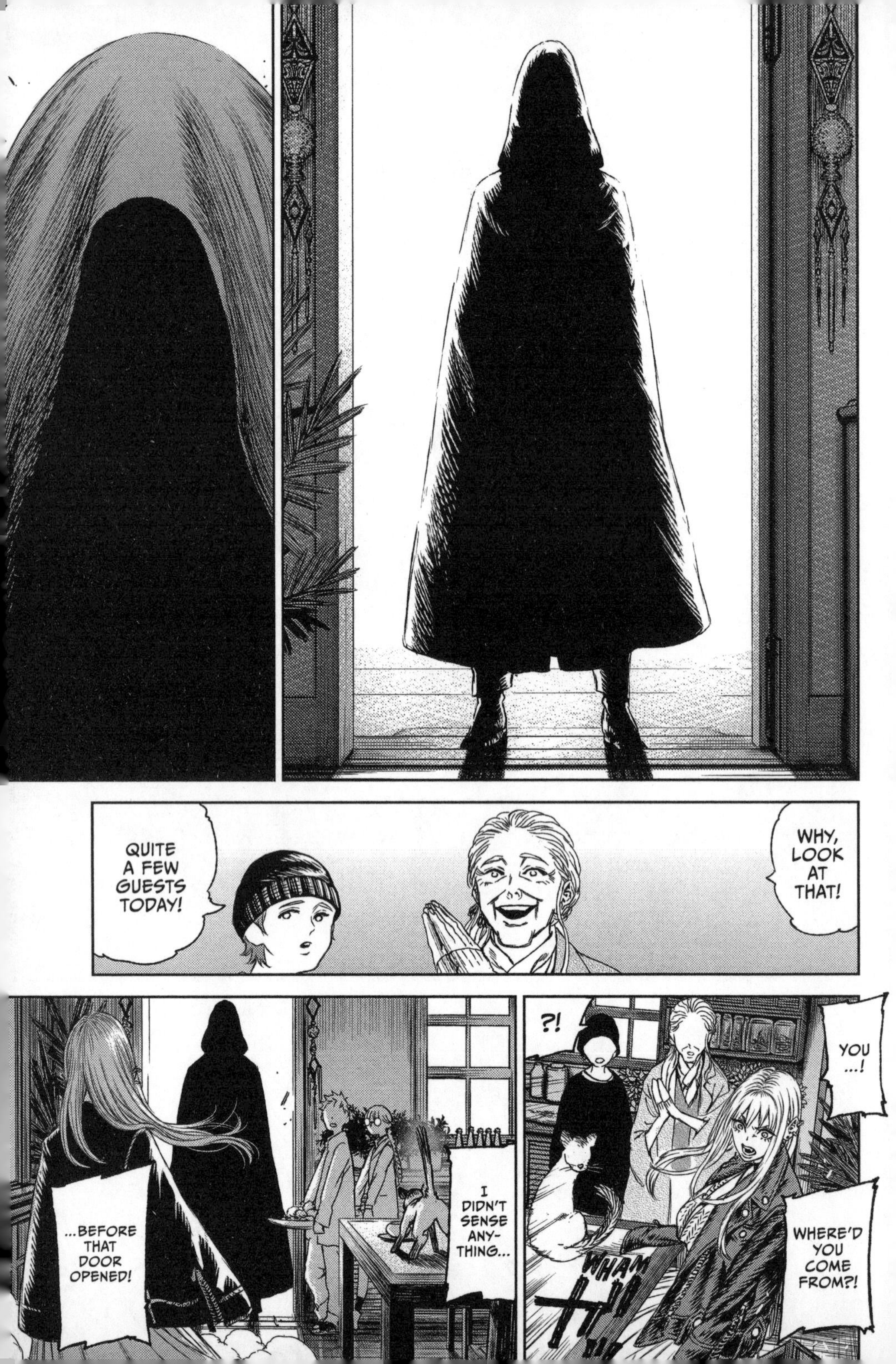
WHY, LOOK AT THAT!
QUITE A FEW GUESTS TODAY!
YOU ...!
?!
WHERE'D YOU COME FROM?!
WHAM
I DIDN'T SENSE ANYTHING...
...BEFORE THAT DOOR OPENED!

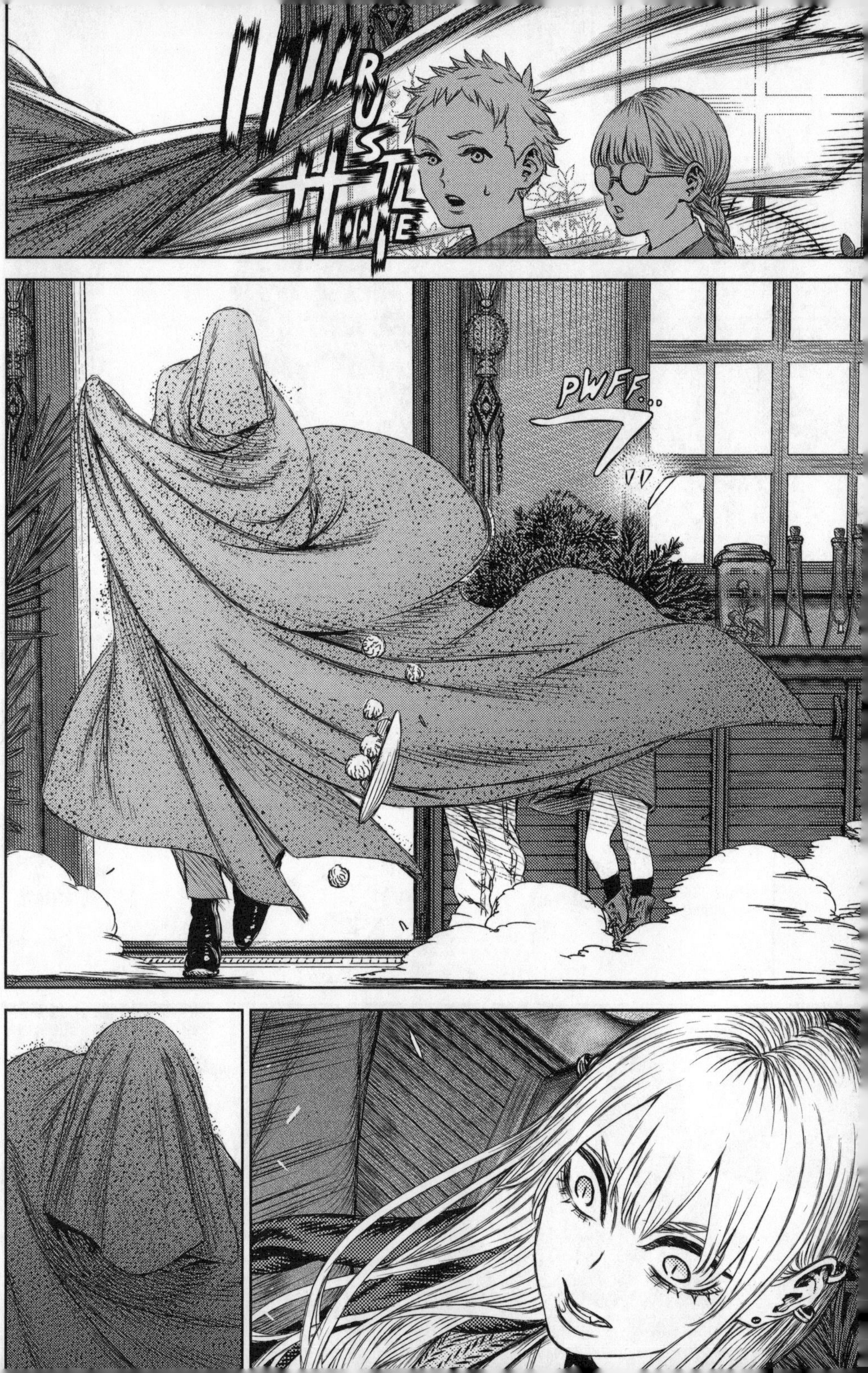
RUSTLE
PWFF...

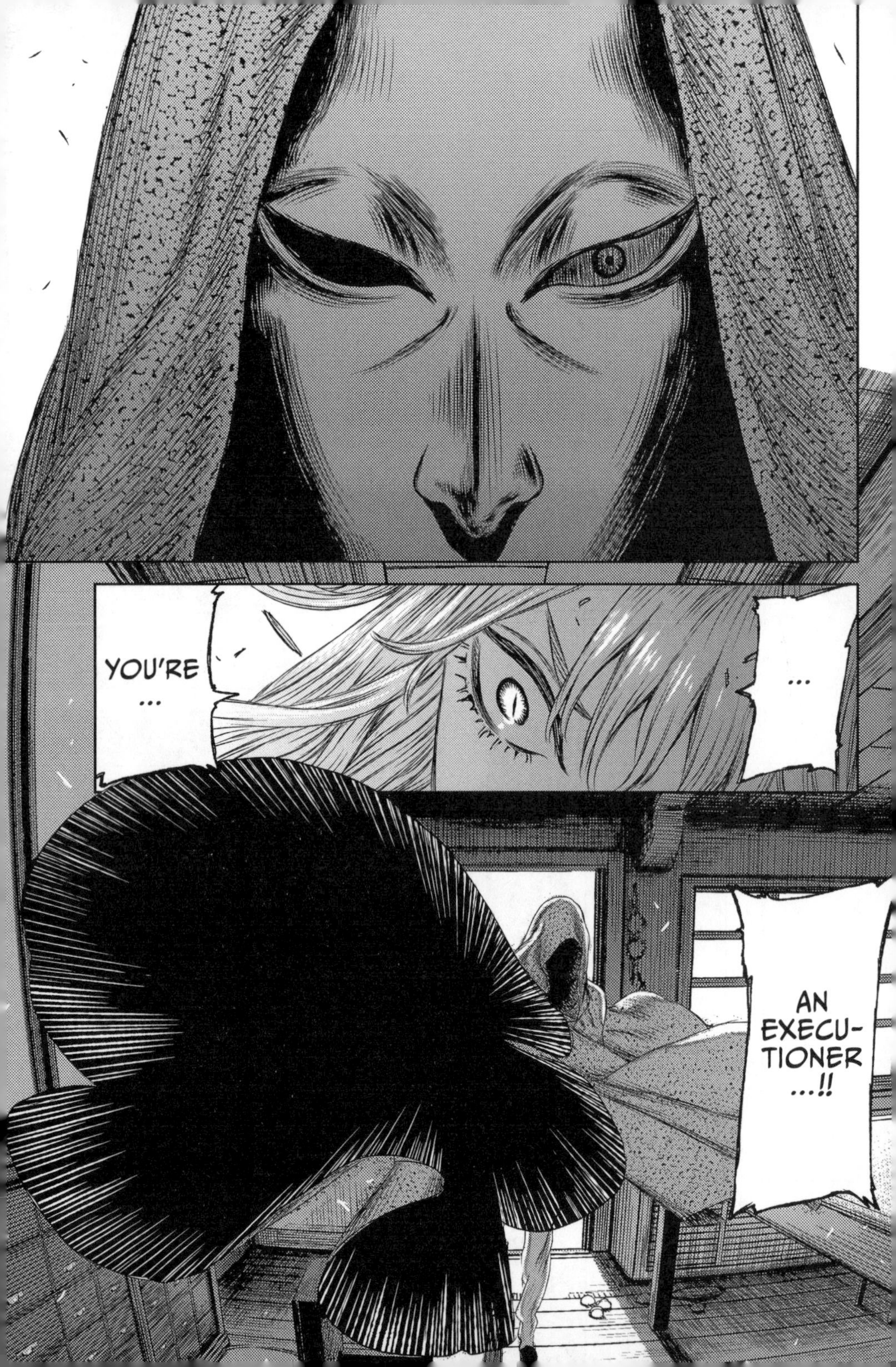
...
YOU'RE ...
AN EXECU- TIONER ...!!

ARF!
ARF!
ARF!
ARF!
ARF!
ARF!
ARF!
ARF!
ARF!
ARF!
ARF!
ARF!

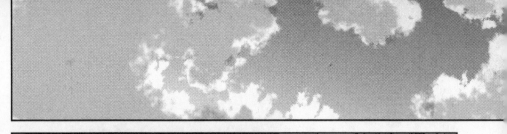

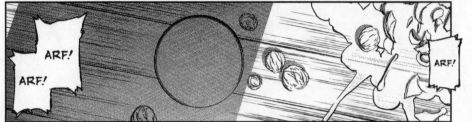

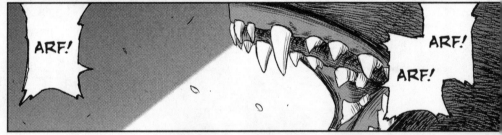

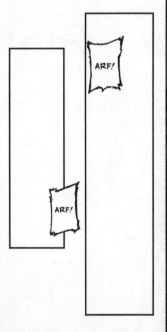

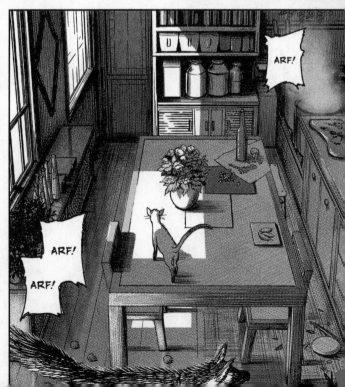

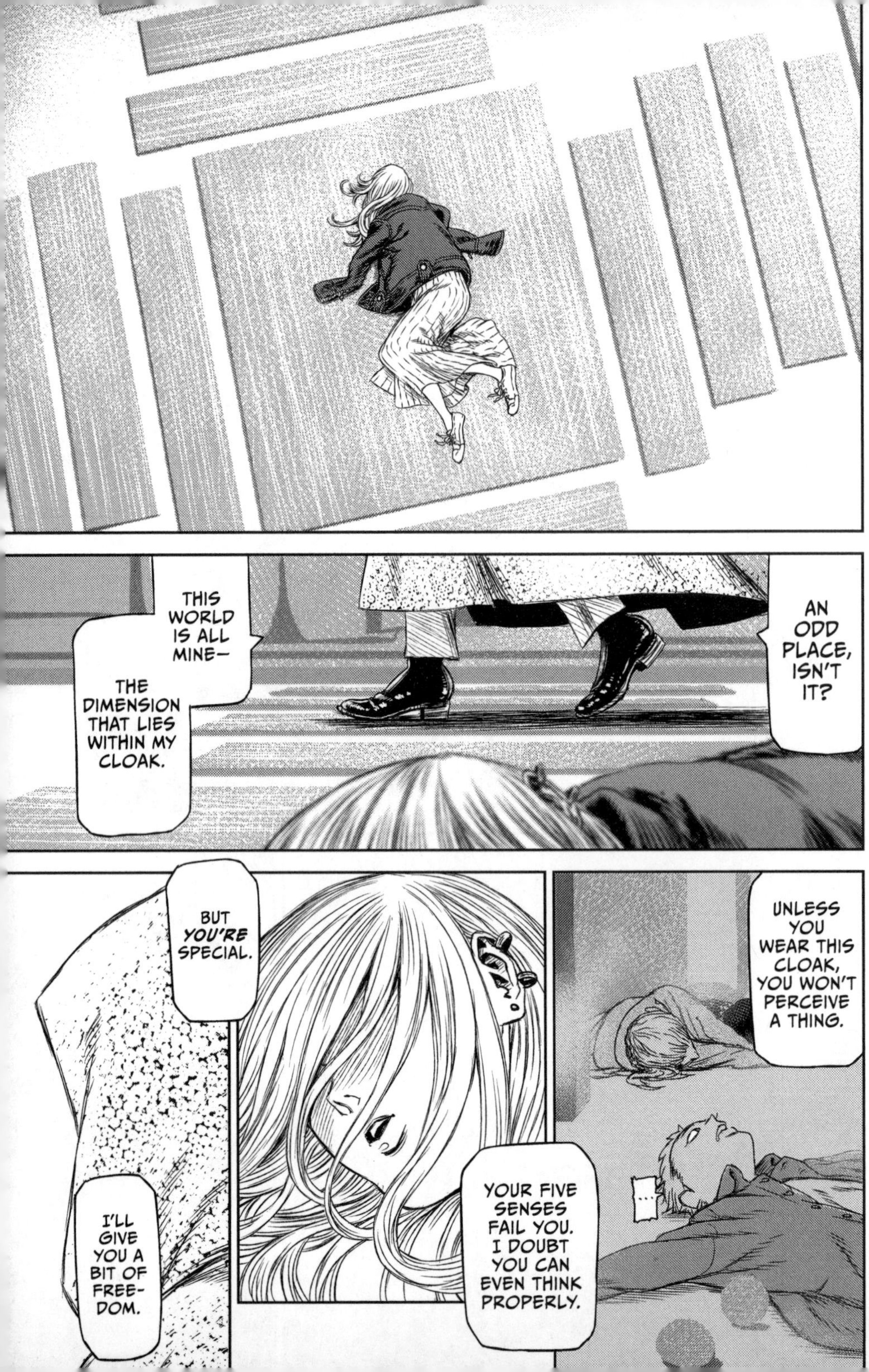

AN ODD PLACE, ISN'T IT?
THIS WORLD IS ALL MINE—
THE DIMENSION THAT LIES WITHIN MY CLOAK.
UNLESS YOU WEAR THIS CLOAK, YOU WON'T PERCEIVE A THING.
...
YOUR FIVE SENSES FAIL YOU. I DOUBT YOU CAN EVEN THINK PROPERLY.
BUT *YOU'RE* SPECIAL.
I'LL GIVE YOU A BIT OF FREE-DOM.

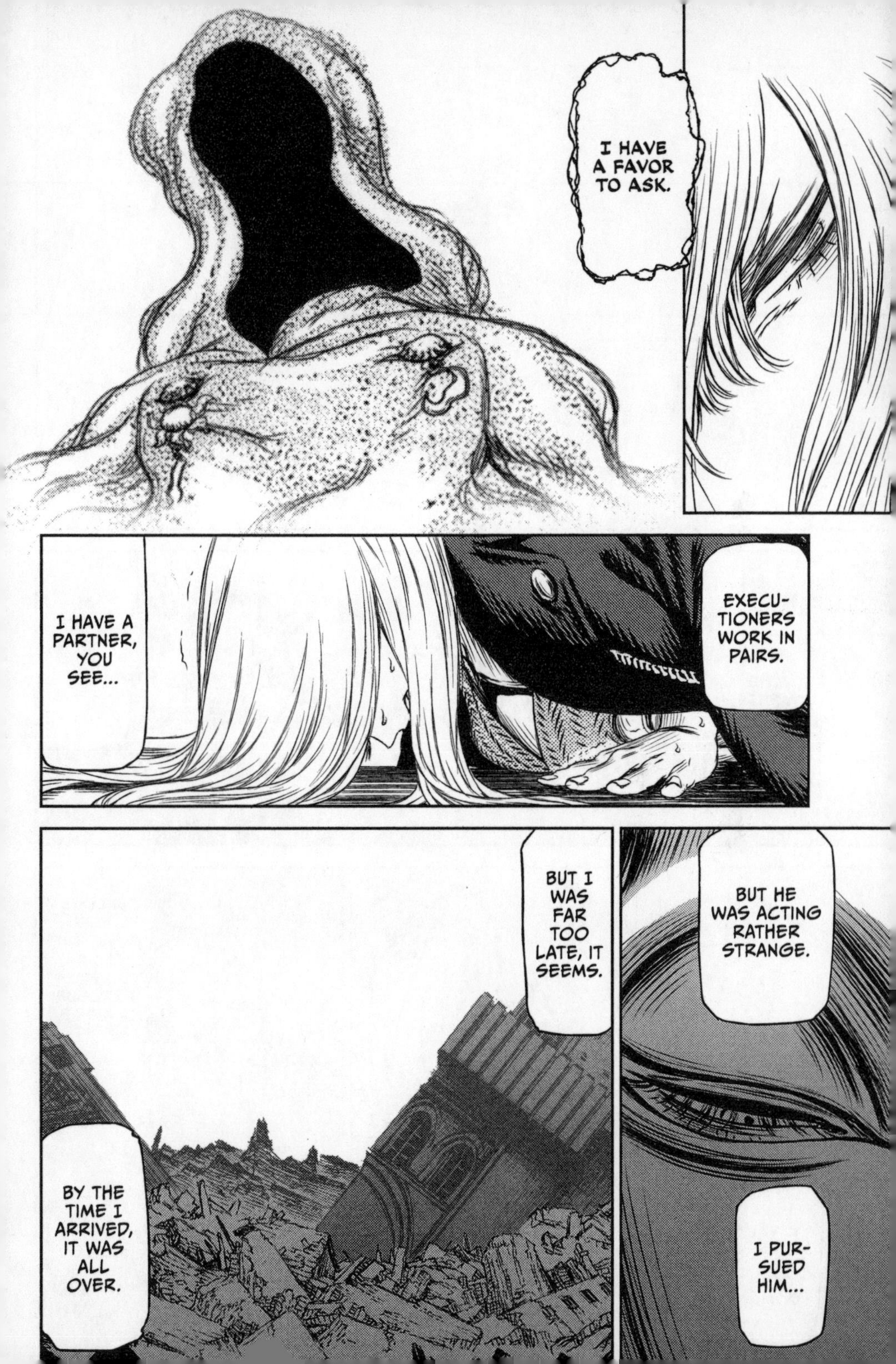
I HAVE A FAVOR TO ASK.
EXECU-TIONERS WORK IN PAIRS.
I HAVE A PARTNER, YOU SEE...
BUT HE WAS ACTING RATHER STRANGE.
I PUR-SUED HIM...
BUT I WAS FAR TOO LATE, IT SEEMS.
BY THE TIME I ARRIVED, IT WAS ALL OVER.

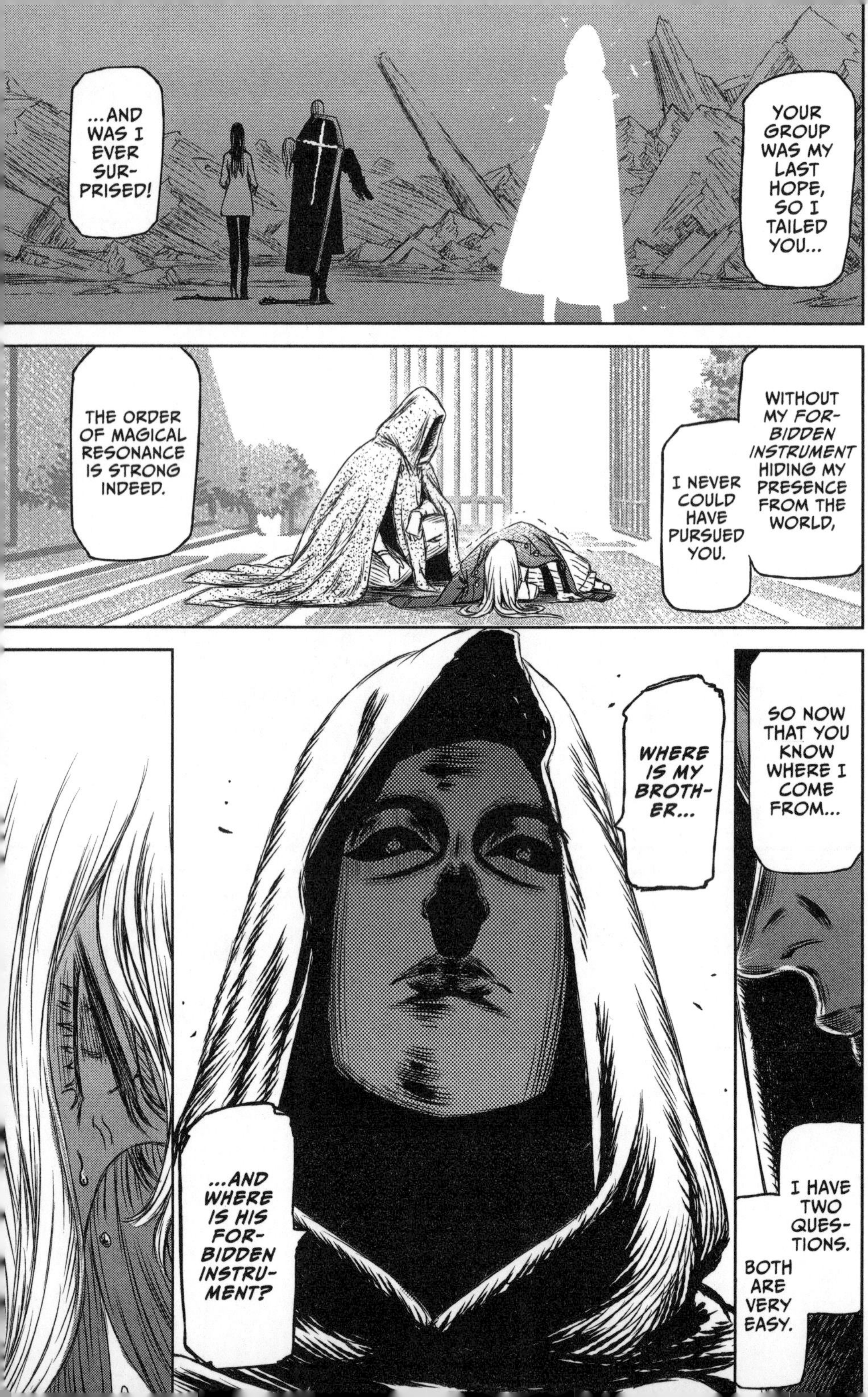
YOUR GROUP WAS MY LAST HOPE, SO I TAILED YOU...
...AND WAS I EVER SURPRISED!
WITHOUT MY *FORBIDDEN INSTRUMENT* HIDING MY PRESENCE FROM THE WORLD,
I NEVER COULD HAVE PURSUED YOU.
THE ORDER OF MAGICAL RESONANCE IS STRONG INDEED.
SO NOW THAT YOU KNOW WHERE I COME FROM...
I HAVE TWO QUESTIONS.
BOTH ARE VERY EASY.
WHERE IS MY BROTHER...
...AND WHERE IS HIS FORBIDDEN INSTRUMENT?

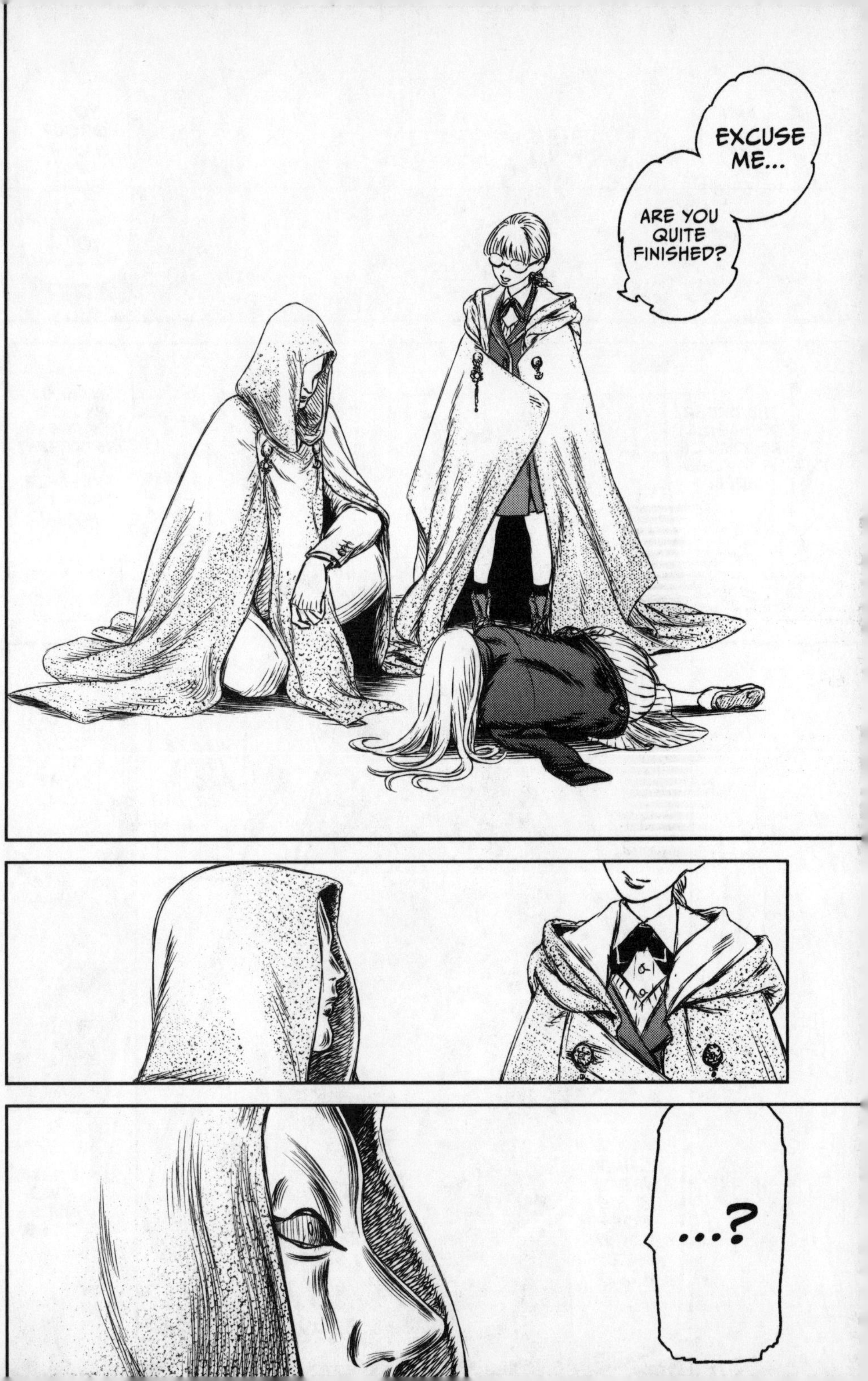
EXCUSE ME...
ARE YOU QUITE FINISHED?
...?

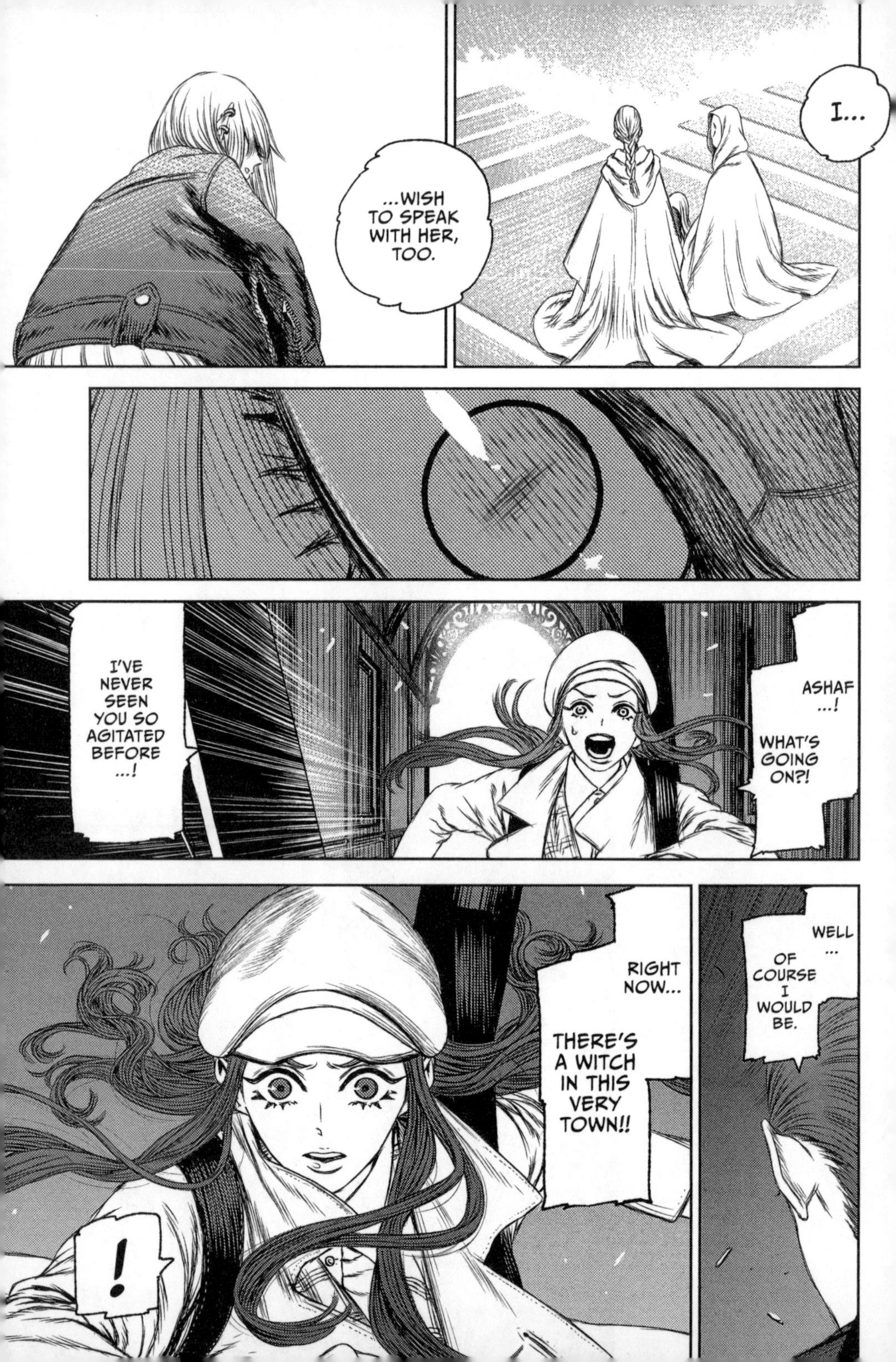
I...
...WISH TO SPEAK WITH HER, TOO.
ASHAF ...!
WHAT'S GOING ON?!
I'VE NEVER SEEN YOU SO AGITATED BEFORE ...!
WELL ...
OF COURSE I WOULD BE.
RIGHT NOW...
THERE'S A WITCH IN THIS VERY TOWN!!
!

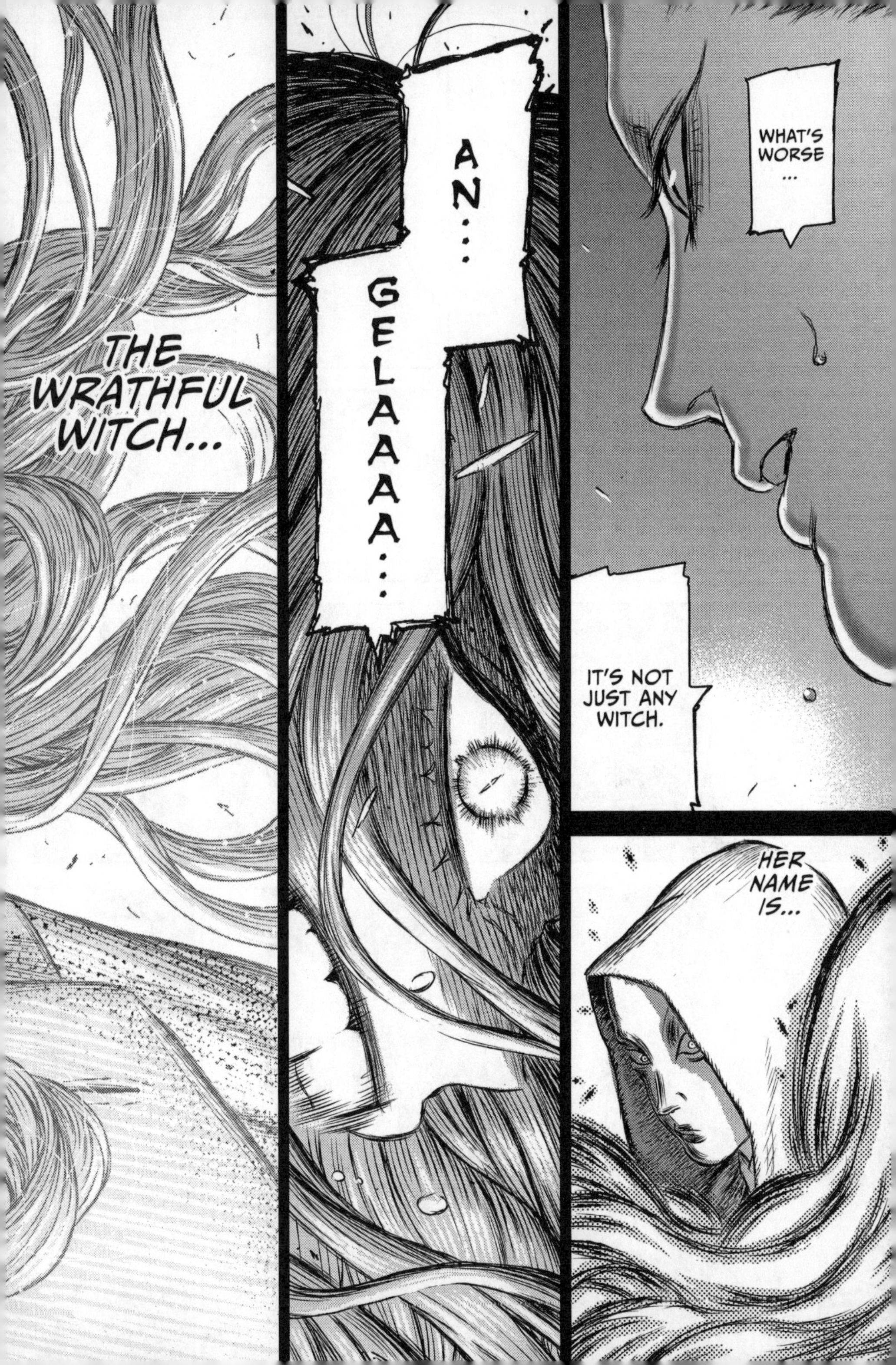
WHAT'S WORSE ...
IT'S NOT JUST ANY WITCH.
HER NAME IS...
AN... GELAAAA...
THE WRATHFUL WITCH...

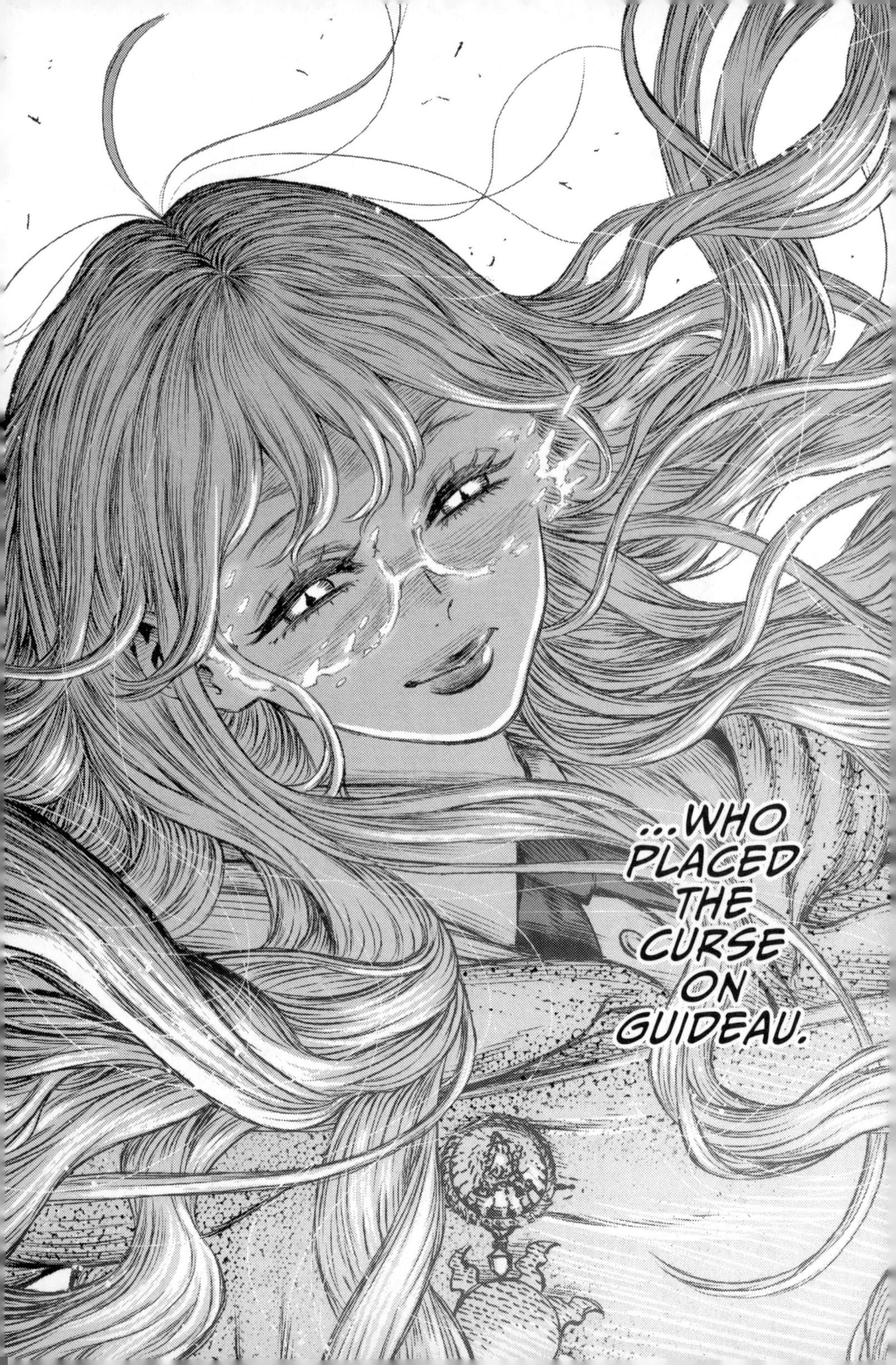
...WHO PLACED THE CURSE ON GUIDEAU.

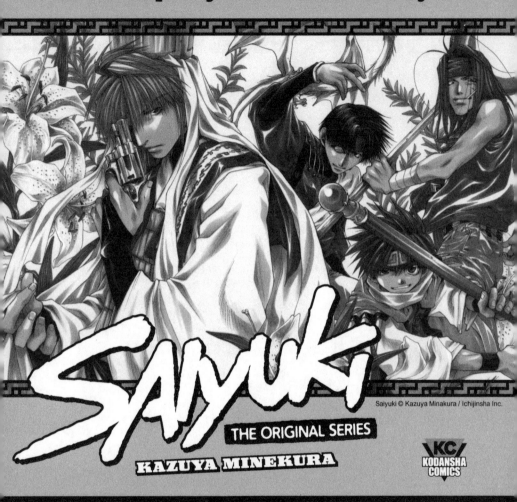